Loeb Classical Monographs / In Memory of James C. Loeb

Athenian Bronze Allotment Plates

By JOHN H. KROLL

Harvard University Press   Cambridge, Massachusetts   1972

The Loeb Classical Monographs are published with
assistance from the Loeb Classical Library Foundation.

Distributed in Great Britain by Oxford University Press, London

Library of Congress Catalog Card Number 79–162636
SBN 674–05092–4

Printed in the United States of America

To My Classics Teachers at Oberlin

Contents

Tables

Photo Credits

The following have provided photographs and have kindly granted the author permission to reproduce them.

Athens,
> Agora Excavations, American School of Classical Studies: Figs. 29, 53, 55, 76, 78, 79, 168, 171, 172, 173, 181, 189, 205, 207, 209, 240, 241, 242, 244, 255, 260, 261, 268, 280, 281, 284, 290, 299, 303, 304
> École française d'archéologie: Figs. 312–315
> National Museum: Figs. 52, 152

Basel, Antikenmuseum: Figs. 9, 47, 66, 82, 97, 122, 133, 145, 165, 166, 193, 227, 317

Berlin (East), Staatliche Museen, Antikenabteilung (negative nos. 425 and 2809): Figs. 17, 49, 127, 177, 229, 232

Hannover, Kestner-Museum: Fig. 25

London, British Museum (courtesy of the Trustees of the British Museum): Figs. 60, 68, 101, 143

Munich, Antikensammlung: Figs. 158, 222, 223

Newcastle upon Tyne, University Museum of Classical Archaeology: Figs. 64, 65

New York,
> Brooklyn Museum: Fig. 149
> Metropolitan Museum of Art: Fig. 6

Oxford, Ashmolean Museum: Fig. 156

Paris,
> Professor Georges Daux: Fig. 11
> Cabinet des Médailles: Figs. 3, 23, 56, 57, 88, 103, 136, 137, 138, 148, 202, 212, 215, 225, 233, 234, 262, 310
> Musée du Louvre: Fig. 309

Philadelphia, University of Pennsylvania Excavations at Porto Cheli: Fig. 307

Thessalonika, Archaeological Museum: Fig. 13

Toronto, Royal Ontario Museum: Fig. 62

Urbana, University of Illinois Classical and European Culture Museum: Fig. 35

All photographs not listed above are by the author. A complete set of his negatives is on file in the offices of the Agora Excavations, Athens.

Abbreviations

PERIODICALS

AA. Archäologischer Anzeiger, Beiblatt zum Jahrbuch des Deutschen Archäologischen Instituts

AllLitZeit. Allegemeinen Literatur-Zeitung

AJA. American Journal of Archaeology

AJP. American Journal of Philology

ArchEph. Ἀρχαιολογικὴ Ἐφημερίς

AthMitt. Mitteilungen des Deutschen Archäologischen Instituts, Athenische Abteilung

AZ. Archäologische Zeitung

BAntF. Bulletin de la Société nationale des antiquaires de France

BCH. Bulletin de correspondance hellénique

BdI. Bollettino dell'Instituto di Corrispondenza Archeologica

BSA. British School at Athens, Annual

CR. Classical Review

Deltion. Ἀρχαιολογικὸν Δελτίον

HSCP. Harvard Studies in Classical Philology

NC. Numismatic Chronicle

Polemon. Πολέμων

RA. Revue archéologique

REG. Revue des études grecques

TAPA. Transactions and Proceedings of the American Philological Association

BOOKS and ARTICLES

Akerblad, *AttiAccRom* 1, 1 (1821). J. D. Akerblad, "Sopra alcune laminette di bronzo trovate ne'cortorni di Atene, Dissertazione letta nell'Accademia d'Archeologia al Campidoglio li 30 Giugno 1811," *Atti dell'Accademia Romana d'Archeologia* 1, Pt. 1 (1821), 39–73

AthPol. Aristoteles, Ἀθηναίων Πολιτεία, ed. Hans Opperman (reprint with additions, Stuttgart: Teubner, 1961)

Bechtel. Fredrich Bechtel, *Die historischen Personennamen des Griechischen bis zur Kaiserzeit* (Halle: Max Niemeyer, 1917)

Bernoulli, *Katalog.* J. J. Bernoulli, *Museum in Basel: Katalog für die antiquarische Abteilung* (Basel, 1880)

Bonner-Smith I. R. J. Bonner and Gertrude Smith, *The Administration of Justice from Homer to Aristotle*, 2 vols. (Chicago: University of Chicago Press, 1930–1938), I

Bruck, *AthMitt* 19 (1894). Silvius Bruck, "Zur den athenischen heliasten Täfelchen," *AthMitt* 19 (1894), 203–211

Bruck, *Philologus* 52 (1893), and *Philologus* 54 (1895). Silvius Bruck, "Über die Organisation der athenischen Heliastengerichte im 4. Jahrh. v. Chr.," Pt. 1, "Die Meldung zur Heliasie," *Philologus* 52 (1893), 295–317; and Pt. 2, "Die Heliastentäfelchen," *Philologus* 54 (1895), 65–79

Busolt-Swoboda. George Busolt, *Griechische Staatskunde*, 2 vols., Vol. II revised by Heinrich Swoboda [Iwan v. Müller's *Handbuch der Altertumswissenschaft*, IV.1.1] (Munich: C. H. Beck, 1920–1926), II

Caillemer, DarSag, "Dikastai". Exupère Caillemer, s.v. "Dikastai," in Ch. Daremberg and Edm. Saglio, eds., *Dictionnaire des antiquités grecques et romaines*, 10 vols. (Paris: Hachette, 1887–1919), IV, Pt. 1, 186–200

CIG. Augustus Boeckh, *Corpus Inscriptionum Graecarum*, 4 vols. (Berlin, 1828–1877)

Curtius, *RhM* 31 (1876). Carl Curtius, "Attische Richtertäfelchen des Berliner Museums," *Rheinisches Museum für Philologie* 31 (1876), 283–286

Davidson and Thompson, *Pnyx Small Objects* I. G. R. Davidson and D. B. Thompson, *Small Objects from the Pnyx: I* [*Hesperia*, Suppl. VII] (Athens: American School of Classical Studies, 1943)

Dodwell, *Tour* I. Edward Dodwell, *A Classical and Topographical Tour through Greece, during the Years 1801, 1805, and 1806*, 2 vols. (London, 1819), I

Dornseiff-Hansen. Franz Dornseiff and Bernhard Hansen, *Rückläufiges Wörterbuch der griechischen Eigennamen* [Berichte über die Verhandlungen der sächsischen Akademie der Wissenschaften zu Leipzig, Philologisch-historische Klasse, Band 104, Heft 2] (Berlin: Akademie-verlag, 1957)

Dow, *BCH* 87 (1963). Sterling Dow, "Dikasts' Bronze Pinakia," *BCH* 87 (1963), 653–687

Dow, *HSCP* 50 (1939). Sterling Dow, "Aristotle, the Kleroteria, and the Courts," *HSCP* 50 (1939), 1–34

Dow, *Prytaneis.* Sterling Dow, *Prytaneis: A Study of the Inscriptions Honoring the Athenian Councillors* [*Hesperia*, Suppl. I] (Athens: American School of Classical Studies, 1937)

Dumont, *RA²* 17 (1868). Albert Dumont, "Sur quelques tablettes du tribunal des Héliastes," *RA*, 2d Ser., 17 (1868), 140–146

Fritz-Kapp, *Constitution of Athens.* Kurt von Fritz and Ernst Kapp, *Aristotle's Constitution of Athens and Related Texts* (New York: Hafner, 1950)

Girard, *BCH* 2 (1878). Paul Girard, "Les tablettes judiciaires du Musée du Varvakeion," *BCH* 2 (1878), 524–539

Guarducci, *Epigrafia*. Margherita Guarducci, *Epigrafia Greca*, 2 vols. (Rome: Instituto Poligrafico dello Stato, 1967–1969)

Hicks, *Manual*. E. L. Hicks, *A Manual of Greek Historical Inscriptions* (Oxford, 1882)

Hicks–Hill, *Manual*. E. L. Hicks and G. F. Hill, *A Manual of Greek Historical Inscriptions* (new and revised ed., Oxford: Clarendon Press, 1901)

Hommel, *Heliaia*. Hildebrecht Hommel, *Heliaia: Untersuchungen zur Verfassung und Prozessordnung des athenischen Volksgerichts, insbesondere zum Schlussteil der Ἀθηναίων Πολιτεία des Aristotles* [*Philologus*, Suppl. 29.2] (Leipzig: Dieterich, 1927)

IG II. Ulrich Koehler, ed., *Inscriptiones Graecae*, II: *Inscriptiones Atticae aetatis quae est inter Euclidis annum et Augusti tempora*, 5 pts. (Berlin, 1877–1895)

IG II². Johannes Kirchner, ed., *Inscriptiones Graecae*, II–III (editio minor): *Inscriptiones Atticae Euclidis anno posteriores*, 6 fasicules (Berlin: G. Reimer; W. de Gruyter, 1913–1940)

Jones, *Democracy*. A. H. M. Jones, *Athenian Democracy* (Oxford: B. Blackwell, 1957)

Jongkees, *BABesch* 20 (1945). J. H. Jongkees, "Twee atheenische Dikastentesserae," *Bulletin van de Vereenining tot Bevordering der Kennis van de Antike Beschaving* 20 (1945), 7–10

Koumanoudes, *ArchEph* 1887. A. S. Koumanoudes, "Πινάκια δικαστικά," *ArchEph* 1887, 53–35

Kroll, *BCH* 91 (1967). J. H. Kroll, "Dikasts' Pinakia from the Fauvel Collection," *BCH* 91 (1967), 379–396

Lipsius I. J. H. Lipsius, *Das attische Recht und Rechtsverfahren*, 3 vols. (Leipzig: O. R. Reisland, 1905–1915), I

Meisterhans-Schwyzer. Konrad Meisterhans, *Grammatik der attischen Inschriften*, 3d ed. prep. by Edward Schwyzer (Berlin: Weidmann, 1900)

Meletopoulos, *Polemon* 3 (1947–48). I. A. Meletopoulos, "Δικαστικὰ πινάκια καὶ «χαλκία»," *Polemon* 3 (1947–1948), 33–40, with σύμμεικτα, κβ´

Michon, *BAntF* 1908. Étienne Michon, *BAntF* 1908, 352–360 (untitled paper on a "tablette d'héliaste athénien," read to the Société nationale des antiquaires de France, December 23, 1908)

P.A. Johannes Kirchner, ed., *Prosopographia Attica*, 2 vols. (Berlin: G. Reimer, 1901–1903)

Pape-Benseler. W. Pape and G. E. Benseler, *Wörterbuch der griechischen Eigennamen* (3d ed., Brunswick, 1863)

Rayet, *AnnAssEtGr* 1878. Olivier Rayet, "Tablettes d'héliastes inédites," *Annuaire de l'Association pour l'encouragement des études grecques* 1878, 201–207

de Ridder, *Bronzes du Louvre II*. André de Ridder, *Les Bronzes antiques du Louvre*, 2 vols. (Paris: Leroux, 1913–1915), II: *Les Instruments*

Robert, *Coll. Froehner*.   Louis Robert, *Collection Froehner*, I: *Inscriptions Grecques* (Paris: Bibliothèque Nationale, 1936)

Ross, *AllLitZeit 1837*.   Ludwig Ross, "Über attische Gräber und Gräbschriften," *AllLitZeit 1837, Intelligenzblätter* Nos. 84–85, 690–710

Ross, *Demen von Attika*.   Ludwig Ross, *Die Demen von Attika und ihre Vertheilung unter die Phylen*, edited by M. H. E. Meier (Halle, 1846)

Sandys, *Constitution of Athens*.   J. E. Sandys, *Aristotles' Constitution of Athens* (2d ed., London: Macmillan, 1912)

Stähelin, *AA 1943*.   Felix Stähelin, "Attische Richtertäfelchen in Basel," *AA* 1943, 16–19

Sundwall, *Nachträge*.   Johannes Sundwall, *Nachträge zur Prosopographica Attica* [Öfversigt af Finska Vetenkaps-Sosietetens Forhandlingar 52 (1909–1910)] (Helsinki: Simelii Arfvingars Boktryckeriaktiebolag, 1910)

Teusch, *De sortitione*.   Theodor Teusch, *De sortitione iudicum apud Athenienses* (Göttingen, 1894)

Vischer, *Beiträge*.   Wilhelm Vischer, *Epigraphische und archäologische Beiträge aus Griechenland* (Basel, 1855)

Vischer, *Kleinigkeiten*.   Wilhelm Vischer, *Epigraphische und archäologische Kleinigkeiten* (Basel, 1871)

Vischer, *Kleine Schriften* II.   Wilhelm Vischer, *Kleine Schriften*, 2 vols. (Leipzig, 1877–1878), II

Walters, *Catalogue*.   H. B. Walters, *Catalogue of the Bronzes, Greek, Roman, and Etruscan, in the Department of Greek and Roman Antiquities, British Museum* (London, 1899)

Preface

During the opening decade of the nineteenth century two inscribed bronze nameplates (**61** and **92** below) were excavated from tombs in the Peiraeus. Their identity was uncertain until a few years later when they came to the attention of the Swedish antiquarian J. D. Akerblad. In a paper read in Rome on June 30, 1811, he announced that they must be examples of the bronze πινάκια, which, according to the lexicographers and scholiasts, were used by Athenian jurors for admission to the courts.

There was much about these small objects to excite the interest of students of Athenian antiquities. Apart from their bearing the names of jurors and letters that were thought to pertain to the specific courts to which the jurors were assigned, many of the *pinakia* were stamped with what soon seemed to be a bewildering number of official seals. The first systematic catalogue of pinakia, which had come to number some forty-seven whole and fragmentary examples, was published in 1878 by Paul Girard and was particularly important for his observations on the way that certain of the seals were treated. These observations, to be credited to Girard's firsthand knowledge of pinakia in Athenian collections, have remained the only valid generalizations about the seals down to the present time.

The recovery and publication in 1891 of Aristotle's *Athenaion Politeia* at once put the study of the Athenian *dikasteria* on a wholly new footing and had an immediate impact on investigation of the pinakia. This was largely through two articles in *Philologus* (1893 and 1895) by Silvius Bruck, who, more than any scholar before or since, exploited the pinakia as primary evidence for reconstructing the Athenian court system. Although most of his deductions have not stood the test of more complete evidence, his empirical approach to the objects admirably pointed in the right direction. Bruck re-examined the pinakia in Berlin and Athens, and his third article on pinakia (*AthMitt* 1894), in the form of addenda and corrigenda to the sixty-seven pinakia catalogued by Ulrich Koehler in *IG* II, is still useful. In more recent years Bruck's work has been eclipsed by Hildebrecht Hommel's *Heliaia* (1927), but although this was a much sounder treatise on the Athenian courts, its treatment of the pinakia was in some ways less satisfactory than Bruck's. Hommel derived almost all of his knowledge of the pinakia directly from Bruck and, having no independent control over this evidence, was rather capricious in accepting or rejecting what Bruck had to say.

After the appearance of *Heliaia* and an updated catalogue of ninety-two pinakia by Johannes Kirchner in *IG* II² (1931), knowledge of the pinakia entered a new phase. The American excavations on the Pnyx and in the Athenian Agora began. Louis Robert published the Froehner Collection in Paris. And the pinakia in the smaller Rhousopoulos-Pfuhl and Meletopoulos Collections in Basel and the Peiraeus were published. (All three were the first collections of pinakia to be published with photographs.) Thus the available material began to increase at an unprecedented rate. But, in respect to pinakia, doubtless the most important event since the rediscovery of the *AthPol* was Sterling Dow's identification and elucidation of Aristotle's *kleroteria* as "allotment-machines." For the first time the actual use of pinakia could be appreciated, and the pinakia could be understood in the specific context of Athenian allotment procedures. Professor Dow's interest in the kleroteria naturally extended to the bronze pinakia, and in an important article devoted to them (*BCH* 1963) he recently demonstrated that the number of reinscribed pinakia had been vastly underestimated and that the overall record was in need of much improvement if further progress was to be made. Hence the present study, which is an enlarged and thoroughly revised version of my Harvard doctoral thesis submitted in the spring of 1968. (A summary of the thesis was published in *HSCP* 73 [1969], 316–319.)

The study has two purposes: to make available a dependable and fully illustrated record of the surviving pinakia and to explore in what ways this record illuminates the mechanics and development of Athenian democratic government in the fourth century B.C. It has seemed best to deal with these two aspects separately. Thus constitutional matters and the general sifting of evidence are taken up in Chapters I–VI, while the pinakia are listed and studied individually in the Catalogue that follows these chapters.

For the time, freedom, and travel that the several stages of this work have required, I am greatly indebted to the American School of Classical Studies in Athens and to the Department of Classics, to the Committee on Sheldon Traveling Fellowships, and, especially, to the Society of Fellows, all of Harvard University. It is hard for me to imagine how the study could have been completed without the financial assistance so generously provided by them.

Professor Dow's part at the outset and his continuing encouragement and criticisms cannot be acknowledged too appreciatively. It was he who introduced me to the pinakia. I am grateful also to David Lewis, who kindly read the manuscript for the Harvard University Press and who suggested a number of valuable improvements. Mabel Lang, Homer Thompson, and T. Leslie Shear, Jr., are to be thanked for their interest and for putting the unpublished Agora material at my disposal. And two Athenian private collectors, Helen Stathatos and Paul Kanellopoulos, were as generous with warm Greek hospitality as with their pinakia.

In addition, the curators and technicians of twenty museums have been involved and have often gone to considerable inconvenience on my behalf, particularly in response to my requests for having pinakia cleaned. My gratitude goes then to the successive directors of the National Museum in Athens, Mr. and Mrs. Ch. I. Karouzos, George Dontas, V. G. Kallipolites, and members of their staff, Evi Touloupa, Maria Petropoulakou, and Andreas Mavrogannis; Mando Karamessini-Oikonomidou, director of the Numismatic Museum, Athens ; D. I. Lazarides, formerly in charge of the Peiraeus Museum; Ph. M. Petsas in Thessalonika; Georges Le Rider and Monique Mainjonet of the Cabinet des Médailles; Pierre Devambez and Georges Ville of the Louvre; Elizabeth Chirol in Rouen; Ernst Berger, Margo Schmidt, and K. J. Faltermeier of the Antikenmuseum, Basel; Dieter Ahrens, Günter Kopcke, and Klaus Vierneisel of the Antikensammlung in Munich; Ursula Blaschke of the Staatliche Museen, Berlin; Margildis Schülter of the Kestner-Museum, Hannover; J. H. C. Kern in Leiden; J. H. Jongkees in Utrecht; D. E. L. Haynes of the British Museum; H. W. Catling of the Ashmolean; B. B. Shefton, Newcastle-upon-Tyne; Neda Leipen of the Royal Ontario Museum; Dietrich von Bothmer and Brian Cook of the Metropolitan; J. D. Cooney, Bernard von Bothmer, and Jean Keith of the Brooklyn Museum; and O. A. Dodson and E. C. McClintock, Jr., of the University of Illinois. The officials of the National Museum, Athens, and Drs. Cooney and Schülter courteously granted permission to include unpublished pinakia in their keeping.

Among other scholars who provided invaluable assistance I should especially like to thank Herbert Bloch, A. L. Boegehold, M. L. Clarke, Georges Daux, Thomas Drew-Bear, D. H. Gill, G. M. A. Hanfmann, M. H. Jameson, B. D. Meritt, C. A. Nordman, Dina Peppas-Delmousou, Olivier Picard, H. S. Robinson, Demetrios Schilardi, C. G. Starr, Arthur Steinberg, Jochen Twele, J. S. Traill, Rolf Westman, and Eugene Vanderpool.

Miss Patricia M. Fox of the Harvard University Press could not have been more patient and helpful in preparing an immoderately difficult manuscript for printing.

And, finally, I should like to thank my wife, Sandra, who continually helped in more ways than she knows.

Athenian Bronze Allotment Plates

I The Literary Evidence

Testimonia

All notices on pinakia in the lexicographers and scholiasts[1] are clearly derived from one or both of the two passages quoted below and thus attest that no primary literary source is missing.

Our *locus classicus* is Aristotle's description of the impaneling of jurors in *AthPol* 63–65 (completed between 329/8 and 325/4 B.C.),[2] which begins by introducing the personnel and equipment required for the allotment: the archons, the kleroteria, chests, staves, and so forth; finally the dikasts themselves (63.3) and the dikasts' pinakia (63.4), which were then made of boxwood:

> ἔχει δ᾽ ἕκαστος δικαστὴς τὸ πινάκιον πύξινον, ἐπιγεγραμμένον τὸ
> ὄνομα τὸ ἑαυτοῦ πατρόθεν καὶ τοῦ δήμου καὶ γράμμα ἓν τῶν στοιχείων
> μέχρι τοῦ κ· νενέμηνται γὰρ κατὰ φυλὰς δέκα μέρη οἱ δικασταί,
> παραπλησίως ἴσοι ἐν ἑκάστῳ τῷ γράμματι.

Each juror has a pinakion of boxwood, inscribed with his name, the name of his father, the name of his deme, and one of the letters of the alphabet up to "K." For the jurors from each tribe are divided into ten sections, about the same number under each letter.[3]

---

1. Harpokration, s.v. πινάκιον = Souidas, s.v. πινάκιον; Hesychios, s.v. χαλκοῦν πινάκιον; Photios, s.v. πινάκιον; and the scholia on Aristophanes *Ploutos* 277.

2. Or on the more cautious dating, which dismisses the argument from the absence of quinqueremes at 46.1, 329/8–323/2 B.C., see Sandys, *Constitution of Athens*, xlix; and James Day and Mortimer Chambers, *Aristotle's History of Athenian Democracy* (Berkeley and Los Angeles: University of California Press, 1962), 196–197. A lowering of the upper terminus to 326/5 has been suggested by B. D. Meritt ("Note on Aristotle, *Αθ.Πολ.*, 54," *AJP* 61 [1940], 78) on the strength of the inscription Dow, *Prytaneis*, no. 1. But since the inscription is now downdated to the time of the twelve *phylai* (J. S. Traill, "Two New Prytany Inscriptions from the Athenian Agora," *Hesperia* 38 [1969], 421, n. 11), we must return to the traditional terminus of 329/8. Most recently, J. J. Keaney has argued that the treatise was composed about 335–333 but was brought up to date in several particulars in the early 320s ("The Date of Aristotle's Athenaion Politeia," *Historia* 19 [1970], 326–336).

3. Translation of Fritz-Kapp, *Constitution of Athens*, with minor alterations. That this is the correct meaning of κατὰ φυλὰς δέκα μέρη is clear from the account of chests and kleroteria in Sections 63.2 and 64.

In the paragraphs that follow (64–65), we are told how the pinakia functioned in the allotments. Each candidate goes to the court entrance of his phyle and deposits his pinakion in the chest marked with his section-letter; the pinakia in each chest are then inserted into one of the vertical rows of slots (κανονίδες) in the phyle's kleroteria; the allotment is run; and those candidates whose pinakia were selected are subsequently allotted to the various courts on which they will sit. Their pinakia were returned to them at the end of the court day when they were paid, while the rejected candidates got back their pinakia as soon as the allotment was concluded. By now all of this is familiar and calls for no further elaboration here. Thanks to Sterling Dow's reconstruction of the kleroteria,[4] Aristotle's account of the allotment procedure is at last able to speak for itself.

The other mention of pinakia in a contemporary source occurs in Demosthenes 39 (*Mantitheos against Boiotos Concerning the Name* I, about 348 B.C.) 10–12. Because it is a quarter century earlier, refers to pinakia of bronze, and informs that pinakia were not used exclusively in a dikastic context, the passage invaluably supplements the information provided by Aristotle. The speaker, Mantitheos, son of Mantias, of Thorikos, is pleading that his half brother, who happens to have the same name as himself, should be compelled to take another name; for, so long as both have the same name, it would be impossible to distinguish between them should one or the other be allotted to some public office.

πρὸς Διός, ἂν δ᾽ ἀρχὴν ἡντινοῦν ἡ πόλις κληροῖ, οἷον βουλῆς, θεσμοθέτου,
τῶν ἄλλων, τῷ δῆλος ἡμῶν ὁ λαχὼν ἔσται; πλὴν εἰ σημεῖον, ὥσπερ
ἂν ἄλλῳ τινί, τῷ χαλκίῳ προσέσται· καὶ οὐδὲ τοῦθ᾽ ὁποτέρου ἐστὶν
οἱ πολλοὶ γνώσονται. οὐκοῦν ὁ μὲν αὐτόν, ἐγὼ δ᾽ ἐμαυτὸν φήσω τὸν
εἰληχότ᾽ εἶναι. λοιπὸν εἰς τὸ δικαστήριον ἡμᾶς εἰσιέναι . . . καὶ ὁ τῷ
λόγῳ κρατήσας ἄρξει . . . τὶ δ᾽, ἂν ἄρα (δεῖ γὰρ ἅπαντα ἡμᾶς ἐξετάσαι)
ἅτερος ἡμῶν πείσας τὸν ἕτερον, ἂν λάχῃ, παραδοῦναι αὐτῷ τὴν
ἀρχήν, οὕτω κληρῶται, τὸ δυοῖν πινακίοιν τὸν ἕνα κληροῦσθαι τί ἄλλ᾽
ἐστίν; εἶτ᾽ ἐφ᾽ ᾧ θάνατον ζημίαν ὁ νόμος λέγει, τοῦθ᾽ ἡμῖν ἀδεῶς
ἐξέσται πράττειν;

Or, by Zeus, suppose the state is allotting to any office, for example, that of *bouleutes, thesmothetes,* or any of the rest; how will it be clear which one of us has been allotted?—unless some mark shall be attached to the bronze [sc. plate], as there might be to anything

4. Dow, *Prytaneis,* 198–215; *HSCP* 50 (1939), 1–34. For further discussion, see J. D. Bishop, "The Cleroterium," *Journal of Hellenic Studies* 90 (1970), 1–14.

else; and even then people will not know to which of us two it belongs. Well then, he will say that he has been allotted, and I shall say that I have. The only course left is for us to go into court ... and he who shall prevail by his words will hold office. ... But suppose again (for we must examine every phase of the matter), one or the other of us persuades the other, in case he is chosen, to yield the office to him, and so is allotted. What is this but one man being chosen by lot with two pinakia? Shall it, then, be permitted us to do with impunity a thing for which the law appoints the penalty of death?[5]

Although Mantitheos' argument would be equally applicable in the case of dikastic allotments, he ignores dikastic sortitions altogether and speaks of pinakia solely in connection with the annual allotments to the higher state magistracies. Nevertheless, owing to the primacy of *AthPol* 63–65 in all writing about pinakia from the ancient lexicographers to the present, the supposition has always been that the pinakia to which Mantitheos refers and the dikastic pinakia defined in the *AthPol* were essentially the same, the only difference being that by the time of Aristotle, the material of the pinakia had been changed from bronze to boxwood. Mantitheos, it is assumed, was really alluding to dikastic pinakia, but happens to inform us that these dikastic pinakia were used in various other Athenian alloments independent of the courts. No one seems to have been bothered by the fact that this assumption is tenable only if Mantitheos and his brother were enrolled as *dikastai* and were entitled to own dikastic pinakia.

The passage requires that by about 348 B.C. all Athenian citizens, or at least all citizens who were qualified and disposed to participate in the annual allotments for the state magistracies, had bronze pinakia, whether they were enrolled as dikastai or not. The status of dikastes was contingent on the swearing of the heliastic oath, which, as we know from Isokrates 15.21, was administered annually (ὀμνύναι μὲν καθ' ἕκαστον τὸν ἐνιαυτόν). The status, therefore, like the status of nearly all other positions in the Athenian government, was annually conferred;[6] surely all Athenians over age thirty did not annually swear the oath and become enrolled as dikastai as a matter of course. The two laws preserved in Demosthenes 24.22 and 27 (353 B.C.), which specify that *nomothetai* were to be chosen "from those who have sworn the heliastic oath"

---

5. Translation of A. T. Murray, *Demosthenes* IV (Cambridge, Mass.: Harvard University Press, 1936), with minor alterations.

6. According to W.S. Ferguson (*Hellenistic Athens* [London: Macmillan, 1911], 474–476), the sole exception was the office of the *athlothetai*, which was held for a four-year term (*AthPol* 60.1).

(ἐκ τῶν ὀμωμοκότων τὸν ἡλιαστικὸν ὅρκον), imply that the Athenian citizenry was divided into men who had sworn the annual oath (the dikasts) and those who had not. If at this time all pinakia were dikasts' pinakia and could have belonged only to members of the former group, how could members of the unsworn group have participated in nondikastic allotments? Are we to believe that membership in the body of dikastai was a prerequisite for obtaining any other position in the state? A more reasonable solution would be to discard the assumption that all pinakia were necessarily dikastic, in favor of the hypothesis that by the middle of the fourth century, although dikastic pinakia were issued to dikasts, another type of pinakion was issued to Athenians not enrolled as dikastai. Chapter III will show that this hypothesis is proven by the extant bronze pinakia. But I have raised the point here to emphasize that even if we had no pinakia to back it up, the hypothesis would remain a natural inference from the literary information at our disposal. Mantitheos apparently did not think of his and his brother's pinakia as being dikastic, and it is entirely possible that they were not.

The unwarranted assumption that all Athenian pinakia were necessarily dikasts' pinakia is only one misconception that has clouded discussion of the subject. Another fallacy, which also goes back to the lexicographers and scholiasts, has been the tendency to regard the pinakia as jurors' identification cards or, worse, "tickets." This view, universally held in the nineteenth century, has been slow to die even after the discovery of the *AthPol* clarified the role of pinakia in the mechanics of Athenian allotment procedure. Bruck, writing with full knowledge of *AthPol* 63–65, thought of pinakia as jurors' *legitimationsmarke*, used primarily for admission to the courts and only incidentally for allotments.[7] And Hommel also committed himself to this position when he followed Bruck in assuming that pinakia were used by Athenian dikastai in the period before the dikastai were actually allotted by pinakia.[8] It may now seem superfluous to affirm that the pinakia were nameplates designed expressly to be used in automated allotments on kleroteria, but the point can hardly be overemphasized. The literary evidence does not allow for any other interpretation or use of the objects.

Similarly, the testimonia speak of pinakia in connection with only two kinds of Athenian sortitions: the impaneling of dikasts at the beginning of each court day, and the annual selection of magistrates. As will be shown in Professor Dow's forthcoming republication of the stone kleroteria, most of which are Hellenistic, allotment by pinakia and kleroteria spread to other Athenian institutions and was probably being used, for example, in the allotting of

---

7. Bruck, *Philologus* 52 (1893), 300; *ibid.*, 54 (1895), 64.
8. Hommel, *Heliaia*, 43–44.

proedroi (*AthPol* 44.2) during the period of the twelve tribes. But for the fourth century our evidence is limited to the sources quoted above and to the extant bronze pinakia, and none of this evidence, so far as I have been able to determine, requires us to look beyond the courts and the annual allotting of magistrates.

Chronological Inferences

Pinakia in bronze are mentioned by Demosthenes about 348, but by the time of the *AthPol* bronze dikasts' pinakia had been superseded by wooden ones. Accordingly, it has been proposed that wood was substituted for bronze in 339 as a consequence of the emergency before Chaironeia[9] or that Aristotle's attention to the humble detail of boxwood suggests the change was more recent still and should be placed as late as about 330 B.C.[10] The former theory, however, has nothing to recommend it, and the latter inference could be mistaken. For the lower termini of bronze pinakia we had best rely on chronological data provided by the pinakia themselves.

Concerning the introduction of bronze pinakia the literary evidence is more abundant and useful. The highest probable upper terminus is 388, the date of Aristophanes' *Ploutos*, which mentions the eagerness of dikasts to be enrolled ἐν πολλοῖς γράμμασιν (1166–1167) and contains other references to jurors' γράμματα (277 and 972) that make good sense only if understood in light of Praxagora's mock allotment of dikasts to courts by panels (γράμματα) in *Ekklesiazousai* 681–688 (392 B.C.). Praxagora used kleroteria (the term first

---

9. *Ibid.*, 40, whence Bonner-Smith I, 375. The theory takes B. V. Head's conventional date of 339 for the first regular Athenian bronze coinage (*Historia Numorum²* [Oxford: Clarendon Press, 1911], 376) and argues that this was an emergency war coinage in preparation for Chaironeia and that a shortage of bronze for the coinage caused the Athenians to call in and melt down all bronze pinakia. However, Head's date of 339 is merely an informed guess, which may well be approximately correct (to within about a decade), but has no more claim to precision than the latest opinion that the Athenians began to strike a regular bronze coinage about the time of Alexander (E. S. G. Robinson and M. J. Price, "An Emergency Coinage of Timotheos," *NC⁷* 7 [1967], 2). Even so, it is highly improbable that the coinage was begun specifically as a war measure, since emergency coinages at Athens and elsewhere were ordinarily of precious metals, especially gold, and the gold issue formerly associated with Chaironeia (Head, *Historia Numorum²*, 375) is now pretty reliably attributed to the crisis under Lachares in the early third century B.C. (E. T. Newell, *The Coinages of Demetrius Poliorcetes* [London: Oxford University Press, 1927], 133–134, n. 4). Finally, Athens would have been in a sorry state indeed if its available supply of bronze was so depleted that bronze pinakia had to be melted down for the manufacture of small coins. But although 339 was a year of political crisis, Athens' material resources remained intact.

10. Dow, *BCH* 87 (1963), 657.

occurs in this passage), but they were apparently simple ones, which allotted jurors *en bloc*, not individually, and did not employ pinakia.[11]

That the developed system of allotment by pinakia had been introduced by the 350s is generally assumed from Isokrates 7.54, which dates from that decade and represents the needy of Athens swarming in front of the law-courts in the hope of being allotted. And the assumption is supported by a riddle from Euboulos' *Sphiggokarion* about kleroteria which allot men "one by one."[12] This lost comedy cannot, unfortunately, be dated closely, but it was surely written no later than Isokrates 7 and could have been produced as early as the 370s or 380s.[13]

In view of the above determinations, recent commentators have seized on 378/7 as the most probable year for the reform that brought the allotment procedure described by Aristotle into being. This was a pre-eminent year of reform generally.[14] But G. M. Calhoun has presented a more specialized argument for connecting the reorganization of the dikasteria with the events of this year; he reasoned as follows:[15]

> Now we know that at sometime between 388 and the middle of the fourth century the system of drawing dicasts for the courts was changed, so that the ten sections into which the available dicasts were grouped were no longer assigned *en bloc* to the several courts, but the courts were filled from the whole heliaea without regard to sections. No attempt has been made, so far as I am aware, to fix the date of this important change more precisely, or to suggest for it any other motive than the general desire to make the bribery of dicasts more difficult. However, a very cogent reason for the change

11. On the early fourth-century organization of the dikasteria suggested by these passages and conventionally dated from 403/2, see Hommel, *Heliaia*, 115–126; Bonner-Smith I, 367–372. The short-lived, transitional period that Hommel hypothetically interposed between the times of the *Ploutos* and the inauguration of the fully developed system of impaneling dikasts (*Heliaia*, 124–125, whence Bonner-Smith I, 372, 373, n. 1) must of course be rejected, based as it was on Bruck's mistaken view that the earliest pinakia antedated allotment by pinakia (see below, p. 11).

12. Athenaeus 10.450b = J. M. Edmonds, *The Fragments of Attic Comedy*, 3 vols. (Leiden: E. J. Brill, 1957–1961), II, 130–133. The riddle is discussed by Dow, *HSCP* 50 (1939), 10–12; and Bishop, "The Cleroterium," 10.

13. The sole evidence is a joke about Kallistratos (Athenaeus 10.449f = Edmonds, *Fragments of Attic Comedy*, II, 130–131), whose career extended from the 380s until his exile in 361; in 355 he returned to Athens and was put to death.

14. See Hommel, *Heliaia*, 129–131; Bonner-Smith I, 373–374. The view of Gustave Glotz ("L'epistate des proèdres," *REG* 34 [1921], 1–19) that the institution of the proedroi dates from this year, however, has recently been called into question by D. M. Lewis ("Notes on Attic Inscriptions," *BSA* 49 [1954], 31–34).

15. G. M. Calhoun, "Oral and Written Pleading in Athenian Courts," *TAPA* 50 (1919), 191–192.

can be discovered, and that too in a year when important constitutional reforms were taking place at Athens. In the archonship of Nausinicus, 378/7 B.C., Athens was organizing her second league and straining every nerve to prepare for war with Sparta. It was a time of reform and reconstruction for the three leading states of Greece. Athens completely reorganized her fiscal system and established the symmories. Furthermore, a resolution was passed providing for the enrollment of 20,000 hoplites and 500 cavalry, and for manning 200 triremes.[16] Whatever may have been the available man power of Athens at this time, mobilization on such a scale would strain her resources to the utmost. The dicastic sections would undoubtedly be so reduced that a single section would often not suffice for the trial of even a private suit. If an attempt was to be made to prevent the complete suspension of the courts, a way had to be found in which to meet the exigencies of the situation. What could have been more effective than the change of which we have been speaking, to disregard the sections and empanel courts from all the dikasts who presented themselves? I can think of no time in which this reform would have been more urgently needed than in the year 378/7.

Calhoun's observation that written complaints and evidence were introduced in the courts sometime very close to 378/7 completes his argument for a general reform of Athenian court procedure in this year.

As Hommel has since remarked,[17] Calhoun is probably correct in attributing the developed system of allotment to a need for greater flexibility in the impaneling of dikasts. Presumably the problem of thwarting bribery of whole courts would have been solved by the early fourth-century system of allotting full sections of dikasts to the courts and would not itself have been a sufficient cause for a further reorganization of the dikasteria after 388. And in Chapter IV we shall see from wholly independent considerations that 378/7 is certainly about the right time for the introduction of bronze pinakia. Thus Calhoun's historical construction would seem to be much stronger now than when it was originally formulated.

16. Diodoros 15.29.7. Polybios (2.62.6), a more reliable authority, gives a force of 10,000 men and 100 triremes, but even these more conservative figures do not seriously affect the general thrust of Calhoun's argument.
17. Hommel, *Heliaia*, 130–131, with 128.

II The Material Evidence

To date, some 175-odd Athenian bronze allotment plates and fragments have been recovered from Greek soil. This is nearly double the number catalogued in the *Editio Minor* in 1931, but it still represents only a minute sampling of the tens of thousands that must have been manufactured and used during the middle quarters of the fourth century. In one sense, the sampling is somewhat greater than is indicated by the number of survivals, for over five-sixths of them are known or suspected palimpsests, that is, pinakia that have been used by more than one owner. Of these, the majority are multiple palimpsests, having had a minimum of three, not infrequently four, and in several attested cases as many as five or six successive owners. Since each reuse of a pinakion was in practice equivalent to its original use, and since the total number of recorded or suspected uses is roughly three times greater than the total number of surviving pinakia, it is fair to say that the palimpsests theoretically triple the amount of extant material. This gain, however, is only theoretical and is more than offset by the fact that our knowledge of most of the survivals is far from complete. Over a dozen pinakia have vanished since they were first and, with few exceptions, inadequately recorded. Fully two-thirds of the remaining survivals are fragments. And on the many palimpsests, erasure has usually been successful enough to deprive us of full readings of the earlier texts and all too often makes it impossible to determine exactly how many earlier inscriptions a given pinakion may have had.

Only three survivals (**144–146**) exhibit fundamental idiosyncracies of detail that cannot be paralleled on at least several other pinakia. All are fragments and might conceivably be less problematic if we knew what their missing right ends looked like. The rest of the pinakia conveniently arrange themselves into six more or less well-defined typological groups and show that however small and imperfect our sampling numerically, on the whole it does seem to be reasonably representative of the different types of pinakia and of the behavior of their various physical details.

Provenience

With only five or six exceptions,[1] complete pinakia with known circumstances of discovery have been recovered from the graves of their last owners.[2] Like a child's knucklebones or doll, a young man's strigil, a lady's mirror, and other common furnishings in Greek burials, pinakia were valued possessions and—what is perhaps of greater importance—symbolic of their owners' way of life. Even today it is hard to think of a more appropriate symbol of an Athenian's nearly professional involvement in democratic government. In heroic times the Greek aristocrat was buried with his bronze sword and armor; in the quieter, democratic fourth century an Athenian might be buried with his bronze allotment plate. I say "might be" because, as institutionalized reuse of pinakia implies, it was probably not strictly legal to bury a pinakion with its deceased owner. Since the pinakia were issued by the state and ordinarily reverted back to the state to be reissued, they must technically have remained state property and should have been returned upon an owner's demise. In this light it is not surprising that more whole pinakia have not been found, and we should feel a certain indebtedness to those families who thought more of their dead than of legal formalities. In two instances, graves have yielded a pair of pinakia belonging to a single owner (**29/125** and **149/150**).[3]

1. These are: **104**, said to have been found on the south slope of the Acropolis; **146**, excavated on the Pnyx; **47**, **96**, and **131** (the last may not be complete), excavated in the Athenian Agora; and **66**, which was excavated from earth within a necropolis where it was presumably buried with an owner before being removed by grave robbers or subsequent grave digging in the area. Except for **66** and **96**, all of these are short, reused pieces of pinakia that were originally of normal length; they are "complete" only as regards their last use.

2. These are: **16, 37, 61, 62, 73, 88, 92, 93, 113, 119, 129, 149-150, 152, 153,** and **157**. They and the fourteen other whole pinakia whose place of discovery has been reported without any specific mention of graves come from a sizable number of necropoleis, occasionally at some of the more remote demesites (for instance, **16** and **37** from Erchia), but scattered mostly in the immediate environs of the city. The only cemetery known to have yielded more than two pinakia is the vast gravefield that extended from the northern Peiraeus westward to Aigaleos (see Dodwell, *Tour* I, 430–467; and Arthur Milchloefer in E. Curtius and J. A. Kaupert, *Karten von Attika*, 8 vols. [Berlin, 1881—1895], II, 7–8). It has produced at least nine. To judge from its size and proximity to the Peiraeus, one would imagine that this was the chief cemetery of the Athenian urban poor, who had the greatest stake in democracy and would have treasured their pinakia most highly. Thus far, no pinakia have appeared in the systematically excavated graves in the Kerameikos. In spite of the corrosive wetness of the soil, the Kerameikos graves have preserved bronze objects of other kinds; and I have been assured by the present excavators that burials there continued uninterruptedly through the whole of the fourth century. The absence of pinakia therefore may have something to do with the social and economic status of the persons who could afford to have been buried in the choice lots in the excavated area close by the city gates. Although the matter has yet to be proven, such persons may have belonged to the Athenian upper crust and may have been less ardent democrats—or at any rate cared less about being buried with their pinakia—than Athenians buried elsewhere.

3. Bruck listed four pairs (*AthMitt* 19 [1894], 207, no. 17; *Philologus* 54 [1895], 77). But one of them involved only a single pinakion (**83**) that was erroneously counted as two; and his

The only graves that contained pinakia and have been excavated with enough care to preserve a record of associated ceramic finds are those which yielded **113** and **119** and the small black-glaze lekythoi illustrated in Figs. 209 and 219. Such lekythoi are currently being studied by Dr. Klaus Vierneisel of the Kerameikos excavations on the evidence of the stratified fourth-century burials in the Kerameikos (which themselves can be dated with reference to such more or less fixed points as the fortifications of 338, the sculptural style of stelai which stood over certain graves, and the like). I have discussed our two lekythoi with Dr. Vierneisel, and have gratefully drawn on his unpublished chronology (see *ad* **113** and **119**, below). In addition to these two gravegroups involving pottery, the inscribed stele that was erected over the tomb containing **68** is extant (Fig. 121), as is the one that may have stood over the tomb containing **124** (Fig. 231).

Burials account for nearly all the complete surviving pinakia and probably for some of the fragmentary examples, the missing remainders of which were overlooked when the contents of a grave were removed. None of the fragments, however, have been reported as coming from graves, and the evidence at hand strongly suggests that the majority of them did not. Of the twenty-five-odd specimens that turned up in random contexts in the American excavations on the Pnyx and in the Athenian Agora, all but three or four (see n. 1 above) are fragments or scraps of pinakia that presumably broke and were discarded in antiquity.[4] The same probably applies also to **7**, a large fragment of an Athenian pinakion excavated from the ruins of Olynthos. Finally, two fragments of unknown provenience, **9** and **76**, surely did not come from graves, as the last name on each has been erased. Both belonged to pinakia that broke while being erased for a further use, were discarded, and were discovered in the last century apparently as surface finds. These, then, are the fragments whose circumstances of discovery are either known or can be inferred. It is reasonable to assume that most of the other fragments likewise are discards from pinakia that broke in the course of use and that they ultimately appeared on the antiquities market after being picked up as surface finds, much like the profuse numbers of bronze coins that are continually being found by the present-day inhabitants of most classical sites.

For the most part, the pinakia and pinakia fragments recovered in the Pnyx and Agora excavations come from contexts that are too late or too loosely dated to have any useful chronological implications. The exceptions

---

fourth pair was comprised of **50** and **71**, two fragments which he mistakenly assumed to have come from a single grave (see **71**).

4. Thus Dow, *BCH* 87 (1963), 659. For a pinakion that broke and was mended in antiquity, see **62**.

are **130**, which was found beneath a floor that the excavator has dated at about 350 or a little later; and **105**, **132**, **161**, and **164**, all fragments from the filling of the Third Assembly Place on the Pnyx, which is now attributed to the building program of Lykourgos and dated "tentatively to the closing years of his active career, i.e., to the period 330–326 B.C."[5] The above-mentioned fragment from Olynthos traveled to that site and was lost or discarded there sometime before Philip's destruction of the city in 348.

Typology and Sequence

As soon as pinakia began to be discovered in the early decades of the last century, it was at once apparent that they differed among themselves in respect to the technique and position of their section-letters, their inscriptional format, and, above all, in the number and variety of the official seals stamped on them. Some pinakia bear from one to four seals in differing combinations and arrangements; others lack seals entirely. From this and from the fact that the types of the seals were thought to have been more numerous than they actually are, many commentators inferred that all of the bronze pinakia were originally issued without seals and that the seals were added one at a time in the course of a pinakion's use. According to this interpretation, any pinakion without seals would have received seals if the pinakion was used over an extended period by an owner who eventually qualified for whatever the seals happened to represent. Pinakia without seals and pinakia with seals were typologically alike, but the owners of the latter happened to have had longer and more active public careers. This view, first put forward by Carl Curtius in 1876,[6] was seriously criticized by Girard only two years later,[7] but was revived by Theodor Teusch (who seems to have been ignorant of Girard's fundamental article)[8] and was subsequently accepted by J. H. Lipsius[9] and as late as 1927 by Hommel.[10]

In reply to Curtius, Girard pointed out that the pinakia without stamped seals were apparently never intended to receive any. He noted that the stampless pinakia were characteristically inscribed with a large section-letter at the middle of one end so as to preclude the later addition of a seal at that end. And as for the pinakia with stamped seals, he observed that whereas

5. H. A. Thompson and R. L. Scranton, "Stoas and City Walls on the Pnyx," *Hesperia* 12 (1943), 300–301.
6. Curtius, *RhM* 31 (1876), 286.
7. Girard, *BCH* 2 (1878), 530.
8. Teusch, *De sortitione*, 54–55.
9. Lipsius I, 150, n. 50.
10. Hommel, *Heliaia*, 42–43.

the square seals with the device of a double-bodied owl are irregularly positioned, often weakly stamped, and appear to have been added in haste as
cachets de contrôle during the course of a pinakion's use, the round seals that
copy the reverse type of Athenian triobol coins (owl standing frontally,
surrounded by an olive wreath and the letters ΑΘΕ or ΑΘΗ) were carefully
positioned and struck and would seem therefore to have been stamped on
pinakia at the time of manufacture, before the pinakia were inscribed.

These findings were seconded by Bruck, who proceeded to explain the
typological differences of the pinakia in terms of a chronological development.[11]
He believed the large holes drilled or punched toward the right ends of many
pinakia were for hanging the pinakia on kleroteria; noting that the pinakia
with triobol seals at their left ends were usually provided with such holes
and that the stampless pinakia were not, he proposed that the former were
contemporary with kleroteria and that the latter were used during an earlier
period before kleroteria were introduced. The pinakia with triobol seals
stamped at the right belonged to a transitional period between the two
larger groups. Bruck, of course, was led astray by his erroneous interpretation
of the "carrying-holes." Pinakia were inserted into kleroteria, not hung on
them. And, as we shall see, his sequence of earlier stampless and later stamped
pinakia was the reverse of what it should have been. The vastly greater evidence at our disposal confirms, nevertheless, that his approach to the seals was
basically sound. The typological differences among the pinakia cannot be
understood except as the result of specific stylistic phases in an overall chronological progression.

The pinakia that were used without stamped seals may be dealt with first.
The nucleus of this group (herein Class VI pinakia) consists of thirty pinakia
(**114–143**) that never received a seal, although most of them are palimpsests
and obviously had been used for a substantial amount of time. Their format
is of the simplest: owner's name inscribed in two lines and a large, inscribed
section-letter usually positioned at the middle of the left or right end. As
Girard recognized, such large, centered section-letters left no room for the
addition of a seal at one end. These are the only pinakia known to have been
issued without at least one stamped seal, and there is nothing to suggest that
a seal or seals might have been added to them later. They were, obviously,
never intended to have seals.

I have referred to such pinakia as the nucleus of Class VI since they are
supplemented by a number of other pinakia that were originally provided
with seals but that in the course of reuse lost their seals through erasure and

11. Bruck, *Philologus* 54 (1895), 67–77.

thus became converted to stampless Class VI pinakia (for example, **23**, **27**, **33**, **34**, **36–38**, **40–42**, **46–48**, **54**, **59**, and **61**). At the time that these converted pinakia lost their seals, most of them acquired a large, centered section-letter of the Class VI variety. Such converted pinakia imply that any stamped pinakion would ultimately become stampless if kept in circulation and re-used over a long enough period of time; they demonstrate, therefore, that the stampless pinakia are, as a group, later than the pinakia with stamped seals. We may thus speak of two fundamental phases of Athenian pinakia: an earlier phase during which stamped seals were a standard feature; and a later phase, which dispensed with seals. Apparently, after a certain point in time, the stamped seals were simply discontinued.

As discussed in the concluding sections of this chapter, there is now abundant evidence to affirm that Girard and Bruck were correct in maintaining that the seals on the stamped pinakia are behaviorally of two types: those which were stamped on pinakia at the time of manufacture, before the pinakia were inscribed; and those which were added later during the course of a pinakion's use. The former, which may also be defined as seals that regularly occur on all pinakia of a given class, I shall refer to as "primary" seals; the latter, which generally appear on some but not on all pinakia of a particular class, may be conveniently designated as "secondary" seals. There are only two varieties of primary seals, the triobol seal and a gorgoneion.

When all of the stamped pinakia are arranged into stylistically homogeneous groups, the following formats of seals, section-letters, and owners' names emerge.

Class I (**1–5**):

[A] <u>nomen: dem.</u> (T)
[O]

—A single primary seal, a T(riobol) seal with the ethnic **AΘE**, at the right.
—Section-letter stamped at the middle of the left end.
—Owner's name inscribed in a single line.
—Secondary seal, O(wl standing right in incuse square), stamped toward the right.

Class II (**12–19**):

—Primary seal and stamped section-letter format as in Class I.
—Owner's name usually inscribed in two lines (but note that the one-line arrangement was retained on **12**, whose triobol seal is die-linked to the triobol seal on three more typical Class II pinakia, **13**, **16**, and **17**).
—Secondary seal (omitted from **12–15**) of the D(ouble-bodied owl) type.

Class III (**20–45**):

—Two primary seals, both G(orgoneion) seals; one stamped at each end.
—Section-letter stamped or inscribed in the upper left corner.
—Owner's name inscribed in two lines.
—Secondary seals do not occur.

Class IV (**61–77**):

—Two primary seals: T(riobol) seal with the ethnic AΘE or AΘH at the lower left corner, and a G(orgoneion) seal at the right.
—Section-letter stamped (or, in several late uses, inscribed) in the upper left corner.
—Owner's name inscribed in two lines.
—D(ouble-bodied owl) secondary seal (not present on **61**, **72**, and **75**).

Class V (**78–113**):

—Seal and section-letter format as in Class VI. Triobol seal ethnics in AΘH. (Secondary seals not present on **78–82**).
—Owner's name inscribed in two lines, with added pierced holes. For the alphabet, see Table 1.

One needs only to glance at the above diagrams to see that the pinakia of Class I have every claim to being the earliest in the full pinakia series. This is most apparent from their one-line textual format, which was the natural arrangement to adopt at the outset. Names were, and are, customarily written in a single line. The one-line arrangement, however, made uneconomical use of the available space on pinakia and left no room for patronymics. Once the Athenians had some experience in inscribing pinakia, these limitations were recognized, and texts in one line were permanently abandoned. The two-line format, adopted already for the second texts on the reused Class I pinakia **4** and **5** and for the first texts on most Class II pinakia remained the standard arrangement down through the latest bronze pinakia of Class VI.

Lesser indications of the priority of the Class I pinakia are the unique form of the Class I secondary seal, which does not occur in other classes (in Classes II, IV, and V it was replaced by the doubled-bodied owl secondary seal); the unparalleled high relief (from careful, heavy stamping) of the triobol seals on **3–5**; and the exceptional 0.38-centimeter thickness of **1**. The last two items imply a certain lavishness in manufacture that was not expended on other pinakia.

Comparatively speaking, the pinakia of Class I form a remarkably homogeneous group. This is surely not fortuitous, for, being the earliest pinakia, they should in all probability date to the year when allotment by pinakia was instituted. In that year, thousands of pinakia had to be made up and issued for the first time, and, manufactured and inscribed together, all would have looked very much alike. The Class I pinakia are almost certainly survivals from this original reform issue.

The Class II pinakia are essentially a continuation of the Class I type and can be distinguished from that class only by their texts in two lines (when they have texts in two lines; the one-line arrangement was retained in the first use of **12**) and by the double-bodied owl form of their secondary seals (but, again, when they have secondary seals; **12–15** do not).[12] Like their two-line inscriptions, their double-bodied owl secondary seals occur in later classes but not in Class I. Classes I and II are closely related with respect to their seal and section-letter format, and together precede the remaining stamped pinakia, which are characterized by being stamped with two primary seals. The Class II pinakia should be pinakia distributed in the years between the initial Class I issue and the time when pinakia began to bear two primary seals.

12. Thus there is a problem in ascertaining whether a pinakion like **6**, which has an earliest text in a single line but which lacks a secondary seal of any kind, should be categorized as a Class I or as a Class II pinakion (see below, p. 47). A similar problem would be presented by **12** were it not that its triobol seal is die-linked to the triobol seals on three archetypal Class II pinakia.

In the period of two primary seals the sequence of classes becomes less simple. On the one hand there are the Class IV and V pinakia, which continue and complete the series of triobol seal pinakia begun in Classes I and II. The pinakia of Classes IV and V were also stamped with a triobol primary seal, but on them this seal was moved into the lower left-hand corner (the stamped section-letter having been raised into the upper left corner) in order to accommodate a new type of primary seal, a gorgoneion seal, at the right. Thus, the introduction of this gorgoneion seal was responsible for the change from one to two primary seals after the issue of the Class II pinakia.

The introduction of the gorgoneion seal was responsible also for the appearance of a wholly new kind of pinakion (Class III), which not only lacked a triobol seal but which was stamped with two gorgoneion seals, one at the right and the other in the lower left corner, as if to emphasize this lack. These are no reasons for thinking that the Class III pinakia disrupted or succeeded the sequence of triobol seal pinakia at any point, that is, that they belong within or followed the progression of the Class I, II, IV, and V pinakia. The Class III pinakia are triobol-*less* pinakia, and, unlike the pinakia of Classes I, II, IV, and V, did not receive secondary seals. Both factors set them apart and strongly suggest that they stood outside of and were used parallel with the triobol seal pinakia, or, more correctly, parallel with the triobol-gorgoneion Class IV and V pinakia, for the Class III pinakia would hardly have been stamped with two gorgoneion seals unless they were contemporaneous with other pinakia having a primary seal at each end.

The two innovations involving the appearance of the gorgoneion seal following the issue of the Class II pinakia—the addition of this seal to triobol seal pinakia and the introduction of the Class III pinakia with two gorgoneion seals—were not likely to have been unrelated either causally or in time. Considered together they imply that, for whatever purpose the gorgoneion seal was devised, when it came into being, it was introduced on the triobol seal pinakia and the Class III pinakia simultaneously.

That some of the Class III and IV pinakia were manufactured and issued at about the same time is concretely attested by a die-link between the gorgoneion seals on certain pinakia of these classes. The die in question (described *ad* 21, below) was used for striking the gorgoneia on 21 and 25 (Class III), on 62 (originally stamped as a Class III pinakion, but converted to a Class IV pinakion, presumably before the pinakion was first issued, by the over-stamping of its left-hand gorgoneion with a triobol seal), on 70 (the right end of a Class IV pinakion with a secondary seal), and on 51 (a right end which could have belonged equally to a pinakion of Class III or IV). One die-link between certain Class III and IV pinakia should mean that these classes shared other gorgoneion dies in common. But, unfortunately, too few of the gorgoneion seals on the handful of Class IV survivals are well enough preserved to allow more such die-links to be positively identified. As I have indicated in the Catalogue, it is possible that the die that struck the gorgoneion seal on **22** (Class III) may be the one used on **59** (Class III or IV) and **63, 65,** and **66** (all Class IV); although unproven, this possible link at least serves to point up the general stylistic similarity of the gorgoneion seals on many pinakia of the two classes.

A second detail that underscores the parallelism between the Class III and IV pinakia is to be found in the change of technique in their section-letters: the earliest pinakia (Classes I and II) were provided with stamped section-letters; on the latest bronze pinakia (Class VI) the section-letters are inscribed. Within Classes III and IV, however, are found both pinakia issued with stamped letters (for example, III: **20–27**; IV: **62, 63, 65, 68, 73–77**) and pinakia whose earliest texts were provided with inscribed section-letters (such as, III: **28–31**; IV: **72**), all of which would indicate that the change in technique occurred at a time when pinakia of both classes were current. The Class III and IV pinakia with stamped section-letters, of course, represent the earlier phase of these classes. (It was in this phase that the positively established die-link occurs.) Those with inscribed section-letters—and to these we must add the later uses of the earlier Class III and IV pinakia whose original stamped section-letters were eventually replaced with inscribed letters (for instance, III: the last uses of **23–26**; IV: the last uses of **63** and **65**)—should belong to the very latest phase, not only of the Class III and IV pinakia but to the very latest phase of pinakia with stamped seals altogether. After such uses with seals and small inscribed section-letters, Class III and IV pinakia, if reused still later, tended to lose their seals through erasure, began to acquire large inscribed section-letters, and were reused as stampless Class VI pinakia (for example, III: **38** and **42**; III or IV: **46**; IV: **61**). The implications are that the parallel Class III and IV pinakia spanned the entire period of pinakia with two primary seals, between the Class II pinakia on the one side and the stampless Class VI pinakia on the other.[13]

The relative chronology of pinakia with two primary seals is complicated further by a comparatively large number of survivals that form a kind of

---

13. For the sake of clarity, I am intentionally oversimplifying. As shown below in the discussion of section-letters, some Class III pinakia with inscribed section-letters apparently continued to be issued after the triobol seal pinakia were discontinued.

subgroup of the Class IV pinakia but that, for ease of reference, I have catalogued separately under the rubric of Class V. Their format is identical to the
format of Class IV pinakia with stamped section-letters: section-letter
stamped in the upper left corner, triobol seal in the lower left corner, gorgoneion seal at the right end, and, frequently, a double-bodied owl secondary
seal stamped toward the right. They are set apart from the Class IV pinakia,
first, by the specialized and highly uniform technique and alphabet with
which they were inscribed, and, second, by the rigorously consistent style of
their primary seals. Their lettering (diagrammed in Table 1) is characterized
by the addition of pierced holes at the terminations of straight strokes, on
crossbars, and on the curved sides of rounded letters. Their triobol and gorgoneion seals are respectively so much alike that I have been unable to determine from the seals themselves whether the pinakia were all stamped with a
single triobol seal and a single gorgoneion seal die or whether (as is more
probable) by a number of virtually identical triobol and virtually identical
gorgoneion dies. Such homogeneity in style of seals is unmatched in any
other class, and since it is accompanied by an equally remarkable consistency
in the way the Class V pinakia were inscribed, it is apparent that the Class V
pinakia were manufactured, stamped, inscribed, and issued together, either
in a single year or in a limited number of consecutive years.

It is apparent also that the Class V pinakia cannot be placed either at the
very beginning or at the very end of the triobol-gorgoneion (Class IV) series
and that they therefore represent an interruption in this series. The evidence
here is quite varied. Each of the following observations must be taken into
account.

(1) We have seen that uses of Class IV pinakia can be divided into two
groups: those uses belonging to an earlier phase with stamped section-letters,
and those belonging to a later phase during which section-letters were
inscribed. The Class V pinakia were issued with stamped section-letters and
normally retain these letters for as many as two uses subsequent to their
original use (see **84, 95, 104,** and **107,** all with three uses). Thus the Class V
pinakia are to be associated with the earlier phase of Class IV and cannot be
the latest triobol-gorgoneion pinakia.

(2) The same conclusion is independently derived from a consideration of
the texts on Class IV pinakia which are inscribed "in imitation of Class V
lettering," that is, texts (listed and discussed below) inscribed with punched
serifs rather than the permanent, fully pierced holes characteristic of the
standard Class V texts. The texts inscribed in imitation of Class V lettering
must belong to a time soon after the issue of the Class V pinakia; it is not
surprising, therefore, that the largest number of such texts occur in the

second or third uses of reused Class V pinakia. Such texts occur on Class IV pinakia also and thereby provide a chronological fix between certain uses of these pinakia and the Class V issue. If texts inscribed in imitation of Class V lettering appear in late uses of much-reused Class IV pinakia, they would indicate that the Class V pinakia were not issued until late in the same series of pinakia stamped with a triobol and gorgoneion seal; whereas, if these texts occurred in earlier uses of Class IV pinakia, it would mean that the Class V pinakia were issued early relative to the Class IV pinakia as a whole. As it happens, the texts that imitate Class V lettering on two Class IV pinakia, **68** and **71**, occur in early uses and could very well belong to the original uses of the pinakia.

It should be noted, however, that on **62** (a Class IV pinakion that was stamped with the above-mentioned gorgoneion seal die that has been identified on certain other pinakia of Classes III and IV) a text in imitation of Class V lettering does not appear until a second use. Of itself, this does not prove that the first use of the pinakion must have antedated the Class V issue (as we see from **111**, a Class V fragment with a regularly inscribed text in a second use followed by a third text in lettering imitating the Class V technique), but it clearly strengthens the possibility. In sum, the few texts on Class IV pinakia that are inscribed in imitation of Class V lettering evidence the earliness of the Class V pinakia in the full triobol-gorgoneion series without implying that the Class V pinakia were necessarily the earliest pinakia in the series.

(3) Another link between specific uses of Class IV and V pinakia is provided by the behavior of the square double-bodied owl secondary seals which were stamped on many but not on all pinakia of these classes. At the end of the present chapter, we shall see that there are strong reasons for thinking that each type of secondary seal was valid for and dated to a very limited period of time, of probably no more than a single year, and that each secondary seal itself applied only to a single use of a pinakion, namely that use during which the seal was added. If this reasoning is correct, all uses of Class IV and V pinakia that received a square double-bodied owl seal should be contemporary with each other. Since this seal was added to a number of Class V pinakia in a first use (**85-91**), the seal would, like texts inscribed in imitation of Class V lettering, date not long after the Class V pinakia were newly issued. At least two Class V pinakia were not stamped with the seal until after their first use (**83** received one in a second use, **84** in a second or third use), the implication being that both pinakia had been reinscribed within the time that elapsed between the Class V issue and the date of the seal. Since the seal was stamped on some of the Class IV pinakia during early uses also (for example, **62, 63,**

and **70**, although **69** did not receive the seal any earlier than its third use), we again have reason to feel confident that early uses of Class V pinakia and early uses of many Class IV pinakia were more or less contemporaneous.

(4) Items (1)–(3) establish that the issue of the Class V pinakia occurred early in the series of pinakia stamped with a triobol and a gorgoneion seal. That the Class V pinakia were not the earliest pinakia in this series, however, is suggested by the ethnics of the Class V triobol seals. The triobol seal ethnics on the Class I and II pinakia read AΘE, and this spelling (which duplicates the ethnic on triobol coins) appears also on a number of the triobol seals on Class IV pinakia (**61–64**), of which two (**62** and **63**) are known to have had early uses with stamped section-letters and thus belong to the earlier phase of Class IV. (All traces of the original section-letters of **61** and **64** have disappeared through erasure.) On the Class V pinakia, however, the spelling of the ethnic is AΘH, which occurs also on two Class IV pinakia. Of these two, **73** appears to have been stamped as a Class V pinakion—both of its primary seals are from Class V dies—but not to have been issued and inscribed until later, when the pierced hole lettering associated with the Class V pinakia had been formally abandoned. The other, **72**, although stamped with a triobol seal from a Class V die, bears a gorgoneion seal that is not of the Class V type and happens to be the one Class IV pinakion that is known to have been first issued in the latest phase of Class IV, for, upon issue, its original stamped section-letter was erased and replaced with an inscribed section-letter. Both Class IV pinakia with triobol seal ethnics in AΘH (that is, with triobol seals from a Class V die or dies), then, were apparently issued later than the Class V issue; the obvious implication for the Class IV pinakia with triobol seal ethnics in AΘE is that their first uses should precede the Class V issue, as certainly did the Class I and II pinakia, whose triobol ethnics are invariably spelled AΘE.

This is logical enough and doubtless correct in principle. No exceptions can be proven, although (since there are no compelling a priori reasons why an early triobol seal die with an AΘE ethnic might not have been returned to use after AΘH ethnics were introduced in Class V) the possibility of an occasional exception cannot be excluded altogether.

(5) The other factor that argues that the Class V pinakia were not issued until after the issue of at least some Class IV pinakia is the absence of any surviving Class III pinakia that have been stamped with gorgoneion seals of the distinctive Class V type, that is, by a Class V gorgoneion seal die. Presumably, when the Class V pinakia were manufactured, no Class III pinakia were manufactured to accompany them, so that if the Class V pinakia were the earliest triobol-gorgoneion pinakia, they would not only have antedated all

of the Class IV pinakia (many of which had triobol seal ethnics in AΘE) but all of the Class III pinakia (which share one or more gorgoneion seal dies with Class IV pinakia) as well. As there is every good reason to suppose that the gorgoneion seal was introduced on the earliest Class III pinakia and on the earliest triobol-gorgoneion pinakia simultaneously, such a sequence is virtually unthinkable.

It is unfortunately true that our knowledge of the Class IV pinakia is severely limited by the small number of extant examples, their frequently poor state of preservation, and by the circumstance that most of them are much-erased palimpsests. To take only one troublesome example, if **63** had no more than its four attested uses, there would be an obvious difficulty in reconciling the AΘE ethnic of its triobol seal (in all probability a sign of pre-Class V manufacture) with the chronological implications of its double-bodied owl seal, which was stamped no later than the earliest of these four uses and which itself dates after the Class V issue. Was the AΘE triobol seal here stamped during the post-Class V period? Or, could it be that the pinakion was manufactured and stamped with primary seals before the Class V issue, but was not issued and first used until much later? Neither solution, I suppose, is untenable. But, for all we can tell, the pinakion may have had five uses altogether, with a first use dating from before the Class V issue and a second use, to which the secondary seal was added, belonging to the post-Class V period. Similar uncertainties arise in regard to the detailed histories of most other Class IV survivals and do not permit us to go beyond the handful of dependable observations listed above.

Considered together, these observations provide a sequence for the pinakia of Classes IV and V that may be summarized as follows:

Upon the introduction of the gorgoneion seal, the first triobol seal pinakia to have been manufactured and issued were the Class IV ones with stamped section-letters and with triobol seals that continue the AΘE ethnic of the Class I and II pinakia.

The issue of these early Class IV pinakia was soon interrupted by the issue of the specially inscribed Class V pinakia (triobol seal ethnics in AΘH).

Following the Class V issue, Class V pinakia and Class IV pinakia, many in various stages of reuse, circulated side by side. Some Class V pinakia were still being used with their original pierced hole inscriptions intact; others were already receiving second and third texts either in imitation of Class V lettering or inscribed conventionally, as also were contemporary uses of Class IV pinakia. It was during this post-Class V period that the double-bodied owl seal was added to many of these triobol seal pinakia. Certain Class II pinakia, although issued before pinakia began to bear two primary seals, were also being reused during this period, as we see from **17**, which received a text in imitation of Class V lettering and a double-bodied owl seal in its last use, and from **16** and **18**, whose double-bodied owl seals were presumably not added until a later use either.

In the very last phase of the triobol-gorgoneion pinakia, the pinakia began to receive inscribed section-letters instead of stamped ones.

Such then are the key observations and deductions from which an overall sequence of the pinakia can be reconstructed. Three main phases have been distinguished: an initial phase of pinakia stamped with a single (triobol) primary seal (Classes I and II); an intermediate phase of pinakia with two primary seals (Classes III–V), which began with the introduction of the gorgoneion seal; and a final phase of stampless pinakia (Class VI). The pinakia with stamped seals divide themselves vertically into two groups: those stamped with the triobol seal (Classes I, II, IV, and V) and those from which the triobol seal was excluded (Class III). It remains to ask what happened to this division after the stamped seals were discontinued. Did the stampless Class VI pinakia continue the triobol group, the group without the triobol seal, or both groups together? But before attempting an answer to this and the many other problems raised in the preceding pages, it will be helpful to review the various physical aspects of the pinakia in closer detail.

Size, Erasure, and Carrying-holes

The plates were cast or cut[14] to dimensions measuring on the average about 11 centimeters in length, about 2 centimeters in width, and about 1.5 to 2.5 millimeters in thickness. Even in the more homogeneous Classes I and V, variations of about 1 centimeter in length and 1 millimeter in thickness are not uncommon. The greatest concentration of pinakia with exceptional thicknesses of about 3 millimeters are found in Class I (the thickness of **1** measures 3.8 millimeters) and among the Class I or II pinakia and fragments (**6–11**). The greatest concentration of exceptionally thin pinakia (thickness under 1 millimeter) occurs in Class VI, but there is no real consistency in these or in any other class. Widths, of course, were limited by the widths of the slots in kleroteria and tend to be more regular.

The original dimensions of reused pinakia have normally been altered by

14. If the raised ridge of metal along the lower edge of **94** is to be correctly identified as a casting line, such as are found on many kinds of ancient bronzes, we may assume that all of the pinakia with substantial thicknesses were cast, probably individually, in shallow, open molds. Thin pinakia like **29**, **52**, and others in Class VI, on the other hand, were almost certainly cut from large hammered bronze sheets.

erasure. As one sees from the many heavily striated palimpsests (for example, **5, 16, 22, 23**), pinakia with stamped seals were ordinarily erased by filing or scraping (subtracting) the requisite metal from the upper surface. The striations could in turn be polished away with fine abrasives, as presumably on **4, 17, 21**, and other palimpsests with relatively smooth surfaces, but the reduction in thickness usually remains as a telltale sign of erasure. Although filing or scraping was a relatively laborious way of erasing bronze, it was the least destructive and was employed to preserve as much of the metal as possible for further uses.

The other common technique of erasure was by hammering (compression), which not only reduced a pinakion's thickness, but distorted its width (see **121**, whose original thickness and width are preserved at the left) and often distended lengths (to nearly 14 centimeters on **96**). There are exceptions (as on **68, 73**, and probably **76**, all Class IV pinakia), but for the most part this more destructive technique was employed primarily in connection with the stampless Class VI pinakia and late Class VI uses of pinakia that were originally stamped (for example, **36, 38, 61**, and **96**).

A more refined type of erasure by hammering is found on **62** and **63**, both stamped (Class IV) pinakia. The letters of the earliest recorded text (text *a*) on each were meticulously peened out stroke by stroke with a hammer and a small blunt tool.

In general, it was not until the stampless Class VI period that segments of broken pinakia were reinscribed and reused (see **47, 128, 131**, and **146**). In the period of stamped pinakia, when primary seals were passed on from one use to the next, a pinakion was effectively invalidated if an end with a primary seal had broken away (but see **104**). Similarly, it is only in the Class VI period that we find opisthographic palimpsests (see **34, 59, 119, 120, 134, 135**, and **172**), since stamped pinakia were necessarily reinscribed on the face that contained their primary seals.

Several surviving pinakia have notches cut into their ends: a single notch in each end of **66, 92, 96**, and in the preserved end of **134**; two notches in the preserved ends of **57** and **89** and apparently in both ends—described as "trilobated ends"—of the lost pinakion **155**; and perhaps the three notches in the preserved end of **19**. These notches, I assume, were to fit nails in a workbench in order to hold the plates firmly in place during inscribing or erasure.

The isolated drilled holes (diameter normally 3–4 millimeters) on twenty-seven survivals were doubtless for receiving a thong or string for carrying, perhaps about the neck.[15] These holes occur on occasional pinakia of Classes

15. Thus Dow, *BCH* 87 (1963), 655. A loop or knotted cord could be slipped out the hole when the pinakion was submitted for allotment.

II (**15**, **16** [at the left], and **17**), IV (**63**, **66**, and **73**), and VI (once only, on **122**), but are characteristic only of Class V where they appear on seventeen out of twenty-three complete pinakia and right and middle fragments. The hole on **17**, a Class II pinakion reinscribed in imitation of Class V lettering, therefore, was probably not added until the last, Class V-like use of the pinakion. And it may be that the carrying-holes on other Class II pinakia also were not added until the later uses of these pinakia.

Lettering

The pinakia, including those of Class V before their letters were elaborated with pierced holes, were inscribed with a punching technique, a straight punch or chisel being used for rectilinear strokes and punches with a curved section for rounded letters or parts of letters. The punches were held perpendicular to the metal and struck from above with a mallet. The technique is most readily detected from rounded letters that were impressed with a tubular ring punch (for example, the omicron, phi, and omega in the last inscription on **18**, all from the same punch) or with a half-round punch (note the last text on **92**, where the first omicron in line one is clearly composed of two interlocking half-round impressions). Segments of circles for betas, rhos, and omegas were obtained from a full ring punch by holding the punch at a slight angle to the surface so that only a part of the ring would actually be impressed into the metal. The lengths of straight lines were also controlled by striking a straight punch at various angles to the surface. Indeed, it seems that all straight strokes on a given pinakion were normally produced with the same straight punch (rather than with one long punch and one short one) since few long strokes or few short strokes ever have the same exact lengths, and since short strokes (including the "dots" in the middle of thetas, see **21**, **119**, **167**) usually have a wedge-shaped profile and a tapering depth caused by the edge of a punch that was tilted up. On very thin pinakia, such as **122**, **123**, and **126**, such punching curved the metal surrounding the letters upward and left an imprint of the letters visible on the back of the plate.

From an epigraphical point of view, the most significant aspect of this punching technique is the effect it had on letter forms, for to a considerable degree the shapes of letters, curvilinear letters in particular, were determined by which punching tools the letterer happened to use.[16] To take an extreme

16. With the exception of Georges Daux, scholars have shied away from dating specific pinakia from the style of their lettering. In his publication of **6** (Class II), *q.v.*, Daux ventured that the letters of text *b* belong to the second quarter of the fourth century, which accords quite well with our more precise chronological criteria for pinakia with stamped seals discussed at the end of Chapter IV.

example, the rho on **91** has an archaic look because the letterer chose to make its loop with two straight punch marks instead of using a rounded tool. Other, though less striking, instances of curved strokes made with a series of straight punches are found on **4, 83, 134** Side B, and **174**. The inconsistent forms of the phis in the last inscription on **84**, on the other hand, result from the letterer's being well equipped with two different full round punches, a small ring punch and another with an oval face; the curved arms of the upsilon in the demotic may have been punched with still a third, half-round tool. Another effect on letter forms is illustrated by the Hellenistic-looking pi in line two of **61**. In making the right-hand vertical the letterer did not hold his punch at a high enough angle with the accidental result that the stroke is almost as long as the vertical on the left. Inscribed section-letters were frequently punched at a larger scale and sometimes with thicker strokes than letters in the corresponding owner's name (for example, on **26, 28, 36, 64, 77, 122**, and **126**). Such differences in scale and texture are not, of course, to be attributed to different "hands" but merely to the same letterer's use of different sized punches or his varying control of a single punch.

The punching technique was undoubtedly the fastest and most efficient method of inscribing bronze. Another ancient technique, that of incising with a sharp cutting blade that is dug into the metal at the beginning of a stroke and pushed to its completion, involved obvious problems in the cutting of rounded letters and required, moreover, that the object being inscribed be locked firmly in a vise or embedded in pitch to counteract the force of the cutting tool.[17] The only inscriptions in our catalogue that appear to have been incised are the slovenly scratched text *b* of **56** and the letters (?) on the dubious **181**.

A third common technique of inscribing bronze was by stippling, or by forming letters with rows of closely placed punched dots, as on the pinakia from Thasos (Figs. 310–315).[18] Stippling was employed on two surviving Athenian pinakia for adding a patronymic to a nomen and demotic that had originally been inscribed by ordinary means (**59**, text *d*; **68**, text *c*). These patronymics were presumably added by owners of the pinakia, who adopted this technique because it required no specialized tools or practice.

Indeed, from the variety and occasional poor quality of the lettering on

17. This technique can usually be detected by the unevenness of circular letters, by burrs of metal at the end of strokes, and by the V-shaped profile of the strokes themselves, especially at their ends. On both techniques, see Stanley Casson, "Early Greek Inscriptions on Metal: Some Notes," *AJA* 39 (1935), 510–517; and Herbert Maryon, "Metal Working in the Ancient World," *ibid.*, 53 (1949), 115–118.

18. Probably the largest single group of bronze inscriptions lettered in this way are those from the sanctuary at Dodona: Constantin Carapanos, *Dodone et ses Ruines*, 2 vols. (Paris, 1878), II, pls. 23–33.

pinakia, it has been unanimously assumed that the pinakia were always inscribed by the owners themselves.[19] A few of the more ineptly inscribed texts might have been (such as text *c* on **4**, text *b* on **56**, text *c* on **104**, and text *b* on **121**); if so, the inscribing of these exceptional texts was unofficial, as will be shown presently. Overall, however, the amateurishness of the lettering is more apparent than real. Many texts look (or, before cleaning, looked) irregular not because they were carelessly inscribed, but because they occur on heavily corroded or damaged pinakia (see, for example, **89**, **124**, and **125**). And considering the large numbers of pinakia that had to be inscribed at time of issue and the limitations imposed by the punching technique, which made for an inevitable variety of letter forms, the lettering is of a rather high level—if not always by the best lapidary standards then at least in comparison with grafitti on ostraka and the like.

The pinakia with state seals were stamped before issue and thus were manufactured under state auspices. One supposes that the Athenian government hired professional bronzesmiths for this work, much as it employed masons for inscribing public documents on stone and craftsmen for work on public buildings. Since the lettering on pinakia was produced with a standard technique and involved the application of specific metalworking tools, it is apparent that the pinakia were also inscribed by professionals and therefore almost certainly at public expense. This applies to the later uses of palimpsest pinakia as well as to original uses. (As is implied by the retention of primary seals from one use to the next, a reused pinakion was a reissued pinakion, that is, a pinakion that had reverted back to the state, had its old text erased, and was inscribed for a new owner as if the pinakion were new.) It applies to the stampless Class VI pinakia, which were inscribed with the same professional lettering as the stamped pinakia. And it should apply even to the wooden dikastic pinakia mentioned in the *AthPol*. For a government that paid its juries, assemblies, and young hoplite ephebes, distributed theoric gifts, and provided for invalids would surely not have left its citizens to obtain and inscribe allotment plates at their own expense. However little a bronze (or wooden) pinakion and its inscribing may have cost, the expense, if paid privately, would have been tantamount to a fee for participation in the public life of the democracy.

Class V Lettering and Class V

Any doubt about the state's responsibility for the inscribing of pinakia should at once be dispelled by consideration of the elaborate and highly

19. E.g., by Bruck, *Philologus* 54 (1895), 65; Hommel, *Heliaia*, 39; and Dow, *BCH* 87 (1963), 659.

regular lettering of the Class V pinakia. The technique involved the addition of pierced holes at terminations of straight strokes, on crossbars of alphas and etas, and on the curved sides of rounded letters, with a fixed pattern of holes for each letter of the alphabet (see Table 1). In principle, the holes were positioned so as to define, in as much as possible, the shape of any given letter with a minimum number of points, and a distinction was maintained between internal, partially pierced holes (for the center of thetas, the crossbars of alphas and etas, and the terminations of middle strokes of epsilons, sigmas, mus, and xis) and fully pierced holes for the outside corners of letters. For curved letters, the Athenians did the best they could. The circumference of omicrons and thetas received three full holes in any arrangement, omegas full holes at the extremity of each tail and a third hole at the apogee of the curved stroke, and rhos and phis similarly a full hole at the center of their curved sections. No betas or psis are extant. The hourglass-shaped profile of many of the full holes informs that the holes were normally punched through with a sharp point first from the front and then opened wider with a second piercing from the back. The full holes of a few of the finer pinakia, such as **86**, may have been drilled, however.

Although the holes are incidentally responsible for making these the most aesthetically pleasing of all pinakia, the holes were clearly not conceived as decorative serifs, which in any case do not appear in Athenian lapidary inscriptions until the end of the fourth century B.C. and did not become common until more than a century later.[20] Whether in lettering on stone or bronze, serifs were not added to the crossbars of alphas and etas, much less to the round segments of curvilinear letters.[21] And decorative serifs, moreover, would hardly have been painstakingly pierced completely through pinakia. Since the letters had to be inscribed on the plates, however lightly, by ordinary means before the holes were added,[22] the piercing of the holes must have at least doubled the time and cost of inscribing the Class V pinakia and could hardly have been justified by any reason short of a purely practical one. Probably no one would argue that the technique made the Class V pinakia more legible than pinakia that were conventionally inscribed. A more

20. Thus Sterling Dow, "The Purported Decree of Themistokles: Stele and Inscription," *AJA* 66 (1962), 356.

21. There is a partial exception that proves the rule. The short dedicatory text on a bronze candlestick found at Dodona (Carapanos, *Dodone*, II, pl. 25, no. 3) is serifed with punched dots at the terminations of strokes and with two punched dots on the loop of the one curvilinear letter, an omega. No dots, however, were added to crossbars. The pinakion from Sinope (Fig. 309) has true, partially punched serifs, but they may be in imitation of the Athenian Class V lettering, as are certainly the serifs on the Athenian pinakia listed in the following section.

22. The strokes of the Class V letters are finer than they would have been if they were not reinforced by the holes.

Table 1   The Class V alphabet, including typical variants*

Α	Three full holes plus a partial hole on the crossbar.
	(Beta unattested)
Γ	Three full holes. Attested on **94**.
Δ	Three full holes.
Ε Ε Ε Ε etc.	Four full holes plus a partial hole at the termination of the middle bar. The upper and lower horizontals frequently tend to diverge.
	(Zeta unattested)
Η Η Η Η etc.	Four full holes plus a partial hole on the crossbar. Only rarely do the terminal holes describe a perfect rectangle.
Θ Θ Θ etc.	Three full holes in any arrangement (and usually close together to give a small radius) plus a partial hole at the center.
Ι	Two full holes.
Κ Κ Κ etc.	Four full holes.
Λ	Three full holes.
Μ Μ	Four full holes plus a partial hole at the center. Attested on **78** and **79**.
Ν Ν Ν Ν etc.	Four full holes, often asymmetrically positioned. Sides are often slanted.
Ξ	Four full holes plus a partial hole at each end of the middle horizontal. Attested on **79**.
Ο Ο Ο etc.	Three full holes in any arrangement, usually close together to give a small diameter.
Π	Four full holes.
Ρ	Three full holes.

* The more irregular variants owe their asymmetry to imprecise placing of the pierced holes.

Table 1—continued

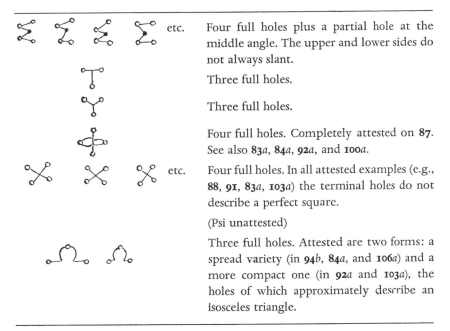

etc.	Four full holes plus a partial hole at the middle angle. The upper and lower sides do not always slant.
	Three full holes.
	Three full holes.
	Four full holes. Completely attested on **87**. See also **83***a*, **84***a*, **92***a*, and **100***a*.
etc.	Four full holes. In all attested examples (e.g., **88**, **91**, **83***a*, **103***a*) the terminal holes do not describe a perfect square.
	(Psi unattested)
	Three full holes. Attested are two forms: a spread variety (in **94***b*, **84***a*, and **106***a*) and a more compact one (in **92***a* and **103***a*), the holes of which approximately describe an isosceles triangle.

utilitarian purpose would seem to be called for, and in this light the only genuinely plausible explanation is the one first advanced by Albert Rehm and later embraced by Hommel and Kirchner: that the pierced holes were to fix the names of owners so that the names could not be erased and replaced.[23] Inscribed letters could be erased from the bronze; the pierced holes could not.

Given this deduction, one may ask why the Athenians went to such lengths to prevent reinscribing when in fact the inscribing of pinakia (in whatever use) was performed by the state, and why, if the Class V pinakia were not meant to be reinscribed, so many of these pinakia have survived as palimpsests. Obviously, the state would not prevent itself from reinscribing pinakia, and, as the many reused Class V survivals prove, many Class V pinakia did revert back to the state and were reissued to new owners. The answer to both questions must be, then, that the pierced lettering was specifically

23. Albert Rehm, review of William Larfeld, *Griechische Epigraphik, Berliner Philologische Wochenschrift* 36 (1916), 300; Hommel, *Heliaia*, 41; Kirchner, in his introduction to the pinakia, *IG* II², ii 2, p. 402. The old view, that the holes were to allow the pinakia to be sewn on dikasts' clothes as permanently visible badges of identification, was justly ridiculed by Bruck, who, however, was unable to replace it with a reasonable theory of his own; he suggested that a string for attaching the pinakia to kleroteria was supposed to be threaded through the holes (*Philologus* 54 [1895], 75, 77).

intended to discourage erasure and reinscribing of pinakia by private persons, as would have occurred if a pinakion was unofficially transferred from its rightful owner, who had received it from the state, to a fellow citizen who had no legal claim to it. So long as the state was responsible for issuing and inscribing pinakia, any private transfer of ownership would have been illegal. The pinakia mentioned in the preceding section as having been reinscribed by apparently unpracticed hands may well have been reinscribed privately; we shall see that uses of several pinakia that changed hands among members of the same deme are also suspect.

There are inconsistencies in the application of the pierced hole technique. Texts **80**, **84***a*, **89**, **91**, **93***a*, **94***b*, **96***a*, and **105***a* were inscribed with alternating fully and partially pierced letters. And occasionally, usually at the very beginning or end of a line, holes that should have been fully pierced through the bronze have been only partially pierced, or, less often, vice versa (see, for example, the sigmas and epsilon on **85**). But these inconsistencies are minor and are to be expected. Altogether, the uniformity of the Class V lettering is undeniable. With only the troublesome exception of **94** (with a fully pierced text in its second use, see below), such lettering was employed only for the first uses of Class V pinakia, which are further united by the characteristic styles of their triobol and gorgoneion seals. These considerations combine to show that the Class V pinakia were manufactured, stamped, and inscribed together within a restricted period of time and in all probability are survivals from a reform issue specifically designed to eliminate the apparently widespread practice of illegal reuse.

About this reform there will be more to say in Chaper IV, but for the present two further inferences are in order. First, if the reform was at all thoroughgoing, it would presumably have required that all currently circulating pinakia with conventional lettering—or, rather, all currently circulating pinakia with triobol seals, since the two-gorgoneion pinakia of Class III, being a different kind of pinakia, would not have been affected—be withdrawn and that the theoretically unerasable Class V pinakia be issued in their place. It is clear that if conventionally inscribed pinakia had continued to be used alongside the Class V pinakia, the effort expended on the inscribing of the latter would have been for naught. And, second, since the inauguration of the reform would have involved a massive initial issue of these specially inscribed pinakia, we may assume that most of the surviving examples belonged to this initial issue and therefore were first used together in a single year. Of course, if the reform had been maintained for more than a year, additional Class V pinakia would have been issued in successive years to supplement the large number already in circulation, but, as we see from the second texts on

Class V pinakia, which were either inscribed conventionally or in imitation of Class V lettering, the Athenians apparently reverted to inscribing pinakia by more ordinary means very soon after the Class V reform was put into effect. Like many ambitious experiments, the reform was of short duration. Precisely how short—whether for one, two, or even three years—there is no way of determining. If the reform lasted for only one year, all of the Class V pinakia were issued in that year; if for only two or three years, it would make little difference from our point of view inasmuch as the pinakia issued to supplement the initial issue would have been comparatively few in number. There would still have been only one major reform issue, and, since it is convenient to speak of a Class V issue in the singular, I think we are justified in continuing to do so without implying that the reform was necessarily restricted to a single year.

Lettering in Imitation of Class V Lettering

The following texts were inscribed with partially punched holes added to terminations of letters and in many cases to crossbars and curved letters: Class II, **17***b*; Class IV, **62***b*, **68***a*, **71***a*, and **74***b*; Class V, **81***b*, **83***b*, **94***a*, **101***b*, **107***b*, **108***b*, **111***c* and **112***c*; Class VI, **140** (last use); unclassified but related to Classes IV and V, **144***a* or *b*; from Class IV or V, **159***a*.

Five of these texts (**17***b*, **68***a*, **83***b*, **94***a*, and **111***c*) are known to have received punched dots on crossbars, curved letters, or both and thus were clearly intended to imitate the pierced lettering of Class V pinakia. On **62***b* and **140** the punched dots, being omitted from crossbars or curvilinear letters, have become mere decorative serifs, but the inspiration for the serifs was presumably the same. The remaining texts are not well enough preserved to allow us to determine how closely their letters imitated the standard Class V alphabet.

All of these texts should be later than the Class V issue. And since their punched dots do not penetrate completely through the metal and could not have served the purpose of the pierced holes they copied, it is reasonable to suppose that (with the probable exception of **140**, from a Class VI pinakion and hence later than the other texts under consideration) they were inscribed at a time when the Class V lettering had been functionally abandoned but when many Class V pinakia were still being used with their original inscriptions intact. One assumes that the Class V lettering was imitated not only for its decorative properties but also because, once introduced in the Class V issue, its appearance came to be temporarily regarded as typical of lettering on pinakia, or at least typical of lettering on pinakia that were stamped with triobol seals, for texts in imitation of Class V lettering are not found on Class III pinakia.

As one could predict, the largest number of such texts occur in second or third uses of Class V pinakia. Those texts which do often incorporate pierced holes from the original inscription and sometimes have letters that were grotesquely distorted in order to take advantage of as many of the original full holes as possible (see especially **111c**). The second and third texts on most Class V pinakia were inscribed conventionally, however, and it should be noted that **111** and **112**, both Class V pinakia that received a text in imitation of Class V lettering in a third use, were conventionally inscribed during their intermediate second uses. Thus the period following the Class V reform was one of considerable irregularity with respect to the inscribing of pinakia. Pinakia with original Class V texts, pinakia inscribed in imitation of Class V lettering, and conventionally inscribed pinakia were apparently being used side by side.

I have already remarked on the value of texts inscribed in imitation of Class V lettering for fixing the chronological relationship between the Class V issue and uses of particular pinakia of Classes II and IV. Such lettering in the last text of **17**, a Class II pinakion that was originally issued before the Class V pinakia and that was presumably withdrawn from use at the time of the Class V reform, shows that the pinakion was reinscribed and returned to use soon after the reform, when the Class V lettering had ceased to be functional. The same probably applies to **62**, a Class IV pinakion with a triobol seal ethnic in ΑΘΕ and therefore probably first issued before the Class V reform, but reused with a text imitating Class V lettering after the reform.

It remains to say something about the one extant pinakion with a fully pierced, Class V-like text in a use later than its original use. This is **94**, on which the usual order of a Class V text followed by a text inscribed with added punched dots in imitation of Class V lettering is reversed. Its primary seals were stamped with Class V primary seal dies, showing that the pinakion was manufactured with the regular Class V pinakia, and, because of the fully pierced lettering of its second text, I have felt obliged to classify **94** with them. The second text on **94**, however, should be somewhat later than the first texts on regular Class V pinakia simply because the first text of **94** cannot date from before any of the regularly inscribed pinakia whose lettering it imitates. Presumably, the pinakion had two texts which should be categorized as being in imitation of Class V lettering, both of which were inscribed at a time when pierced lettering was no longer obligatory. The second of these was provided with pierced holes gratuitously to give an almost perfect imitation of Class V lettering—"almost perfect" since the strokes of the letters are deeply impressed into the metal, like the strokes of conventionally inscribed letters and the letters of the second text of **83**, a text inscribed in close imitation of Class V lettering but with punched holes that do not perforate completely through the metal. By the best Class V standards, the pierced holes of text **94***b* are rather irregularly treated, especially in the epsilons of the first line; this factor may also result from the lateness of the text relative to the Class V issue. For another pinakion stamped with Class V primary seals, but apparently not issued until after the Class V lettering had been officially abandoned, see **73**, which did not receive a text with pierced holes in any use.

Arrangement of Texts

A canonical format for the inscribing of owners' names is found only in Class I:

a.   NOMEN: DEM.

On most, and probably all Class I pinakia, nomen and curtailed demotic were separated by an interpunct.

We have seen that the one-line arrangement gave way to texts in two lines, which were better suited to the space available on pinakia. There was a brief time after the Class I issue when texts in one line and texts in two lines were used interchangeably (see **10**), but the two-line format soon won out and was retained on all subsequent pinakia.[24]

Patronymics are included in about half of the names inscribed in two lines and occur in any one of several positions. With the exception of format "e," which is primarily associated with the elaborately inscribed Class V pinakia, there is no apparent correlation between the various two-line arrangements and particular classes. It was presumably left to the owner to specify whether his patronymic should or should not be included and to the letterer to decide on the convenient format. I list the arrangements according to frequency of occurrence:

b.   NOMEN
      DEMOTIC

c.   NOMEN PATRONYMIC
      DEMOTIC

24. With the possible and virtually negligible exception of **177**.

d.	NOMEN	Positively attested in 13 instances.
	PATRONYMIC DEMOTIC	

e.	NOMEN PATRO-	Positively attested in 10 instances, all
	NYMIC DEMOTIC	but two of which (**14** and **139**) occur on Class V pinakia.

f.	NOMEN	Positively attested in 9 instances.
	DEMOTIC PATRONYMIC	

Attested once each.

g.	NOMEN DEM-	**102** (Class V)
	OTIC	

h.	NOMEN DEMOTIC	**122**, text *a* (Class VI) (Possibly also on
	PATRONYMIC	**177**)

Patronymics and demotics are frequently abbreviated, patronymics when space required, demotics often even when sufficient room remained for a full spelling. In one instance, on **104**, text *c*, a nomen may have been abbreviated, but this is a highly problematic piece, and my conclusions about it may be mistaken. Interpuncts were used about two-thirds of the time, regardless of class or use, to separate two elements of a name in the same line. In five instances two parts of a name in the same line are divided by a space.

The sole text with three lines (text *c* on **68**) was initially inscribed in two regular lines according to format "b" above; the patronymic in between was added later and in stippled letters.

Tribal Affiliations of Successive Owners

In regard to owners' names, it may be worth noting finally that successive owners of reused pinakia were ordinarily from different phylai. Out of thirty-nine extant palimpsest pinakia on which the demotics of two or more successive owners can be read or can be restored with some degree of probability, no more than ten can be suspected of having successive owners belonging to the same phyle. The figures break down as follows:

a. Twenty-nine pinakia with successive owners from different phylai.

b. Three or four pinakia with successive owners from the same deme.

7 (Class I or II: last two owners from Phlya)
18 (Class II: last two owners from Paiania)

63 (Class IV: last two or three owners from Phyle)

?73 (Class IV: last two [?] owners from Phaleron)

c.   Four to six pinakia with successive owners from the same phyle.

6 (Class I or II: both owners from Akmantis)

34 (Class III in stampless reuses: last two owners from Akmantis)

40 (Class III in stampless reuses: last two owners from Aigeis)

96 (Class V in stampless Class VI reuses: last two owners from Aigeis)

?105 (Class V: if the deme of the penultimate owner was Halai Araphenides and not Halai Aixonides, the last two owners would be from Aigeis)

?123 (Class VI: if my tentative restoration of the first demotic is correct, both owners were from Oineis)

The body responsible for the manufacture and stamping of pinakia was doubtless the state at large, and not, for instance, the separate phylai or demes.[25] On the other hand, as is clear from the account of section-letters given in *AthPol* 63.4, which requires that each owner be assigned to one of the ten allotment sections of his phyle upon or before receiving his pinakion, the actual issuing of pinakia was performed on a tribal basis. Thus, at the time the pinakia were issued, each phyle must have received from the state a quota of blank pinakia that the officers of the phyle were in turn responsible for distributing to individual owners. (Presumably a number of bronze-smiths were assigned to each phyle to do the inscribing that was a part of the distribution process.)

The above figures show merely that the two steps involved in getting new pinakia from the state to the individual owners—the apportionment of blank pinakia among the ten phylai and the ultimate issue by the phylai to the owners—applied also in the case of reused pinakia. When a pinakion was surrendered by a former owner, it did not remain in his phyle to be rein-scribed for another member of that phyle, but instead reverted back to the state at large, which had it erased and then treated it as if it were a newly manufactured pinakion. That is, once erased, it would be thrown together with all other blank pinakia and randomly apportioned out to a phyle at the

25. If proof is needed, it will be found in certain pinakia that were stamped with the same section-letter die but that were issued to members of different phylai: **78** and **88**, both stamped with the same zeta die, although **78** was first used by a member of Erechtheis and **88** by a member of Kekropis or Aigeis; and **86** and **87**, stamped with the same eta die, but first used by a member of Leontis and a member of Aiantis, respectively. If the record of original owners' names and of primary seal and section-letter dies were more complete, we would doubtless be able to point to many other instances of pinakia that share common dies from the time of manufacture but that were first inscribed for members of different phylai.

time of the next distribution. In this way a pinakion circulated purely by chance from one phyle to another through the agency of a central state authority.

There can be little question that the few pinakia that happened to find their way back to their previous owner's phyle but not to his deme (item "c" above) did so fortuitously. It is highly improbable, however, that chance was operating in the case of the three or four surviving pinakia that had fellow demesmen as successive owners (item "b"). One rather suspects that such pinakia, like the several pinakia that were unprofessionally inscribed, changed hands privately between acquaintances, without the official mediation of the government. And, indeed, it so happens that at least one of these palimpsests (7) was only partially erased when the owner's name was changed so that the previously inscribed demotic was passed on from one owner to the next; whoever did the erasing and reinscribing knew who the next owner would be—a circumstance that could never have occurred if the pinakion had reverted back to the state for erasure and legal reuse.

One last point. From the cyclical movement of pinakia from state to phyle to owner back to the state and so on, as outlined above, it is apparent that a palimpsest pinakion was not reinscribed and reissued immediately after being surrendered by a former owner. An interval must have elapsed between the time when it was returned to the state for erasure and when it was passed with other blank pinakia back to a phyle for reissue. For reasons which will emerge in Chapters IV and V, this interval could probably not have been less than a full year and in some instances may have lasted for two, three, or even more years. But for the present it is sufficient to observe that the amount of time spanned by a reinscribed pinakion from the moment it was manufactured until it broke or was buried with its last owner included not only the years during which it was actually being used but also the time when it lay blank in the hands of the state between its several uses.

Section-letters

Section-letters from A through K, as on the wooden pinakia described in *AthPol* 63.4, occur on all the bronze pinakia with the apparent exception of at least one from the Class VI period and perhaps a few in Class III. On the earlier pinakia, the letters are stamped in an incuse field; on the later pinakia they are inscribed. The inscribed letters were added to pinakia at the same time as the owners' names and were regularly changed with each change of name. Conversely, stamped letters were added to pinakia together with primary seals before the pinakia were inscribed and were normally retained without change for as many uses as a pinakion had until the time when inscribed letters replaced stamped letters.[26]

One letter (eta) calls for special comment. Whether stamped or inscribed (see **30**, **38**, **44**, and **105**), it was invariably rendered in the monogrammatic form ⋈ = HT(A), which, as A. L. Boegehold has lucidly explained,[27] was originated to distinguish etas from zetas on round dikastic tokens and was subsequently retained for use on other dikastic equipment.

The priority of stamped section-letters to owners' names in first uses is demonstrated by **28** (Class III) and **72** (Class IV), both manufactured with a stamped letter that was replaced with an inscribed letter when the pinakia were first issued. The priority of stamped letters to owners' names in reuses is amply proven by the many palimpsests that retained their original stamped letter for one or more uses subsequent to their first use, for example, **4** (Class I), **18** (Class II), **21** (Class III), **68** (Class IV), and **84** (Class V).

On a few pinakia (**11**, **16**, **22**, **107**, and **146**) an original stamped letter has been replaced with a second stamped letter. According to the principle that stamped section-letters ordinarily preceded owners' names, one assumes that the original letters on most of these pinakia were altered between uses, that is, while the pinakia were in an erased state before being reinscribed.[28]

The priority of stamped section-letters to owners' names was recognized by Bruck, who interpreted it as an indication that Athenians were allotted to

26. **96** (originally a Class V pinakion) and the unclassified **145** are the only surviving pinakia on which the regular sequence of stamped section-letter followed by an inscribed one is reversed. The last two uses of **96**, each with a different stamped letter, seem clearly to be stampless Class VI uses, however. And since **145** is without a stamped seal in its lower left corner (at least during the final use which received the stamped letter), its last use too can be classified as a Class VI use. Thus both pinakia imply that, although it was customary to provide Class VI pinakia with inscribed section-letters, there was no real reason why their section-letters could not have been stamped, providing a set of dies for the stamping happened to be available. Another pinakion that may have received one or more stamped section-letters during the Class VI period is **146**, which is even more anomalous than **96** and **145**. All three of these pinakia are highly irregular and, so far as I am able to judge, have no bearing on the larger chronological deductions discussed in the present chapter.

27. A. L. Boegehold, "Aristotle's *Athenaion Politeia* 62, 5: The 'Official Token,'" *Hesperia* 29 (1960), 395–396.

28. The one proven exception here is **146**, whose last section-letter (it is stamped twice, once at each end) was clearly added after the inscribing of the last owner's name. But this last use probably belongs to the Class VI period when section-letters were regularly changed with every change in ownership. Since the last two section-letters on **96** and the last one on **145** date from the Class VI period as well (see n. 26, above), each of them also was very likely added with, rather than before, the inscribing of an owner's name.

tribal sections by a random drawing of uninscribed pinakia.[29] Thus, at the time of issue, each phyle placed all of its blank pinakia in a container; every member of the phyle who was to receive a pinakion drew one; and the letter stamped on the pinakion he drew assigned him to his particular section. The pinakion was subsequently inscribed with his name.

Whatever truth there may be in this theory concerning the issue of the earlier pinakia, it cannot apply during the period when pinakia were provided with inscribed section-letters. For on these later pinakia, section-letter and owner's name were inscribed by the same hand and were obviously added together. During the later period, therefore, men were assigned to tribal sections by some means other than by drawing blank pinakia. We shall see in Chapter V that during this later period an Athenian's membership in an allotment section had become permanent, much like his membership in his deme and phyle, and that it was probably the change from temporary to permanent membership in tribal sections that was ultimately responsible for the change from stamped to inscribed section-letters.

Inscribed section-letters first appear on pinakia with two primary seals (Classes III–V). On such stamped pinakia the letters are usually small and placed in the upper left corner so as not to encroach on the left-hand seal in the corner below (for example, **24, 25, 28, 29, 63, 65**, and **72**). But note the large section-letter inscribed above the unerased gorgoneion seal on **26**. Later, in the stampless Class VI period, there is less consistency in the sizes and positions of inscribed section-letters; although the section-letters were customarily larger and located toward the middle of the left (for example, **115–120**) or right (such as **38** use *c*, **126** and **127**) ends of pinakia, it is not uncommon to find small inscribed section-letters positioned in the upper or lower corners (upper: **23, 33, 40**, and **114**; lower: **34** use *b*, **46** use *c*, and **125**). The lack of consistency in late section-letters was such that a few rare Class VI uses were even provided with stamped section-letters (see nn. 26 and 28, above).

Comparatively few inscribed section-letters are to be found on the surviving Class IV and V pinakia. For lack of a proven exception to the contrary, it appears that all of the triobol-gorgoneion pinakia were manufactured with stamped section-letters. Most of those that were reused retained their original stamped letters for several uses subsequent to their original uses, and if they received an inscribed section-letter at all, it was not ordinarily until a third or fourth use at the earliest (see **63, 65, 77, 81**, and **105**). Inscribed section-letters, therefore, were not introduced until late in the triobol-gorgoneion

29. Bruck, *Philologus* 54 (1895), 65; whence Hommel, *Heliaia*, 38.

series. Moreover, since none of the Class IV or V pinakia are known to have had more than one use (or, possibly in the case of **96**, two uses) with a small inscribed letter and with both primary seals intact, we may conclude that inscribed section-letters first appeared shortly before the triobol-gorgoneion pinakia were discontinued.

Among the extant Class III pinakia, however, uses with inscribed section-letters are more plentiful than ones with stamped section-letters and imply that the inscribed section-letter phase of these gorgoneion-gorgoneion pinakia was more prolonged than the corresponding phase of the triobol-gorgoneion pinakia. Indeed, the Class III pinakia admit of division into two typological subgroups: an earlier group of pinakia which were manufactured with stamped section-letters (**20–28**) and which therefore were first issued contemporaneously with the pinakia of Classes IV and V and a group of later Class III pinakia which were manufactured and issued after inscribed section-letters had superseded stamped ones (**29–35**).[30] On the pinakia of the second group, the upper left-hand corner was left vacant at the time of manufacture and was ordinarily filled in with an inscribed section-letter when the name of the owner was added. The pinakia of the second group have no counterpart among the pinakia of Classes IV and V and were apparently issued after these triobol-gorgoneion pinakia had been discontinued. Thus to judge from the technique of section-letters on the pinakia stamped with two primary seals, the parallelism between the triobol-gorgoneion and the gorgoneion-gorgoneion pinakia that I have discussed above, actually applies only from the introduction of the gorgoneion seal to the point when inscribed section-letters replaced stamped section-letters. Shortly after that point, the former series was terminated while the Class III pinakia continued to be issued and used for some time afterward.

This later continuation of the Class III pinakia helps to explain why so many from this class were ultimately converted to stampless Class VI pinakia (see **23, 27, 33, 34, 36–42**, and **45**). By way of contrast, comparatively few of the pinakia from Classes IV and V were ever used as late as the final Class VI period. **61** was certainly used that late, as is clear from its last, large section-letter that was inscribed directly over its erased triobol seal; and **96** (see n. 26, above) apparently had an exceptional three or four Class VI uses. But the only other possible candidates are **64, 77, 81**, and **105**, and since the triobol seals on these have not been totally erased and since their last section-letters are relatively small and do not encroach on the seals, it is not altogether clear whether their last uses should be categorized as stamped or stampless.

30. It is uncertain to which of the two groups the remaining Class III pinakia, **36–45**, all heavily erased palimpsests, belong.

To return to the later group of Class III pinakia, those manufactured without section-letters, I remarked above that they ordinarily received inscribed section-letters at the time when they were inscribed for an owner. This was clearly the case with **29** and **30**, but some qualification is called for, since it appears that certain other pinakia of this group may have been employed without section-letters for one or more uses. There is no trace of a properly inscribed section-letter from any of the three attested uses of **32**. And there are reasons for thinking that when **31**, **33**, and **34** were manufactured they may not have been intended to receive section-letters: the left-hand gorgoneion seal on each of these pinakia was stamped toward the middle of their left ends, so as to leave little or no room for a regularly inscribed section-letter in the upper left corner; and on **33** and **34** the existence of a section-letter during the first use is highly doubtful on material grounds. Beyond this, however, it is impossible to go. All four of these pinakia are well-erased palimpsests, two are fragments, and, as I have explained in more detail in the Catalogue, the absence of a section-letter on **32–34**, although apparent, cannot be conclusively proven.

The one extant pinakion that seems almost certainly to have been used without a section-letter is **47** in its final Class VI use. One such use implies that other Class VI pinakia probably lacked section-letters also. For reasons explained in the Catalogue, some possible candidates are **121** and **122** in their first uses and **129–131**, but these are problematic pieces and could equally have been provided with section-letters. All Class VI left ends that lack section-letters (such as the last uses of **27** and **45**, **129** and **130**) may well have belonged to pinakia whose section-letters were inscribed at their right ends. In our present ignorance, the only permissible conclusion is that omission of a section-letter is attested on a single Class VI survival and can be suspected on some of the later pinakia of Class III.

For what it may be worth, I should point out that the only known instances of repetition of stamped section-letter dies occur on Class V and related pinakia. The same alpha die was used on **85** and **94**; the same zeta die on **78**, **88**, and **144**; and the same eta die on **86**, **87**, **106**, **110**, and possibly on **79** and **80**. At the same time, two beta dies in Class V are attested by **93** and **107**; two gamma dies by **83** and **91** and **109**; and two epsilon dies by **95** and **104**. From this we conclude that the manufacture of the Class V pinakia involved two or possibly more dies for each section-letter, although certainly not many more than two since the frequency with which a single die reoccurs in the relatively small number of Class V survivals would probably not be as great as it is had a considerably larger number of dies been employed.

Primary Seals

The triobol and gorgoneion seals, which regularly appear on all pinakia of a respective class and which were—like the stamped section-letters—stamped on pinakia at the time of manufacture, I have designated as "primary" seals to distinguish them from "secondary" seals or seals that were stamped in the course of a pinakion's use and then generally not on every pinakion of a given class. That the gorgoneion seal was added always at the time of manufacture, before the first owner's name was inscribed, is apparent from **20** and **31** (Class III), **72** (Class IV), and **80** (Class V), the original inscriptions of which encroach on the gorgoneia at the right. Should the gorgoneia have been stamped after the inscribing of the first owners' names these seals would have been stamped higher or lower to avoid contact with the names. By analogy with the gorgoneion seals (and stamped section-letters) the triobol seals were doubtless added to pinakia at the time of manufacture also, as is independently demonstrated by the positioning of stamped section-letters and triobol seals at the extreme left and right ends of the earliest (Class I) pinakia, normally with part of the stamps off the edges of the pinakia in order to leave the maximum possible space for the addition of long one-line texts. On Class I pinakia that happened to be inscribed with names that filled the entire space (for example, **2** and **4**), it is impossible to ascertain whether the stamping preceded or followed inscribing, but **1** and **3**, with shorter texts, are more telling. If the names on these last pinakia had preceded the stamps, the stamps would have been positioned with reference to the names and presumably would not have been partially struck off the ends of the plates. Thus the priority of primary seals (and stamped section-letters) to names in first uses was no different from the priority of the seals (and stamped letters), which had already been stamped for first uses, to names in subsequent uses. As we have noted, a stamped pinakion retained its primary seals for all subsequent uses until it might be converted to a stampless pinakion in the Class VI period.

The triobol seals on the Class I and II pinakia and the Class IV pinakia **61–64** precisely duplicate the reverse type of fourth-century Athenian triobol coins and could have been struck with dies engraved and originally used for the minting of coins:[31]

31. Having looked at the triobol coins in all of the major published collections and in the large national numismatic cabinets in Athens, Paris, London, and New York, I have yet to find one that was struck from a die used on the surviving pinakia. On the style of fourth-century triobols, see Margaret Thompson, "A Hoard of Athenian Fractions," *American Numismatic Society Museum Notes* 7 (1957), 1–11, with pls. 1–3. The triobols in the

Incuse circle containing erect, facing owl, wings folded, surrounded by an olive wreath of two branches (one branch curving down on each side of the owl) and the three letter ethnic A or A .
                                                                                           E Θ   Θ Ǝ

The arrangement of the ethnic is without significance on the coins or the pinakia, as the two patterns are found interchangeably on both.[32] And since the pre-Eukleidian spelling of the ethnic was retained on all regular Athenian coinages down to the Roman period, no chronological importance can be attached to it either. The triobol seals on these earlier pinakia display a fairly wide variation in the shape and proportions of the owl and in the number of leaves on the olive branches, and this too is precisely what one finds on the coins. In the Catalogue eight different seal dies with AΘE ethnics have been positively distinguished. Their infrequent repetition (only one is known from more than one pinakion; it occurs on **12**, **13**, **16**, and **17**, all Class II pinakia) indicates that there must have been many others.

The triobol seals on the Class V pinakia and the related **72**, **73**, and **74** are all of a rigidly consistent type (best exemplified by the seal on **78** and described below, p. 178), bear the ethnic $\smash{\genfrac{}{}{0pt}{}{A}{H\,\Theta}}$, and therefore could not have been struck with dies borrowed from the Athenian mint.[33] The proportions and feathering of the owls, the regular arrangement of six leaves on each olive branch, and the size and placement of the letters in the legend are so

---

hoard evidence a marked deterioration in style, which began apparently not long before the hoard was buried, sometime near the end of the century. Compare the finer style of the worn triobols nos. 3–7, 8–10, and 16 with the cruder style of nos. 19–59, which had been exposed to very little circulation. The three triobols in a smaller hoard from Agios Ioannis Rentis published by Mando Karamessini-Oikonomidou (*Deltion* 18 [1963], Χρονικά, 50, with pl. 56) are all of the finer style. Since this smaller hoard can be dated to the second quarter of the fourth century by the shape of the lamp in which the coins were found, it confirms that the crude style did not begin until sometime in the second half of the century. All of the triobol seals on the pinakia, including those of Class V, clearly belong to the period of the finer style.

32. A third arrangement, $\smash{\genfrac{}{}{0pt}{}{A}{\Theta\,E}}$, also appears on the fourth-century coins, although infrequently.

33. The triobol-like bronze coins struck by Timotheus at Olynthos sometime between 363 and 359 B.C. also bear ethnics in AΘH (E. S. G. Robinson and M. J. Price, "An Emergency Coinage of Timotheos," *NC*[7] [1967], 1–6). Although these coins were contemporary with the Class V pinakia (see the concluding section of Chapter III, below), this chronological proximity is probably fortuitous and need not imply that the variant ethnic on the coins was borrowed from the seals on pinakia, or vice versa. As Robinson and Price observe, the coins differ from regular Athenian issues in several other stylistic respects and owe these variations primarily to the fact that their dies were engraved at Olynthos by local artisans. Caillemer, DarSag, "Dikastai," 193, fig. 2413 (whence Sandys, *Constitution of Athens*, frontispiece) illustrates a lead token stamped with a triobol device containing the ethnic $\smash{\genfrac{}{}{0pt}{}{A}{\Theta\,H}}$. The token was probably used in a dikastic context, but is undated.

much alike on all of these seals that I have been unable to differentiate individual dies. Not that minute variations in internal measurements do not exist. They do, but there is no clear consistency in the variations, and the degree of divergence is never emphatic enough to be necessarily attributable to variant dies. Making allowance for minor distortions of the seals caused by occasional faulty striking and slight bending of the surface of the pinakia, one could argue that all of the Class V triobol seals may have come from a single die. Actually, however, they were almost certainly struck with an unknown number of essentially identical dies, all probably cut by a single die engraver. The evidence here is provided by the dies of the Class V section-letters. Since each of the ten section-letters involved more than one die, it follows that more than one die was used also for the triobol seals. If all of the Class V triobol seals were better struck and preserved, several dies presumably could be identified.

These triobol seal dies were doubtless commissioned specifically for the manufacture of the Class V pinakia, and I assume that their AΘH ethnics are to be understood in terms of the scrupulousness and innovation that characterize the issue as a whole. It was only natural that the Athenians at first began to stamp the triobol device on pinakia with dies that reproduced the device exactly as it was known from coins. Or perhaps dies were conveniently borrowed from the mint for this purpose. Either practice, however, would have been highly questionable from the standpoint of Athenian mint officials, for in antiquity, as now, coin dies should have remained safely in the custody of the mint, and copies of them should not have been identical copies. Even if no one seriously feared that dies employed with the pinakia might be stolen and illicitly used for forging coins, the abstract possibility existed. The obvious course, then, was to alter some detail on the pinakia dies, and the AΘH ethnic, which is without parallel on the coins and yet does not affect the appearance of the seals in any fundamental respect, served this purpose admirably. That this step was taken in conjunction with a major innovation in the inscribing of pinakia is not surprising. The pierced lettering of the Class V pinakia reflects a reassessment of one policy governing the production and issue of pinakia; the Class V triobol seal ethnics in AΘH reflect a minor reform of another.

The gorgoneion seals can, similarly, be divided into two groups: one involving the pinakia of Classes III and IV and characterized by a comparatively large number of widely differing gorgoneion seal dies; and a Class V group, in which, as with the Class V triobol seals, we meet with only one seal type, with the impossibility of distinguishing dies, and with the attendant conclusion that however many dies were used, all of them were practically identical in appearance and were probably engraved by a single artisan who was specifically commissioned to cut dies in preparation for the Class V issue.

The Class V gorgoneion (best illustrated also on **78** and described in more detail below, p. 178) is rather refined in appearance, having a circular profile, short, smooth bands of hair, carefully modeled facial features, and the maximum four pairs of snakes growing out of the hair and chin and filling the comparatively wide field between the head and the edge of the surrounding incuse circle. The incuse fields of some of the Class V gorgoneia have assumed a slightly ovoid form (for instance, on **78**, **87**, **93**, and **94**), but since the dies used for striking these seals were themselves surely circular and not ovoid in section, such seals must have been distorted by bending on the surface of the pinakia. Other Class V gorgoneia appear to be missing their incuse fields or snakes, but these and other anomalies are to be attributed to incomplete striking or poor preservation and, again, not to any inherent variety in the dies. As in the case of the Class V triobol seals, were it not for the multiplicity of dies used for the Class V section-letters, one would be tempted to argue that all of the Class V gorgoneia came from only a single gorgoneion seal die.

In marked contrast, the variation among the gorgoneia on the Class III and IV pinakia is extreme. The gorgoneia on **20** have small, round, finely featured faces and bushy hair; those on **21** are larger, and their chins are more pointed. The gorgoneion on **22** has smooth, long hair; those on **28** smooth, shorter hair and very marked V-shaped chin profiles. The gorgoneia on **29** and **30** are exceptionally large, coarsely featured, and bushy haired. Those on **31–32**, **39**, and **44** are abnormally small, and so forth. I have been able to differentiate a minimum (there were certainly more) of thirteen dies altogether, and the only thing they have in common is that none are of the refined Class V type. Most are not even remotely similar to the gorgoneia of Class V. Such diversity is the natural result of the lack of established prototypes. Unlike the triobol seals, the gorgoneion seals had no numismatic antecedents, and one presumes that, in the absence of a model, each die engraver commissioned to make up the gorgoneion dies followed his own stylistic inclinations in producing them.

Secondary Seals

Conspicuously absent from the Class III pinakia, secondary seals were added only to pinakia with triobol seals. Although there are three varieties, the distinction is chronological, the behavior of the several types being essentially the same. Chronologically, the order is owl-in-square seal, double-bodied owl seal, and sphinx (?) seal. It will be convenient, however, to treat the double-bodied owl seals first, since they are by far the most satisfactorily documented.

DOUBLE-BODIED OWL SEALS

(Classes II, IV, and V):

> Incuse square containing a double-bodied owl and the letters A A, one at each side of the owl's head.
> Variant, which occurs on **16** (Class II), use *b*, only: Incuse circle containing a double-bodied owl and the letters A A.

These seals are modeled after the double-bodied owl in incuse square reverse type of fourth-century Athenian silver diobols, which bear the ethnic A (above the owl's head) Θ E (interchangeably in the field above the owl's two backs) and a small olive spray hanging from each upper corner of the square.[34] On the pinakia seals, however, the ethnic and olive leaves of the coins have been compressed into two alphas, which are normally tilted and hang from the upper corners like leaves of an olive spray.[35] I assume that this simplification of the coin type was intended, like the AΘH ethnics on the Class V triobol seals, to keep the dies used for pinakia distinguishable from coin dies. But at the same time it makes it awkward for us to refer to the seals as "diobol" seals. The unique double-bodied owl seal on **16** carries the divergence one step further; being stamped in a circular field, it is twice removed from the numismatic prototype.

A remarkably large number of dies were employed for the stamping of the double-bodied owl seal. An exact count is precluded by the poor preservation of many examples, but in all twenty or so instances where substantial remains of the seal have survived (the seal is attested on thirty-two pinakia altogether), I have been able to detect only two cases of die linkage: between the seals on **83** and **93** and between those on **65, 85,** and **86.**

---

34. Examples in J. N. Svoronos, *Les monnaies d'Athènes* (Munich: F. Bruckmann, 1923–1926), pl. 17, nos. 34–36, pl. 21, nos. 53–62; see also the two hoards referred to in n. 31, above.

35. The double-bodied owl seal on **62** just might reproduce the coin type in full. Not enough of the seal's field survives, however, to decide positively for or against this possibility, and until another seal from the same die should come to light, I believe that we are obliged to assume that the seal was regular, that is, that its ethnic was AA, not AΘE.

The behavior of the seals may be summarized in three observations: First, the seal was added to a majority (about two-thirds) but not all surviving pinakia of Classes II, IV, and V. Second, the seal was added after the name of the first owner was inscribed and often was not stamped until a second or even a later use. Clear instances of stamping after the first use are provided on **16**, **17**, **69**, **83**, and **84**. Before the use receiving the secondary seal, **69** is known to have had two uses; nor may **84** have been stamped with the seal until its third use. Third, when the seal was added, it was frequently stamped upside down (on **65**, **71**, **73**, **87**, and **93**) or at a tilt (for example, on **18** and **92**; on the latter the seal was also weakly impressed and located exceptionally far to the left), as if added in haste. On **97** the seal was stamped on the back.

OWL-IN-SQUARE SEALS

(Class I):

> Incuse square (about 0.8 × 0.8 centimeter average) containing an owl standing right, head facing; in the field behind the owl's head, a spray of two olive leaves; at the lower right, the ethnic AΘE reading downward.

These earlier secondary seals reproduce the well-known reverse type of classical Athenian tetradrachms, which at a reduced scale was used also for drachms (incuse field about 1.1 centimeter square), obols (incuse field in the fourth century about 0.7–0.8 centimeter square), and hemiobols (incuse field about 0.5 centimeter square).[36] The dimensions of the seals' incuse squares closely approximate those of the obols and make it entirely possible that the seals were stamped with actual coin dies. Indeed, I have refrained from calling the seals "obol" seals only because it is not altogether accurate to use numismatic nomenclature in describing the later double-bodied owl seals. The four extant examples of the owl-in-square seal (on **2–5**) are each from a different die.

Behaviorally, the seals are analogous to the double-bodied owl seals in at least two respects.

It is obvious from the position of the seal on **3**, at the middle of the plate's width in the space between the demotic and the triobol seal that the seals were added after owners' names; had the name been longer, this space would

---

36. Cf. Svoronos, *Monnaies d'Athènes*, pl. 21, nos. 27–42 (drachms), pl. 22, nos. 1–6 (obols), and nos. 24–28 (hemiobols).

have been occupied by the inscription, and the seal would have been stamped below the name, as it is on the other Class I pinakia. In the second place, on **2**, **3**, and **5** the owl-in-square seal was stamped at a tilt, and on the last the seal is also upside down.

What then about the first behavioral characteristic of the double-bodied owl seals? On analogy with the Class II, IV, and V pinakia, one would expect that some of the pinakia from the Class I issue did not receive a secondary seal. Are we entitled to say that the owl-in-square seals were added to a majority but not to all of the pinakia of this issue? We could do so without hesitation if we could be sure that **6**, which lacks a secondary seal, was issued as a Class I pinakion. There are good reasons for thinking that it may have been since it was first inscribed with a text in one line, and the die of its triobol seal may in fact be linked to the triobol seals on the unmistakable Class I pinakia **3** and **5**. This possible die link is, nevertheless, far from proven, and in view of the fact that at least one Class II pinakion (**12**, see n. 12, above) is known to have had an original text inscribed in one line, the identification of **6** as a Class I pinakion cannot be regarded as certain. The problem quite frankly is that in the absence of secondary seals, we cannot now make a clear distinction between pinakia that belong to the initial Class I issue and Class II pinakia (from supplementary issues) that were inscribed with one-line texts. We must be content to classify **6** ambiguously as a Class I or II pinakion and to acknowledge that, although certain pinakia from the Class I issue probably did not receive an owl-in-square seal, the matter has yet to be confirmed.

SPHINX (?) SEAL

(Occurs in a late use of **73**, a Class IV pinakion, only):

Incuse square containing a feline, probably a sphinx, seated right.

For the identification of the animal represented, see my remarks concerning **73** in the Catalogue.

The seal was stamped at a tilt and, as is indicated by the depth of its relief, was apparently not added until the last use (or one of the last uses) of the pinakion. Compare the shallow, barely preserved relief of the double-bodied owl seal that is next to it and that would seem to have been stamped during an earlier use, well before the addition of the sphinx (?) seal.

The sphinx (?) seal is unique, and since it stands outside the repertory of obviously official Athenian symbols, as are known, for example, from silver coins, Bruck assumed that it was a private seal of the pinakion's last owner.[37] This solution is not without its attractions, but I suspect that the matter is more complex. In the first place, the seal was stamped onto the pinakion with a metal die and could not have been impressed with a stone signet such as were ordinarily used by private persons for wax sealings on correspondence, belongings, and so forth. It is doubtful that many Athenians kept a signet die for the purpose of stamping metal. Secondly, as we know from Athenian bronze and lead tokens, which display a vast range of symbols (among them the sphinx),[38] the Athenians appropriated all kinds of common symbols for official use whether they happened to have any specific associations with Athens or not. We may note also that the sphinx was adopted as an Athenian coin type on an issue of bronze coins of the first century B.C.[39] But perhaps the strongest argument against regarding the sphinx (?) seal as the seal of a private owner is that there are no real reasons why it should be disassociated from the secondary seals discussed above. They are surely official, and by analogy the present seal should be official as well.

It is evident that the owl-in-square seal was used for only a brief period of time. The seal is found only on pinakia that were issued together in the year when allotment by pinakia was instituted and was added apparently during the earliest uses of these pinakia; this at least is the implication of **1–3**, each of which received an owl-in-square seal during its first use. By the time Class II pinakia began to be issued, the owl-in-square seal had become obsolete. A very limited span may be assumed too for the sphinx (?) seal, for it is known only from one pinakion.

In keeping with the above, one is led to suspect that the amount of time during which the double-bodied owl seal was employed was very limited also. The fact that this seal is found on pinakia of three different classes poses no argument against this possibility, since, as we have seen in our discussion of texts inscribed in imitation of Class V lettering, specific uses of the Class II, IV, and V pinakia overlapped each other. Although all Class II pinakia and at least a nucleus of the Class IV ones were first issued before the Class V issue, many of these pinakia were still in circulation in various stages of reuse in the years following the issue. It was within these years, of course, that many Class V pinakia were stamped with a double-bodied owl seal in a first or

37. Bruck, *Philologus* 54 (1895), 72.
38. See Mabel Lang and Margaret Crosby, *The Athenian Agora* X: *Weights, Measures and Tokens* (Princeton: American School of Classical Studies at Athens, 1964), 101, no. L 155 a–b.
39. Svoronos, *Monnaies d'Athènes*, pl. 80, nos. 18–21. For the date of the coins and possible relevance of the sphinx type, see Chapter III, n. 10, below.

second use (and possibly in the case of **84** in a third use). And it was then too
that **17**, a Class II pinakion that was last inscribed with a text in imitation of
Class V lettering, was stamped with its double-bodied owl seal. About this
there can be no doubt; the seal could not have been added until after the
pinakion was last erased. Can we then say that all other (Class II and IV)
pinakia that received a double-bodied owl seal did not do so until the post-
Class V period also? An affirmative answer follows, I think, from consideration of the seals' ethnic, which represents a departure from the diobol coin
type on which the seal is based. To judge from the change in ethnic of the
triobol primary seal, pinakia seals that display an intentional modification of
a numismatic device are not to be expected until after the Class V issue (thus
the owl-in-square seal, the one type of secondary seal that unquestionably
antedates this issue, was not subjected to such modification).

Admittedly, a complication is introduced by the double-bodied owl seal in
a circular field that had been stamped on **16**, a Class II pinakion, during its
second use. Had this seal appeared on a Class V pinakion, one would un-
hesitatingly assume it to be a mere die variant from the normally square
double-bodied owl seals. And indeed I believe it should still be so considered,
especially since its device is doubly removed from the diobol coin type.
Nevertheless, the occurrence of a unique variant in an early use of an early
type of pinakion at least invites the suspicion that the variant may be earlier
than the other double-bodied owl seals. But even if it were earlier, this would
still not pose any objection to the possibility that all of the square double-
bodied owl seals belong to the same limited span in the post-Class V period,
since, for all we can tell, the round seal may then not have been so much a
variant as a different type of secondary seal altogether and could therefore
be considered apart from the numerous square seals.

Thus far we have reviewed the material evidence that allows that each
type of secondary seal was of limited duration. Let us now attack the problem
from a different angle by considering the behavior of the seals against the
background of pinakia reuse. Secondary seals were stamped on many but not
on all pinakia of certain kinds and thus served to distinguish these pinakia
from other pinakia of the same kind. The seals, therefore, were in some way
exclusive. Since the seals were always added after an owner's name was
inscribed, we deduce that the exclusiveness of the seals was restricted further
and pertained only to particular owners, namely, the men who were in possession of the pinakia at the time when the seal was added. Accordingly, the
seals should not have remained valid for more than a single use; if they did,
and if their designation was indiscriminately transferred to later owners
every time pinakia bearing the seal were reinscribed, one would be hard put

to explain how the seals could have had any exclusive effect in the first place.[40]

To be sure, the secondary seals were physically retained into later uses; I know of no instance where one was deliberately voided by erasure. But this does not necessarily imply that the seals continued to remain in effect. On the contrary, the very circumstance that none were obliterated or canceled intentionally can be taken as an indication that the seals had ceased to be relevant for subsequent owners; it was unnecessary to void seals that had already become invalid. A sure indication, however, is provided by **63**, whose double-bodied owl seal was inscribed over by the name of the owner subsequent to the owner for whom the seal was stamped—even though the name of the second owner could have easily been abbreviated by one or two letters to avoid encroaching on the seal. After one use, the seal had apparently lost its value and was inscribed over as if it did not exist. Still later, this secondary seal was erased with the erasure of the second name.

Now, if each secondary seal could be valid for no more than a single use of a pinakion, all secondary seals of a given type could have been employed only between the time that the seal type was introduced and the time that any pinakion that was stamped with such a seal was transferred to a subsequent owner. Chapter IV shows that transfer of pinakia took place at rather frequent intervals and in some cases occurred after the minimum interval of a single year. Hence the maximum allowable span for the use of each seal type should be one year also.

For the owl-in-square seal, this year could be the very one in which the Class I pinakia were issued, or it could possibly be the second or third year after the year of issue. The year in which all double-bodied owl seals were stamped on pinakia cannot date long after the Class V issue, for it is a year when many Class V pinakia were still being used by their first owners. On the other hand, since some pinakia received a double-bodied owl seal in a use that was inscribed with conventional letters or with lettering in imitation of Class V lettering (such as **16–18, 62, 63, 65–71, 73, 83,** and **84**), the year of the double-bodied owl seal belongs after the Class V lettering had been formally abandoned, somewhere, I would imagine, between about three to six years after the Class V reform. The sphinx (?) seal dates from a year that is later still, for it was added to **73** after the pinakion's double-bodied owl seal.

---

40. It is illogical to suppose that, at the time a pinakion with a secondary seal was re-inscribed for a new owner, pains were taken to ensure that the new owner qualified for whatever the seal happened to represent (and that owners who did not so qualify received pinakia without the secondary seal). For if such were the case in respect to the reissue of pinakia with a secondary seal, why were the seals not stamped, like primary seals, before the pinakia were issued originally?

III Meaning of the Stamped Seals: Dikastic and Nondikastic Pinakia

Of all aspects of the pinakia, none have remained as enigmatic and challenging as the stamped seals. Explicit guidance from the literary sources is lacking, and in the past nearly the same could be said about the published records of the pinakia themselves. In *IG* II² one reads of an owl seal with the legend KO *vel* ΛO, or $\begin{smallmatrix} Z \\ I \end{smallmatrix} \begin{smallmatrix} \bar{\pi} \\ O \end{smallmatrix}$ (II², 1848 = **93**), of seals with the head of Athena (II², 1852 = **28**) or of a woman (II², 1839 = **81**), and of several seals that defied identification (II², 1842, 1865, 1875, and 1891 = **37, 36, 27,** and **29,** all Class III pinakia with gorgoneion seals). And before Bruck the record was riddled with many more errors; for example, two pinakia (**37** and **149**) were thought to have been stamped with a seal in the form of a crescent moon.

In view of this seemingly vast repertory of devices, it is no wonder that much theorizing about the seals has drawn on the mere multiplicity of seal types and on the observation that the seals occur on various pinakia in various numbers. Thus Curtius proposed that a seal was stamped on a dikast's pinakion every time the juror sat in court.[1] And from an equally superficial acquaintance with the seals, but with reference to the nondikastic allotments in Demosthenes 39.10–12, Teusch, followed by Lipsius and Hommel, submitted that each seal represented a different Athenian magistracy and was stamped on the pinakia of citizens who had been allotted to it.[2] According to Hommel, the frequently occurring triobol seals (which he, like most others, called simply "owl" seals) may have signified membership in the boule, and the double-bodied owl seals a second term as *bouleutes*.

Primary Seals

When Girard inferred that the triobol seals were stamped on pinakia before the pinakia were inscribed and put into use, he ventured no deductions. The implications, however, were obvious enough. As first stated by

1. Curtius, *RhM* 31 (1876), 286.
2. Teusch, *De sortitione*, 54–55; Lipsius I, 150, n. 50; Hommel, *Heliaia*, 42–43.

Olivier Rayet,[3] they are simply that any such seal should be a seal of certification, at once witnessing that a pinakion was officially issued and protecting against forged imitations. In other words, such a seal would have served the same purpose as governmental seals affixed to documents, money, standard weights, and in general to official things of all kinds in all eras. Only Rayet, apparently not having read Girard with sufficient care, believed that all of the seals were stamped on pinakia before issue and that all of them consequently were validating seals. It was thus left for Bruck to restrict Rayet's reasoning to Girard's observation about the behavior of the triobol seal (vis-à-vis secondary seals). Since all pinakia were presumed to be dikasts' pinakia, and since a triobol-like device was suitable for the stamping of such pinakia—three obols constituting a juror's stipend—Bruck concluded that the seal was the *Hauptstempel der Richterlegitmation,* whose function was to certify the legitimacy of the dikasts' pinakia and the dikastic status of their owners.[4]

This is perfectly logical, and, although I have warned in Chapter I, above, that it is mistaken to assume that all the bronze pinakia are necessarily dikastic, the truth is that not all stamped pinakia were provided with a triobol seal. As for Bruck's remark that a triobol seal was appropriate for validating dikasts' pinakia, the point can hardly be overemphasized. In the entire repertory of Athenian symbols, no device could have been more ideally appropriate. Beginning in 424 B.C., or shortly before, when the *dikastikon* was raised to three obols, τὸ τριώβολον and τὸ δικαστικόν became virtually synonymous, as seen in the frequent references to τὸ τριώβολον in Aristophanes, whether the references have an explicitly dikastic context or not.[5] At *Knights* 255, the heliasts are called the "brotherhood of the triobol," φράτερες τριωβόλου. And, unlike the *ekklesiastikon,* which was gradually augmented in the course of the fourth century, the dikastikon remained fixed at three obols as late as the time of the *AthPol.*[6] It is not surprising, therefore, that the

3. Rayet, *AnnAssEtGr* 1878, 204.
4. Bruck, *Philologus* 54 (1895), 69, 74–76.
5. Aristophanes, *Knights* (424 B.C.) 51, 800; *Wasps* (423 B.C.) 609, 684, 690, 1121; and *Birds* (415 B.C.) 1541.
6. *AthPol* 62.2 and 68.2. From its inauguration at one obol shortly after 404/3, the ekklesiastikon rose quickly to three obols by 392 (*AthPol* 41.3; Aristophanes, *Ekklesiazousai* [392 B.C.] 293, 301). How long the stipend remained at this sum is unknown, but it continued to be raised so that by the 320s it had doubled to a drachma for ordinary sessions and nine obols for *kuria* assemblies (*AthPol* 62.2). Hence the association of the triobol and the ekklesiastikon was temporary and never as strong as the older, centurylong association of the triobol and dikastikon. The amount of the *bouleutikon* is known only for the later fourth century when it stood at five obols. A useful survey of these *misthoi* is to be found in J. J. Buchanan, *Theorika, A Study of Monetary Distributions to the Athenian Citizenry during the Fifth and Fourth Centuries B.C.* (Locust Valley, N.Y.: J. J. Augustin, 1962), 14–27.

only numismatists who have dealt with pinakia, C. T. Seltman[7] and J. H. Jongkees,[8] assumed independently of Bruck and without reference to the seal's behavior that the triobol seal must have been indicative of membership in the body of dikastai.

The purpose of the triobol seal was certification, and because of the dikastic significance that the seal would have had for every fourth-century Athenian, we have good reason for thinking that the certification was specifically dikastic. Let us then take this interpretation of the triobol seal and test it by seeing whether it throws any meaningful light on the more problematic gorgoneion seals.

Unlike the triobol device, a gorgon's head had no institutional or numismatic associations at Athens, at least not during the fifth through second century B.C. As the centerpiece of Athena's aegis, it was, like her owls, an attribute of the goddess and hence symbolic of her city. It was possibly in this connection that the device was adopted in the sixth century B.C. for the obverse type of the latest series of Athenian *Wappenmünzen*,[9] and again in the first century B.C. for the obverses on an issue of Athenian bronze coins.[10]

7. C. T. Seltman, "Pinakia Dikastika," summary of a paper read at a meeting of the Cambridge Philological Society, Feb. 19, 1931, *Cambridge University Reporter* 61 (1931), 752. Seltman states "that the triobol-device . . . was a voucher guaranteeing his three-obol pay for jury-service to a dikast. Probably the diobol-device [our double-bodied owl seal] surcharged on some of the tickets was likewise a guarantee of *theoretic* pay." For this last notion Seltman presumably drew on the old and now discredited association of the *diobelia*, which is known from late fifth-century inscriptions, with the fourth-century *theorikon* (see Buchanan, *Theorika*, 35–48).

8. Jongkees, *BABesch* 20 (1945), 10.

9. Thus C. T. Seltman, *Athens, Its History and Coinage before the Persian Invasion* (Cambridge: Cambridge University Press, 1924), 50. These coins (*ibid.*, plate XIV; Svoronos, *Monnaies d'Athènes*, plate 1, nos. 69–75), the earliest Athenian ones with both an obverse and reverse type, are now recognized as the immediate precursors of the earliest Athenian owl coinage (C. M. Kraay, "The Archaic Owls of Athens: Classification and Chronology," *NC*[6] 16 [1956], 45–47). The gorgoneion was, of course, the pre-eminent apotropaic device throughout the Greek world, and I would rather imagine that this apotropaic aspect, rather than any specific connection with Athena, accounts for the great gorgoneion seen by Pausanias (1.21.3) on the wall of the Acropolis. Gorgoneia, along with dozens of other common Greek symbols, also occur on Athenian *kollyboi*, lead tokens, and clay tesserae (full references in Lang and Crosby, *The Athenian Agora* X, 103, L 182–183).

10. Svoronos, *Monnaies d'Athènes*, plate 25, nos. 22–28. On the date of the issue (and that of the related bronze issue with a sphinx obverse [Chapter II, n. 38, above]), see the chronology implied by M. J. Price, "The New-Style Coinage of Athens: Some Evidence from the Bronze Issues," *NC*[7] 6 (1964), 27–36, especially Table II. Both the gorgoneion and sphinx bronze issues have been associated traditionally with the New Style silver coins which bear gorgoneia and sphinxes as magistrates' private symbols (see most recently, Margaret Thompson, *The New Style Silver Coinage of Athens* [New York: American Numismatic Society, 1961], 529). But the correctness of this association cannot be affirmed until some kind of final consensus is reached as to the date of the two issues of silver involved (on the present lack of consensus on the New Style silver as a whole, see Price, "New-Style Coinage," 28, 35–36, with references). If the bronze and silver coins should turn out to be unrelated, the gorgoneion and sphinx on the bronze should probably be interpreted as symbolic

Still, the best indication that the gorgoneion was regarded by the Athenians as an official emblem is its appearance on the pinakia alongside the unquestionably official owl seals.

Girard did not have the material nor Bruck the eye to appreciate the behavior of the gorgoneion seal. Bruck, for example, failed to identify the gorgoneia on two of the better preserved Class III pinakia that he examined (**28** and **29**) and from his unimproved record believed that the gorgoneia were secondary seals, like double-bodied owl seals, and that both types may have pertained to special commercial, military, or religious courts.[11] In retrospect, the most thoughtful solution was that of Jongkees, who proposed that if the triobol seal denoted membership among the dikastai, then the gorgoneion, the next most common seal and the one occurring once on some pinakia and twice on others, indicated membership in the boule and, in accordance with the theorizing of Teusch and Hommel, was stamped on the pinakia of citizens who served as bouleutai for one or two terms.[12] As all others, however, Jongkees was unaware of the gorgoneion's behavior as a primary seal.

We now know that the gorgoneia, like the triobol seals, were stamped on pinakia before the pinakia were inscribed and issued. This should make them in some way seals of certification also. In addition, our analysis of the chronological sequence of the stamped pinakia has revealed three further circumstances of the seals' behavior, each of which any interpretation of the gorgoneia must explain. First, absent from the Class I and II pinakia, the gorgoneion seal is a latecomer, not appearing until after allotment by pinakia (with triobol seals) was firmly established. Second, when the gorgoneion seal is introduced, it appears on a wholly new type of pinakion (Class III), which not only lacks a triobol seal, but is stamped with two gorgoneia as if to exclude the addition of a triobol seal at either the right or left end. Third, when the seal is introduced, it is at the same time combined with the triobol seal of Classes I and II on the composite triobol-gorgoneion pinakia of Classes IV and V.

These requirements for a theory of the gorgoneion seal are exact and relatively complex, so much so that if a simple interpretation can be found to account for them all, the validity of the interpretation is practically assured.

A theory begins to emerge when we substitute the word "dikastic" for "triobol" in the three statements above. Assuming that the triobol seal denotes membership in the body of dikastai, it follows that the owners of

---

of Athena and Athens, the gorgoneion as explained above, the sphinx perhaps as a reference to the sphinx on the helmet of the Parthenos (Pausanias 1.24.5).

11. Bruck, *Philologus* 54 (1895), 70–73.

12. Jongkees, *BABesch* 20 (1945), 10.

the Class I and II pinakia were dikasts, that the owners of the Class III pinakia, from which the triobol seal was excluded, were not dikasts, and that the owners of the triobol-gorgoneion Class IV and V pinakia were dikasts who simultaneously shared the nondikastic status of the Class III owners. This last status cannot be connected with a particular Athenian magistracy, a special court, or any other institution that involved a restricted number of Athenians, for (to cite only one objection to all of these proposals) it was a status held by every dikast once the gorgoneion seal was introduced, that is, during the years when the Class III, IV, and V pinakia were employed. Since the status denoted by the gorgoneion seal should apply to all enrolled dikastai as well as to a sizable group of Athenians who were owners of Class III pinakia and not enrolled as dikastai, it is hard to imagine what the status could be unless it was simply citizenship. But why a seal to represent citizenship, and why would it have been added to the pinakia of dikastai?

All becomes clear, I believe, when the primary seals are considered in light of the allotments in which pinakia were employed. From the literary testimonia discussed in Chapter I, two such allotments are known: the dikastic allotments held every court day and the annual allotments to the state magistracies. As I have explained with regard to Demosthenes 39.10 12, these two kinds of allotments presuppose two kinds of pinakia: those belonging to citizens sworn as dikastai and those belonging to citizens who were not but who needed pinakia to participate in the magisterial allotments. If this situation applied when bronze pinakia bore validating seals, it presumably would have called for two kinds of seals: a dikastic seal for the jurors' pinakia and a validating seal for the pinakia belonging to men who were citizens, but not enrolled as jurors. Since it can hardly be coincidental that among the surviving bronze pinakia two such types of pinakia and two such seals can be identified, we need not hesitate to conclude that, whereas the triobol seal indeed certified pinakia used in dikastic allotments, the gorgoneion seals certified pinakia used in the annual allotments open to all citizens.

From historical probability alone, one naturally assumes that allotment by pinakia was invented to solve specific problems posed by the dikastic allotments held at the beginning of every court day, by far the most frequent and, because of the large numbers of candidates to be chosen as quickly and mechanically as possible, the most intricate and demanding of Athenian allotments. Pinakia and large kleroteria were eventually adopted for the annual allotments of magistrates, but not until after they had been devised, tried, and proven in their original employment with the dikasts. This no longer need be a matter of informed conjecture, however, for it is precisely what the absence of the gorgoneion seal on the earliest extant pinakia demonstrates.

To review the stamped pinakia once more, they are to be understood as follows:

(1) The earliest pinakia were exclusively dikastic. When the Athenians reorganized the dikasteria, instituted allotment by pinakia, and had to issue pinakia to jurors for the first time, they protected against forgeries by stamping the pinakia with an official seal. Any seal would have sufficed, but a triobol device was chosen because of its traditional associations with the dikasteria; hence the form of the earliest (Class I and II) pinakia with a triobol seal at the right.

(2) Later, once allotment by pinakia and kleroteria had captured the fancy of the Athenians and it was decided to appropriate this procedure for the annual elections of state officials, a new kind of pinakion, distinguished by a new kind of seal, had to be issued to eligible Athenians not sworn as jurors. This new seal was the gorgoneion seal, selected probably because it was devoid of institutional connotations, and the new pinakia the pinakia of Class III.

(3) At the same time, rather than provide each dikast with two pinakia, one stamped for each kind of allotment, the Athenians began to add the new gorgoneion seal to the pinakia of dikasts (Classes IV and V), which henceforth were to be good for use both in the annual magisterial allotments and in the more frequent allotments to the courts. Thus the dikastic pinakia came to be stamped with two primary seals, the dikastic triobol seal being moved over to the more prominent left end to make room for the nondikastic gorgoneion seal at the right.

In keeping with this new format, the nondikastic pinakia received two identical gorgoneion seals, in order to emphasize that their owners could participate only in nondikastic allotments.

Secondary Seals

It is clear from the foregoing that the owl-in-square, double-bodied owl, and sphinx (?) seals, which appear only on pinakia stamped with a triobol seal, must in one way or another have been used in connection with the courts. Thus we may dismiss immediately any interpretation of these seals that does not take their essential dikastic nature into account, such as Hommel's tentative suggestion that the double-bodied owl seals might have to do with the boule or Seltman's attempt to link the double-bodied owl seals with theoric payments (see n. 7, above). I observed at the end of the preceding chapter that the purpose of the seals was in some sense exclusive. We can now proceed one step further: since the seals were stamped on many but not on all dikastic pinakia, they obviously served to mark out certain dikastic pinakia from other dikastic pinakia.

The owl-in-square seal and the double-bodied owl seal behave similarly; each occurs on a relatively large proportion of the dikastic pinakia that survive from a particular chronological period. It is probable, therefore, that each of these two seal types had the same function, but discharged it at a different time, or, rather, in a different year, for we have seen that each secondary seal type was probably employed only for a single year, after which it became meaningless and obsolete. According to the absolute chronology developed at the end of this chapter and the next, these two years—one dating to or shortly after the year of the Class I issue, the other falling not long after the Class V issue—would have been separated by a span of at least a decade. That the function of the two secondary seals was the same is again suggested by the numismatic connotation of the seals' devices, the owl-in-square seal being copied from the reverse type of a one-obol coin, the later double-bodied owl seal from diobol coins.

Whether the sphinx (?) seal is to be regarded as a still later counterpart of the owl-in-square and double-bodied owl seals is less clear. It is known from only one extant pinakion, is not derived from a coin type, and may have been used in some other, related or unrelated, connection. Indeed, we would do well to remember in the following discussion that we have not proven that the sphinx (?) seal was official. There is still an outside chance that Bruck was correct in declaring it to be the seal of a private owner.

Having stated these considerations for an interpretation of the secondary seals, I remain uncertain about what they must mean. According to Bruck, such secondary seals were stamped on the pinakia of dikastai who were qualified to sit on special courts or, perhaps in the case of the diobol-like double-bodied owl seals, special judicial commisions, the members of which would have received two obols pay.[13] The tentative tone of Bruck's discussion attests to the difficulty of convincingly demonstrating what particular courts or commissions these should be. Violations of the Mysteries were tried by dikastai who had been initiated into the Eleusinian rites (Andokides 1.28, Pollux 8.123), and, if Lipsius' interpretation of Lysias 14.5 is correct,[14] military

13. Bruck, *Philologus* 54 (1895), 70–73.
14. Lipsius I, 143; cf. Plato, *Laws* 12.943A. As an explanation for secondary seals, Bruck was particularly attracted to the old view, based on Demosthenes 35.43, that mercantile cases were heard by expert dikasts (thus Th. Thalheim, s.v. Δικασταί, in *Paulys Real-Encyclopädie der klassischen Altertumswissenschaft*, ed. George Wissowa [Stuttgart: J. B. Metzler, 1894–], v, 569). But no one would now maintain that Demosthenes' reference

tribunals may have been heard by dikasts who served with the defendant on the campaign in question. Are we to believe that in two or three separate years, all Eleusinian initiates or all participants in a campaign who were enrolled as jurors had their pinakia stamped with a seal so that a special court of them could be allotted? It is possible, but not, I think, an especially compelling solution. As for Bruck's dikastic commissions, he could point only to the board of ten *hieropoioi* that was allotted out of the dikastai in 421/0 (*IG* I², 84, lines 19 and 20), but there is no reason to believe that any special eligibility was required for it beyond enrollment as a dikastes.

Another approach would be that the secondary seals stood not for qualifications of certain jurors but rather for actual participation in some specially allotted body of dikastai, like the above-mentioned board of ten or, better, the nomothetai.[15] A committee of nomothetai was chosen only in years when it had some specific legislation to consider; thus the establishing of such committees would perhaps suffice for the occasion of seals that were used in several separated years. Committees of nomothetai varied in size according to the business at hand and in one year included as many as 1,001 dikasts (Demosthenes 24.27); this might allow for the fact that the owl-in-square and double-bodied owl seals occur on a large proportion of pinakia in two years and the sphinx (?) seal on a small proportion in another year. As for why seals might have been stamped on the pinakia of nomothetai, one supposes that a year's nomothetai had to sit on more than one day and might have had their pinakia stamped so that they could be identified and admitted at a later session. I do not know whether this interpretation is any more convincing than the previous one. But it should be noted that unless we are willing to assume that nomothetai or dikasts in any kind of irregular court were paid differently than dikasts sitting in a normal session—which seems to me quite unlikely— neither interpretation would account for the possible numismatic implications of the owl-in-square and double-bodied owl seals. This is also true of my provisional suggestion that the secondary seals might have been stamped on the pinakia of jurors who had been specially allotted as courtroom attendants—such as the keepers of the water clock and men in charge of the ballots,

---

to the commercial expertise of his audience pertained to a limited group when, as Lipsius has pointed out (I, 143, n. 31), it is obviously a comment on the ability of Athenian juries at large. Another special kind of court (not mentioned by Bruck) which conceivably could have been composed of regular dikastai with special qualifications, such as age, are the ephetic homicide courts, but about the qualifications of the *ephetai* we know nothing for certain, and there is no firm basis for assuming that they were allotted from the regular dikastai. For an exemplary discussion, see D. M. MacDowell, *Athenian Homicide Law in the Age of the Orators* (Manchester: Manchester University Press, 1963), 48–57.

15. On nomothetai, see Demosthenes 24.21–22, 25–27, 33; and Aischines 3.38–40; cf. Busolt-Swoboda, 1011.

known from *AthPol* 66.2–3—and served to ensure that these positions would be fairly rotated among all the jurors;[16] for such attendants too were surely not paid any differently than the other dikasts.

A simpler and possibly more attractive interpretation of the owl-in-square and double-bodied owl seals is that they were validating stamps added to the pinakia of all dikasts who were enrolled in two particular years. All dikastic pinakia lacking such a seal would, for one reason or another, simply not have been in use during either of the two years when pinakia had to be so validated. The interpretation would admirably explain the high proportion of dikastic pinakia that were stamped with one of the two seals, and it is not hard to understand why validating stamps of this kind would have been employed. As will be seen in the next chapter, the enrolling of dikasts on an annual basis presented a theoretical problem in the control of pinakia that would have been alleviated by the use of annual control stamps. Our seals are, of course, not annual, but belong to two rather widely separated years. And other difficulties with the present interpretation are that it, too, allows neither for the seals' numismatic connotations nor for a parallel interpretation of the sphinx (?) seal as a validating seal, since it is highly improbable that only one pinakion has survived from the year when this last seal was being used.

Such difficulties are not insuperable. Perhaps owl-in-square validating seals were tried out in the year after the first issue of pinakia, but were found to be unworkable or unnecessary and so were abandoned until much later when they were tried out again, and again were abandoned. The owl-in-square and double-bodied owl devices need not have been selected with reference to money paid out. And, as stated above, the sphinx (?) seal perhaps ought to be disassociated from the other secondary seals. Nevertheless, until some new evidence should be able to substantiate further this or any other theory, I believe we are obliged to recognize that the difficulties exist and that an interpretation of the secondary seals is at present beyond any decisive solution.

Period of Stampless Pinakia

A division of the stamped pinakia into dikastic and nondikastic groups explains the behavior of their primary seals and, as will be seen in the

16. J. H. Kroll, "Pinakia Dikastika: A Summary History of Athenian Bronze Allotment Plates," a paper read at the Sixty-eighth General Meeting of the Archaeological Institute of America, abstract in *AJA* 71 (1967), 191. On these attendants, see D. M. Lewis, "Dedications of Phialai at Athens," *Hesperia* 37 (1968), 370, lines 15–19, with commentary, 373.

following chapters, much more besides. But before we can turn to problems of absolute chronology and thence to purely constitutional matters, it remains to deal with four interrelated questions concerning the sequence and interpretation of pinakia after the stamped seals were discontinued. They are, in the order in which I shall treat them here: were the stampless Class VI pinakia dikastic or nondikastic? How do the wooden dikastic pinakia known from the *AthPol* fit the sequence of bronze pinakia? Why were stamped seals discontinued on the bronze pinakia? And, finally, what is the meaning of the two pairs of pinakia that were found in single graves and belonged to single owners, **29/125** and **149/150**.

An answer to the first question follows naturally from the particularly close affiliation of the Class VI pinakia with the stamped nondikastic pinakia of Class III. We observed in our discussion of section-letters (above, p. 39) that the Class III pinakia continued to be issued and used after the series of bronze pinakia with triobol seals (that is, dikastic pinakia) had been terminated and that, as a result, most of the stamped pinakia that ultimately lost their seals and were reused in the Class VI period come from Class III. It was noted also that only in Classes III and VI do we find pinakia that may have lacked section-letters. For more explicit testimony on the special relationship of these two classes, however, we must turn to the above-mentioned pairs of pinakia. It is regrettable that both pairs were lost during the last world war and that our knowledge of the second is limited to what can be deduced from Ross's rough transcription. The transcription (Fig. 273) shows that one of the two pinakia (**150**) was almost certainly a Class VI pinakion—at least in its last use—and suggests that the other (**149**) was probably a Class III pinakion in a final Class VI reuse. The first pair, known from excellent photographs, was comprised of one Class III pinakion (**29**) and one Class VI pinakion (**125**) and clarifies precisely how the two classes were affiliated. The Class III pinakion in the pair demonstrates the nondikastic status of the owner concerned and therefore of the Class VI pinakion that had subsequently come into his possession.[17] Everything points inevitably to the same conclusion: the stampless Class VI pinakia were a direct continuation of the nondikastic pinakia of Class III. Thus we can now trace the nondikastic pinakia through three stylistic phases: a phase of stamped pinakia with stamped section-

---

17. This assumes of course (as I have assumed throughout) that anyone who became enrolled as a dikast had to exchange his nondikastic pinakion for a dikastic pinakion, and, similarly, that any dikast who retired from the courts had to exchange his dikastic pinakion for a nondikastic one. Hence an Athenian would not have owned both a nondikastic and a dikastic pinakion at the same time. The assumption follows naturally from the fact that the vast majority of burials involving pinakia (and all those involving stamped dikastic pinakia) contained only one pinakion.

letters (the earlier Class III pinakia); a phase of stamped pinakia with inscribed section-letters (the later Class III pinakia); and a final phase of stampless pinakia (Class VI).

But if this is so, what happened to the pinakia of jurors during the latest phases of the nondikastic pinakia? Bronze dikastic pinakia can be traced only through the first of these stylistic phases and were discontinued soon after inscribed section-letters were introduced. Since we have no other bronze pinakia to parallel the later nondikastic pinakia, the dikasts' pinakia contemporary with them must have been those of boxwood.

That Class VI pinakia were being used as late as the time of the *AthPol* (when we know dikasts' pinakia were of wood) is all but proven by **114**, a Class VI pinakion that was buried with its sole owner, Nikostratos, the son of Nikostratos, of Acharnai, sometime after the spring of 330 B.C. when he celebrated a choregic victory in the Greater Dionysia. Although we have no way of ascertaining exactly when Nikostratos died and was buried with his pinakion (he may or may not be the Nikostratos of Acharnai listed in a manumission inscription of the later 320s; in any case his brother Pythodoros was still alive at age sixty in 325/4), the date of his victory provides the latest known *terminus post quem* for the interment of a bronze pinakion; and the *terminus* implies an actual burial date that must be very close to, contemporary with, or even later than the completion of the *AthPol* between 329/8 and 325/4 (or 323/2, see Chapter I, n. 2, above).[18]

However this may be, the coexistence of wooden pinakia for dikasts and stampless bronze pinakia for citizens not enrolled as dikasts at the time of the *AthPol* admirably explains why Aristotle troubled to specify that in his day jurors' pinakia were of boxwood. In the following chapter it will become clear why wood was particularly well suited for dikasts' pinakia and bronze for pinakia belonging to citizens who were not dikasts.

The change from bronze to wooden dikastic pinakia was surely responsible for the corresponding change in the nondikastic series from the stamped pinakia of Class III to the stampless pinakia of Class VI. After the bronze dikastic pinakia were retired in favor of wooden ones, the gorgoneion seals on Class III pinakia were no longer essential for distinguishing nondikastic from dikastic pinakia and were eventually abandoned. The seals would, of course, have continued to serve as guarantees of official issue, but in view of the unspecialized allotments in which the Class III pinakia were used, such

18. Also cf. Philostratos of Kolone, the last owner of the lost pinakion **158**. If the pinakion was a Class VI one and was recovered from a grave—both circumstances are at least not improbable—the owner should be identical with the well-known orator who died (and therefore would have been buried with his pinakion) about 330 B.C., a date again close in time to the composition of the *AthPol*.

certification was essentially gratuitous from the beginning.[19] Unlike the dikastic pinakia, which could belong legitimately only to those Athenians who were duly sworn and enrolled as jurors, a nondikastic pinakion could be owned by any Athenian, and, practically speaking, it made little difference whether the pinakion was issued by the state or was procured privately. Anyone allotted to a magistracy with a nondikastic pinakion was subject to scrutiny before being confirmed in office, and the scrutiny, rather than the validity of the pinakion per se, protected against the selection of unqualified candidates. Conceived negatively as nondikastic seals, the gorgoneion seals (and the expense of adding them to pinakia) became superfluous after bronze dikastic pinakia and their triobol seals had been discontinued. The Athenians seem to have been slow to appreciate this fully, for stamped Class III pinakia with inscribed section-letters continued to be manufactured and issued for a time after the cessation of dikastic pinakia in bronze. In respect to the dropping of seals from the nondikastic pinakia, therefore, cause preceded effect by some interval.

The grave-group composed of **29** and **125** attests that the introduction of stampless nondikastic pinakia was not marked by a withdrawal of the stamped ones. Rather, the stamped Class III pinakia in various degrees of reuse continued to be employed side by side with stampless pinakia down into the Class VI period. As for the question of how certain Athenians managed to obtain a second nondikastic pinakion, I would imagine that one was theirs for the asking. Certainly no one would submit more than one pinakion in an allotment; as we learn from Demosthenes 39.12, to do so was to risk the penalty of death. Presumably the second pinakion was a spare, obtained perhaps when the other was temporarily misplaced. Whatever the circumstances, the important fact is that both of our extant pairs are pairs of nondikastic pinakia. Such pinakia had virtually no intrinsic value and were not subject to the kind of strict regulation that applied to dikastic pinakia and that will be discussed below.

Chronological Termini

The bronze pinakia mentioned in Demosthenes 39.10–12 should probably be identified as nondikastic pinakia either of the stamped Class III or stampless Class VI variety. Demosthenes' speaker, Mantitheos, avoids mention of dikas-

---

19. That the gorgoneion came to be tacitly regarded as superfluous even on the dikastic Class IV and V pinakia is implied by the Class II pinakia **16–18**, which never received a gorgoneion seal and yet were reused during the post-Class V period (see above, pp. 21–22, 32, 48–49), when the gorgoneion had become a standard fixture on the pinakia of dikasts.

tic allotments—again, the most frequent allotments in Athenian public life—very likely because neither he nor his brother was enrolled and sworn as a dikastes. The speech in any event belongs after bronze pinakia were adopted for magisterial allotments, and its date therefore gives a *terminus ante quem* of about 348 for the introduction of the nondikastic gorgoneion seal.

Mantitheos suggested that in order to distinguish his pinakion from his brother's, a σημεῖον might be attached to one of them; to judge from the context, he apparently thought the σημεῖον would be a novelty so far as pinakia were concerned. It would be mistaken, of course, to argue from this that the pinakia involved must have lacked seals; σημεῖον denotes a mark of any kind and not necessarily a stamped seal or signet (σφραγίς). Nevertheless, I believe the following evidence shows that it is entirely possible that the speech was delivered at a time when wooden pinakia were already being used by dikasts and when late Class III or stampless Class VI pinakia were being used by citizens who were not dikasts.

For other *termini ante quos* we must depend primarily on archaeological contexts and associated finds which help fix the dates that particular pinakia went out of use and found their way into the ground.

a. For example, according to the unpublished chronology of Dr. Klaus Vierneisel of the Kerameikos excavations, the small lekythos interred with **119** gives a *terminus ante quem* of about 338 for this Class VI pinakion, which had two uses before being buried with its second owner. Working back from 338 and allowing a minimum of a few years for each of the pinakion's uses, we find ourselves already in the neighborhood of the date of the Demosthenic speech (about 348). When we reflect that the actual burial date of the lekythos may well have been earlier than 338 (Vierneisel believes the most probable date is around 350) and that each use of the pinakion could have been longer than a few years, the contemporaneity of the Class VI pinakia and Demosthenes 39 becomes even more likely. Since the change from dikasts' pinakia of bronze to dikasts' pinakia of wood occurred some years before the change from stamped nondikastic pinakia to stampless nondikastic pinakia, the conclusion that dikasts' pinakia were of wood already by 348 would seem to be inescapable, providing of course that Vierneisel's chronological estimate, based on his long experience with grave-groups from the Kerameikos, is accurate.

b. Identical deductions follow from the context of **130**, another Class VI pinakion, which probably had more than one use before being lost or discarded near the Agora and covered over with a floor that the excavator assigned to around the middle of the fourth century B.C. or a little later on the evidence of the latest potsherd from under the floor. Admittedly, one sherd, itself rather roughly dated by comparison with ceramic shapes found at Olynthos, is a slender reed. But it is all we have in this particular instance, and the high chronology it implies for all pinakia is in general agreement with our other data.

c. Of all the relevant contextual evidence, the most dependably dated is the small palmette lekythos found in a grave group with the Class V pinakion **113**. Vierneisel is confident that the lekythos was interred about 360 or a little earlier, and certainly not later than 350. This, in turn, places the issue of the Class V pinakia before mid-century, probably by as much as a decade or more, and strengthens a relatively high chronology for stamped pinakia of all types.

d. The fill of the final reconstruction of the assembly place on the Pnyx, which has yielded fragments of four pinakia, is dated later in the century, about 330–326 (see above, p. 11) and thus adds little to the above. Two fragments from the fill (**161** and **164**) cannot be identified as to class. Of the others, one (**105**) is from a Class V pinakion that broke and was discarded after its last use with an inscribed section-letter, possibly as a stampless Class VI pinakion; the other (**132**) belonged to a Class VI pinakion with at least two uses before breaking.

e. In view of our *terminus ante* of about 360 for the Class V issue (item "c"), the *terminus* of 348 for the Class I or II fragment from Olynthos, **7** is seen to be too late to help narrow the chronological possibilities for these earlier classes.

f. Relevant gravestones: Kirchner's *med. s. IV a.* dates for two gravestones connected with late uses of late dikastic pinakia support the estimate that bronze dikastic pinakia were supplanted by wooden pinakia at about that time. One of the stones was erected over the tomb containing **68**, a much-reused Class IV pinakion; if accurately dated, the stone fixes the interment of the pinakion at the middle of the century. The other was probably the tombstone of the last owner of **111**, a fragment of a Class V pinakion with a total of three uses; although the fragment may have been a surface find and may not have come from its last owner's grave, Kirchner's date for the stele (and thus for the death of the pinakion owner buried beneath it) at least gives a *terminus ante* for the pinakion's last use, which was dikastic.

As shown in Tables 2 and 3, the yield of prosopographical connections involving men known from the extant pinakia is quite modest. The number of these connections that has a direct bearing on the chronology of the pinakia is more limited still. Apart from the usual uncertainties that arise from the frequent absence of patronymics and the ever present possibilities of homonyms, the reliability of our identifications of particular owners with Athenians attested from dated inscriptions on stone depends to a considerable degree on the dates we independently arrive at for the various types of pinakia. Such identifications are, moreover, relevant for purposes of chronology only when they pertain to last owners of whole pinakia and can give us *termini post quos* for the burial of the pinakia.[20] I list here the six or seven identifications which are both probable and immediately germane to the present inquiry.

g. Nikostratos, son of Nikostratos, of Acharnai, was buried with **114**, a Class VI pinakion, after 331/0, see above, p. 61. (Cf. Philostratos of Kolone, n. 18, above.)

h. Eukolion, son of Pyrrakos, of Anagyrous, was buried with **23**, which was originally a Class III pinakion, but was last used with its seals erased as a Class VI pinakion. Eukolion is known to have served in the boule in 367/6 (and was born, therefore, prior to 396) and is very probably the Euko[lion] of Anagyrous who is mentioned in an inscription pertaining to liturgies in the 380s. Neither of these dates informs us when he died; nor does either necessarily rule out a date of death after the middle of the fourth century, but the second date is sufficiently early to suggest that he and his pinakion were more likely to have been buried before or near the middle of the century rather than substantially later and thus generally supports a high chronology for the beginning of the Class VI pinakia.

i. Two less certain identifications relating to the 370s may also be adduced as being in favor of a relatively high chronology: Epikrates of Gargettos, the last owner of **105** (a Class V pinakion last used with an inscribed section-letter possibly in the Class VI period), is probably to be identified with a trierarch of 377/6; and Lysistratos, son of Kephisodoros, of Melite, a post-Class V owner of the Class IV pinakion **68**, is probably the brother of the Onetor, son of Kephisodoros, of Melite, who moved a decree in 376/5.

j. Although a patronymic is lacking on **78**, it is highly probable that the sole owner of this Class V pinakion was another bouleutes of the year 367/6 (cf. item "h"). If so, and if—as will be determined in the next chapter— dikastic pinakia were owned on a short-term basis, 367/6 must be regarded as

---

20. For example, although the second owner of **4**, a Class I pinakion, is probably to be identified with the Protarchos Peiraieus known to have been alive in about 342/1, this is no guarantee that he did not own the pinakion many years before that date. The pinakion had three uses altogether and was buried with its third owner, who almost certainly had died before 342/1 (by which time dikastic wooden pinakia had replaced bronze ones). On the crucial distinction between last owners, who died in possession of pinakia, and earlier owners of reused pinakia, who were still alive when they parted with pinakia, see Chapter IV, below.

the *terminus post quem* of the Class V issue. The owner, Thucydides of Upper Lamptrai, could not have died and been buried with the pinakion before that date; nor presumably could he have obtained the pinakion (that is, become enrolled or re-enrolled as a dikastes) until after his term on the boule was terminated.[21] Thus on the available evidence we arrive at a date between 367/6 and about 360 (the latter being the *terminus ante* provided by the lekythos buried with **113**, item "c") for the Class V issue.

k. We have seen that some Class V pinakia have as many as two uses with their primary seals intact subsequent to their original use and that stamped bronze dikastic pinakia continued to be issued after the Class V issue. The change to dikastic pinakia of wood is later still. That the change occurred after 356/5 is implied by the Class IV pinakion **62**, whose last owner, Deinias of Halai (his name inscribed with punched serifs in imitation of Class V lettering), should probably be identified with an *epimeletes* of the dockyards of that year. Neither the pinakion nor *IG* II², 1622, the pertinent naval document that gives the date, bears patronymics. But unless additional evidence should come to light to show that the identification is unsound, I believe that we are obliged to accept it, and therefore the year 356/5 as the *terminus post quem* for Deinias' death, for the burial of his pinakion, and hence for the beginning of dikastic pinakia of wood.

How much later did he die? If we can trust the contextual data for the interment of **119** and **130** (items "a" and "b"), which indicate that the introduction of wooden pinakia should be dated as early as possible, probably as early as 348 or before, the burial of Deinias and his pinakion should have occurred within a very few years after 356/5. And this, happily, is in large measure confirmed by the above-mentioned *IG* II², 1622, which records that during the period 345/4–342/1 (lines 379–385) the debt of fifty-five drachmas owed by Deinias for his activities in 356/5 was paid by a certain Philokrates of Oa (lines 513–519). To be sure, Philokrates is not specified as Deinias' heir. But all of Deinias' colleagues of 356/5 who are known from the inscription (lines 402–404, 417–419, 479–482, and 545–548) paid their fifty-five

---

21. Unless we are to believe that an Athenian could hold the titles of bouleutes and dikastes simultaneously. But that surely is unlikely. The bouleutai were required to meet every day except holidays and received five obols per diem for so doing (*AthPol* 43.3, 62.2). Hence there was neither time nor any incentive for a bouleutes to act as a juror, and we may safely assume that anyone nominated to the boule for a particular year would not have sworn the dikastic oath in that year and consequently would not have retained the right to keep a dikastic pinakion. Moreover, if the dikastai were annually allotted, as I shall argue in Chapter IV, it becomes extremely doubtful whether they could hold any other position in the state during the year they served as dikastai. I know of no evidence to support the contention of W. S. Ferguson (*Hellenistic Athens* [London: Macmillan, 1911], 25, n. 3) that a dikast could also serve as a regular magistrate.

drachmas themselves, and the clear implication is that Deinias did not do the same because in the later 340s he was no longer alive.

In light of the above determinations, it is only natural that a few potential identifications must be abandoned. One of these is Kirchner's equation of the owner of **2**, a Class I pinakion, with a *diaitetes* of 325/4, whose nomen and demotic are the same. The diaitetes did not reach age thirty and become eligible for enrollment as a dikastes until 354, and, as we now know, the Class I pinakia were issued many years before that date. If related to the owner of the pinakion, the diaitetes must have been a younger relative, probably a grandson. Similarly, Lysanias of Eupyridai, sole owner of the Class V pinakion **86**, cannot be identified with the Lysanias, son of Lysiades, of Eupyridai who served as bouleutes in 335/4 without doing violence to the evidence that places the Class V issue during the 360s (items "c" and "j"). In the next chapter we will see that each use of a dikastic pinakion ordinarily lasted for only several years at most, so that a man buried with such a pinakion would not have received it much before his death. But even if dikastic pinakia were owned for more substantial amounts of time, the identification would still be doubtful, for, had the bouleutes of 335/4 obtained the pinakion in the 360s, he presumably would have had to surrender it (and his title as dikastes) when he was allotted to the boule and could not have been buried with it later (see n. 21, above). That 335/4 is unquestionably too late to be a *terminus post quem* for the Class V issue is clear, moreover, not only from the archaeological criteria cited above but also from the circumstance that the Class V pinakia were issued within a few years after the gorgoneion seal was introduced on the earliest Class III and IV pinakia, which themselves must have been issued before about 348, the date of Demosthenes 39. Again, we apparently have to do with relatives. A bouleutes of the 330s who can be identified with the owner of an extant pinakion is Demostratos of Euonymon, bouleutes in 336/5 (or about that year) and the last owner of **118**, which is a Class VI pinakion.

Future finds will have the most to contribute in the area of absolute chronology. For the present, a chronology must be based on the following more or less fixed points:

Class I, after 388, the date of Aristophanes' *Ploutos* (see Chapter I, above).

Class V, after 367/6 (item "j") but before about 360 (item "c").

Change from dikastic pinakia of bronze to dikastic pinakia of wood, after but apparently not long after 356/5 (items "a", "b", and "k"); approximately 350 would seem to be a fair estimate (cf. item "f").[22]

Coexistence of wooden dikastic pinakia with nondikastic pinakia of bronze, from around 350 to the oligarchic revision of the constitution in 322/1, which abolished sortitions (cf. item "g").[23]

Thus, stamped dikastic pinakia of bronze, together with the stamped section-letter phase of the Class III pinakia, are seen to span roughly the second quarter of the fourth century, wooden dikastic pinakia and the later nondikastic pinakia (most uses of Class III pinakia with inscribed section-letters and the Class VI pinakia) roughly the third quarter.

In order to complete our chronology, it remains to obtain estimates for the actual date of the Class I issue and for the introduction of the gorgoneion seal. Such estimates depend, however, on a fuller understanding of pinakia reuse and are best postponed until the end of the next chapter.

22. As the purpose of the change was no doubt to save money (see below), the change may be plausibly connected with the general economic tightening up under Euboulos, who began to dominate Athenian politics in 354, after the financial exhaustion of the Social War.

23. On the curtailment of sortitions in 322/1, see Ferguson, *Hellenistic Athens*, 22–23, 25, 39–40. With the exception of a brief interlude in 318, an oligarchic constitution was in force for some fifteen years, until the downfall of Demetrios Phalereus in 307. Since none of the surviving Class VI pinakia can be suspected on prosopographical or other grounds of belonging to the restored democracy, all allotments run on kleroteria after 306 apparently employed pinakia of wood. About sortitions in the third century we know only that in the 280s the courts were still being filled by allotment (*IG* II², 1163, lines 9–10: κλήρωσις τῶν δικαστηρίων), presumably as in the time of Aristotle. The extant stone kleroteria that can be dated all belong to the second century B.C. (Dow, *Prytaneis*, 198–205, nos. I–IV).

IV Reuse, and the Organization of the Athenian Dikasteria in the Fourth Century B.C.

Most students of the Athenian courts have accepted references to six thousand dikastai in sources pertaining to the fifth century as evidence for a fixed number of dikasts; they have supposed that the six thousand were allotted afresh every year and—at least since Hommel's criticisms—that an annual enrollment of this number nominally persisted into the early fourth century when the dikasts were allotted to courts in sections.[1] The dependability of these references has from time to time been called into question, most recently by A. W. Gomme.[2] But even if Aristophanes' mention of six thousand dikastai (*Wasps* 662) is suspect because of the ambiguous and exaggerated context, and even if the recurrence of the figure in *AthPol* 24.3 was a direct borrowing from Aristophanes, as Gomme argues, there still remain the six thousand judges referred to in Andokides 1.17, a passage that cannot be dismissed lightly on account of the religious overtones of the trial. Since the case involved a *graphe paranomon*, which ordinarily would be tried before regularly enrolled dikastai, we cannot assume with Gomme that a special jury of initiates was impaneled. It would seem to me that this last passage lends credence to the others and that the evidence for the fifth century still tends to favor the traditional theory of a fixed annual enrollment of six thousand. This number, incidentally, was recognized by the Athenians as constituting a quorum of the demos for ostracisms and the granting of *adeia*.[3]

However this may be, since the discovery of the *AthPol* there has been nearly universal agreement that neither a fixed number of jurors nor an enrollment

---

1. Hommel, *Heliaia*, 109–111, 118–125; Bonner-Smith I, 224–226, 230, 246, 365, 370. Before Hommel it was commonly assumed (e.g., by Bruck, *Philologus* 52 [1893], 299; Teusch, *De sortitione*, 49–51; Lipsius I, 138–140; Busolt–Swoboda, 1156–1157) that pinakia were introduced at the beginning of the fourth century and that it was then that open enrollment was substituted for a fixed enrollment of six thousand.

2. A. W. Gomme, review of Hommel, *Heliaia*, CR 44 (1930), 60. Other skeptics are Max Fränkel, *Die attischen Geschworenengericht* (Berlin, 1877), 1–20, 88–89; Caillemer, DarSag, "Dikastai," 187–188; R. W. Macan, review of Gustav Gilbert, *The Constitutional Antiquities of Sparta and Athens*, CR 10 (1896), 200–201.

3. R. J. Bonner, "The Minimum Vote in Ostracism," *Classical Philology* 8 (1913), 223–225. See also Bonner-Smith I, 194, 213; Russell Meiggs, "A Note on the Population of Attika," CR 78 (1964), 2–3.

of all jurors on an annual basis continued after the introduction of pinakia and the allotment system described by Aristotle.[4] *AthPol 63.3* states that those over age thirty, not in debt to the state and not ἄτιμοι are permitted to be jurors (δικάζειν δ' ἔξεστιν). This is ordinarily taken to mean that for most of the fourth century the number of dikasts was not fixed, and that any qualified citizen could become enrolled as a juror merely by presenting himself. On the frequency and circumstances of enrollment the *AthPol* is silent, but proof of permanent, lifelong membership in the body of dikastai was assumed from the pinakia. Without exception, they were believed to have been permanent possessions of their owners, a pinakion being issued to an Athenian when he was first enrolled as a juror, used by him until he died, and then buried with him.

The discovery of pinakia in graves was particularly persuasive in this respect since one naturally supposes that what was buried with a man was a lifelong possession to which he had grown dearly attached.[5] To this Bruck systematically added the following considerations:[6]

The pinakia look, and were, carefully inscribed as if they were intended to be permanent. The Class V pinakia with their pierced hole lettering clearly were not meant to be reinscribed and were expected to be used for a considerable time. Bruck might have also mentioned that permanence is also implied by the very use of bronze rather than some more perishable material.

If ownership were not permanent, but annual, some means, such as annual stamps, would have been required for distinguishing the pinakia of one year's dikasts from the next's, but the stamped seals on the pinakia are too few in type to have served in this way. In the absence of annual stamps, each year it would have been necessary to call in every last pinakion, but such regulation would have been exceedingly difficult if not impossible to enforce.

On the pairs of pinakia from the same grave and belonging to the same owner, the section-letter is also the same, thus suggesting that membership in a section was continuous throughout a man's lifetime.

The number of reinscribed pinakia was thought to be small. Bruck knew of only five or six in 1893,[7] of only thirteen two years later.[8] Most pinakia were believed to have had only one, and therefore a permanent, use.

From his conviction that ownership of pinakia and an Athenian's attendant enrollment as a dikastes were permanent, Bruck argued that every dikast swore the heliastic oath only once in his life, at age thirty when he was first

4. Cf. Hommel, *Heliaia*, 36; Bonner-Smith I, 372; and others cited in n. 1, above.
5. Thus Fränkel, *Attischen Geschworenengericht*, 106.
6. Bruck, *Philologus* 52 (1893), 300–303.
7. *Ibid.*, 301.
8. Bruck, *Philologus* 54 (1895), 78, n. 39.

enrolled, that is, when he was assigned to a section and received his pinakion.[9] Hommel disagreed only on this last point, correctly observing that the reference in Isokrates 15.21 to the annual swearing of the heliastic oath (see above, p. 3) must be read to mean that the oath was administered annually to all dikasts, both those who were newly enrolled and those who had been formally enrolled (and had received their pinakia) in previous years.[10]

We now know that reuse, far from being exceptional, was very much the rule. Over five-sixths of the surviving pinakia have been reinscribed either before burial with an owner or before they broke and were discarded. Of these about half are known to have been reinscribed more than once, that is, had three or more uses. Nine (**18, 57, 58, 63, 68, 69, 82, 97,** and **172**) positively or very probably had a minimum of four uses; **59** and **81** had at least five uses, and **96** at least six. These figures, however, must be regarded as conservative minima. As often as not traces of earlier uses have disappeared after repeated or thorough erasure and can no longer be counted. Of those pinakia which are known to have had two or more or three or more uses, many must have had more than two, or more than three. A pinakion with more than six uses is not unthinkable, although the number of such pinakia could never have been large for the purely practical reason that the bronze plates would rarely remain strong and usable after being subjected to erasure on six different occasions. Indeed, the mere durability of the metal seems to have been a primary factor in limiting the number of times a pinakion could be reused.

That more of the surviving pinakia were not reused or not reused more frequently is to be attributed to their popularity as grave furnishings. Pinakia that were buried with their owners—and these include almost all pinakia that have survived whole and virtually all examples with a single use—were in effect withdrawn from circulation. Had any of these whole pinakia with only one or two uses not been interred with their last owners, they would probably have been reused again and again until they too would have broken. Thus, in respect to reuse, whole pinakia with few uses are exceptional and misleading, whereas multiple palimpsests and much-reused fragments—scraps of pinakia so heavily reused that they broke, could not be used any longer, and were discarded—represent the norm.

From this it becomes apparent that bronze pinakia were generally not owned for an Athenian's full adult life, nor, in the case of jurors, from age thirty until they died. Assuming that the earliest pinakia were not issued until after 388 B.C. and that the latest bronze pinakia are no later than 322/1, we

9. Bruck, *Philologus* 52 (1893), 303–305.
10. Hommel, *Heliaia*, 37, 44.

see that bronze pinakia could have spanned at most a period of only sixty-seven years. And there is no reason to think that any particular pinakion was ever employed for more than a part of this entire time. With the possible exception of **12**, a Class II pinakion, none of the surviving Class I or II pinakia can be suspected of having been reused as late as the stampless Class VI period; they broke or were buried with a last owner with their triobol seals intact and thus before dikastic pinakia were changed to wood. And since pinakia from the later classes were not issued until sometime after the earliest possible date for the Class I issue, and since most of these that have survived doubtless broke or were buried before the latest possible year of Class VI pinakia, neither would any of them have spanned the full sixty-seven-year maximum. Consequently, those pinakia which were not buried with their first or second owners came to be reinscribed for three, four, five, and even six owners within a space of considerably less than sixty-seven years. It is clear that reuse was not only common in terms of overall numbers of uses, but, in view of the chronological limitations involved, must have taken place at fairly frequent intervals.

Reuse of Dikastic Pinakia and the Principle of Annual Ownership

That reuse occurred at very frequent intervals on some of the bronze dikastic pinakia (the nondikastic pinakia of Classes III and VI may best be discussed separately) can be ascertained from those pinakia which were re-inscribed in such a way as to betray the lingering influence of the inscriptional format or technique used when the pinakia were first inscribed. The best examples of such palimpsests are the several Class V pinakia reinscribed in imitation of the Class V technique (see above, p. 31). It seems only reasonable to suppose that the second, or in the cases of **111** and **112**, the third, texts on these pinakia were added within only a few years after the Class V issue, when the influence of the technique would have been strongest. Indeed, it is tempting to argue that the two texts on **83** were inscribed within no more than two or three years of each other; the second text imitates the Class V technique with extreme care and is, moreover, the text to which the secondary seal, a seal that dates shortly after the Class V issue, belongs. One is similarly justified in assuming that such texts as **7b** and **10c** (texts of one line) and **6b** (a two-line text both lines of which are abnormally low), all belonging to later uses of Class I or (early) Class II pinakia originally inscribed in one line, were added within only a few years after the initial Class I issue, for, as we know from later texts on other Class I palimpsests, the one-line format was abandoned and forgotten soon after that issue.

The chronological termini reached at the end of the preceding chapter require us to conclude that the frequent reuse of these particular palimpsests was not atypical of the dikastic pinakia as a whole. At least eight surviving Class V pinakia (**81, 84, 95, 96, 104, 107, 108,** and **111**) are known to have had a minimum of three uses with their triobol seals intact and thus had a minimum of three uses before bronze dikastic pinakia were replaced with pinakia of wood. If I am correct in dating the issue of these Class V pinakia to a year between 367/6 and about 360 and the change from bronze to wooden dikastic pinakia in the neighborhood of 350, each of these pinakia would have undergone at least three uses within a space of no more than ten to fifteen years, with a maximum average duration of only about three to five years for each use. Since some allowance should be made for an interval, probably of at least one year, between each use—an interval during which a pinakion was erased and put aside until the next distribution by phylai (see above, p. 36)—the actual average for each use must be lowered further.

The evidence from Class IV tells much the same story. One or possibly two pinakia from this class are known to have four stamped dikastic uses subsequent to the time of the Class V issue. **63** had three such uses subsequent to a use that was stamped with a double-bodied owl seal, a seal that dates after the Class V issue. (The last one or two owners, however, may have obtained the pinakion illegally [see above, pp. 35–36]; thus there is no certainty that all of the four uses can be counted as typical uses.) And if the use of **68** inscribed in imitation of Class V lettering is the first (and not the second) of the four visible uses on the pinakion, this pinakion too would have had four uses in the estimated ten to fifteen years between the Class V issue and the change to dikastic pinakia of wood.

It must be admitted that chronological precision here is impossible. Our dates for the Class V issue and the introduction of wooden dikastic pinakia are estimates hedged about with "circas." But one very good cause for thinking that they are probably not far wrong is that the results they provide about the duration of uses of Class IV and V pinakia tally with the conclusion independently derived from a consideration of Class V pinakia reinscribed in imitation of Class V lettering and from several Class I pinakia with later texts showing the influence of the one-line format. The conclusion in both cases is that each use of a stamped bronze dikastic pinakion lasted for not more than a "few" years, and this, I believe, should mean anywhere from one to, say, five or six years, depending on circumstances of the particular uses.

What does such frequent reuse of jurors' pinakia imply? In the first place it makes it wholly unnecessary to suppose that the ownership of dikastic pinakia during the period when bronze pinakia were employed was on any

but an annual basis. On the compelling evidence of both the annual administration of the heliastic oath and the organization of the Athenian constitution
around annual terms of office generally, an annual enrollment of all Athenian
jurors has traditionally been assumed for the earlier period of the courts.
And were it not for the past conviction that pinakia were issued on a permanent, lifelong basis, doubtless the same would have been assumed for the
time of the bronze pinakia.

Incidentally, in speaking of annual ownership and enrollment, I do not
wish to suggest that a pinakion might not have been used by an owner for
more than a single year. That some dikasts did retain possession of their
pinakia for more than one year is clearly demonstrated by the presence of
the square double-bodied owl secondary seal on some of the Class V pinakia
having only a single use (**85–91**). This seal could not have been stamped on
them until a year or more (I have estimated three to six years) after the
pinakia were originally issued, for between the time of the Class V issue and
the stamping of the seal, two other Class V pinakia (**83** and **84**) are known to
have changed owners (**84** perhaps twice). Annual enrollment would not preclude a man's being enrolled for two, three, or more years in succession. But
it would entail that when a dikast did become re-enrolled and retained
possession of his pinakion for another year, the pinakion was in effect reissued
to him, rather as if the pinakion would have been reissued to another citizen
if its former owner did not happen to become re-enrolled.

Against the concrete testimony of the palimpsest pinakia, the arguments
against such annual ownership and enrollment carry little weight. The
Athenians who were buried with pinakia need not have owned the pinakia
for longer than the year in which they died. And although there is certainly
some truth in Bruck's contention that new pinakia may not have been
intended to be reused—surely the theoretically unerasable Class V pinakia
were not—it is much more to the point that the pinakia, including the Class
V ones, were reused, in some cases within a year or two after they were
initially issued. I would imagine that at the time of the first (Class I) issue,
little attention was given to the needs of the coming years: what was to be
done with the pinakia of retired dikasts; how new pinakia were to be sup-
plied. The first issue would have been experimental enough in its own right.
Bronze was chosen to ensure durability. In any event the solution for the
following years was obviously dictated by economic considerations; it was
immeasurably more efficient to erase and reinscribe old pinakia (for each
piece only a matter of minutes) than to melt them down and to manufacture
new ones. Similarly, the Class V issue signaled a minor reform whereby all
dikasts were to have a theoretically unerasable pinakion, but, after the initial

year or years, the program was abandoned, perhaps because the trouble and expense required to maintain it was not felt to be justified. The Class V lettering could only have been intended against illegal erasure and not against erasure by the state, and there is no reason to presume that names inscribed with this lettering were to be "permanent" for any longer than a single year. When the reform Class I and V pinakia were issued, they were probably not intended to have more than one use, but they were not necessarily intended to be used for more than one year either. As Thucydides has taught us, forethought was never a hallmark of the Athenian demos.

Bruck's observation that the pairs of pinakia belonging to the same owners and having the same section-letters prove permanent membership in the tribal sections is also fundamentally sound, but again only so far as it goes. For as we have seen, both such pairs are nondikastic and tell us nothing about membership in dikastic sections. As for Bruck's concern for how the annual issue of pinakia could have been controlled without stamping pinakia with annual seals, I suggested in the preceding chapter that the owl-in-square and double-bodied owl seals might possibly have been just such revalidating stamps, although for only two separate years. There will be more to say about this question of control below, but for the present it is enough to point out that it is no more proof against annual ownership of pinakia than is the hypothetical problem of keeping unenrolled men from participating in the courts proof against the theory that the courts were organized around annual terms of the dikastic office in the fifth and early fourth centuries.

Reuse of Nondikastic Pinakia

The two pairs of nondikastic pinakia, **29/125** and **149/150**, with their repetitions of section-letters, attest that membership in the nondikastic sections and therefore the issue of the nondikastic pinakia were on a long-term or permanent basis. This is as it should be. Such pinakia were employed in allotments held only once a year.

Yet the nondikastic pinakia were reused, and some of them were reused at frequent enough intervals to make it plain that each of their particular uses could not have spanned an owner's full adult life. According to our dates for the Class VI pinakia (beginning soon after about 350 and ending in 322/1) the maximum span for a pinakion of this class would be in the area of twenty-five years. It is unlikely, of course, that any Class VI pinakion was ever employed for this entire period; most such pinakia were surely issued after and broke or were buried before the absolute outside chronological limits. But even taking the full twenty-five-year span and dividing it by the three uses of the

Class VI pinakia **128**, **133**, and **134**, an average of about eight years emerges for each use. The average for the two uses of **119**, the reused Class VI pinakion interred with a lekythos dating from before 338, should be lower still. Clearly, if the duration of the uses of these particular pinakia was greater than that of average uses of dikastic pinakia, the difference could not have been more than a couple of years.

There is some evidence, nevertheless, that tends to suggest that reuse of nondikastic pinakia was, on the whole, somewhat less frequent than reuse of dikastic pinakia. Since none of the Class III and Class VI pinakia were inscribed with texts similar to Class I or (with the possible, though weak, exception of **140**) Class V texts, this sort of criterion cannot be brought to bear. But it is relevant to note that no positively identified Class III or Class VI pinakion is known to have had more than three uses.[11] To be sure, this does not mean that some might not have undergone more than three. We should never feel confident that all uses of a heavily erased palimpsest have been detected. But the same possibility of undetected uses exists in the case of dikastic palimpsests that are known to have had a minimum of three uses, and yet within the dikastic pinakia we do find pinakia with definite traces of four, five, and six uses. I believe therefore that the absence of surviving nondikastic pinakia with more than three positively attested uses may well be a fairly meaningful indication that nondikastic pinakia were, in general, subjected to less reuse in terms of actual numbers of uses than were the dikastic pinakia.

In terms of the relevant chronological limitations, this inference takes on a greater significance. The maximum span for the circulation of a Class VI pinakion, again, is about twenty-five years, but for some Class III pinakia, which began to be issued shortly before the Class V issue (between 367/6 and about 360) and could have been reused as valid nondikastic pinakia all the way through the Class VI period down to 322/1, we have a maximum of roughly half a century. Thus, whereas dikastic pinakia are known to have undergone three and four stamped dikastic uses within a period of only about ten to fifteen years, it would appear that the nondikastic pinakia were less often used in a possible space of twenty-five to fifty years.

If I have read the above evidence correctly, the results should probably be interpreted as follows: nondikastic pinakia were issued on a permanent basis and could have been used for their owner's full adult life. In view of the

11. All but three of the pinakia listed above as having four or more than four uses are positively from the dikastic Classes II, IV, or V. The exceptions are the right-hand fragments **57**, **58**, and **59**, which typologically could belong to either Class III or IV; their very number of uses, however, suggests that they too were probably dikastic and therefore come from Class IV pinakia.

general tendency of the nondikastic pinakia to be reused with less frequency than their dikastic counterparts, doubtless some of them were. Uses of a number of nondikastic pinakia, however, apparently lasted no longer than the average use of an annually issued dikastic pinakion. I rather imagine—though this is only a guess couched in the most general terms—that the majority of nondikastic uses fell in between these two extremes, that is, were reused at intervals substantially less than the several decades of a man's full adult life but somewhat more than the one to several years of dikastic uses.

The apparent contradiction between the long-term issue of nondikastic pinakia and the shortness of many of their individual uses is resolved when we reflect that the turnover of these pinakia was inextricably bound up with the turnover of dikastic pinakia, which were issued *and* used on a short-term basis. For every change in ownership among the dikastic pinakia, resulting from a man's joining or retiring from the body of dikastai, there was a corresponding change of ownership among the nondikastic pinakia. When an Athenian joined the body of dikasts and obtained a dikastic pinakion he would have to surrender his nondikastic pinakion; when he retired from this body, his dikastic pinakion was exchanged for a nondikastic one.

Thus those who may have owned nondikastic pinakia for relatively long periods, say a decade or more, were Athenians who for one reason or another did not become enrolled as dikastai within that time. This group may or may not have included all eighteen- to twenty-nine-year-olds. Should nondikastic pinakia have been issued to all male Athenians when they came of age, there would have been a space of about a decade in every citizen's life during which he possessed a nondikastic pinakion and was unable to exchange it for a dikastic one. But it is possible that the thirty-year age limit attested for bouleutai and dikastai may have applied to eligibility for all state magistracies,[12] in which case citizens under age thirty probably would not have been eligible to receive pinakia of any kind. In any case, however, long-term ownership of nondikastic pinakia presents no difficulties. There would always have been men who were simply not inclined to participate in the courts. Athenians who owned nondikastic pinakia for very short periods, on the other hand,

---

12. Thus Ulrich Kahrstedt, *Studien zum öffentlichen Recht Athens,* 2 vols. (Stuttgart: W. Kohlhammer, 1934–1936), II. *Untersuchungen zur Magistratur in Athen,* 18; whence C. Hignett, *A History of the Athenian Constitution* (Oxford: Clarendon Press, 1952), 224. As Kahrstedt notes, the possibility receives no small support from the fact that Alkibiades was elected to his first generalship very shortly after he turned thirty. I doubt whether the thirty-year age qualification for assistants at the Herakleian games at Marathon can be used to resolve this issue (see Eugene Vanderpool, "An Archaic Inscribed Stele from Marathon," *Hesperia* 11 [1942], 333–337). These ad hoc officials were apparently chosen from the spectators at the games and cannot be considered magistrates in any conventional sense.

were men who joined or rejoined the body of dikastai within a very short interval after the pinakia were issued to them.

Cause of Reuse

The picture of the Athenian dikasteria that emerges from the above discussions is very different from that envisaged by Bruck, Hommel, and others. Instead of a relatively stable body of lifelong jurors, each of whom received a pinakion at age thirty and used it perpetually until he died, we now know that during the second quarter of the fourth century the Athenian dikastai was a fluid, constantly changing body of men, whose members retained pinakia for comparatively brief periods of time. Men were continually joining the body and retiring from it, often, it seems, after only one or two years of jury service.

The pivotal question, then, is how to account for the retirement of jurors after such brief intervals. I think we can safely say that, for the most part, this was not a matter of personal choice. Given the remuneration and pleasures of a dikastes, one would find it difficult to explain why all Athenian jurors would have habitually resigned from the body if they did not have to. Even the richer citizens had civic and class interests to be protected in the courts. And while every Athenian had something to gain by each year swearing the oath and becoming enrolled as a dikast, he had nothing to lose; for a juror was free to exercise the rights of his office only when he wished. Nor do I believe that one can satisfactorily account for the periodic retirement of the dikasts by their being allotted to other positions in the state; it is very doubtful that such positions could have been obtained with the kind of regularity called for by the frequent turnover of the dikastic pinakia.

So far as I have been able to judge, the one plausible solution is to be found in a reconsideration of another fundamental assumption usually made about the organization of the Athenian dikasteria after pinakia had been introduced: that the body of dikasts was then unlimited in size and open without restriction to all qualified applicants. The argument from *AthPol* 63.3, on which the assumption rests, may correctly pertain only to a time later than the bronze dikastic pinakia and can no longer be supported by the assumption—based exclusively on the pinakia—that membership in the dikasteria was for life. On the contrary, the evidence of the pinakia now strongly favors an annual enrollment of a limited number of dikasts, which is to say an annual allotment of that number, precisely as has been conjectured for the Athenian courts in the fifth century.

An organization of the dikasteria around annual allotments would provide a context in which the frequent turnover and exchange of dikastic and non-dikastic pinakia was a regular and inevitable occurrence. Each year, by the mechanical working of the lot, a substantial number of dikasts would have been retired and new men accepted in their place. The dikastic pinakia issued on an annual basis, from the allotment of one year to that of the next, came to be reinscribed for new owners every time their former owners were allotted out of the body of dikastai. The permanently issued nondikastic pinakia would have belonged not only to citizens who did not wish to become dikastai but in any given year to those who wanted to be but who were not lucky enough to get allotted.

An annual allotment of dikasts also would have ensured that all dikastic pinakia were returned at the end of the court year, at least in the period when nondikastic pinakia had been introduced and all annual allotments were performed by means of kleroteria and pinakia. Without submitting his pinakion for the allotment, a man could not expect to be reallotted for the following year. He would retain the pinakion but no longer the legal title to it and presumably would be subject to some kind of prosecution if he attempted to use it. About this last point there is some difficulty raised by the Class V pinakia, which imply that dikastic pinakia were sometimes used by men not properly enrolled and sworn as dikasts. But whatever the precise legal background of this practice, it furnishes the most compelling evidence in favor of an annual allotment of dikasts.

The problem of ensuring that men not enrolled for a given year be excluded from participating in the courts must have been faced and solved in the fifth and early fourth centuries before the use of pinakia. One supposes a list of sworn dikasts and penalties against misrepresentation were maintained.[13] The issue of the elaborately inscribed, unerasable pinakia of Class V, however, would suggest that with the introduction of pinakia such safeguards as may have applied earlier were relaxed. As I have argued in Chapter II, the Class V pinakia constitute an issue of a single year or a limited number of years and were specially inscribed to protect against the erasure of the names of the assigned owners and illegal reuse of the pinakia. The precaution informs us of a loophole (probably slow to be discovered and not widely exploited until after the Athenians had several years' experience with the pinakia) that made

---

13. Thus Teusch (*De sortitione*, 56), who believed that such lists were discontinued after the introduction of pinakia. Hommel (*Heliaia*, 45–46) cautions that although official lists were common and although Aristotle mentions an *ἀπογράφεσθαι* of jurors at *Politics* 1297a.24, there is no concrete evidence for such lists at Athens during any period. Bruck (*Philologus* 52 [1893] 299–300), was not sure that lists were kept either, but opines that even if they were during the time that pinakia were being used, the pinakia rather than the lists served as the main check on legal enrollment in the body of dikasts.

it tempting for enrolled dikasts to sell their pinakia to unenrolled men and to permit such men to replace them in the body of dikastai.[14]

Who were these unregistered men who made it a practice to buy their way into the dikasteria? We may confidently exclude those under age thirty, state debtors, and *atimoi*, for although they were liable to severe punishment for serving as jurors, there was no scrutiny of the dikasts before they assumed office, and such citizens who were legally disqualified could risk becoming enrolled (*AthPol* 63.3; Demosthenes 24.123). The debtor Pyrrhos, cited in Demosthenes 21.182, served as a dikastes until he was brought to trial and condemned to death, and there is no reason to think that he was not officially enrolled and not issued a pinakion.[15]

On the traditional assumption that all qualified applicants were automatically accepted as dikasts, our unregistered citizens who obtained pinakia from their rightful owners would have to be those who simply failed to apply in any given year but later changed their minds and wanted a pinakion to hold them over until the next annual enrollment. But such men could never have been many and would hardly have been enough to cause the Athenians to experiment with elaborate, theoretically unerasable pinakia. If, on the other hand, a limited number of dikastai were chosen every year from all applicants, the number of rejected, would-be dikasts would have been substantial; not only would they have provided a ready market for valid pinakia, but men who had no intention of serving as jurors would probably have been tempted to participate in the annual sortition in the hopes of obtaining a pinakion that could be sold—or, in the case of family or friends, given—to a less lucky fellow who had desperately wanted to be allotted. In sum, the Class V lettering would seem to make good sense only if dikastic pinakia were issued on a restricted basis, which is to say if during the second quarter of the fourth century, roughly the period of bronze dikastic pinakia, the number of dikasts was limited and filled by annual allotments.

In retrospect, this deduction cannot be regarded as surprising. Fifth-century references mention six thousand dikastai and imply a fixed annual enrollment of this number. The reference at *Ploutos* 1164–1167 to men trying to get en-

14. One such illegal use may be 4*c*, which was not inscribed professionally. All pinakia reused successively by members of the same deme (listed and discussed above, pp. 34–36) are highly suspect. It is significant that all such pinakia belong to one or another of our dikastic classes. From *AthPol* 62.1 we know of an analogous selling of state offices, but in this case the guilty parties were the demes responsible for allotting the offices rather than individual officeholders who had already become confirmed in their position.

15. Since the speech was composed soon after 349/8, the case of Pyrrhos, still fresh in the minds of Demosthenes' audience, almost certainly took place at a time when pinakia were being used. On the date of the speech, see Raphael Sealey, "Dionysius of Halicarnassus and Some Demosthenic Dates," *REG* 68 (1955), 96–101, who proposes that the section containing the reference to Pyrrhos was set down in 352/1.

rolled in more than one dikastic *gramma* provides a somewhat more implicit testimony that in 388 the enrollment of dikastai still involved some kind of predetermined quota and that to make up the quota each year the Athenians had resorted to a practice of multiple enrollment. Thus an annual quota of dikasts was apparently maintained at least down until the introduction of pinakia, and since such a quota admirably helps to explain the frequent turnover of the surviving dikastic pinakia as well as the rationale behind illegally inscribed pinakia and the Class V issue, it seems only just to conclude that a fixed enrollment was retained through the time during which these pinakia were being used.

The conclusion, however, runs head on into three long-held assumptions concerning the decline of population in late fifth-century Athens and its supposed effect on the organization of the courts. Briefly stated, the assumptions are:[16]

The losses suffered by the Athenian populace during the second half of the Peloponnesian War (that is, after 415, the year for which Andokides 1.14 attests a jury of six thousand) seriously hampered the annual enrolling of six thousand dikastai and were ultimately responsible for the multiple enrollments attested in 388. Hommel emphasizes the gravity of Athenian losses at Arginousai; Bonner and Smith, those from the Sicilian disaster.[17] The latter suggest, too, that the return of large numbers of Athenians to the countryside at the end of the war further reduced the supply of applicants for the dikasteria.

Although the legal quota of six thousand dikastai was nominally retained after 403/2, when dikasts began to be allotted to courts by sections, the number of applicants was so low that multiple enrollments were required merely to keep up a basic working minimum of five thousand required by an organization of ten sections of five hundred dikasts each. A classic statement of this position was given by Gustav Gilbert: "As there can hardly have been 5,000 Heliasts in all at this time, we must assume 500 [per section] to have been a theoretical total, only realized by allowing Heliasts to belong to several sections at once."[18]

The still later arrangement of allotting dikasts individually to courts by means of pinakia provided a happier solution to the shortage of dikasts. Not only did it make for greater flexibility in impaneling courts on any given

16. Cf. Hommel, *Heliaia*, 120–125; Bonner-Smith I, 365–370.
17. Hommel, *Heliaia*, 121; Bonner-Smith I, 366.
18. Gustav Gilbert, *The Constitutional Antiquities of Sparta and Athens*, Eng. trans. (New York, 1895), 395.

day (its real purpose), but it eliminated the need for annual quotas and multiple enrollments altogether. Henceforth all qualified applicants were automatically accepted as dikasts, and we hear nothing more of fixed totals.

There is an undeniable logic to this reconstruction, which posits a gradual evolution from a rigid enrollment of six thousand, through a more flexible system involving plural registration, to the final, completely elastic organization of open enrollment. But, as we have seen, open enrollment is not easily reconciled with the evidence of the pinakia. The introduction of pinakia may well have made the enrollment of a fixed quota unnecessary, but an allotted quota was apparently retained all the same.

As for the supposedly drastic shortage of jurors, the pinakia imply that the Athenian population could not only support a fixed quota of dikasts by the second quarter of the fourth century, but provided more than enough applicants each year, enough in fact that no Athenian could expect to be reallotted for more than a few years in succession before the lot went against him and his place in the body of dikastai fell to another citizen. Between 388, when multiple enrollments are indirectly attested, and the introduction of pinakia around 378/7 (see below), there intervened a space of a decade, during which the population was increasing, and with it the numbers of men applying to join the dikasteria. By the 370s, too, any mass exodus to rural Attika as may have occurred at the end of the Peloponnesian War was presumably being offset by a reverse migration back to the city (see n. 21, below). But even so, the impact of the war on the early fourth-century courts was probably never as great as is usually alleged on the strength of *Ploutos* 1164–1167. The references to six thousand dikastai in the *Frogs* (422 B.C.) and Andokides 1 (alluding to the spring of 415),[19] after all, do not pertain to a time when the manpower of Athens was near its height; both postdate the sharp decline in population brought by the years of plague. Losses did occur after 415 (A. W. Gomme estimates a fall from 29,000 males aged eighteen to sixty in 425 to 22,000 in 400),[20] and unless we throw out the one plausible interpretation of *Ploutos* 1164–1167, some kind of shortage of dikastai as late as 388 should be assumed. The shortage, however, need not have been serious. Nor are we obliged to assume that multiple enrollments were necessarily employed to maintain a minimum of five thousand jurors, when they could just as well have been

19. At this time, moreover, a large portion of the army and fleet was away on the Sicilian expedition (cf. Douglas MacDowell, *Andokides, On the Mysteries* [Oxford: Clarendon Press, 1962], 182–183). For the numbers of Athenian ships and men on the expedition, see Thucydides 6.43.

20. A. W. Gomme, *The Population of Athens in the Fifth and Fourth Centuries B.C.* (Oxford: Blackwell, 1933), 26.

used to support a legally constituted dikasteria of six thousand. Indeed, the latter is much the more probable in light of the pinakia, which imply a fixed enrollment with more than enough applicants by the 370s. The pinakia do not tell us how many men were annually being enrolled at that time, but there is no cause for supposing any change from six thousand. The figure was sanctioned by tradition as constituting an official quorum of the Athenian demos (see n. 3, above) and for that reason alone can be expected to have been retained.

I do not believe that a final decision in this matter can be reached by an appeal to estimates of population. There are so many imponderables, and, as Gomme repeatedly stresses, until the last quarter of the fourth century such estimates for the size of the Athenian lower classes—always the backbone of the dikasteria—are extremely tenuous. Still, I find nothing in current figures for the fourth century that would make it impossible for the population to have maintained an annually allotted dikasteria of six thousand.[21]

To sum up, the testimony of the pinakia invites certain modifications in the conventional interpretation of *Ploutos* 1164-1167 and our understanding of the dikasteria in the early fourth century: Although the passage in the *Ploutos* suggests that the Athenians were having difficulties enrolling a full complement of dikasts about 388, these difficulties may have been minimal. This full complement was probably six thousand, as earlier. By the 370s, when the impaneling of dikasts was reformed by the introduction of allotment by pinakia, such difficulties had vanished, and it was then possible to allot an annual total of six thousand dikasts out of an abundance of applicants, as had been done at least down through 415.

21. The problem is to determine the number of male citizens from age thirty on. For 323, when the evidence is most complete, Gomme gives a male population from age eighteen to sixty of 28,000 (*ibid.*, 18, 26). Adding a factor of 10 percent to obtain an approximation of males from eighteen to beyond sixty (cf. *ibid.*, 18, 76), and subtracting from this about a third of the original 28,000 to eliminate males from eighteen to twenty-nine, we end up with a total of about 22,000 citizens eligible to serve as dikasts. Performing the same operation on Gomme's much more tentative estimates for the male citizenry ca. 400, we get a total of about 17,000 eligibles. In "The Population of Athens Again," *Journal of Hellenic Studies* 79 (1959), 66–68, especially n. 6, Gomme defends his calculations against the substantially lower figures of Jones, *Democracy*, 76 *et passim*. Jones's more traditional estimate of 21,000 adult males (argued also by Chrysis Pélékidis, *Histoire de l'éphébie attique* [Paris: Éditions E. de Boccard, 1962], 283–294) would give something like 15,000 men eligible for the dikasteria. On population questions further, see Felix Jacoby, *Die Fragmente der griechischen Historiker*, 3 Pts. (Leiden: E. J. Brill, 1923–1955), Pt. IIIb, i, 464–466 (Philochoros frag. 119), with notes, ii, 375–379. Most jurors were city dwellers, as the places of discovery of most pinakia confirm (see Chapter II, n. 2, above). Gomme estimates that by the later fifth century about half of the Athenian population was concentrated in the city and that by 330 the proportion had risen to about three-quarters (*Population of Athens*, 47). But we must remember that the body of dikasts would have included men who did not sit in the courts regularly but who nevertheless became enrolled so they could participate when they wished and, in the case of rural Athenians, when they happened to be in town.

The Organization of the Dikasteria at the Time of the *AthPol*

It is essential to recognize the chronological limitation in the preceding discussion, for after about 350, when dikastic pinakia of bronze gave way to pinakia of wood, our material evidence for the organization of the courts is drastically reduced. We may confidently assume that the dikasts continued to be enrolled on an annual basis down through the time of the *AthPol*; it had always been so, and the last chapters of the *AthPol* are compatible with any term of the dikasts' office. The later dikastic pinakia of boxwood were better suited for short-term annual issue than were the more expensive pinakia of bronze. New wooden ones could have been made up and distributed each year and could have been discarded at the year's end. Or were they too reused? One of the advantages of wooden pinakia is that they could be inscribed (presumably with paint) and erased more easily than metal ones, and boxwood, being an exceptionally hard and durable variety of wood, might have been worth reusing. But whether the wooden pinakia were reinscribed or not, the fact remains that for temporarily issued pinakia the permanence of bronze was sensibly sacrificed for the cheapness of wood. Because nondikastic pinakia were issued on a permanent basis and were used in allotments held only once a year, it was equally sensible that they remained of bronze. Reuse of the Class VI pinakia (in some cases at intervals of less than eight years) suggests that the perpetual movement of men in and out of the body of dikastai, and hence the annual allotments responsible for this movement, continued well into the third quarter of the fourth century.

Aristotle's silence regarding the heliastic oath and enrolling of jurors generally is to be understood in light of his specialized concern with court procedures and the allotments that took place on the days when the courts were in session. The sentences devoted to the qualifications of the jurors in 63.3 comprise a brief digression, which serves to introduce the dikastai as a final ingredient—like kleroteria, chests, acorns, and colored staves—requisite for the allotments described in Sections 64 and 65. The digression is patently incomplete as a definition of the dikastai. It tells who were allowed to be dikasts (δικάζειν δ' ἔξεστιν) but not how they became dikasts. There must have been a yearly enrollment of some kind, for an Athenian was not qualified as a dikast until he had at least sworn the oath (cf. the definition of the dikastai as the "sworn" in the laws quoted in Demosthenes 24.22, 27, see above, pp. 3–4). And if mention of the essential oath was omitted from the *AthPol*, we have reason to question whether other features of the enrollment might not have been omitted as well, more specifically whether dikasts were still being allotted as they were earlier in the fourth century.

It is to be regretted that the material evidence is not more decisive in this regard. For all we can tell, reuse of nondikastic pinakia could have slowed down or ceased toward the end of the Class VI period; thus it can be argued that the annual body of dikastai was opened to all qualified citizens, without sortitions, at some point in the later 330s or early 320s (during the innovative administration of Lykourgos), as a literal reading of 63.3 would require. But a literal reading is not necessarily to be preferred, especially when its δικάζειν δ' ἔξεστιν is compared with 62.3 (ἄρχειν δὲ τὰς μὲν κατὰ πόλεμον ἀρχὰς ἔξεστι πλεονάκις, τῶν δ' ἄλλων οὐδεμίαν, πλὴν βουλεῦσαι δίς.) where ἔξεστι does not mean that anyone can go and exercise the functions of a military official or of a bouleutes for the second time. It means that one can submit oneself for election, be elected, and serve. If δικάζειν δ' ἔξεστιν was intended in the same way, 63.3 would not be the first passage of the *AthPol* to mislead by unconscious omission.[22]

Since the discovery of the *AthPol*, two authorities, Ulrich von Wilamowitz-Moellendorff and A. H. M. Jones, have maintained, in fact, that a fixed total of six thousand dikastai was annually allotted at the time it was composed.[23] Both ignore 63.3 and argue from other passages in the *AthPol*. Jones cites 27.4, but it is not clear whether the dikastic allotments mentioned there are annual ones or those that took place on days when the courts were in session. The argument of Wilamowitz is more complex and deserves to be summarized in some detail. He drew on 62.1, which states that at some earlier period there were two groups of allotted officials: those who were allotted from the separate phylai, and a second group that was allotted from the demes; by the time of the *AthPol*, however, all magistrates of the second group were also being allotted by phylai, "with the exception of the bouleutai and guards [φρουροί], whom they still give over to the demes." It is hard to disagree with Wilamowitz that the various magistrates in the first category should cover all the various boards of ten (and multiples of ten like the Forty).[24] But who, then,

---

22. At face value, the detailed descriptions of the *ephebeia* at *AthPol* 42.2 and of the diaitetai at 53.4 would have us believe that all Athenians participated in these institutions and not just citizens enrolled in the hoplite census, as we now know from inscriptions to have been the case (Gomme, *Population of Athens*, 11). Aristotle apparently expected his readers to understand that he was referring to the hoplite class only. This is vehemently disputed by Pélékidis, *Histoire de l'éphébie attique*, 113–114, 283–294. But D. M. Lewis has shown that the epigraphical evidence is decisive for the diaitetai ("Notes on Attic Inscriptions [II], *BSA* 50 [1955], 29); and in *AthPol* 53.4 the organization of the latter is intimately linked with the organization of the ephebes.

23. Ulrich von Wilamowitz-Moellendorff, *Aristoteles und Athen*, 2 vols. (Berlin, 1893), I, 200–201 (whence Fritz-Kapp, *Constitution of Athens*, 139, n. *b*); Jones, *Democracy*, 123–124 with n. 145, 37, 49, 80. Six thousand jurors at the time of Aristotle was rather cavalierly assumed by P. S. Photiades ("Περὶ κληρώσεως καὶ πληρώσεως τῶν ἡλιαστικῶν δικαστηρίων," 'Αθηνᾶ 14 [1902], 244), but it is not clear how he thought this number was filled.

24. This, too, is the interpretation of F. G. Kenyon, *Aristotle on the Constitution of Athens*, 3d ed. (Oxford, 1892), *ad loc*. For a radically different interpretation, however, see Mabel Lang, "Allotment by Tokens," *Historia* 8 (1959), 80.

were the officials, in addition to bouleutai and *phrouroi*, who were once allotted from the demes? F. G. Kenyon ventured merely that "they can only have been of very minor importance,"[25] although it is perhaps more to the point that they could hardly have been single magistrates or those on boards of fewer than ten, since these are even less likely to have been conceded to the demes. On analogy with the five hundred bouleutai and the phrouroi (the latter also five hundred in number if they are identical with the phrouroi of 24.3), Wilamowitz argues that the other ἄρχαι should have comprised a numerous body also. Hence he concludes, "nur eine kategorie, allerdings eine sehr wichtige, kann man hierherziehn: die 6000 richter, die zu Aristoteles zeit aus den phylen genommen wurdern."

Despite an unsound supporting argument from the absence of tribal names on pinakia, Wilamowitz' interpretation is just plausible enough not to be taken lightly. It need not be flatly contradicted by 63.3. As for the propriety of designating the office of dikastes as an ἄρχη, Aristotle explains in *Politics* 1275a.22–23 that for lack of better terminology the equation is entirely permissible; 62.1 treats the phrouroi as ἄρχαι. And we may add, finally, that a relationship between the demes and the earlier dikasteria is independently suggested by the fact that the basic Athenian dikasterion consisted of five hundred members.[26] In all other sectors of the Athenian constitution, the number five hundred appears in connection with bodies that were drawn on a proportional basis from the separate demes. In addition to the five hundred bouleutai and phrouroi mentioned above, we know that five hundred candidates for the archonship were annually nominated by the demes in the earlier fifth century (*AthPol* 22.5) and that a special committee of five hundred nomothetai was elected, by demes, in the year 403/2 (Andokides 1.82–84). It becomes tempting to argue, therefore, that the regular Athenian courts also consisted of this number because they too were originally chosen on a proportional deme basis. Twelve such separately allotted dikasteria, each with a composition identical to that of the boule of five hundred, would have yielded a full complement of six thousand dikastai.

This is not to say that 62.1 can be treated as proof that jurors were annually allotted in the 320s. The passage, like Jones's 27.4, is inexplicit in far too many important details. But whether Wilamowitz' and Jones's interpretations are correct or not, an allotted enrollment of six thousand dikastai at the time of the *AthPol* must still be recognized as a distinct possibility.

---

25. Kenyon, *Aristotle on the Constitution of Athens, ad loc.*
26. *AthPol* 68.1, cf. Harpokration s.v. ἡλιαία; Demosthenes 24.9; Pollux 8.123. That a dikasterion consisted of five hundred men in the fifth century is implied by Plutarch, *Perikles* 32, where a jury of 1,500 (presumably three dikasteria) is mentioned.

Absolute Chronology

At the end of Chapter III we reviewed the available archaeological and prosopographical data that have a direct bearing on absolute chronology. These data happen to pertain almost exclusively to particular uses of Class IV, V, and VI pinakia and provide a tentative dating between 367/6 and about 360 for the Class V issue as our earliest more or less fixed point. It is unfortunate that such independent chronological evidence is lacking for all pinakia earlier than this issue. But in the present chapter we have been able to arrive at a basis for estimating the duration of individual uses of dikasts' pinakia, and by working back from Class V, we can now attempt to narrow the chronological possibilities for the introduction of the Class I pinakia and the subsequent introduction of the gorgoneion seal. Chronological precision, obviously, is out of the question. Our estimates must be anchored ultimately to the Class V issue, which itself is inexactly dated. And since individual uses of dikastic pinakia can have lasted anywhere from one to several years, the space between the Class V reform and earlier events must also be expressed in terms of higher and lower allowable limits. Still, some kind of working estimates are called for.

We may begin with the introduction of the gorgoneion seal. As stated in Chapter II, the seal appears on the earliest Class III and IV pinakia simultaneously, and since none of the surviving Class IV pinakia with pre-Class V uses are known to have had more than one or two such uses before the pinakia were temporarily withdrawn at the time of the Class V reform, the introduction of the seal apparently belongs very shortly before the reform. Beginning with our established dating for the Class V issue, and allowing a minimum of about two years for the pre-Class V uses of the earliest Class IV pinakia and a maximum of probably no more than five or six years, we see that the earliest Class III and IV pinakia can hardly have dated before the late 370s at the earliest and in all probability were issued somewhere in the 360s. Hence if we assign the beginning of the Class III and IV issues to between about 370 and about 362 (the latter date being two years before our round lower terminus for the Class V issue), we are not likely to be far wrong.

The Class I pinakia can be presumed to be survivals from the initial reform issue in the year when allotment by pinakia was introduced. One of these pinakia, **5**, is known to have had at least three uses before it broke;[27] thus if we allow a minimal one year for each use and an additional year during which the pinakion was erased and lay fallow in the hands of the state between each

---

27. I think it best in this connection to omit consideration of **4**, whose third use appears to be irregular (see n. 14, above).

use, we arrive at a figure of about five years for the minimum longevity of the Class I pinakia. A maximum of about fifteen years cannot be logically excluded, but I would imagine that a more reasonable high approximation would be in the neighborhood of a decade.

The Class II pinakia are stylistically a direct continuation of the Class I type. To judge from **12**, some of them were even inscribed with texts of one line, which surely indicates that the earliest pinakia of this class began to be issued very shortly after the initial Class I issue, presumably as supplements to the Class I pinakia already in circulation. That is, as the original total of Class I pinakia gradually diminished over the years through breakage, burial with deceased owners, and any number of other causes, the Class II pinakia were manufactured and issued to make up the loss. Hence the earliest uses of all or most of the Class II pinakia must have overlapped with uses of Class I pinakia —very much as the later uses of such Class II pinakia as were stamped with a square double-bodied owl seal overlapped Class IV and V pinakia in the post-Class V period. This overlapping of the Class II pinakia with pinakia of earlier and later classes substantially reduces the number of years to be added to the estimates suggested for the duration of Class I pinakia in determining the amount of elapsed time between the initial Class I issue and the first issue of Class III and IV pinakia. Another factor that cautions against allowing a generous additional time for the Class II pinakia is to be found in the repetition of a single triobol seal die on a relatively high proportion of the Class II survivals (**12**, **13**, **16**, and **17**). Such a high incidence of die linkage is approximated on the Class V pinakia, which were unquestionably manufactured and issued within a very brief space of time and can be paralleled by a group of Class III and IV pinakia that share a single gorgoneion seal die and that also can justly be assumed to have been issued within a very short time of each other (see above, pp. 16–17). Accordingly, it would appear that all or most of the Class II pinakia were probably first issued over a limited period as well.

Thus in attempting an estimate of the time occupied by the Class I and II pinakia together, before the introduction of the gorgoneion seal, little, if any, separate time should be allotted to the Class II pinakia in addition to the estimates already derived for Class I. If we grant no extra time for the Class II pinakia, our Class I estimates of five to ten to fifteen years would apply to the full space between the Class I issue and the first issue of Class III and IV pinakia. Well they might, since it is just possible that all pre-Class IV uses of the Class II pinakia could have been subsumed in the minimum five years suggested for the three attested uses of **5**. But even if we allot a few additional years for the Class II pinakia, only our lower Class I estimate should probably be revised (say, from five up to seven or eight years); a maximum of fifteen years would still be a very generous allowance for all Class I uses plus all uses of Class II pinakia before the advent of the gorgoneion seal. A round decade, though perhaps no longer a safer maximum, can be regarded as a reasonable middle estimate in any event.

For the time between the Class I and the first Class III and IV issues, we are justified, then, I believe, in assuming a five to eight year minimum and a maximum of about fifteen years. Adding these figures to our termini for the appearance of the gorgoneion seal, we see that the introduction of allotment by pinakia probably fell somewhere between about 385 (370 + 15) and about 367 (362 + 5). Or if we should try for closer approximations by taking the middle ten-year estimate, the limits would be reduced to around 380 (370 + 10) and around 372 (362 + 10), respectively.

Whether one prefers the former, more conservative calculations or the narrower ones, two observations are inescapable. Both relate to chronological points discussed at the end of Chapter I. First, these limits agree remarkably well with the assumption that the pinakia can hardly belong as early as 392 or 388, the respective dates for the *Ekklesiazousai* and the *Ploutos*. This is, of course, as it should be. But it is reassuring nevertheless to have independent evidence that the organization of the dikasteria implied by certain passages in these plays does in fact antedate the introduction of pinakia. Second, our limits rather neatly bracket the year 378/7 and thus strongly re-enforce the historical case for attributing the introduction of pinakia to that year. Indeed, since this close correspondence between a year that has been suggested from historical probability and a limited range of possible years independently derived from the pinakia is not likely to be fortuitous, I believe we are obligated to accept 378/7—or, to be on the safe side, about 378/7 [28]—as the probable absolute date for the Class I issue.

Unfortunately, since we still do not know exactly how much time elapsed between the Class I issue and the introduction of the gorgoneion seal, between the latter and the Class V issue, and so forth, a fixed point of around 378/7 at the beginning of the pinakia series does not allow us to adjust our dates for the later classes any more precisely than we have above. And so until more evidence should permit us to modify or narrow our present determinations, we must be content with the following:

in or about 378/7   Class I issue (soon supplemented by the addition of Class II pinakia)

28. Calhoun's argument for 378/7 (see Chapter 1, n. 15, above) does not exclude dating the reform of the dikasteria to a year or so after the foundation of the Second Athenian Confederacy.

between about 370 and about 362	Initial issue of Class III and IV pinakia
between 367/6 and about 360	Class V issue
about 350	Dikastic pinakia of bronze discontinued; henceforth dikastic pinakia are of wood
shortly after 350	Beginning of Class VI pinakia
322/1	End of democracy; discontinuance of bronze non-dikastic pinakia; temporary cessation of wooden pinakia

V   Tribal Sections in Annual Allotments

Sections in the Allotment of Magistrates

Our knowledge of Athenian allotment procedure has, up to this time, been limited chiefly to the allotments for impaneling dikasts at the beginning of each court day (*AthPol* 63–64). These allotments proceeded by phylai and were structured around the division of each phyle's dikasts into ten sections (μέρη, γράμματα) lettered from A to K. The allotments were run on kleroteria so constructed that each of a phyle's ten sections was provided with a single vertical row of slots (κανονίς) to receive the pinakia marked with the section's letter. That this organization and kleroteria design date from the very beginning of allotment by pinakia (about 378/7) is assured by the earliest surviving bronze pinakia, which, like the wooden dikastic pinakia of Aristotle's day, bear section-letters. As Hommel has correctly stressed, however, the division of each phyle's dikasts into ten sections was not essential to the allotment process.[1] Each pinakion did not have to be preassigned to one of the ten slot rows in a phyle's kleroteria in order for the rows to be filled. The sections were essentially a legacy from the earlier system of impaneling juries when whole grammata of dikastai were allotted directly to the several courts. But since sections did serve to structure and speed the later procedure—no small consideration for allotments that had to be conducted as expeditiously as possible at the opening of every court day—it is not hard to see why they were retained.

According to Demosthenes 39.10–12, by the middle of the fourth century bronze pinakia were also being used in the massive allotments that each year filled the boule, the board of archons, and presumably, therefore, all other city magistracies open to the lot. We have seen that allotment by pinakia was appropriated for these annual sortitions after it had been invented and tried out in connection with the impaneling of jurors and that when it was appropriated, in the 360s or late 370s, every Athenian citizen had to be provided with a pinakion. While men enrolled and sworn as jurors henceforth used their dikastic pinakia in the annual allotments as well as in those held on court days, the rest of the citizenry was issued nondikastic pinakia which

---

1. Hommel, *Heliaia*, 37.

were stamped with two gorgoneion seals to ensure that they would be submitted only in the annual sortitions. Still later, after dikastic pinakia began to be made of boxwood, the earlier nondikastic pinakia (Class III) were superseded by the stampless ones of Class VI. It remains to ask, if the Class III and VI pinakia really are to be identified as nondikastic pinakia, how are we to explain the fact that they, too, bear section-letters from A to K?

Only one answer is permissible, I believe: tribal sections must have been adopted for use in the annual magisterial allotments. This is not quite so farfetched as it might first appear. For at *AthPol* 8.1 Aristotle writes that in his day the archons, who were allotted by phylai, were selected by a double sortition that first eliminated all but ten of a phyle's applicants and then made a final selection from these ten:

> *Τὰς δ' ἀρχὰς ἐποίησε κληρωτὰς ἐκ προκρίτων, οὓς ἑκάστη προκρί-*
> *νειε τῶν φυλῶν. προύκρινεν δ' εἰς τοὺς ἐννέα ἄρχοντας ἑκάστη δέκα,*
> *καὶ του[των ἐκ]λήρουν· ὅθεν ἔτι διαμένει ταῖς φυλαῖς τὸ δέκα κληροῦν*
> *ἑκάστην, εἶτ' ἐκ τούτων κυαμεύειν.*

[Solon] established the rule that magistrates were allotted out of candidates nominated by each of the phylai. In regard to the nine archons, each phyle nominated ten, and among these they cast the lot. Hence the custom still survives with the phylai that each of them allots ten and then they allot again from these men.[2]

Most of the other annual administrative officials were organized in boards of ten like the "nine" archons and were certainly allotted, one representative from each phyle, in the same manner.

To be sure, *AthPol* 8.1 does not specify that the preliminary allotments within each phyle were organized around divisions of the phylai into ten sections. But ten candidates were chosen within each phyle, and since pinakia with section-letters were being used in magisterial allotments at the time of the *AthPol* (wooden pinakia by men enrolled as dikasts and Class VI bronze pinakia by others), I think there can be little serious doubt that these pre-liminary sortitions were run exactly like the ordinary dikastic allotments of *AthPol* 63–64, and on the same kind of kleroteria.[3] The sole procedural varia-

2. Translation of Fritz-Kapp, *Constitution of Athens*, with minor alterations.
3. The officials who administered the two kinds of allotments were also the same: in both cases each phyle's representative on the board of archons, compare *AthPol* 59.7 and 63.1 (impaneling of jurors) with Aischines 3.13 (*thesmothetai* in charge of the annual allotments).

tion was in the number of men to be selected. For the impaneling of jurors, each section furnished one-tenth of a phyle's quota of dikasts for a given court day, the number of white cubes dropped in the tube of each kleroterion having been determined by dividing this quota by ten. In the preliminary sortition for a phyle's representative on a board of magistrates, every section furnished only one candidate; therefore only one white cube would have been deposited among the cubes used with each kleroterion.

The second part of the double sortition was presumably run by means of pinakia too;[4] at least this is the implication of Demosthenes 39.10, which appears to refer to the final selection of a phyle's representative on the board of archons (and adds that pinakia were also used in the allotting of bouleutai). But, of course, in the final runoff between the candidates who had been allotted, one from each section, the tribal sections would have played no part, any more than they could have in the selection of bouleutai, who were allotted not by tribes but by demes. The sections were of value only for mass allotments within phylai. In both the impaneling of dikasts and in the preliminary sortition of magistrates the function of the sections was to permit a limited number of men to be chosen from the hundreds of applicants of an entire phyle with all possible fairness and speed.

We can now trace three stages in the employment of allotment sections. The original sections, parodied in Praxagora's allotment of grammata of banqueters in the *Ekklesiazousai*, were divisions of dikasts instituted for the purpose of allotting dikasts *en bloc* to specific courts. As Hommel assumed on analogy with the later system, these early fourth-century grammata were probably ten in number, probably contained an equal number of dikasts from each phyle, and were very likely an outgrowth of the fifth-century dikasteria, which possibly consisted of ten courts of annually assigned jurors.[5] In 378/7 or thereabouts, when the early fourth-century procedure was supplanted by the system that impaneled dikasts by pinakia and large kleroteria, the grammata were retained, although merely as a means of organizing the dikasts of each phyle into divisions that ensured that the impanelings would proceed quickly and with a minimum of confusion. Finally, with the

4. In *AthPol* 8.1 Aristotle departs from the verb κληροῦν and uses κυαμεύειν to describe this final allotment, but the latter term need not be taken literally to mean that the ten candidates actually drew beans or lots of some other kind. κυαμεύειν had long been closely associated with the selection of archons and bouleutai (cf. its many appearances in the passages quoted in Sandys, *Constitution of Athens*, apparatus to *AthPol* 8.1); its occurrence here is appropriate if only for this time-honored association.

5. Hommel, *Heliaia*, 111, 116; cf. Bonner-Smith I, 367, 370, but who argue for twelve panels of dikastai in the fifth century, 233–248. Twelve panels of five hundred men each would in fact be correct if the dikasts were then allotted by demes, as suggested above, pp. 85–86.

wholesale adoption of this new system of allotment for the annual sortition of
magistrates, at some point in the 360s or late 370s, the grammata passed out
of an exclusively dikastic context and, together with pinakia and kleroteria,
became a standard part of mass tribal allotments of all kinds. Every adult
Athenian (it is uncertain at which age, see above, p. 77) was, henceforth,
assigned to one of the ten allotment sections of his phyle, to remain in it for
the duration of his life.

It is, unfortunately, impossible to assess the full historical impact of this
last reform on the annual selection of magistrates. The preliminary allotment
of ten candidates in each phyle current at the time of the *AthPol* must go back
at least to the introduction of tribal sections in nondikastic sortitions with the
advent of Class III pinakia, about 370–362. We have no way of knowing,
however, whether the preliminary allotment of ten was instituted at that
time or had existed earlier,[6] but was run by some other allotment procedure
(for example, by the drawing of beans or lots) and without regard to sections.
Should the preliminary allotment of ten have antedated the Class III reform,
the introduction of pinakia and tribal sections would have affected only the
mechanics of the selection.

Sections in the Enrolling of Dikasts

This is not the place to attempt a step-by-step reconstruction of the entire
series of the magisterial sortitions held each year in Athens. But one related
matter, the annual enrollment of dikasts, does call for close consideration
since it is intimately bound up with the turnover of pinakia and has been
touched on repeatedly throughout the preceding chapters. As we will see
after first considering the requirements of the enrollment during the period
of the Class I and II pinakia, it, too, must have been affected by certain
changes brought about by the Class III reform.

The enrollment, as I envisage it, would have proceeded in three stages,
beginning with the determination of the next year's dikasts. I have argued
in the last chapter that down at least through the middle of the fourth century,
if not as late as the time of the *AthPol*, the number of Athenian dikastai re-

---

6. It could not have been earlier than 457/6 when each phyle's representative on the
board of archons was still being allotted out of a group of fifty nominees (πρόκριτοι) who
were elected by the demes in the phyle (*AthPol* 26.2 with 22.5). Thus after 457/6, but no
later than about 370–362, there occurred three innovations in the preselection of candidates to the archonships: the selection was transferred from the demes to the phylai;
allotment (κλήρωσις) was substituted for nomination (πρόκρισις); and the number of
candidates was reduced from fifty to ten per phyle. As I hope to demonstrate elsewhere,
the first and second of these innovations are intimately related and were doubtless put
into effect together.

mained fixed at six thousand and that this total was annually filled by a sortition among all qualified applicants. Before the Class III reform this sortition would have been by drawing beans or by some other rudimentary procedure and in all probability was run off by the separate phylai.[7] It was during this first step that the pinakia of all former dikasts who were not to be re-enrolled (that is, who were rejected in the sortition) were collected to be returned later to some central agency in the state which was responsible for erasing them and ultimately for redistributing them to the phylai to be used again as new pinakia (see above, p. 35); for the next step was unquestionably carried out by the phylai.

This step involved the issuing of pinakia of new dikasts and the assigning of new dikasts to sections. Each phyle was provided with a supply of uninscribed pinakia, presumably an equal number stamped with each section-letter, for this purpose. Precisely how the pinakia were distributed and men assigned to sections we can only guess, but we would probably not be far wrong, if, like Bruck and Hommel (see Chapter II, n. 29, above), we assume that the blank pinakia were simply drawn from a chest by the new enrollees themselves and that the section-letters stamped on the pinakion that a man happened to draw determined by chance the section to which he would belong. If there were no concern for keeping the sections in exact balance, all of a phyle's blank pinakia could have been placed in the chest. But if—as I consider the more probable—the sections were to be maintained at equal strength, it would first have been necessary to count how many formerly enrolled dikasts remained in each section and how many vacant places in each section had to be filled to bring the sections again into balance; then, for each vacant place, a pinakion with the appropriate section-letter was thrown in the chest, and the drawing commenced. After each new enrollee had drawn a pinakion, it was inscribed for him on the spot. We may note that such a procedure did not require the keeping of a written register of each phyle's dikasts. The sections could be balanced by simple arithmetic and a drawing of pinakia, and a dikast's pinakion would have been certification enough that he had been duly enrolled.

I assume that the swearing of the heliastic oath on Mt. Ardettos was the final step,[8] but, for all we can tell, it conceivably could have taken place between the first two steps.

It should be obvious how much the first two steps would have been

7. Of course, if dikasts were allotted by demes during the fifth century, it is possible that this procedure might have been carried over into the earlier part of the fourth century. For purposes of the present discussion, however, it makes very little difference what arrangement was in effect prior to the Class III reform.

8. Thus also Hommel, *Heliaia*, 44–45.

simplified after about 370–362, when all Athenians not enrolled as dikastai had been provided with a nondikastic pinakion. To begin with, the selection of the next year's dikasts could have been performed on large kleroteria by pinakia and tribal sections, each section yielding one-tenth of a phyle's annual quota of dikasts. Since these sortitions would have been closely modeled on the impaneling of dikasts, little imagination is required to suggest how the allotments could have progressed.

All qualified members of a phyle who wished to apply for the position of dikastes submitted their pinakia to the chests marked with their section-letters, the dikasts of the past year their dikastic pinakia, all other applicants their nondikastic pinakia. The pinakia then were inserted, by sections, in the slots in the kleroteria, and the sortition proper was run according to the procedure detailed in *AthPol* 64. Sixty white cubes (equal in number to a phyle's quota of dikasts divided by ten) were dropped down the tube of each kleroterion and allotted perfectly even totals of pinakia from each section. The men allotted out of each section automatically comprised a full dikastic section for the coming year. "As the archon draws out the cubes, the herald calls those who have been allotted. . . . The person who has been called steps forward." If he had submitted a nondikastic pinakion, it was handed over to an attendant who inscribed a blank dikastic pinakion for him and then placed his void nondikastic pinakion aside to be returned to a central authority later. Finally, the pinakia of unaccepted men were returned or exchanged in like manner, so that all of these men left the sortition with nondikastic pinakia.

So much is hypothesis only. But the most significant innovation in the reconstruction is the least dependent on it and in fact would apply even if the body of dikasts was not subject to an allotment and was open without restriction to all qualified applicants. This is that once every Athenian was permanently assigned to a section in his phyle for general allotment purposes, he would have remained in it upon becoming a dikast, with the result that the entire business of assigning newly enrolled jurors to dikastic sections was dispensed with. After the creation of the larger tribal sections, around 370–362, a man's membership in a dikastic section was predetermined by his membership in the larger section, and the dikastic sections became, in effect, merely specialized subdivisions of the general sections, that is, subdivisions containing all members of the general sections who happened to have become enrolled as dikasts.[9]

9. I am unable to account satisfactorily for the one or more nondikastic pinakia that lack a section-letter (see above, p. 40). Did it or they belong to a brief span during which the nondikastic sections were allowed to lapse, or to men who intentionally were not assigned to sections so they could fill in whatever section in their phyle happened to be underrepresented at a given allotment? Whatever the answer, it may be enough to note that uses

This by-product of the Class III reform accounts for, I believe, the change from stamped to inscribed section-letters on the bronze pinakia. The stamped section-letters may be viewed as a legacy from the period of Class I and II pinakia when the dikastic sections were readjusted afresh each year. As suggested above, new dikasts may have allotted themselves to sections as they drew blank pinakia prestamped with section-letters. After every Athenian was permanently assigned to a section without regard to his becoming a dikast, however, his affiliation with a section became a part of his public identity, analogous, though on a much humbler scale, to his deme and tribal affiliations. It would make no difference what letter appeared on a pinakion that was issued him, for if the letter did not correspond to the section to which he was preassigned, it could be inscribed over when his name and demotic were added. We have seen (above, pp. 38–39, 61) that the change from stamped to inscribed section-letters did not take place until sometime after the Class III reform, not in fact until just before bronze dikastic pinakia were discontinued in favor of dikastic pinakia of boxwood. But effect need not follow cause directly, and making allowance for native Athenian conservatism, which would have resisted alteration of the physical appearance of pinakia, it should not be surprising that stamped section-letters were retained longer than they needed to be.

That dikasts after about 370–362 were preassigned to dikastic sections by virtue of their membership in the larger tribal sections may or may not have some bearing on the question of whether the body of dikasts was still being allotted at the time of the *AthPol*. At 63.2 Aristotle writes that "the jurors are divided into ten sections, about the same number ($\pi\alpha\rho\alpha\pi\lambda\eta\sigma\iota\omega\varsigma$ $\iota\sigma\iota$) under each letter," which at first glance might seem to rule out an annual allotting of dikasts at that time, inasmuch as annual allotments should theoretically have yielded perfectly even numbers of dikasts from each tribal section. Accordingly, it could be argued, if membership in the body of dikastai had become completely voluntary, unbalanced dikastic sections would have inevitably resulted from the differing numbers of men who each year applied for enrollment from the various general sections.

The difficulty with this argument, however, is that factors other than voluntary enrollment could have been responsible for slightly unbalanced dikastic sections. In the course of a year, even perfectly balanced sections would have changed as members died or became incapacitated by illness. And, as

---

without section-letters are extremely few in number and that they occur only on non-dikastic pinakia from the stampless Class VI period or perhaps in other cases from the late, inscribed section-letter phase of Class III.

Dow has discussed at some length with reference to the dikastic allotments of *AthPol* 64,[10] it is doubtful whether sections were ever adhered to strictly in mass allotments on kleroteria. Since men voluntarily submitted themselves for such allotments, different sections within each phyle were bound to be represented in slightly differing strengths, with the result that some vertical rows on each kleroterion would be filled with more pinakia than other rows. The only fair solution for the more heavily represented sections was to remove their excess pinakia and place them in the vertical rows of other sections until all of the vertical rows contained an equal number of pinakia. Thus (to illustrate the consequences with only two sections of a phyle), if more men applied from section A than applied from section B, some of the A applicants could expect to be allotted out of the B row. In the case of the annual allotting of dikasts, this kind of compensation would have had precisely the same effect as voluntary enrollment from the larger general sections—and for the same reason: differences in the number of applicants from each of the larger general sections would have resulted in differences in the final dikastic sections. In view of the alternative possibilities which lay behind the uneven dikastic sections of *AthPol* 63.2, I do not think that the passage can be used to advance the question of dikastic enrollment in the 320s beyond where we left it in the preceding chapter.

10. Dow, *HSCP* 50 (1939), 23–34.

VI   Summary and Rates of Survival

About 378/7, probably in that very year, the Athenians reorganized their system of impaneling jurors. Whole sections of dikasts had previously been allotted to the several courts. But with the advent of the reform, the jurors were to be allotted individually (actually, by fives)[1] by an intricate mechanical procedure that employed allotment plates and kleroteria and that has been described for us at some length by Aristotle. Only after a juror was selected by this procedure would he then become assigned to the court on which he was to sit. As G. M. Calhoun has argued, the purpose of the reform was apparently to introduce a greater flexibility in the impaneling of juries at a time when the Athenians were contemplating a grandiose revival of empire and the heavy demands on their manpower that would have been required to maintain it.

When the reform was put into effect, every Athenian dikast had to be provided with a pinakion. The pinakia issued in that year are those of our Class I, with a triobol seal stamped at the right to certify that the pinakion was official, a section-letter stamped at the left, and the dikast's name inscribed through the middle of the plate. Sometime later—it is uncertain whether during the same year or a year shortly thereafter—many or all of these pinakia were stamped with an owl-in-square seal, the meaning of which is unknown.

The reform of about 378/7 did not go so far as to abolish the fixed quota of six thousand dikastai, which continued to be allotted each year as it had in the fifth century. Thus the pinakia issued in connection with this reform should have been originally six thousand in number. Of this total, only five positively identified Class I examples and an uncertain number of the six indefinitely classified Class I or II pinakia have survived, making for a survival rate of about one in five hundred to one thousand. Although this rate of survival may seem surprisingly low, it is in fact quite in keeping with survival rates that have been estimated for certain Greek coinages, which range anywhere from one in four hundred to one in twelve thousand to twenty thousand.[2] Such estimates, to be sure, are restricted to coins in precious metals, whose

---

1. On this distinction, see Dow, *HSCP* 50 (1939), 23–34.
2. For a convenient summary of the work that has been done in this area, see Margaret Thompson, *The New Style Silver Coinage of Athens* (New York: American Numismatic

rates of survival are determined by economic laws governing the circulation and melting down of coins, chance hoard finds, and the like. But chance must have played an equally large part in the burial and discovery of pinakia, and since the pinakia continued to revert back to the state after each use, doubtless most of them ultimately came to be melted down also. When we reflect that we have only a minimal idea of how many triobol seal dies were used in the manufacture of Class I pinakia and that each die was probably used to stamp (at least) many hundreds of pinakia,[3] we may easily believe that our handful of Class I survivals represents an original issue of thousands.

Each year, all qualified men who wanted to become enrolled among the six thousand dikastai for the next year submitted themselves for the annual allotment of that number. Those who were accepted by the allotment received a pinakion, or, if they had been allotted and enrolled as dikasts in the previous year, were reissued their former pinakion. All former dikasts whom the allotment rejected had their pinakia taken away to be erased and eventually to be reissued to new dikasts later. Because some pinakia broke or were buried with dikasts who died while in office, and as others of the original Class I issue were put aside to be erased before being reissued, their number had to be supplemented over the next several years. The pinakia made to supplement them are those of our Class II, which differ from the Class I pinakia in only one formal respect: when first issued, most were inscribed with a text of two lines, which allowed room for a patronymic and for a more satisfactory arrangement of owners' names generally. Texts in two lines began to appear in the second and later uses of the Class I pinakia; these uses were contemporary with earlier uses of the Class II pinakia. Some of the

---

Society, 1961), 709–722; see also E. J. P. Raven, "Problems of the Earliest Owls of Athens," in C. M. Kraay and G. K. Jenkins, eds., *Essays in Greek Coinage Presented to Stanley Robinson* (Oxford: Clarendon Press, 1968), 40–58. Numismatists have long recognized that the relative size of an issue of ancient coinage must be estimated not from the number of coins surviving from the issue but from the number of different dies attested on the extant coins. Since each obverse or reverse die can be assumed under normal conditions to have struck an equal number of coins, an issue survived by only five coins, each struck with a different obverse die, should in all likelihood have been five (or more) times as large as an issue that is survived by hundreds of coins, of which all are from only a single obverse die.

3. According to the recent experiments of D. G. Sellwood ("Some Experiments in Greek Minting Technique," *NC*[7] 3 [1963], 228–230), it is estimated that a tempered bronze reverse die of tetradrachm size could have been used for striking upward to four thousand silver coins, if the flans were struck unheated and with an average of three hammerblows per impression. Bronze is a harder substance than silver, and other variables in striking are involved, such as different sized dies and probably fewer blows in the stamping of Class II–V pinakia (on the Class I pinakia, see above, p. 15) than were used in the minting of coins; thus it would be wrong to appropriate Sellwood's figure for estimating the number of pinakia that could have been stamped with each identified primary seal die. But even so, the figure does serve to suggest that the total number of pinakia represented by each triobol and gorgoneion seal die could very well have been somewhere in the thousands.

Class II pinakia were stamped with a double-bodied owl secondary seal, but this seal was not added to them until much later when these pinakia were being reused during the post-Class V period.

Although we do not know exactly how long after 378/7 the period of Class I and II pinakia lasted, I have estimated that the span was probably in the neighborhood of about ten years. Nor can we be sure how many Class II pinakia there may have been originally, whether as many as the Class I pinakia or a fewer number. The seven positively identified Class II survivals are on the whole much better preserved than the survivals from Class I and show that a minimum of three triobol seal dies were used in their manufacture. But as with all of the stamped classes, our record of primary seal dies is so incomplete that we have no firm basis for calculating the actual total of dies that may have been employed.

Allotment by pinakia proved to be an immediate success, and it was not long before another constitutional reform introduced this procedure into the great annual allotments fundamental to the theory and practice of Athenian democracy: the allotments that filled the boule, the numerous boards of ten, and all other city magistracies open to the lot. I would add to this list of annual sortitions the yearly selection of six thousand dikastai. This second reform dates probably from the end of the 370s or from the earlier 360s and was responsible for the invention of a new kind of pinakion for issue to all Athenians not enrolled as jurors. These were the Class III pinakia, which were stamped with a gorgoneion seal at each end. Such pinakia must have existed in vast quantities, for not only was the number of Athenians eligible to receive one large at any given time, but the period during which these nondikastic pinakia were manufactured dates from the time of the Class III reform (between about 370 and 362) until after the middle of the fourth century, a period of some fifteen to twenty-plus years. From the many thousands of Class III pinakia that were manufactured during this time, there have survived twenty-seven positively and probably identified examples (**20–45** and **149**) and a large share of the fifteen left or right ends that are classified as having come from Class III or IV pinakia (**46–60**). A minimum of thirteen different gorgoneion seal dies are attested on these survivals, by far the largest number of primary seal dies known from any of the stamped classes.

The section-letters on the Class III pinakia demonstrate the thoroughness with which the dikastic system of allotment was transferred to the annual sortition of magistrates. Not only was the technique of allotment by pinakia adopted, but with it the organization of candidates into ten tribal sections. As a result, every adult Athenian became permanently assigned to one of ten general allotment sections in his phyle.

Another result of the Class III reform was the change in appearance of dikastic pinakia. Since Athenians enrolled as jurors would now be able to use their pinakia in two different kinds of sortitions, these pinakia began to be stamped with two different primary seals: the triobol seal, which certified eligibility for participation in the frequent dikastic allotments held at the beginning of each court day; and the new gorgoneion seal, which certified eligibility for the annual magisterial sortitions.

The earliest dikastic pinakia to bear two primary seals are the Class IV pinakia with triobol seal ethnics in AΘE. They were manufactured contemporaneously with the earliest Class III pinakia and originally may have comprised a reform issue of six thousand. If so, all currently circulating Class I and II pinakia, that is, pinakia bearing only a single primary seal, would have been withdrawn and the new triobol-gorgoneion pinakia issued in their place. The evidence here is slight, however. Only seventeen positively identified Class IV pinakia have survived. On only seven of these is the ethnic of the triobol seal legible, and on only four (**61–64**) does the ethnic read AΘE. It is clear, moreover, that later uses of most Class IV pinakia date from after the Class V issue, when they may have received a double-bodied owl secondary seal, a text in imitation of Class V lettering, and in some cases even an inscribed rather than a stamped section-letter. Thus it may be that there was a massive issue of six thousand dikastic pinakia with two primary seals in the year of the Class III reform, but that our evidence for these six thousand has been drastically curtailed by the impact of the Class V issue shortly thereafter, for the Class V issue required that all regularly inscribed dikastic pinakia be retired from circulation. Some of the withdrawn Class IV pinakia were returned to use later, as were certain Class II pinakia, but many others may have been melted down. For the present, one can only hope that our knowledge of the relative sequence of the Class IV pinakia and the circumstances governing their low rate of survival will be improved by future discoveries.

The issue of dikasts' pinakia was closely regulated. From the beginning they were stamped with a triobol seal to ensure that no one would attempt to forge them. But this did not prevent men from obtaining pinakia illicitly. One had only to acquire a duly issued pinakion and to replace the name of its legal owner with one's own name. Since this practice would have been hazardous if authorities could check the names of owners of pinakia against a list of all properly enrolled dikasts, I would assume that such a list was not kept. But it is apparent, at any rate, that by the 360s the practice had become so prevalent that the state had to do something about it. The measure taken was the issue of the Class V pinakia, which were inscribed with added pierced holes to make them nontransferable in fact as well as in principle. On the present evidence, the issue of the Class V pinakia is to be dated between 367/6 and about 360.

Thirty-six Class V pinakia and fragments are extant. Originally there must have been six thousand, or more if the reform continued into a second or third year. That their rate of survival is much higher (by a factor of more than three) than the survival rate calculated for the Class I pinakia, which were originally issued in the same number, can be explained by a combination of factors. The first factor, which pertains only to Class V survivals with one use, is their undeniable attractiveness, which doubtless caused them to be the most treasured pinakia and therefore the pinakia that were buried with deceased owners in the greatest numbers. Second, the custom of burying pinakia with deceased owners can be expected to have increased as time went on. And a third factor is that the Class V pinakia apparently were allowed to remain in circulation for a decade or more before being subjected to the kind of withdrawal that I have suggested for the Class I and II pinakia at the time of the Class III reform and that surely took place for many Class IV pinakia at the time of the Class V issue. The only known occasion for a withdrawal of Class V pinakia is when dikasts' pinakia of boxwood were instituted, about 350.

The issuing of the specially inscribed Class V pinakia did not continue for long. Perhaps the Athenians realized that illegal transfer of pinakia could be more easily prevented by keeping an official list of jurors and by periodic checking. In any case, the Class V pinakia began to be reused with conventional lettering (sometimes with punched dot serifs in imitation of Class V lettering) within a few years after they were first issued. Until about 350, as the number of Class V pinakia gradually diminished through breakage, burial, and the like, the supply of dikasts' pinakia was maintained by bringing old Class II and IV pinakia out of retirement and by the manufacture of new Class IV pinakia with triobol seal ethnics in AΘH (cf. **72–74**). In one year during this post-Class V period, many, if not all, of the dikastic pinakia in use were stamped with a double-bodied owl seal; **73** received its sphinx (?) seal in a still later year. The purpose of these secondary seals has yet to be determined. Later still, the section-letters on both dikastic and nondikastic pinakia began to be inscribed at the same time as the owners' names were added, instead of being stamped before issue, as previously. Finally, sometime very close to the middle of the fourth century, dikastic pinakia of bronze were discontinued in favor of cheaper and more practical ones of boxwood.

The pinakia used by Athenians not enrolled as jurors, however, remained of bronze as late as the time of the *AthPol*. Class III pinakia with inscribed section-letters were being issued after mid-century, but, once it was recognized that their gorgoneion seals had outlived their usefulness, the Class III pinakia began to lose their seals in reuse and began to be supplemented by the stampless nondikastic pinakia of Class VI. The Class VI pinakia had a long duration, from shortly after 350 to the establishment of oligarchic government in 322/1. Like the Class III pinakia, they must have existed in huge numbers. But since they were manufactured as supplements to the many Class III pinakia that were being reused in the third quarter of the fourth century, the thirty extant Class VI pinakia and fragments (to which must be added probably the majority of the nine lost pinakia **150–158**) do not comprise the sum total of all pinakia that have survived from this time. Fully half of the extant Class III pinakia, as well as such originally dikastic pinakia as **61** and **96**, had lost their seals through erasure and had last been used during the Class VI period also.

Our survey comes to a close with the abolition of democratic allotments in 322/1. Stone kleroteria from later centuries attest that allotment by pinakia continued to be practiced in Hellenistic Athens, but all later Athenian pinakia were of wood and have perished.

Catalogue

Catalogue

Introduction

The pinakia are listed by classes and various subgroups within the classes. Within the subgroups, pinakia with particular idiosyncracies in common are listed together when possible; whole pinakia and larger fragments precede smaller fragments; pinakia with one or a few uses precede palimpsests with many uses; and pinakia with regular or especially distinct features generally precede problematic or exceptional examples. I have resorted to alphabetizing by section-letters only twice, for a few pinakia in Classes V and VI, when no other criteria could be applied.

Nearly all of the palimpsest pinakia are illustrated with one or more tracings designed to show the visible remains of earlier, partially erased inscriptions. These tracings were made by drawing on xerographic copies of photographs of the pinakia. The xerographic copier used is that manufactured by the Xerox Corporation.

With respect to the entries themselves in the Catalogue, the following should be noted:

Berlin Pinakia. The nine pinakia formerly in the Staatliche Museen, Berlin, are no longer extant. One has been lost since 1897; the others have not been located in East or West Berlin since they were presumably packed away for safekeeping during the last war. Six of the Berlin pinakia had been photographed, however. And so far as I have been able to determine, the photographs sent to me were printed exactly to actual size and permit precise measurements to be taken from them.

Museum Numbers. The inventory numbers here given for the pinakia in the National Museum, Athens, supersede the Archaeological Society Museum numbers that appear in *IG* II and II².

The numbers of the pinakia in the Froehner Collection in the Cabinet des Médailles are those assigned in Froehner's handwritten inventory kept at the Cabinet.

Provenience. The coordinates for the finding places of the specimens from the Agora excavations correspond to the grid that appears at the back of all volumes of *The Athenian Agora.*

Those pinakia in the National Museum, Athens, for which no provenience is given in the present catalogue are listed in the museum inventory either without a known provenience or as having been purchased on the Athenian antiquities market.

Condition. Such pinakia as those in Basel, in the Peiraeus and National Museums, Athens, and many from the Agora and Pnyx excavations have been "stripped" by electrolytic or electrochemical reduction, which has removed all traces of corrosion from both their front and back sides. Other pinakia, such as **4, 18, 61**, and the cleaned pinakia in the Cabinet des Médailles were treated more cautiously, by solvents, so as to remove only as much of the corrosion products as was deemed necessary, and then only from the inscribed surface. "Recent" cleaning refers to cleaning undertaken in 1966–1970 for benefit of the present study.

On the patination (oxidation) and cleaning of bronze generally, see H. J. Plenderleith, *The Conservation of Antiquities and Works of Art: Treatment, Repair, and Restoration* (London: Oxford University Press, 1956), 232–247.

Measurements. L(ength), w(idth), and th(ickness) are given in centimeters. Thicknesses and widths are frequently reported from both ends of palimpsest pinakia in order to emphasize the degree of tapering and spread caused by erasure.

Texts and Commentary. These are conceived primarily as a commentary on the photographs and tracings, which must always be allowed to bear the burden of proof.

I should emphasize that my observations are based on a firsthand examination of the extant pinakia in their present (cleaned or uncleaned) state, except in the following instances. I have not seen **13** (Hannover), **38** (Newcastle-upon-Tyne), and **88** (Oxford), but each has been cleaned and is known to me from photographs. Others I have not seen since they have last been cleaned: **18** (Urbana), **119** (Munich), **34, 63, 111, 118**, and **122** (Cabinet des Médailles, Paris), and all twelve examples in Basel. But, again, I have been sent excellent photographs, written confirmation of problematic details, and, from Basel and Paris, plaster casts, which leave practically nothing to be desired.

Seals and Stamped Section-Letters. My study of these has been directly from plaster casts that I have made of the left and right ends of the extant Class I–V pinakia. Measurements from the casts were taken with a Bausch and Lomb micrometer loupe containing a scale in tenths of millimeters.

Class 1

Section-letter stamped at center of the left end; triobol seal (ethnic AΘE) at the right. Nomen and curtailed demotic, usually separated by an interpunct, inscribed in one line through the middle of the plate. Secondary seal: owl-in-square seal.

WITH SECONDARY SEAL

1 (Figs. 1–2)   Athens, National Museum, Inv. Bronze 8122 (left half only). From *Πεδίον Ἄρεως*, Athens, according to the museum inventory; Koumanoudes says merely *βορειοανατολικῶς τῶν Ἀθηνῶν*. A. S. Koumanoudes, *ArchEph* 1887, 55–56, no. 3, whence our Fig. 2 Cf. S. Bruck, *AthMitt* 19 (1894), 208, no. 22. (*IG* II 5, 905b; II², 1871)

Complete. Broken in two. The right half is now lost. The left half is covered with a crusty green and reddish patina. L. 11.3 cm. (Koumanoudes), w. 2.3 cm., th. 0.38 cm.

One use:

$$\boxed{E}\ \ N\iota\kappa o\phi\tilde{\omega}\nu : \ ^{\backprime}Y\beta\acute{\alpha}(\delta\eta s)\quad \textcircled{\scriptsize T}$$
$$\boxed{O}$$

T(riobol) seal. With $\underset{\underset{\bullet}{E}}{}\overset{[A]}{}\underset{\underset{\bullet}{\Theta}}{}$. *O(wl-in-square) seal.*

Section-letter. Incuse field 0.95 × 0.8 cm.

Thanks to Koumanoudes' careful drawing, the loss of the right half has not deprived us of knowledge of the stamped seals, which in every respect conformed to the standard Class I format. With regard to the triobol seal, the drawing reproduces the lower part of the left-hand olive branch, below it two or three horizontals of what must be an epsilon in relief, and, in the lower right of the seal, the upper segment of a theta.

From the drawing, Bruck (followed in *IG* II and II²) interpreted the square seal as a double-bodied owl seal, but the drawing clearly shows a single owl, body to the right, head in the right corner facing, legs directly beneath the body—exactly as one should expect on a Class I pinakion. Behind the owl's head is a spray of olive leaves, which in the drawing was made to resemble an ivy leaf pointing away from the owl and which Koumanoudes erroneously described as "some obscure letter." At the right of the owl a diagonal in relief, probably a part of one of the letters of the ethnic.

2 (Fig. 3)   Paris, Cabinet des Médailles, Froehner Collection Inv. 610. Ex coll. Rayet. Drawing published by O. Rayet, *AnnAssEtGr* 1878, 205. Photo by L. Robert, *Coll. Froehner* I, 9, and pl. VII, no 10k. (*IG* II, 913; II², 1886).

Whole. Brown bronze attacked by green disease solidly on the back and in countless pittings on the inscribed surface. Cleaning around the seals at the right since the photograph was taken failed to reveal any further details. The channels of most letter strokes have been filled in, presumably by particles of copper that percolated up through fissures at the bottoms of the channels after the pinakion was buried and began to oxidize. L. 11.0 cm., w. 2.0 cm., th. 0.20–0.28 cm.

One use:

$\boxed{\Theta}$ *Δημήτριος* : *Πτελε(άσιος)*   Ⓣ

$\boxed{\text{O}}$

T(riobol) seal. With $\text{E}\,{}^{[A]}_{\ \ [\Theta]}$. All other details destroyed by corrosion. Diam. 0.12 cm. The seal had previously been declared "indistinct" (Rayet followed in both editions of *IG* II) or "tête à gauche" (Froehner-Robert). Rayet identified the secondary seal correctly, however.

O(wl-in-square) seal. With AΘ[E]. Stamped at a tilt. Head of the owl is larger than in any of the similar seals (i.e., dies) below. Because of weak stamping and corrosion other details are not preserved. Height? × width 0.8 cm.

Section-letter. In quadrangular field with rounded corners, ca. 0.95 cm. square.

In *PA* and the *Editio Minor* Kirchner identified the owner with the Demetrios of Ptelea who was diaitetes in 325/4 (*IG* II², 1926, line 92) and the Demetrios, son of Phil(—?),[1] of Ptelea, who appears in a list of bouleutai (*IG* II², 1746, line 35) formerly dated to the middle of the century, but now known to belong to 303/2 B.C. (*Hesperia* 37 [1968], 1, n. 2, and 13, lines 125 e–f). Both references, however, are obviously too late for the owner of a Class I pinakion, who must have died and have been buried with his pinakion soon after the Class I issue in the first half of the century. The diaitetes and the bouleutes may, of course, be younger relatives.

3 (Figs. 4–5)   Athens, Peiraeus, Archaeological Museum, A. N. Meletopoulos Collection. I. A. Meletopoulos, *Polemon* 3 (1947–48), 37–38, and pl. B′, no. 3.

1. The patronymic has been traditionally restored on analogy with that of a second-century B.C. sculptor, *Δημήτριος Φίλωνος Πτελάσιος*, known from three signatures (see G. A. Stamires, "Greek Inscriptions," *Hesperia* 26 [1957], 265–266, no. 99).

Complete. Broken into three large and two corner fragments. Recently stripped to bare metal, which is rotten and blistered by internal corrosion. L. 11.2 cm., w. 2.2 cm., th., where the surfaces are intact, ca. 0.25 cm.

One use:

   $\boxed{\Theta}$ *Σήλων* : *Πρασι*(*εύς*) $\boxed{\text{o}}$ Ⓣ

T(riobol) seal. Details obscured by the effects of corrosion, but the proportions and measurements of the small, compact owl strongly suggest that the seal may have been struck from the same die as the seal on **5**. Of the ethnic, only the A is legible. Diam. ca. 0.11 cm.

O(wl-in-square) seal. Visible are the profile of the large owl and the letters AΘE. Exceptionally large incuse field ca. 0.9 cm. square.

Section-letter. In quadrangular or circular field, height ca. 1.0 cm.

Neither of the seals at the right was noted by Meletopoulos.

4 (Figs. 6–8)   New York, Metropolitan Museum of Art, Inv. 07.286.95 (Rogers Fund). Purchased in 1907 from a Greek dealer residing in Paris. Notice by G.M.A. Richter, "New Accessions in the Classical Department," *Bulletin of the Metropolitan Museum of Art* 3 (1908), 90, no. 11 (whence *AJA* 12 [1908], 379, no. 4). Regular publication with photograph (before cleaning), G. M. A. Richter, *Greek, Etruscan, and Roman Bronzes in the Metropolitan Museum of Art* (New York: Metropolitan Museum of Art, 1915), 462–463, no. 1831. S. Dow, *BCH* 87 (1963), 668–669 (with references to several additional works in which the pinakion is illustrated), and fig. 2 (photograph after superficial cleaning).

Whole. Inscribed face recently cleaned to bare metal. L. 11.5 cm., w. 2.3 cm., th. 0.25 cm. at ends to 0.15 cm. in center.

Three uses:

a $\boxed{\text{I}}$ *Ἀριστ*[*ο*]*κράτης* : *Στερ*(*ιεύς*) Ⓣ
                              $\boxed{\text{o}}$?

b $\boxed{\text{I}}$ *Πρώταρχος*   Ⓣ
                 Πειραι(*εύς*) $\boxed{\text{o}}$

c $\boxed{\text{I}}$ *Ἐπικράτης*   Ⓣ
                 Σκαβω(*νίδης*) $\boxed{\text{o}}$

T(riobol) seal. With $\frac{A}{E\ \Theta}$. Rounded, compact owl; an exceptional amount of detail is visible, including a slight amount of feathering around the right eye and stippled feathering between the wings. Olive wreath with three pairs of leaves on each branch. Diam. 1.2 cm.

O(wl-in-square) seal. With AΘE. The die is distinguished by its horizontal olive spray. Height 0.75 × width 0.78 cm. I cannot be certain whether the seal was added after the name of the first owner or still later after erasure when the pinakion had been inscribed for the second owner. The latter would explain why the seal was not noticeably affected by the erasure of the letters of text *a* directly above it. But the seal appears to have been carefully positioned with relation to the first inscription, and I imagine that erasure of the letters without damage to the seal was possible. The erasure of the first inscription does seem to have been remarkably controlled.

Section-letter. In a rectangular field (distorted by erasure), 1.05 × 0.7 cm.

Dow was the first to observe that the pinakion is a palimpsest, but in its uncleaned condition he was able to read only the demotic and a few letters of the nomen of text *b*. I owe the recovery of the first inscription and the full text of *b* to D. v. Bothmer, who expertly undertook the final cleaning.

Text a. This is one of the most thoroughly erased yet still completely legible inscriptions detected on any of the surviving pinakia. Only the finest indications of letters remain and, except for the rho at the right, can barely be distinguished from superficial scratches in the metal. For a parallel spelling of the root *Στειρ-*, see *IG* I², 336, line 8.

Text b. The second owner is probably the same Protarchos Peiraieus who appears in a poletai list as an owner of a house in Peiraeus about 342/1 B.C. (*Hesperia* 5 [1936], 401, no. 10, lines 120–121). The owner was not buried with the pinakion and may well have lived on into the 340s after surrendering it.

Text c. The inscription is notable for its orthography and slovenly lettering. It was presumably not added by a professional and may be the work of the last owner himself. A single, straight punch was used for making the curved as well as the straight strokes, but even many of the rectilinear letters are malformed. Other instances of mu omitted from *Σκαμβωνιδ-* occur in *Hesperia* 28 (1959), 216, lines 380 and 384 (from the late 320s B.C.) and *IG* II², 7408 (first or second century A.D.); cf. *IG* II², 11474, and Meisterhans-Schwyzer, 84–85, nos. 5 and 7, with notes.

5 (Figs. 9–10)   Basel, Antikenmuseum, Inv. 1941.126.7. Ex coll. Rousopoulos–
Pfuhl. F. Stähelin, *AA* 1943, 19, and pl. I, no. 7 (photograph before cleaning).
   Right half. Now stripped to bare bronze. L. 5.3 cm., w. 2.0 cm. at right
to 2.2 cm. at left, th. 0.2 cm. at right to 0.1 cm. at left.
   Three or more uses. Repeated erasure evident from the heavy vertical
striations and from the tapering thickness and distended width toward the left.

a   <u>nomen : dem.</u>] *ΑΔ*   Ⓣ
                                    ⬛?

b   – – – – – –]*s*
         – – – – –]   ⬛   Ⓣ

c   – – – –]*ρης*
          – – – –]*H*   ⬛   Ⓣ

T(*riobol*) *seal.* Compact owl with slightly articulated head and proportionally
small body. Olive wreath (preserved on left only) with apparently two pairs
of leaves per branch. Of the ethnic only the A is certain. Diam. ca. 1.1 cm. The
die was very likely the same as used on **3** and conceivably might be the same
as found on **6**.

O(*wl-in-square*) *seal.* With AΘE. Stamped upside down at a tilt. Olive spray
slants down at an angle. Height 0.75 cm.
   Stähelin misidentified the seals as a gorgoneion seal and a double-bodied
owl seal, respectively, and recorded only the letters of the last text.

   Owing to the deep erasure striations throughout the inscribed area, few
traces of earlier names remain. At least two earlier uses are represented, but
there may well have been more. Chances are that the demotic of text *a* was
one of several that terminate –αδ(ης).

Class I or II

6 (Figs. 11–12)   Athens, Paul Kanellopoulos Collection. Georges Daux, "Une
nouvelle tablette athénienne de juge," *Mélanges offerts à K. Michalowski*
(Warsaw: Panstwowe Wydawnictwo Naukowe, 1966), 355–356 (text *b* only),
with photograph.

Whole. Incrusted green patination. Erasure at the center has warped the ends forward. L. 11.0 cm., w. 2.0 cm., th. 0.3 cm.

Two uses:

a $\boxed{\Delta}$ $M\acute{\epsilon}\nu\iota\pi\pi o[s\ \Sigma]\phi\acute{\eta}\tau\tau\iota(os)$ $\textcircled{\scriptsize T}$

b $\boxed{\Delta}$ $\begin{array}{l}\mathring{A}\nu\theta\epsilon\mu\acute{\iota}\omega\nu\ M\epsilon\delta\upsilon(\lambda\acute{\iota}\delta o\upsilon)\\ \Pi\rho o\sigma\pi\acute{a}\lambda\tau\iota(os)\end{array}$ $\textcircled{\scriptsize T}$

T(riobol) seal. With $\begin{smallmatrix}&A\\\Theta&&\exists\end{smallmatrix}$. Small, compact owl. Two pairs of leaves on each olive branch. Diam. 1.1 cm. The seal is closely comparable in style and dimensions to the less well-preserved seals on **3** and **5**. All three seals may be from the same die.

Section-letter. Incuse square 0.9 cm. in height.

Text a. Two weak diagonals within the second mu of text *b* (parallel to the first and third strokes of the mu) must be misstrikings in the inscribing of this letter and do not belong to the earlier text. Both are rather more deep and prominent than the erased letters of text *a*.

Text b. As was observed by Daux, $M\epsilon\delta\upsilon(\lambda\acute{\iota}\delta o\upsilon)$ is written for $M\epsilon\iota\delta\upsilon(\lambda\acute{\iota}\delta o\upsilon)$ (*PA*, 9731–9734). Note the abnormally low position of both lines of the text, which suggests that the letterer was still under the influence of the earlier format of a single, centered line.

FRAGMENTS BROKEN AT THE RIGHT, PRESENCE OR ABSENCE OF
SECONDARY SEAL UNCERTAIN

7 (Figs. 13–16)   Thessalonika, Archaeological Museum, Inv. 1207. Excavated in 1938 from house A viii 3 at Olynthos. D. M. Robinson, "Inscriptions from Macedonia, 1938," *TAPA* 69 (1938), 56–57, and pl. 8, no. 10; *Excavations at Olynthus* X, *Metal and Minor Miscellaneous Finds* (Baltimore: Johns Hopkins University Press, 1941), 500–502, and pl. 164, no. 2562. S. Dow, *BCH* 87 (1963), 669–671, with fig. 3.

Left four-fifths. Ca. 2.5 cm. is missing at the right. Stripped to bare metal. L. 8.7 cm., w. 2.0 cm. at left to 2.3 cm. at center, th. 0.2 cm. at left to 0.13 cm. minimum.

Four texts (= three uses) visible:

a   E $\underset{.}{K}\underset{.}{Y}$ ⟦≋ ⩗⟧[.]Σ $\overset{'}{A}\nu\alpha\gamma[(\nu\rho\acute{\alpha}\sigma\iota\sigma\varsigma)$

b   E $\underset{.}{T}\iota\mu\underset{.}{\rho}\kappa\rho\acute{\alpha}\tau\eta\varsigma$

c   E $T\iota\mu\sigma\kappa\rho\acute{\alpha}\tau\eta\varsigma$
              $T\iota\mu\alpha\nu(\text{—?}):\varPhi\lambda\upsilon\varepsilon\acute{\upsilon}[\varsigma$

d   E $\overset{'}{A}\rho\iota\sigma\tau\sigma\phi\tilde{\omega}\nu$
              υ υ υ υ $\varPhi\lambda\upsilon\varepsilon\acute{\upsilon}[\varsigma$

Section-letter. Large and rectangular, incuse field 1.0 × 0.75 cm.

Robinson printed only one earlier text, the second line of which bears little relation to anything that appears on the pinakion. Working from Robinson's excellent photograph, Dow was able to get to the heart of the matter by correctly detecting most of the earlier letters and seeing that there are at least three texts, two of them containing the same nomen and therefore probably representing only a single use. Actually there are four texts altogether, representing three uses. They may be discussed best by lines.

Line 1 (through the upper third of the plate) poses no problems. Beneath the nomen of the last owner, Aristophon, are the weakly erased remains of the nomen of the previous owner, Timokrates.

Line 2 (through the middle of the plate) also contains two names, both clearly legible toward the right. One terminates in *–ATHΣ* and should go with less distinct traces at the left to give $T\underset{.}{I}\underset{.}{M}\underset{.}{O}KP\underset{.}{A}TH\Sigma$ (the rho survives in a vertical). The other name, inscribed one to two millimeters lower and a little better erased, reads $K\underset{.}{Y}$ ⟦≋ ⩗⟧[.]$\underset{.}{\Sigma}ANA\Gamma$ (cf. Dow's ⟦≋ Y⟦≋[...]$\Sigma A\Gamma A\Gamma$), giving a good one-line text of the Class I type. I realize that the spacing between the sigma and the initial letter of the demotic is extremely slight, but I feel that this objection must be overruled inasmuch as it does not lead to a more acceptable reading. The nomen may have read *Κύκνος*, but the identity of the letters and conjectured spacing at the left of the line are not sufficiently reliable for a confident restoration (the upsilon, for example, looks slightly oversize).

Line 3 (through the lower third of the plate). *TIMAN:ΦΛΥΕΥ* has always been taken to be the patronymic and demotic of the last owner, but, as is shown perfectly well on the photograph and is even more apparent on the pinakion itself, the letters comprising the patronymic are notably weaker than the letters of the demotic (and the nomen Ἀριστοφῶν) and in fact have the closed up and partly broken look of letters that have been subjected to erasure. With the exception of the right-hand vertical of the nu, the strokes of the last three letters of the patronymic, *MAN*, are as faint as the erased strokes in the first line of text *c*. *TI* and the vertical of the nu are bolder, but they belong to the beginning and end of the patronymic, and erasure was frequently less thorough at ends than in the middle of inscriptions (compare the nearly intact sigma at the end of line 1 of text *c*). Now if the patronymic had been erased, as it appears to have been, this would mean that the patronymic and demotic were actually inscribed for the penultimate owner Timokrates; that Timokrates and the last owner both happened to be from the same deme; and that therefore, when Timokrates' name was erased, his demotic was left intact by the letterer to save having to reinscribe the second line.

These deductions receive independent support from the absence of any other suitable candidate for the completion of Timokrates' name. In Fig. 15 I have indicated two fine intersecting diagonals in line 3, which could belong to one of the earlier texts. I have a suspicion that they should be considered scratches, but even if they are not, the thoroughness with which they— and any other hypothetical letters that may have been associated with them—were erased excludes them from being associated with Timokrates' weakly erased nomen in line 1. It was probably not mere coincidence that the pinakion had two successive owners from the same deme. Although the practice was illegal, pinakia did change hands privately and presumably often in such cases between friends and relatives.

Repetition of names. With Dow, I think it is reasonable to assume that Timokrates' nomen was first inscribed through the middle of the plate in error and was erased to be reinscribed higher. Perhaps the letterer originally intended a one-line inscription, but did not leave himself room for a demotic at the right and felt that the space below was inadequate.

I have expressed doubt as to the relevance of the two intersecting diagonals of line 3, shown in Fig. 15. The possibility should be acknowledged, nevertheless, that if they happen to be remnants of an almost perfectly erased inscription, this inscription would probably have comprised a second line of text *b*, in a textual arrangement of two low lines like that of the last inscription on **6**. Even if this were the case, however, none of the other deductions above need be affected. A priori, we may feel quite confident that the pinakion had only one owner named Timokrates, however many times and ways his name was inscribed.

Provenience. The discovery of the fragment at Olynthos has disappointingly few concrete implications. It attests that pinakia traveled with their owners and that this piece must have been brought to Olynthos before the destruction of the city in 348. The latter gives a *terminus ante quem*, to be sure, but other evidence discussed at the ends of Chapters III and IV, above, shows that the pinakion was probably manufactured as much as a quarter of a century before this date. Dow reviews the few details of discovery. The excavators could affirm only that the pinakion was found in a fill in the kitchen of the house.

Presumably it was simply lost or (if the right end broke off in antiquity) discarded by the last owner during a visit to Olynthos. There are no particular reasons for connecting his visit with a known event, such as the Athenian attack on Olynthos under Timotheos between 363 and 359 B.C. or Philip's siege in 348. From Aischines 2.15 we know that Philip found a number of Athenians in the city, yet it is generally believed on the evidence of Suidas (s.v. *Κάρανος*) that any expeditionary force the Athenians might have sent to relieve Olynthos did not arrive until after the city had fallen (see K. J. Beloch, *Griechische Geschichte*, 2d ed., 4 vols. [Berlin and Leipzig: de Gruyter, 1912–1927], III, pt. 1, 496; pt. 2, 279). Olynthos was the commercial and political center of the northwest Aegean, and an Athenian might have journeyed there at any time during the second quarter of the fourth century for any number of reasons.

8 (Fig. 17)   formerly Berlin, Staatliche Museen, Inv. Bronze 6504. C. Curtius, *RhM* 31 (1876), 284, no. 4, with a sketch. (Girard, no. 42; *IG* II, 896; II², 1860)

Left end. L. 4.6 cm., w. 1.9 cm.; from the photograph th. looks regular, ca. 0.2 cm.

One use:

[Δ] *Μνησικλ*[ῆς *vel* –είδης

Section-letter. In field 0.9 cm. high.

The surface of the metal was pitted by corrosion. The shallow-looking hole above and between the section-letter and the initial mu is probably also a pitting. It was omitted from Curtius' drawing and looks too small for a properly drilled carrying-hole.

9 (Figs. 18–19)   Athens, National Museum, Inv. Bronze 8131. Unpublished.

Left end. Recently stripped to bare metal. L. 3.2 cm., w. 1.9 cm. at left to

2.1 cm. at right, th. 0.22 cm. at left to 0.18 cm. at right.
Three uses visible:

a   ⊞ $A[---$

b   ⊞ $\Sigma[---$
         $\Sigma \digamma[---$

c   ⊞ $X\alpha[---$ erased
         $\Sigma o[\upsilon\nu\iota\epsilon\acute{\upsilon}\varsigma?$

Section-letter. In field 0.9 cm. high × 0.8 cm. wide.

Like **76**, this fragment comes from a pinakion that broke as it was being prepared to receive the name of still another owner. It must therefore have been a surface find and did not come from a tomb. I have recorded only the more prominent remains of erased letters. The surface contains a number of other fine lines which should also belong to texts *a* and *b*. That line 2 of text *c* began with a demotic is probable, although by no means certain.

10 (Figs. 20–21)   Athens, National Museum, Inv. Bronze 8080. A. Dumont, *RA*[2] 17 (1868), 144, and pl. V, 5. (Girard, no. 19; *IG* II, 895; II[2], 1859)
    Left end. Recently stripped to bare metal. L. 2.9 cm., w. 2.0 cm. at left to 2.15 cm. at right, th. 0.28 cm. at left to 0.15 cm. at right.
    More than two uses, as required by the heavy erasure which is responsible for the considerable reduction of thickness at the right:

a   △ [Name in one line?

b   △ $N\digamma[---$
         $\grave{\epsilon}\kappa[--- \; vel \; `E\kappa[\alpha\lambda\hat{\eta}\theta\epsilon\nu$

c   △ $K\rho[---$

Section-letter. In incuse field 0.9 cm. square.

The chief interest of this fragment is the disposition of the last text in a single, centered line after an intermediate text inscribed in two lines, which implies that texts of one and two lines were used interchangeably for a time after the Class I issue.

Before cleaning, only the last text was visible. It had been variously read as *KI*[– – – (Dumont) or *KE*[– – – (Girard, *IG* II and II²).

11 (Fig. 22)   Athens, National Museum, Inv. Bronze 8071. S. Bruck, *AthMitt* 19 (1894), 208, no. 2. (*IG* II 5, 912b; II², 1885)

Left end. Recently stripped to bare metal. L. 3.15 cm., w. 2.1 cm., th. 0.2 cm. at left to 0.05 cm. at right.

Three or more uses, as implied by evidence of erasure on more than two occasions:

a   ?   [Name in one or two lines

b   H   Σ[– – –
             ̣[– – – –

c   H   Φα[– – –
             Φα[ληρεύς?

Section-letters. Below the lower edge of the eta section-letter (incuse field roughly 0.9 cm. square) is the edge of another incuse square remaining from an earlier stamped letter (as also on **16**), which was erased by the diagonal striations crossing its field.

The thick vertical depression in line 2 just to the right of the section-letters is not part of an earlier inscription, but marks a sharp decrease in thickness caused by erasure later than the erasure of the original section-letter. This later erasure was abruptly terminated so as to leave the second section-letter intact and shows that the second section-letter belongs with at least the last two uses of the pinakion. Because of the deep erasure striations, positive remains of only one earlier letter are visible, those of a sigma underneath the phi in line 1.

Class II

Similar to Class I pinakia except that names are usually inscribed in two lines, and the secondary seal, when present, is of the double-bodied owl type.

WITHOUT SECONDARY SEAL

12 (Figs. 23–24)   Paris, Cabinet des Médailles, Froehner Collection Inv. 617. L. Robert, *Coll. Froehner* I, 9–10, and pl. VI, no. 10l. S. Dow, *BCH* 87 (1963), 671, and fig. 9.

Right half. Superficial green patina. L. 4.8 cm., w. 2.0 cm., th. 0.3 cm. at right to 0.1 cm. at left.

Three or more uses:

a　　$- - -$]s v $Λαμ\,(πτρεύς)$　　Ⓣ

b　　$- - -$]$ἐλος$
　　　$- - -$]os　　　Ⓣ

c　　$Ἀνδ?$]$ροκλῆς$
　　　$Ἀχα$]$ρνε\,(ύς)$　　　Ⓣ?

$T(riobol)$ *seal*. With　[A]　. Same die as used on **13**, **16**, and **17**, all archetypal
　　　　　　　　　 Θ　Ⅎ
Class II pinakia.

Texts a and b. Dow recorded most letters of the earlier inscriptions and suggested that there may have been three uses, but in his texts he conflated texts *a* and *b* into a single earlier inscription of three lines. Actually, the letters of *a* and *b* differ in their degrees of fineness, the letters of text *a* being clearly the more heavily erased.

　My texts give only the more legible earlier readings. Several fine lines within the demotic of text *a* may represent another, still earlier name running through the middle of the plate, but there is an equal chance some or all of these lines may be mere surface scratches in the metal. Note the rare *vacat* between nomen and demotic of text *a* and the abnormally high position of line 1 of text *b* resulting apparently from the letterer's fear of encroaching on the poorly erased remains of the previous inscription.

Text c. Robert's (undotted) text and restoration

$$[Ἀγα]θοκλῆς$$
$$[Ἀθμ]ονε\,(ύς)$$

fails to take into account both the sharp break at the left (probably caused by verticals that weakened the metal there) and the fact that the loop of the first preserved letter at the left of line 2 is not closed, as it should have been if the letter were an omicron. Both rhos in my restoration are low, but compare the rho in line 1 of **72** and the one in line 2 of **125**. The owner was almost certainly an Acharnian, and, although the completion of line 1 is less positive on material grounds, an Androkles Acharneus is known from a fourth-century B.C. gravestone (*IG* II², 5782) and as the father of the last owner of **121**, a Class VI pinakion, q.v. No Agathokles is attested from Acharnai or Athmonon.

Dow's observation that the pinakion must have been short remains pertinent only to the last use. The earlier inscriptions show that the pinakion was originally of standard length, but may have been broken or cut one to three centimeters from the left before the last name was inscribed. Since the original stamped section-letter would have been replaced, perhaps with an inscribed letter, and since the final sigma in line 1 partially obliterates the triobol seal, the pinakion might have finally been used during the stampless Class VI period. Whether it was or not, this is the only pinakion from Class I or II that can even be suspected of having been used that late.

13 (Figs. 25–26)   Hannover, Kestner-Museum, Inv. 1928.265. Ex coll. C.T. Seltman. Unpublished.

Whole. Cleaned to bare metal. L. 11.1 cm., w. 2.15 cm., th. 0.22–0.27 cm. Two uses attested:

a $\boxed{\text{K}}$ $[-\overset{3-4}{-}-]\,\overline{III}\,[\overset{\text{ca. 2}}{--}]O[\overset{\text{ca. 3}}{--}]\Sigma$ $\circled{T}$
   $[.]X?[---]$

b $\boxed{\text{K}}$ $M\nu\eta\sigma\acute{\iota}\sigma\tau\rho\alpha\tau\sigma\varsigma$ $\circled{T}$
   $\Sigma\phi\acute{\eta}\tau\tau\iota(\sigma\varsigma)$

T(riobol) seal. With $\underset{\Theta\ \ \exists}{\overset{A}{}}$. Same die as used on **12**, **16**, and **17**: owl with wide head articulated from the body. Three pairs of leaves on each olive branch. Diam. 1.13 cm.

Section-letter. Incuse square 0.8 cm. in height.

Two or three faint lines to the right of the sigma of text *a* could possibly belong to a sigma of a still earlier text, but could also be accidental scratches of some kind, as are certainly the two parallel diagonals above the section-letter.

14 (Figs. 27–28)   Athens, National Museum, Inv. Bronze 15173. From "near the church of St. George of the former Second Cemetery" (about halfway on the ancient road from the Diplyon Gate to Plato's Academy), presumably in

Panagiotes Aristophron's excavations in 1931.[2] B. D. Theophaneides, "*Νέα προσκτήματα Ἐθνικοῦ Ἀρχαιολογικοῦ Μουσείου κατὰ τὰ ἔτη* 1930, 1931 *καὶ* 1932," *ArchEph* 1939–1941, *Χρονικά*, 17, no. 5 (transcription of text *b* only).

Whole. Recently stripped to bare bronze. L. 11.2 cm., w. 2.15 cm., th. 0.23–0.28 cm.

Two uses:

a $\boxed{\text{K}}$ ΛΥΣ[Ι]Σ͞PAT $\vert$ Σ T
          Λ*ε̣υ̣*(κονοεύς)

b $\boxed{\text{K}}$ Κλεόφαντος : Κλεάν– T
          δρου ἐκ Κεραμέων

T(riobol) seal. With $\Theta \, ^{\text{A}} \, \dashv$. Small: diam. 1.05 cm. All details at a reduced, delicate scale. Owl with slightly articulated profile. Olive wreath with three closely spaced pairs of leaves on each branch.

Section-letter. Incuse field 0.85 cm. square.

Text a. The restoration that fits the traces, *Λυσ*[*ι*]*οστράτης*, is highly doubtful since names ending –*στρατ.s* regularly terminate in –*os*. Known exceptions are few, non-Attic, and negligible.[3] The troublesome vertical before the final sigma is too sharp and deep to have been an accidental scratch and resembles the other erased strokes in line 1. Absolutely no trace of an erased omicron can, moreover, be found in its vicinity. Hence, to explain the vertical away and to restore *Λυσ*[*ι*]*οστρατ*⟨*ο*⟩*s* or –[*ο*]*s*, it would be necessary to postulate an inscriber's error in text *a* (cf. **40**, text *c*, where one has been corrected) or in text *b*, in which case the vertical would have been a misstrike in the inscribing of the epsilon to its right. An alternate solution would be to read *Λῦσις* as the nomen (a Lysis of Leukonoe happens to be known from a fourth-century inscribed marble lekythos, *IG* II², 6748) and to restore an abbreviated patronymic in the second half of the line. The problem here, however, is finding an

---

2. The church can be made out on the map in *AA* 1934, 137–138, fig. 8, as a black dot on the right side of the broad, shaded avenue. Aristophron is known to have excavated graves along the ancient road near the church. See *Πρακτικὰ τῆς Ἀκαδημίας Ἀθηναίων* 8 (1933), 71, and *AA* 1931, 217.

3. Dornseiff-Hansen lists four, one of which is bogus: a *Σάτρτης* from Kyrene, two variants from Egyptian papyri, and a false *Δαμοστράτης* taken from Pape-Benseler, which cites *BdI* 1844, 145–146 (now *IG* V, 209), line 17. The name in question actually reads *Δαμοκράτης*.

Athenian name that will fit the remains at the right, which I have been unable
to do. Since there is no independent evidence of a use anterior to text *a* that
can be evoked as the source of the difficulty, it has seemed to me best to leave
the line unrestored.

In line 2 the erasure seems to continue beyond the initial *ΛΕΥ*, but I have
been unable to identify any further traces of letters other than the questionable horizontal indicated in the tracing. The horizontal does not fit the only
possible demotic that can be restored from the first three letters and is probably a scratch or crack in the surface resulting from erasure.

15 (Figs. 29–30)   Athens, Stoa of Attalos, Agora Excavations Inv. B 1104.
Excavated in 1954 from Area H/15; Hellenistic-Early Roman context. Unpublished.

Right half. Broken in two. Clean bare bronze. L. 6.0 cm., w. 2.0 cm. at right
to 2.3 cm. at left, th. 0.2 cm. at right to 0.1 cm. at left.

Three uses visible:

a   − − − − − −]ǀǀ
          − − − −]*M* ⸗   Ⓣ

b   − − −]*ης*   Ⓣ   (carrying-hole)
          − −-ε]*ύς*

c   − − −]*ς* : *Διονυσίο*   Ⓣ
          − − −-ε]*ύς*

T(riobol) seal. Ethnic illegible. The surface metal with the relief has flaked
away leaving only the outline of the owl.

A carrying-hole was drilled over the vertical in line 2 of text *a* and therefore
was not added until one of the later uses. Nevertheless, since a carrying-hole
has yet to appear on a Class I pinakion, the hole tends to confirm that this
fragment originally belonged to Class II.

WITH SECONDARY SEAL

16 (Figs. 31–32)   Athens, National Museum, Inv. Bronze 8061. From a grave
near Spata, ancient Erchia. A. S. Koumanoudes, *ArchEph* 1887, 55–56, no. 2,
with a drawing. (*IG* II 5, 911b; II², 1882)

Whole. Cleaned to bare metal. L. 11.6 cm., w. 2.1 cm., th. 0.27 cm. at ends to
0.15 cm. in middle. Erasure in the middle has warped the ends forward.

Three uses visible:

a   □⌐ $O[- -\overset{ca.\ 7}{- - -}]s$ Ⓣ   (carrying-hole at upper left)
        $[- - - - -]$

b   ⌐?⌐ $\underset{.}{N}\epsilon o\kappa\lambda\epsilon i\delta\eta s$ Ⓓ   Ⓣ
        $[-\overset{ca.\ 4}{- -}-]$◪

c   ⌐H⌐ $E\mathring{v}\pi\acute{o}\lambda\epsilon\mu os$ Ⓓ   Ⓣ
        $'E\rho\chi\iota\epsilon\acute{v}s\ T\iota\mu o\delta\acute{o}(.ov)$

T(riobol) seal. With ⊖ $\overset{A}{ᴣ}$. Same die as used on **12**, **13**, and **17**.

D(ouble-bodied owl) seal. In incuse *circle.* With A A. Diam. 1.05 cm. Overlying the sigma from text *a* but encroached upon by the erasure preceding text *c*, the seal clearly was added during the penultimate use.

Section-letters. It is uncertain when the original gamma (incuse field ca. 0.9 cm. square) was partially erased (note the deep striations at the upper left from the erasure) and overstruck with the smaller eta (field ca. 0.85 cm. square).

Text c. Eupolemos' son, Timodo[.]os, was the last owner of **37**, a much-reused Class III pinakion doubtless found in the same burial plot as the present pinakion. A later member of this family was $E\mathring{v}\beta\iota os\ E\mathring{v}\pi o\lambda\acute{\epsilon}\mu ov$ ($'E\rho\chi\iota\epsilon\acute{v}s$), prytanis in 256/5 B.C. (IG II², 678 [= Dow, *Prytaneis*, no. 10], line 33; for the date, see W. K. Pritchett and B. D. Meritt, *The Chronology of Hellenistic Athens* [Cambridge, Mass.: Harvard University Press, 1940], xxi).

17 (Figs. 33–34) Utrecht, Archaeological Institute, Inv. 136. Acquired in 1920 from the Arndt Collection. J. J. E. Hondius, *Supplementum Epigraphicum Graecum* 3 (1927), 37–38, no. 141. J. Kirchner, IG II², 1870 (texts independently derived from a photograph). J. H. Jongkees, *BABesch* 20 (1945), 7–8, and Fig. 5.
    Whole. Brown metal attacked in several areas (where white in the photograph) by bronze disease. A crack, most pronounced on the back runs vertically through the second epsilon in line 1 and the pi in line 2. L. 10.6 cm., w. 2.2 cm., th. 0.28 cm. at ends to 0.20 cm. in center. Erasure has reduced the thickness of the plate between the section-letter and the triobol seal, as shown in the profile, Fig. 34.

Two uses visible:

a $\boxed{\text{E}}$ $[-\overset{ca.\ 3}{--}-]\ \bar{\mathsf{T}}\ [-\overset{ca.\ 4}{--}-]\ \gtrless E$ $\overset{\frown}{\text{T}}$
  $[\,.\,]\ \bar{\mathsf{T}}\ \gtrless \mathsf{f}^{\!\!\!\!-}$

b $\boxed{\text{E}}$ $M\epsilon\nu\epsilon\kappa\rho\acute{\alpha}\tau\eta\varsigma$ Inscribed in imitation of Class
  $\Lambda\alpha\mu\pi\tau(\rho\epsilon\acute{\nu}\varsigma)$ $\boxed{\text{D}}$ $\overset{\frown}{\text{T}}$ V lettering (carrying-hole)

T(riobol) seal. With A . Same die as on **12, 13,** and **16.**
        Θ Ǝ

D(ouble-bodied owl) seal. With A A. Height 0.7 × width 0.75 cm. The seal was stamped in the erased area where the thickness of the pinakion has been substantially reduced. Since the relief of the seal impression has not been affected by any erasure, the seal was clearly added after the pinakion was last erased, that is, during the final use.

Section-letter. Field 0.9 cm. square.

Text a. The traces at the end of line 1 were read *IĘ* by both Jongkees and Kirchner. There is, however, no visible basis for the first two letters in Kirchner's reading, *ΛΛIE*. Within the epsilon are two or three lines that are probably scratches, but could also be remains of a still earlier inscription.

Text b. Even though punched holes are omitted from the crossbars of the etas and the alpha in line 2, the holes in the loop of the rho and in the crossbar of the alpha in line 1 are enough to demonstrate that the "serifs" were inspired by the pierced lettering of Class V pinakia. The secondary seal goes with this Class V-like use, and the carrying-hole may not have been drilled until the last use also, for it is positioned like the carrying-holes on standard Class V pinakia.

18 (Figs. 35–36) Urbana, University of Illinois Classical and European Culture Museum, Inv. 907. Purchased in 1930 from C. T. Seltman. "Said to have been found near the modern village of Liopesi in Attica, on the east side of Mt. Hymettos, the ancient deme of Paiania" (Vanderpool). Eugene Vanderpool, "An Athenian Dikast's Ticket," *AJA* 36 (1932), 293–294, with fig. 1 (photograph before cleaning).
  Whole. The inscribed face has been recently cleaned of most corrosion L. 11.8 cm., w. 2.2 cm. at ends to 2.3 cm. in middle, th. 0.25 cm. at ends to 0.20 cm. in middle.

Probably four uses:

a   Γ $\not\equiv[---\overset{7\text{-}9}{--}----]\underset{.}{s}$ Ⓣ

            $[----------]\underset{.}{O}?$

b   Γ $[\cdot]/[--\overset{ca.\,6}{--}--]s$ Ⓓ? Ⓣ

            $\underset{.}{A}\rho[\alpha]\underset{.}{\phi}[\acute{\eta}\nu]\iota o s$

c   Γ $\underset{.}{\Phi}\alpha\acute{\iota}\delta\iota\mu o s$

            $\Pi\alpha\iota\alpha\,(\nu\iota\epsilon\acute{\upsilon}s)\ \Phi\alpha\nu\underset{.}{\rho}\,(—?)$ Ⓓ? Ⓣ

d   Γ $T\iota\mu o\phi\hat{\omega}\nu$

            $\Pi\alpha\iota\alpha\nu\iota\,(\epsilon\acute{\upsilon}s)$ Ⓓ   Ⓣ

T(riobol) seal. With $\begin{smallmatrix} & A & \\ E & & \Theta \end{smallmatrix}$. Owl with wide head. Three pairs of leaves plus a terminal leaf or berry on each olive branch. Diam. 1.18 cm.

D(ouble-bodied owl) seal. With letters A A. Ca. 0.7 cm. square. There is no way of knowing when the secondary seal was added, but on analogy with the two other Class II pinakia that did not receive a secondary seal until after their first use, this pinakion should not have either.

Section-letter. Field ca. 0.85 cm. square.

Before cleaning, only the last two texts were visible. Further cleaning might help clarify the remains of the two earliest texts, which I have been able to study only from photographs and a plaster cast.

Text a. The earliest visible traces are the slight suggestions of a sigma at the right and a low diagonal at the extreme left. Both appear to have belonged to a line that ran just above the middle of the plate's width. There are no traces of a demotic to the right of the sigma; the demotic would, therefore, have been inscribed along the lower edge of the plate, like the demotic of text *b*. If the broken and unaligned segments of the omicron before the final sigma of text *b* actually happened to belong to two different omicrons, one would go with text *a*.

Text b. Judging from the sigma at the right, line 1 ran just slightly higher than the first line of *a*. The restored demotic is the only one that will fit the traces in line 2: $\underset{.}{A}\not\in[\cdot]\,\bar{\top}[\cdot\cdot]IO\Sigma.$

Text c replaces Vanderpool's reading (before cleaning): Φιλώ[νν]μ[ο]ς /
Παια(νιεύς)νANO. Of the deeply impressed omicron at the end of line 2, only
the upper left segment was touched by erasure.

PRESENCE OR ABSENCE OF SECONDARY SEAL UNCERTAIN

19 (Fig. 37) Athens, Numismatic Museum. Inventoried as a bronze weight,
no. 3348. Unpublished.
   Left end. Green patina. L. 1.9 cm., w. 2.1 cm., th. ca. 0.25 cm.
   Probably more than one use:

a
   [B] [– – –
       [– – –

b
   [B] K⫶[– – –
       K⫶[– – –

Its serrated edge might raise doubts about the identity of this fragment
were there not other Athenian pinakia with notched edges (above, p. 23).
This, however, is the only surviving example with three rather than two
notches. The rounded and worn right edge of the fragment suggests, on the
other hand, that it had been reused in its present broken state during ancient
or more recent times, and the notches might not have been added until this
reuse as something other than an allotment plate.
   A slightly more serious question is raised by the size of the section-letter
(incuse field 0.75 cm. high × 0.8 cm. wide), which is too small for a Class I
pinakion and small but perhaps not too much so for a pinakion of Class II.

Class III

   Two gorgoneion seals: one stamped at the left, usually in the lower left
corner; the other at the right end. Usually with a section-letter, stamped or
inscribed in the upper left corner.

FIRST USE WITH A STAMPED SECTION-LETTER

20 (Fig. 38) Athens, National Museum, Inv. Bronze 8060. Paul Vidal-
Lablache, "Tablette judiciaire du tribunal des héliastes," *Bulletin de l'école
française d'Athènes* 3–4 (Sept.–Oct. 1868), 51–54. (Girard, no. 3; *IG* II, 912; II²,
1884)

Whole. Recently stripped to bare metal. L. 11.2 cm., w. 2.1 cm., th. 0.15–
0.18 cm. even.

One use:

    H *Μειδωνίδης* : *Μείδω* (*νος*?)
    G *Κηφισιεύς*   G

G(*orgoneion*) *seals*. Small, round, finely featured head in incuse circle of
normal 1.0 cm. diameter. Bushy hair terminates in two snakes that are
knotted under the chin; another pair of snakes rises from the crown of the
head in the field above. The same die struck the seal of **52**.

Section-letter. Field ca. 0.8 cm. high × 0.75 cm. wide.

The only other attested possibility for the full patronymic is *Μείδω* (*νίδου*).

21 (Fig. 39) Athens, Peiraeus, Archaeological Museum, A. N. Meletopoulos
Collection. I. A. Meletopoulos, *Polemon* 3 (1947–48), 40, and pl. B′, no. 5
(photograph before cleaning).

Whole. Recently stripped to bare metal. L. 11.0 cm., w. 2.0 cm. at left to
1.9 cm. minimum near center, th. tapers from 0.18 cm. maximum at left to
0.10 cm. at the lower right corner.

Apparently two uses:

a   Θ [------]
       G [------]⸗[---] G

b   Θ *Τεισίας*
       G *῎Ωαθεν*   G

G(*orgoneion*) *seals*. From the best-attested Class III–IV die, which was used also
on **25**, **51**, **62**, and **70**, and possibly on **26** and **48**. Large head (height 0.85 cm.)
with coarse features and bushy hair falling just below ear level. No trace of
snakes. Diam. of field 1.0 cm. The die is distinguished most readily by a
longish, straight cut that separates cheek and hair on the right.

Section-letter. Incuse field 0.7–0.75 cm. square. Before cleaning, the section-
letter was completely hidden by patination and thus escaped Meletopoulos,
who, however, deserves credit for recognizing the gorgoneion beneath.

Text a. The existence of an erased inscription is implied by the diagonal
striations at the right and by a number of short, straight disturbances in the

surface, which seem too numerous to have all been caused by corrosion. Only one of the latter, however, is clear enough to be included in our text: apparently the tail of an erased diagonal in line 2 about one centimeter to the right of the last text. The others cannot be positively distinguished from natural pittings, for which corrosion is responsible, or from accidental scratches. The striations at the right suggest that the entire middle of the pinakion had been filed or scraped and then polished with abrasives to remove all striations from the inscribed area.

22 (Figs. 40–41)   Athens, Peiraeus, Archaeological Museum, A. N. Meleto-poulos Collection. I. A. Meletopoulos, *Polemon* 3 (1947–48), 37, and pl. Β΄, no. 1 (photograph before cleaning).

Left fragment. Recently stripped to bare metal. L. 4.6 cm., w. 2.1 cm. maximum to 1.9 cm. at right, th. 0.18 cm. at left to 0.08 cm. at right.

Two or more uses:

a   Β   Εὐ[– – – –
         Ⓖ   [– – – – –

b   Δ   ’Ολυμπ[– – –
         Ⓖ   ’Αναγ[υράσιος

G(*orgoneion*) *seal.* Large head with coarse features and smooth, long hair that gradually tapers into snakes. Diam. 1.05 cm. The die may be the one used for the seals on **59, 63, 65,** and **66.**

Section-letters. The relief of a flattened beta is plainly visible under the later delta (incuse field, ca. 0.85 cm. square). I assume that the section-letter was not altered until after the first use.

23 (Figs. 42–43)   Paris, Cabinet des Médailles. Anonymous gift. L. Robert, *Coll. Froehner* I, 10, no. 10r (text *b* and measurements). S. Dow, *BCH* 87 (1963), 672, and fig. 4 (photograph before cleaning).

Complete. Broken in two. Recently freed of much of the green patina. L. 11.5 cm., w. 2.2 cm., th. 0.15–0.20 cm. fairly even.

Two uses visible:

a   Θ   [– – –^{ca. 8}– – –] $\overline{\mathit{III}}$ [.]ς   Ⓖ
         Ⓖ   [– –^{ca. 5}–]‖[–^{ca. 5}–] $\frac{1}{2}$ Λ|

b   Ζ: Εὐκολίων: Πυρρά(κου)   Class VI
     Ἀναγυρά(σιος)

G(orgoneion) seals. Heads with pointed, V-shaped jowls; similar in size and shape to the gorgoneia on **28** and possibly from the same die. The seals were quite thoroughly erased together with text *a* and the original section-letter, thus converting the pinakion to a stampless Class VI pinakion in its final use.

Text a. The last owner served as bouleutes in 367/6, [*E*]ὐκολίων Πυρράκο (Ἀναγυράσιος), *Hesperia* 11 (1942), 233, no. 42, line 18,[4] and was probably the Εὐκο[– – –]Ἀναγ[υράσιος who appears in one of the "judicial catalogues pertaining to liturgies," *IG* II², 1928, lines 35–36, dating to approximately the late 380s.[5] As Dow observed, the rarity of names in Εὐκο– permits Εὐκο[λίων] to be restored in II², 1928, with substantial confidence. For other occurrences of the name Eukolion, see *IG* II², 10 B, col. II, line 8; and *AthMitt* 67 (1942), 19–20, no. 19, lines 13–19.

24 (Fig. 44)   Athens, Peiraeus, Archaeological Museum, A. N. Meletopoulos Collection. I. A. Meletopoulos, *Polemon* 3 (1947–48), 37, and pl. B′, no. 2 (photograph before cleaning).

Left end. Recently stripped to bare metal. L. 2.6 cm., w. 2.2 cm., th. 0.2 cm. at left to 0.15 cm. at right.

Two or more uses:

a   Ε̣ Ṃ[– – –
     Ⓖ K[– – –

b   Ζ Ε ͳͽ[– – –
     Ⓖ Φ ͱ[– – –

G(orgoneion) seal. From a die similar to that on **21**, **25**, and others but differing in respect to the size of the monster's head (here 0.9 cm. high in incuse field

---

4. The restoration in the *editio princeps*, [*Λ*]υκολίων *Π. Α.*, is corrected in *Hesperia, Index to Vols. XI–XX* (Princeton: American School of Classical Studies at Athens, 1968), 79, 121.
   5. On the basis of the dated catalogues of this type: *IG* II², 1930 and 1931 = 383/2 B.C., and 1929 = 380/79 B.C. (see *Hesperia* 15 [1946], 160–161, no. 17). D. M. Lewis has proposed that all these documents come from a single monument ("Notes on Attic Inscriptions," *BSA* 49 [1954], 37, no. 10).

of 1.0 cm.), its bushier hair, and more pointed chin. This is the only positive occurrence of the die, but see **41**.

25 (Fig. 45)   Athens, National Museum, Inv. Bronze 8141. S. Bruck, *AthMitt* 19 (1894), 208, no. 1. (*IG* II 5, 907b; II², 1873)
   Left end. Recently stripped to bare metal. L. 3.8 cm., w. 2.1 cm., th. 0.18 cm. at left to 0.08 cm. at right
   Two or more uses:

a   ? [– – – –
     G [– – – –

b   Z Αἰσχ[– – –
     G ’Επιμ[– – –

G(orgoneion) seal. From the same die as on **21**, **51**, and others.

Of the original stamped section-letter only evidence of its erasure remains: a slight concavity in the surface of the upper left corner and a split in the upper edge, both caused by the obliteration of the letter with a blunt tool.
   The slanting line to the right of the section-letter and seal marks a sharp falling off in thickness caused by erasure of the earlier text or texts.

26 (Fig. 46)   Athens, National Museum, Inv. Bronze 8134. Unpublished.
   Left end. Recently stripped to bare metal. L. 2.7 cm., w. 2.5 cm. maximum, th. 0.2 cm. at left to 0.15 cm. at right.
   Three uses evident:

a   ? [– – –
     G [– – –

b   B [– – –
     G [– – –

c   E Δι[– – –   Class VI?
     G ΦΕ[– – –

G(orgoneion) seal. Possibly from the same die as on the preceding pinakion; see **21**.

The substantial split in the left edge combines with a shallow depression in the corner under the later section-letters to show that the original section-letter had been stamped and later erased like the original section-letter of **25**.

Text c. The size of the section-letter is suggestive of a Class VI use.

27 (Fig. 47) Basel, Antikenmuseum, Inv. 1906.774. Ex coll. Vischer. W. Vischer, *Kleinigkeiten*, 15, no. 3, and pl. II, 64 = *Kleine Schriften* II, 286, no. 3, and pl. XV, 64 (drawing before cleaning). J. J. Bernoulli, *Katalog*, 189, no. 1084a. (*IG* II, 908; II², 1875).

Left fragment. Recently stripped to bare metal. L. 4.3 cm., w. 2.2 cm. maximum, th. 0.2 cm. at left to 0.1 cm. at break.

Two or more uses:

a   ⊡ I[– – – –
   ⊙ [.]I[– – –

b   Ἐπίκτ[ητος   Class VI
   Ἐρχι[εύς

G(*orgoneion*) *seal.* Stamped sideways, chin pointing to the right. Probably from the same die as the gorgoneia on **28**. Obliteration of the seal by the time of the last use shows that the pinakion was ultimately used as a stampless Class VI pinakion.

Text a. This may combine traces from more than one earlier use. The depressed and disturbed surface in the upper left-hand corner attests to the original presence of a section-letter stamped in relief. Faint lines forming the top, left side, and bottom of a square around the depressed area may be edges of an erased incuse square or may belong to a later inscribed section-letter such as an epsilon. These faint disturbances in the metal, emphasized or distorted perhaps by coloration of the patina, were read and drawn by Vischer as constituting an inscribed zeta.

Text b. The section-letter for the last use may have been placed at the right of the owner's name (as on **38** and the Class VI pinakia **126–128**), or, since room for a letter is available at the left, a section-letter may have been omitted altogether (as apparently on **47**).

To Vischer's *ΕΠΙΚ/ΕΡΧ* we may add vestiges of letters from the break at the right: a perpendicular in line 2, and, at the right of line 1, a vertical intersected by a horizontal, which leads to the restoration Ἐπίκτ[ητος, the only male name in Ἐπικτ– attested at Athens.

28 (Fig. 48)   Athens, National Museum, Inv. Bronze 8062. Found "in Athens." A. S. Rousopoulos, "Σκεύη δικαστικά," *ArchEph* 1862, 304, no. 380, and pl. 46.1 (a rough sketch). A. Dumont, *RA*² 17 (1868), 145–146. Cf. S. Bruck, *AthMitt* 19 (1894), 203, no. 4. (Girard, no. 4; *IG* II, 888; II², 1852)

Complete. Broken in half. Clean, brown metal. L. 11.1 cm., w. 2.15 cm., th. 0.22 cm. even.

Apparently, only one use. No indication of erasure or earlier letters. Except for several horizontal scratches at the left, which do not have the character of erasure striations, the surface is perfectly smooth and undisturbed.

K̲		before inscription
Ⓖ		Ⓖ

Γ Πεδιεὺς : Θεοξέ(νου)		name added
Ⓖ ʼΕλευσίνιος		Ⓖ

G(*orgoneion*) *seals*. Stamped sideways, chins pointing slightly upward and to the left.[6] The die is characterized by the pointed, V-shape formation of the creature's jowls and the hair rendered in two short, smooth bands. Diam. ca. 0.95 cm. The gorgoneia on **23** and **27** are similar and come from the same die or a closely related die or dies.

Dumont observed that the gamma section-letter was inscribed in a depression in the metal and suggested that the depression was caused by the effacement of an earlier "marque." Upon closer inspection, this "marque" has the unmistakable profile of a kappa in flattened relief; above and to the right of the kappa are lines from the upper and right edges of the incuse square that originally surrounded the letter. As stated above, there is absolutely no

---

6. Because of their orientation the seals have been notoriously misidentified. Rousopoulos interpreted and drew them as representing heads of Athena, whereas Dumont thought that they must be male heads facing left. Finally, Bruck confirmed that the heads are indeed helmeted heads of Athena facing right. In all subsequent references to this pinakion Bruck's word has not been questioned.

evidence for an earlier name that could be associated with the earlier section-letter. The kappa, stamped with the seals before the pinakion was assigned to an owner, was therefore erased and replaced with the gamma when the pinakion was finally issued and inscribed. Note that the vertical of the gamma has the same bent character (caused by careless alignment of two contiguous strikings of a short, straight punch) as many strokes in the owner's name.

The patronymic can be restored Θεοξέ(νου) or Θεοξε(νίδου), but the latter is much less common, and a Θεόξ[εν]ος 'Ελευ(σίνιος) appears as *symproedros* in the temple inventory of the Athenian cleruchs on Samos, 346/5 B.C. (C. Michel, *Recueil d'Inscriptions Grecques* [Brussels: Lamertin, 1900], 678, no. 832, line 13). The cleruch may well have been the father (or the son) of our Pedieus.

FIRST USE WITH AN INSCRIBED SECTION-LETTER

29 (Fig. 49) formerly Berlin, Staatliche Museen, Inv. Bronze 6315. "Im jahre 1873 von Lambros in Athen angekauft" (Curtius). C. Curtius, *RhM* 31 (1876), 284, no. 3 (drawing before cleaning). U. Koehler, *IG* II, 918 (*exscripsit Frankelius*). Cleaned, redrawn, and described by S. Bruck, *AthMitt* 19 (1894), 205, no. 12. (Girard, no. 39; *IG* II², 1891 with corrigenda)

Complete, although much eaten away by bronze disease at the upper and right edges. A number of small, cup-like depressions on the surface were presumably caused by individual pockets of disease. Cleaned to bare metal. L. 9.4 cm., w. 2.0 cm.; from the photograph it seems that the pinakion was exceptionally thin, say, ca. 0.1 to 0.05 cm. (Note that the lowest bar of the epsilon in line 2 pierced all the way through the metal.)

Apparently, only one use. Not the slightest suggestion of erasure or earlier letters can be detected on the excellent photograph.

Θ [Π]ολύμνηστο[ς]
Ⓖ   Φλυε (ύς) Ⓖ

G(*orgoneion*) seals.[7] Same die as used on **50** and probably **47**. Large, wide head with coarse features. Two prominent pairs of confronting snakes' heads, one pair above the crown of the hair, the other growing directly from the chin. Diam. of field 1.0–1.05 cm.

---

7. Curtius misidentified the left-hand seal as an owl seal. The seal at the right was not noticed until Bruck had the pinakion cleaned, but Bruck admitted that even with a magnifying glass he was unable to distinguish what the seals represented. The acknowledged expert on pinakia seals, he was followed by Kirchner. In point of fact, the correct identification of the left-hand seal, by Fränkel, appeared in *IG* II.

The theta section-letter was stamped with the same ring punch used for the other circular letters in the text and thus was clearly added with the owner's name.

Like **36**, the present pinakion is about a centimeter short and quite thin. The right-hand gorgoneia on both pinakia make it certain that their original lengths did not extend further to the right.

This is one of two pinakia belonging to Polymnestos, son of Ari(—?) of Phyla (for the patronymic, see **124**). It and **124** were purchased together and must have come from the same grave.

30 (Figs. 50–51) Athens, National Museum, Inv. Bronze 16308. Unknown provenience. Unpublished.

Complete. Broken in three pieces. Cleaned to brown metal; corrosion has roughened and pitted the surface. L. 11.5 cm., w. 2.1 cm., th. 0.18 cm. even.

Two uses:

a $[.]:EY[.]E[..]|[--]$
         ⓖ $Κο\lambdaωνῆ(θεν)$ ⓖ

b   Ͱ $Β\lambdaεψίδης$
         $Τειθράσιος$ ⓖ

G(*orgoneion*) *seals*. Exceptionally large head and surrounding field (diam. 1.1 cm.). The locks of hair terminate in a pair of snakes which are knotted under the chin. A second pair of snakes grows out of the hair at the crown of the head. The seals on **37** are apparently from the same die. The left-hand seal was largely erased with the earlier name.

Text a. There being in the upper left corner no traces either of a stamped letter or of the kind of emphatic erasure required for the obliteration of a stamped letter, we may be confident that a stamped section-letter was never added to this pinakion. No positive traces of an inscribed section-letter are visible under the later section-letter either,[8] but the former existence of such a letter is attested by the faint interpunct of two horizontal dashes between the later section-letter and the beginning of the owners' names. Interpuncts occasionally separated inscribed section-letters from the names that follow, and this one is too faint to belong to any but an erased earlier use, that is, use *a.*

8. The photograph, which shows two lines curving down and out from the middle vertical of the later eta section-letter, is somewhat misleading in this respect. These "lines" are random configurations in the rough surface of the metal and have nothing to do with letters from either text.

Text b. The name Blepsides is new to Greek prosopography. Our Blepsides may be related to Blepyros, son of Phyleides, of Teithra, who was active in the third quarter of the fourth century (*PA*, 2882 with *Hesperia* 31 [1962], 402, no. 3, lines 13–14).

31 (Fig. 52)   Athens, National Museum, Karapanos Collection Inv. 1198. A. A. Papagiannopoulos-Palaios, "Χαλκοῦν ἐνεπίγραφον πινάκιον ἐν τῇ συλλογῇ Σταθάτου," *Polemon* 4 (1949), 79, note 8.[9]

Whole. Stripped to bare bronze. The metal is slightly bent along the upper left edge within the area of the omega. L. 10.9 cm., w. 2.2 cm., th. 0.17 cm. even.

Apparently only one use:

A Σωταιρίδης   Ⓖ
Ⓖ Σωσάν(δρου) : Πειραιεύ(ς)

G(orgoneion) seals. From the same die used for the gorgoneion of **32**. Small, very finely featured heads with thick, bushy hair and within an exceptionally small field, diam., 0.85 cm. Two snakes knotted under the chin. On **32** it is seen that they extend down from the ends of the hair and that there is a pair of confronting snakes' heads above the head. The left-hand seal is positioned at the middle of the left end, as also on **33** and **34**.

There are no convincing suggestions of earlier letters or of any erasure. The vertical extending up from the seal at the left seems clearly to be a misstrike in the inscribing of the alpha section-letter, whose left diagonal is itself composed of two imperfectly aligned strokes. I assume that the lower stroke of the diagonal was struck out of alignment to the left in order to avoid cutting through the middle of the face of the gorgoneion seal.

The main interest of this piece is the high position of the left-hand gorgoneion, which precluded the addition of a stamped section-letter in the upper corner and makes it clear that the pinakion was manufactured when stamped section-letters had been discontinued. The seal did not, of course, leave proper room for an inscribed section-letter either, and one wonders if the pinakion was originally intended to receive a section-letter of any kind. (Whether or not a section-letter was added would be immaterial, inasmuch

---

9. Papagiannopoulos-Palaios' conjecture that the pinakion might have come from Karapanos' excavations at Dodona is groundless. The Karapanos collection contains many inscriptions from other localities, and the pinakion, moreover, is not mentioned by Karapanos in any of his Dodona publications.

as a pinakion need not have been inscribed until some years after it was manufactured and stamped; **32**, which was stamped with the same gorgone-ion die, may not have received a section-letter in a total of three uses.) Alterna-tively, however, it may have been that once stamped section-letters were discontinued in favor of inscribed ones, less attention was paid to the posi-tioning of gorgoneia at the left and that the gorgoneion at the left of this pinak-ion and at the left of **33** and **34** simply happened to be struck higher than usual.

PRESENCE OF SECTION-LETTER IN THE FIRST USE UNCERTAIN

32 (Figs. 53–54) Athens, Stoa of Attalos, Agora Excavations Inv. B 242. Excavated in 1935 from Area D/9; modern context. Unpublished.

Left half. Cleaned to bare metal. L. 6.3 cm., w. 2.4 cm., th. 0.2 cm. at left to 0.15 cm. at right.

Apparently three uses. Except for the slightly tapering thickness, evidence of erasure is slight.

a 　　　[– – – – – – –

　　ⓖ [. .]Σ[– – – –

b 　　　[‾‾‾nomen patro-‾‾

　　ⓖ α̣[.]έϝο[‾‾dem.‾‾

c 　　　Εὐθύμα[χος

　　ⓖ Ἐρυξιμ[άχου

G(orgoneion) seal. From the same die as the small, bushy-haired gorgoneia of **31**. The erased surface at the beginning of line 2 continues over into the lower right part of the seal, thus linking the seal positively to the earlier uses.

Text a. Unmistakable traces of an erased sigma within and between the less erased epsilon of text *b* and the xi of text *c* imply this use earlier than text *b*.

Text b. Line 2 presumably concludes a patronymic that began in line 1 and terminates –α̣[γ]έϝο(υ) or –α̣[ξ]έϝο(υ).

Absence of section-letter. In line 1 all traces of the names of texts *a* and *b* have been erased and polished away, making it conceivable that an inscribed section-letter or letters was erased away with them. Since the surface above the 'gorgoneion seal is smoother and looks less disturbed than the surface toward the right of the line, however, I am inclined to think that the area above the seal was left vacant in all uses. I doubt, too, that a section-letter would have been added at the right of the owner's name in the first use. Section-letters at the right occur in later uses of Class III pinakia, that is, in uses belonging to the Class VI period (see **38**), but none are attested from early, stamped uses. Because texts *b* and *c* are later, dating possibly from the Class VI period, chances are somewhat greater that one or both of them could have had a section-letter at the right. Nevertheless, these uses, too, may have lacked section-letters.

33 (Fig. 55)   Athens, Stoa of Attalos, Pnyx Excavations Inv. M–2. Excavated from mixed context below the great polygonal wall on the Pnyx, 1930–1931. G. R. Davidson and D. B. Thompson, *Pnyx Small Objects* I, 13, and fig. 12, no. 2.

Left end. Cleaned to bare bronze. L. 5.0 cm., w. 2.1 cm.–1.9 cm., th. 0.2 cm. maximum to 0.05 cm. at break.

Two or more uses. Considerable erasure evidenced by the tapering thickness and the partial effacement of the gorgoneion seal.

a ⒢ *ⵤ*[– – – –
[– – – – –

b Θ *Πάμφι*[λος   Class VI
Πανσί[– – –

G(*orgoneion*) *seal.* Large round head with an exceptionally prominent protruding tongue like the gorgoneion of **56**. Stamped at the middle of the left end.

I list this fragment here because the position of its seal relates it to **31** and **34** and because, as with **32**, there are no traces of a section-letter from its first use (or uses). The pinakion has been heavily erased so that the possibility of an earlier section-letter inscribed into the top of the gorgoneion seal cannot be ruled out. But a slight diagonal (just touching the upper left-hand corner of the initial pi of text *b*) does seem to have survived from an earlier inscription, and it is located just to the right of where such an earlier section-letter would have been located. Though there are uncertainties, this fragment provides our best indication that pinakia with gorgoneia stamped at the middle of their left ends may not have been intended to receive section-letters.

I realize that the fragment could be interpreted as a right end of a pinakion that was stamped with its gorgoneia upside down (as on **28**, **52**, and **71**) and that was subsequently reversed in reuse so as to become a left end (as were **54** and **59**). But, apart from the evidence of **31** and **34**, which prove that gorgoneia were sometimes added at the middle of left ends of Class III pinakia, inverted seals and the inversion of pinakia were rather exceptional phenomena, and chances of both occurring together are not very great.

34 (Figs. 56–57)   Paris, Cabinet des Médailles, Froehner Collection Inv. 609. "Πειραιῶς, 1872."[10] Ex coll. Rayet. O. Rayet, *AnnAssEtGr* 1878, 205 (with a drawing of Side B). L. Robert, *Coll. Froehner* I, 8, and pl. VII, no. 10d (photograph of Side B before cleaning). (*IG* II, 883; II², 1847)

Whole. Both sides recently cleaned of a heavily encrusted patination. Before cleaning there was no reason to suspect that the pinakion was opisthographic. L. 11.0 cm., w. 1.9 cm., th. 0.2 cm. at ends to 0.15 cm. in the middle.

Three (or four) uses evident:

a	? Ⓖ [- - - - - - -] [- - - - - -] Ⓖ		Side A	

b	Γ	O[.]ΛOK[. .] ₹ Σ ἐ[κ Κε]ρᾳ[μ]έ(ων)?	Side A Class VI

c	B	Πίτταλος Προσπάλτιος	Side B Class VI

G(orgoneion) seals. Struck sideways with chins pointing to the left. Still visible are the sunken eyes of the gorgoneion on the right and the relief of the two snakes springing out of the crown of the one on the left. As on **31** and **33**, the left-hand seal is stamped toward the middle of the end.

Text a. The left-hand seal must have been effaced and in its present state before the (unerased) gamma section-letter was inscribed over it. Thus, a use before the addition of the gamma is assured. I have been unable to determine whether the original inscription was provided with a section-letter. As on **31** and **33**, the room available was not sufficient for a section-letter of normal size, and this may indicate that a letter was not intended or added. On the other hand, a fine, vertical groove extending up from the vertical of

10. This is the label, presumably Rayet's, glued on the back of the pinakion, whence the entry in Froehner's inventory reproduced by Robert: "Trouvée au Pirée en 1877" [*sic*].

the gamma of text *b* might survive from an earlier section-letter (which intruded into the seal), but it could easily be illusory, or at best a meaningless line caused by erasure or by the inscription of the gamma.

Text b. The name was inscribed with comparatively wide spacing between letters, as one sees from the space between the omicron (?) and the kappa at the middle of line 1 and in the spacing of the restored demotic.

   Line 1. The nomen may have been rare, since I have been unable to discover any attested name that will satisfactorily fit the remains. The strongest possibility is $Φ[ι]λοκ[λέ]ης$, with an exceptionally wide spacing for the iota, but since there are no traces of a phi's vertical, the first letter would seem to have been a theta or omicron rather than a phi. The diagonal in position 2 seems clearly to be an erasure striation and should not be read as part of the second letter.

   Side B is pitted throughout and contains a few tantalizing suggestions (most notably a possible diagonal under the omicron in line 2) of an inscription anterior to text *c*. These possible traces, however, are not concrete or sharp enough to ensure a fourth text and may be accidental configurations of pittings and marks caused during erasure of the other side, as I think but cannot prove they are.

Text c. Line 1. Rayet's $Θετταλός$, repeated in both editions of the Attic corpus and *PA*, was corrected by Froehner (*apud* Robert). $Πίτταλος$ is rare and, to my knowledge, known only from Athens. There it appears as the name of a public physician of the fifth century: Aristophanes *Acharnians* 1032, 1222, and *Wasps* 1432. An equivalent, $Πίταλλος$, has been discovered inscribed on the retaining wall of the Pnyx (*Hesperia* 1 [1931], 214). The name can be restored in a prytany decree of 235/4: $Πιττα[--](Πρασιεύς)$ (*Hesperia* 11 [1942], 243, no. 47, line 54), although other restorations, e.g. Pape-Benseler's $Πιττακός$, are possible.

35 (Figs. 58–59)   Athens, National Museum, Inv. Bronze 13347 B. "Aus dem Peiraeus." Ex coll. University of Athens. L. Ross, *AllLitZeit* 1837, Intelligenzblätter Nos. 84–85, 689–690, and 710, no. 6. Whence Ross, *Demen von Attika*, 98, no. 174. (Girard, no. 35; *IG* II, 880; II², 1844)

   Whole, except for missing lower right corner. Recently stripped of patination. L. 11.9 cm., w. 2.1–2.2 cm., th. fairly even, 0.18–0.20 cm.

   Apparently two uses:

a   ? $[---\overset{\text{ca. 10}}{-----}]\overset{\vee}{=}\underline{E}\underline{Σ}?$ ⓖ

   ⓖ $[-\overset{\text{ca. 4}}{--}-]\backslash[---]$

b   B   Διονύσιος : Κλεμά (—?)

    Ⓖ Τρικορύ(σιος)   Ⓖ

G(orgoneion) seals. Large heads nearly filling the ca. 1.0 cm. fields. The seals were weakly impressed and the one at the left is double-struck, so that no details of profile or facial relief are preserved. Ross did not detect the gorgoneion at the left, which, before cleaning, was nearly invisible.

Text a. Were it not for the deep right-hand half diagonal within the epsilon of the final name, I would be tempted to doubt whether the pinakion had been reused. All of the other possible suggestions of earlier letters could be regarded as accidental lines formed by scratches and the pitting of the surface. There are no indications of an earlier, inscribed section-letter under the present one.

Text b. The patronymic, however restored, is the only attested Athenian name in Κλε(ι)μα–. The name has been completed Κλε(ι)μά(χου) in all previous editions and *PA*, although Bechtel also gives Κλείμανδρος. For other Trikorysioi named Dionysios, all from the third or second century B.C., see *PA*, 19 (*IG* II², 7542) and *PA*, 4252 (with Sundwall, *Nachträge*, 38, and *Hesperia* 10 [1941], 278, no. 74, lines 29–30).

36 (Fig. 60)   London, British Museum, Inv. Bronze 330. E. L. Hicks, *Manual*, 202, no. 119.3 = Hicks-Hill, *Manual*, 286, no. 151.3. H. B. Walters, *Catalogue*, 49, no. 330. (*IG* II, 901; II², 1865)

Whole. Heavily incrusted green patina; owing to the highly mineralized condition of the bronze, cleaning could not be undertaken. L. 9.7 cm., w. 2.25 cm., th. ca. 0.05 cm.

Two or more uses. The sole evidence of erasure is the obliterated condition of the seals.

a   ?   [– – – –]

    Ⓖ [– – – –]   Ⓖ

b   E   Ἀρχίλοχος   Class VI

      Φαληρεύς

G(orgoneion) seals. Both almost completely effaced, allowing the last use, with a large section-letter, to be classified as a stampless Class VI use. Hicks noted "an imperfect stamp" at the left only.

37 (Fig. 61)   Athens, National Museum, Inv. Bronze 8123 and 8127. From a grave near Spata, the ancient deme of Erchia. A. S. Koumanoudes, *ArchEph*

1887, 53–54, no. 1, with a drawing. Cf. S. Bruck, *AthMitt* 19 (1894), 207, no. 21. (*IG* II 5, 878b; *IG* II², 1842)

Complete. Broken in two. Recently stripped to bare metal. The mottled surface and indistinct character of the letters at either side of the break may be the results of an earlier attempt to clean this area by heating (see **81**, which is known to have been subjected to such treatment). L. 12 cm., w. 2.0 cm., th. 0.15 cm. at right to 0.09 cm. at the middle.

Probably more than two uses:

a   ? [– – – – – – – –]

  Ⓖ [– – –$\overset{7-8}{-}$– – –] : $Ἀλωπε(κῆθεν)$ Ⓖ

b   A : $Τιμόδο[.]ος : Εὐπο(λέμου)$ Class VI
       $Ἐρχιεύς$

G(orgoneion) seals.[11] Of a large-headed variety (diam. of field 1.1 cm.); probably from the same die as the seals on **30**. The seal at the left is almost completely effaced, but can still be identified at the top by the remains of a gorgoneion's wavy hairline. One suspects that such thorough erasure of the left-hand gorgoneion was caused by erasure on more than one occasion and that there were therefore probably more than two uses.

Text a. The remains of the demotic, preceded by an interpunct, read $ΛΛΟΓΕ$. The partial erasure of the epsilon, which was inscribed into the seal at the right, accounts for the seal's partially obliterated condition.

Text b. The damaged condition at either side of the break precludes identification of the crucial sixth letter of the nomen. From the possible traces—a horizontal, beneath which two crossing diagonals and possibly a vertical along the break—one can read a tau (with vertical off center to the left), kappa, or chi. No Timodotos, Timodokos, or Timodochos is listed in the standard prosopographies. The letter must be left unrestored here and in the restoration of the patronymic on **16**, a Class II pinakion last owned by Timodo[.]os' father and doubtless found in an adjacent grave.

38 (Figs. 62–63)   Toronto, Royal Ontario Museum, Inv. 939.42. Purchased in Athens in the 1930s. S. Dow, *BCH* 87 (1963), 674–675, with fig. 5.

---

11. Koumanoudes noted only the seal at the right, which he interpreted as representing a half-moon. The seal was correctly identified by Bruck, who also pointed out but was unable to identify the seal at the left.

Whole. Cleaned to bare metal. L. 13.0 cm., w. 2.2 cm. at right to 2.7 cm. maximum, th. 0.09 cm. at left to 0.05 cm. at the middle.

Three or more uses. Distorted shape and distended length—exceptional by about 1 cm.—attest an extreme amount of erasure, possibly on more than the two occasions required by three uses.

a   ? $[----\overset{10-12}{---}-]O$

Ⓖ $[-\overset{ca.5}{--}-]P[\overset{ca.3}{---}]O\Sigma$ Ⓖ

b   Ⱶ $T[\iota]\mu\acute{o}\sigma\tau\rho\alpha\tau o\varsigma$ Class III or VI

Ⓖ? $['I]\kappa\alpha\rho\iota\epsilon\acute{v}\varsigma$ Ⓖ?

c $\mathring{A}\rho\iota\sigma\tau\acute{\iota}\omega\nu$ Class VI

$T\iota\mu o(—?):\Pi\epsilon\rho\gamma\alpha(\sigma\mathring{\eta}\theta\epsilon\nu)$ B

G(*orgoneion*) *seals.* The one at the right is fairly well preserved and is of the long-haired variety, with a pair of snakes knotted under the chin (diam. of field, 1.0—1.1 cm.). To judge from the dimensions and the character of the creature's eyes and jowls, this seal and the one on **57** would seem to have come from the same die. Although the left-hand gorgoneion has been almost totally obliterated, unmistakable traces of the jowl and hair profiles are visible.

Text a. These readings are new.

Text b. As read by Dow.

Text c. The pinakion is most notable for the positioning of the last section-letter at the right to avoid the poorly erased remains of the earlier section-letter in the upper left-hand corner. Section-letters at the right occur, not uncommonly, on Class VI pinakia (cf. **126–128**).

Another Aristion of Pergase, probably a contemporary of the pinakion's last owner, is $\mathring{A}\rho\iota\sigma\tau\acute{\iota}\omega\nu$ $\mathring{A}\rho\iota\sigma\tau o\nu\acute{\iota}[\kappa o\nu]$ *Π.*, known from a catalogue of uncertain character, *IG* II², 2401, line 9, *post med. s. IV a.* Either he or our owner is to be identified with the Aristion Pergasethen who appears as a lampadephoros on a herm base from Rhamnous, *IG* II², 3105, line 31, *post med. s. IV a.*

39 (Figs. 64–65)   Newcastle upon Tyne, The Greek Museum. Purchased from Sotheby Sale, December 11, 1967 (cf. **91**). B. B. Shefton, "The Greek Museum, University of Newcastle upon Tyne," *Archaeological Reports* 16 (1969–1970), 58, no. 10, with fig. 10 (drawing and profile).

Left four-fifths. Encrusted patination cleaned from surface. Heavily blistered by internal corrosion. L. 7.8 cm., w. 2.2–2.4 cm., th. ca. 0.25 cm.

Two or more uses:

a   Ι   [.]ℵ[– – –
     Ⓖ [– – – – – –]𝖎𝖎𝖎[– –

b   Β   Διϱολις
     Ⓖ? Κρωπίδ(ης)   Class III or VI

G(*orgoneion*) *seal.* Small, finely featured head, diam. ca. 0.6 cm. The seal was apparently subjected to some erasure prior to the last use.

Text b. To my knowledge, the name Διϱολις is without parallel or cognates in Greek prosopography. Hence, before it was cleaned, one was tempted to read line 1 as Δίπολις, which would be composed of regular elements and is listed by Pape-Benseler as a place-name. The cast sent me after cleaning, however, has confirmed that in all probability the circular third letter should be read as a rho. Although the rho has a larger loop than the rho in line 2, the loop is complete, perfectly round (more so than is apparent from the photograph), and seems not to have been accidentally formed by partially erased strokes from an earlier text.

The pinakion may have been last used in its present, broken length.

40 (Figs. 66–67) Basel, Antikenmuseum, Inv. 1906.775. Ex coll. Vischer. W. Vischer, *Kleinigkeiten*, 15, no. 3, and pl. II, 65 = *Kleine Schriften* II, 287, no. 3, and pl. XV, 65. Cf. S. Bruck, *AthMitt* 19 (1894), 206. J. J. Bernoulli, *Katalog*, 189, no. 1084 a. (*IG* II, 922; II², 1896)

Left fragment. Recently stripped to bare metal. L. 4.8 cm., w. 2.0 cm., th. 0.2 cm. at left to 0.05 cm. at right.

Three or more uses:

a   ? [– – –
     Ⓖ [– – –

b   Ι: ℵ⅀⅂̄Ε[– – –   Class VI
     Κολλυ[τεύς

c   Κ   Φείδυλ[λος   Class VI
     Ἰωνίδη[ς

G(orgoneion) seal. Completely erased except for the left profile. Bruck noted but could not identify the seal from Vischer's drawing.

It is obvious that the seal had been erased before use *b* since the erasure that removed the seal was very thorough, involved polishing, and therefore must have preceded the unpolished striations of the more superficial erasure of text *b*.

Line 2 (texts *b* and *c*). At the right, just before the break, are the superimposed strokes of three letters: an eta, belonging to text *c*; under it an unerased omicron; and within both a faint, erased diagonal that must belong to the upsilon in the demotic of text *b*. That the unerased omicron represents a slip in the inscribing of text *c* is clear from its 0.5 cm. outside diameter, which is identical to the outside diameter of the ring punch used for the other circular letters in text *c*. Apparently the letterer of text *c* inscribed ʼΙωνίδος and then corrected it to ʼΙωνίδης.

41 (Figs. 68–69). London, British Museum, Inv. Bronze 1905.6–7.4. "Erwerbungen des British Museum in Jahre 1905," *AA* 1906, 247, no. 21. (*IG* II², Addenda, 1864a)

Left fragment. Recently cleaned to bare bronze. L. 4.2 cm., w. 2.0 cm., th, 0.2 cm. at left to 0.1 cm. at right.

Three or more uses:

a   B [– – –
      Ⓖ [– – –

b   Η *A*⧚[.]∥[– – –   Class VI?
      Ⓖ [<u>ca. 3</u>]∥[– – –

c   E Φιλοχάρ[ης   Class VI
         Ἀχα[ρνεύς

G(orgenion) seal. To judge from the preserved lower profile of the face, the seal was possibly struck from the same die as used on **24**.

Text a. This may not be from the earliest use. Its large beta section-letter intrudes into the gorgoneion seal, perhaps indicating that the seal was no longer respected and that this earliest visible use was inscribed already in the stampless Class VI period.

Text c. An alternative restoration, Φιλοχαρ[ίδης, is possible, but unattested from Athens. A daughter of Philochares of Acharnai is known from a statue dedicated *med. s. IV a. (IG* II², 4024), but the distinct possibility that Philochares was the name of more than one demesman of Acharnai in the fourth century is underlined by two entries for Acharnai in the bouleutic list of 303/2 (*Hesperia* 37 [1968], 12 and 14): [Φι?]λοχάρης (line 85) and Φιλοχα[ρ– –] (line 94). If the fragment was a surface find, and not from a grave, it could have belonged to either of these men before it broke and was discarded.

42 (Figs. 70–72)   Athens, National Museum, Inv. Bronze 8137. Unpublished.
    Left end. Recently stripped to bare metal. L. 3.3 cm., w. 2.3 cm., th. 0.15 cm. at left to 0.10 cm. at right.
    Three or more uses:

a   B   Ko ⫽ [– – –
        © ”Ọαθ[εν– –

b   Θ   ᾽Επι[– – –   Class VI
           Εὐω[νυμεύς

c   K: Λυσ[– – –   Class VI
           ΦΕΝ[– – –

G(*orgoneion*) *seal.* All details obscured.

    Visible are three virtually unerased texts. I suspect that there may have been more. In any case, the centered position of the section-letter of use *b* shows that, by the penultimate use at least, the pinakion was being reused as a Class VI pinakion.

Text a. Line 2. The initial letter may, of course, have been an omega, the tails of which are no longer visible. But there is evidence that the demotic as given above is possible for the fourth century (see S. Dow, "The Attic Demes Oa and Oe," *AJP* 84 [1963], 171).

Text b. Note the inordinately small theta and omega, from the same ring-punch.

Text c. Line 2. The readings seem certain, yet ΦΕΝ or ΦΕ(Ι)Ν are not found in any demotic, nor, to my knowledge, in any roots or terminations of attested Athenian names. Thus an uncommon patronymic, perhaps continued from the end of line 1, may be represented.

43 (Figs. 73–74)   Athens, National Museum, Inv. Bronze 8098. U. Koehler, *IG* II, 882. Cf. S. Bruck, *AthMitt* 19 (1894), 203, no. 2. (*IG* II², 1846)

Left end. Recently stripped to bare metal. L. 2.5 cm., w. 2.1 cm., th. 0.2 cm. at left to 0.18 cm. at break.

Two or more uses:

a   A [– – – –
     ⓖ A[– – –

b   B Εὐ[– – –
     ⓖ ΤⒾ[– – –

G(orgoneion) *seal.* Diam. of field, ca. 0.95 cm. The seal was noted by Koehler and was identified as a gorgoneion seal by Bruck.

44 (Fig. 75)   Athens, National Museum, Inv. Bronze 8086. P. Girard, *BCH* 2 (1878), 533, no. 11. (*IG* II, 911; II², 1881)

Left end. Recently stripped to bare metal. L. 2.3 cm., w. 2.2 cm., th. 0.13 cm. even.

Two or more uses:

a   ? Φ[– – –
     ⓖ Ε[– – –

b   Η ΑⒾ[– – –
     ⓖ Φ[– – –

G(orgoneion) *seal.* Exceptionally small, finely detailed head. Diam. of present field only 0.75 cm. The die does not appear on other surviving pinakia.

There are no visible traces of an earlier section-letter under the eta.

45 (Fig. 76)   Athens, Stoa of Attalos, Agora Excavations Inv. B 56. Excavated in 1932 from Area I/16. Unpublished.

Left end. Cleaned to bare metal. L. 3.2 cm., w. 2.3 cm., th. 0.13 cm. at left to 0.08 cm. at break.

Probably more than two uses. Subjected to much erasure, as seen from the heavy diagonal striations and tapering thickness.

a   Δ Ο[– – –
     ⓖ Ι[– – –

b   Ἀβρ[– – –   Class VI
         Κ[– – –

G(orgoneion) seal. Substantially erased by the final use.

The delta section-letter has been partially erased and thus belongs to a use prior to use *b*. The last use either had a section-letter inscribed at the right of the owner's name, as on **38**, or lacked a section-letter entirely, as apparently did the last use of **47**.

Class III or IV

LEFT END, SEAL INDISTINCT

46 (Fig. 77)   Athens, National Museum, Inv. Bronze 8133. Unpublished.
Left end. Recently stripped to bare metal. L. 3.0 cm., w. 2.1 cm., th. 0.25 cm. at left to 0.12 cm. at right.
Three or more uses:

a   ?   [– – –
⑤ [– – –

b   Ζ   [.] ≥ [– – –   Class VI?
[– – – – –

c   Μολ[– – –   Class VI
Γ: 'Ερχ[ιεύς

S(eal). All that remains is the lower left outline of a circular incuse field, which could conceivably have belonged to a triobol seal, but is more suggestive of a gorgoneion.

Since the erasure of the seal is almost total, whereas the zeta section-letter, which cuts into the top of the seal, is nearly intact, the seal must have been subjected to erasure before the zeta was added; hence my restoration of a use earlier than the use with the zeta.

RIGHT ENDS (OR EQUIVALENTS), WITH GORGONEION SEALS OF A
CLASS III–IV TYPE

From Class III pinakia or Class IV pinakia without secondary seals

47 (Fig 78)   Athens, Stoa of Attalos, Agora Excavations Inv. B 60. Excavated in 1932 from Area F/16; fourth- to early third-century B.C. context. Unpublished.

Broken into two nonjoining fragments, eaten away by corrosion at their upper edges. When found, that is, before cleaning, the left fragment was joined to and folded over the right one. Cleaned to bare metal. L. (estimated) ca. 8.0 cm., w. 2.2 cm. at right, th. 0.18 cm. at right to 0.1 cm. minimum.

Two or more uses:

a $----]$
     $----]$ Ⓖ

b   *Φ[ι]λοκύδης*   Class VI
     ⟨Ἀ⟩λω(πεκῆθεν)

G(*orgoneion*) *seal.* Although it has been fairly well erased, enough remains to show that it was probably struck from the same die as the gorgoneia on **29** and **50**.

The original left end, with the other seal, had broken or was cut off before the last inscription was added. We have, however, the full length of the pinakion in its last use and actually enough of the upper left corner to see that the last use probably lacked a section-letter. Some surface metal has flaked away from the upper left, but the flaking is not sufficiently deep—certainly not at its edges—nor sufficiently large in area to have removed all traces of an inscribed section-letter.

The demotic of text *b* is restored, by emendation, from ΛΞΩ. The right diagonal of the lambda is preserved along the break of the right fragment. The crossbar of the alpha was omitted.

48 (Fig. 79)   Athens, Stoa of Attalos, Agora Excavations Inv. B 700 (left fragment) and B 110 (right fragment). Found May 24, 1933, and April 24, 1933, respectively, in identical levels and contexts in the same Area, K/8. Context dated to second half of fourth century B.C. Unpublished.

Two nonjoining fragments with identically corroded surfaces on both sides, with the same character of lettering, and approximately the same widths and thicknesses. Cleaned to bare metal. B 700: l. 2.2 cm., w. 2.1 cm. at left, th. 0.18 cm. maximum at left tapering to right; B 110: l. 5.3 cm., w. 0.2 cm. maximum, th. 0.15 cm. at right to 0.08 cm. at left.

Two or more uses:

a | [− − − − − − −]
       [Ⓢ − − − − −]εύς   Ⓖ

b   [− − − − − −] ≅ μίδης   Class VI
       Γ [− − − − − −]

G(orgoneion) seal. In the area of the sigma of text *b*. The surprisingly well-preserved profile of the creature's hair is akin to the profile produced by the die used on **21**, **25**, and others. The seal may, therefore, also be from this die.

[S(eal)]. There are no positive remains of a seal on the left fragment. But unless the original left end had broken away, as on **47**, we can confidently assume a gorgoneion or triobol seal had been stamped in the area that is now occupied by the gamma section-letter of text *b*.

It is highly probable that the two fragments belong together. The strokes of the final letters on each are distinctively deep, wide, and, in section, have a relatively flat-bottomed profile. In addition, the two fragments responded to corrosion in the same way, a surface layer, beginning in a notch, having flaked off a right corner of each.

49 (Fig. 80)   Athens, Paul Kanellopoulos Collection. Unpublished.
   Right half. Green patination. L. 5.3 cm., w. 2.3 cm., th. ca. 0.1 cm. even.
   Two or more uses. Considerable reuse, that is, erasure, is suggested by the uneven surface and profile.

a   − − − − − −]
       − − − − − −]   Ⓖ

b   [$\frac{2-3}{-}$]ꙅινος   Class VI
       [Εὐ]ωνυ(μεύς)   Ⓖ?

G(orgoneion) seal. Large head in field 1.0 cm. in diam.

Text b. The spacing between letters in the demotic is wider than between letters of the nomen and implies that the five-letter demotic was centered under the nomen. Symmetry requires that line 2 did not begin with a patronymic, that the nomen in line 1 was probably no more than seven or eight letters long, and that the pinakion was short or broken at the left prior to the last use. The nomen terminated in $-\theta\iota\nu os$, $-\rho\iota\nu os$, or $-o\iota\nu os$, as in, for example, the good Athenian name, $E\check{\upsilon}\theta o\iota\nu os$.

50 (Fig. 81) Athens, National Museum, Inv. Bronze 8074. P. Pervanoglu, "Briefliches aus Athen," *AZ* 22 (1864), 284, and, independently, A. Dumont, *RA*² 17 (1868), 143. (Girard, no. 13; *IG* II, 934; II², 1913)

Right half. Recently cleaned to bare bronze. L. 5.35 cm., w. 2.1 cm., th. 0.17 cm. at right to 0.12 cm. at left.

Two or more uses. Erasure evident from tapering thickness.

a $- - - - - - -]$
   $- - - - - - -]$ Ⓖ

b $- - -]\mu os$
   $- - -]o\ A\chi\alpha\rho(\nu\epsilon\acute{\upsilon}s)$ Ⓖ

G(*orgoneion*) *seal*. Same die as used on **29** and probably **47**.

On Bruck's dubious suggestion that this fragment and **71** may have belonged to the same owner, see **71**.

51 (Fig. 82) Basel, Antikenmuseum, Inv. 1941.126.6. Ex coll. Rousopoulos-Pfuhl. F. Stähelin, *AA* 1943, 19, and pl. I, no. 6 (photo before cleaning).

Right fragment. Recently stripped to bare metal. L. 4.9 cm., w. 2.0 cm., th. 0.2 cm. at right to 0.17 cm. at left.

Two or more uses:

a $- - -]\rho\alpha\tau os$
   $- - -]$ Ⓖ

b $- - -]\omega\nu$ Class VI
   $\overset{\text{dem.}}{- - -}]\upsilon\ \Theta ov\kappa\lambda(\acute{\epsilon}ovs\ \textit{vel}\ -\epsilon\acute{\iota}\delta ov)$

G(*orgoneion*) *seal*. From the same die as the seals on **21**, **25**, and others. Erased and encroached upon by the time of the last use.

Text a. Though visible before cleaning, these letters were not noted by Stähelin.

Text b. Line 1 corrects Stähelin's $\upsilon\nu-$?; line 2 his $\Theta ov\kappa(\upsilon\delta\acute{\iota}\delta ov)$.

52 (Fig. 83) Athens, National Museum, Inv. Bronze 8070. S. Bruck, *AthMitt* 19 (1894), 209, no. 6. (*IG* II 5, 938d; II², 1919)

Right fragment. Recently stripped to bare metal. L. 3.9 cm., w. 2.0 cm. at right to 1.7 cm. at left, th. (minimal) ca. 0.05 cm.

Two or more uses:

a　　－－－]|
　　　　－－－]　　Ⓖ

b　　－－－]εδηs　Ⓖ?　Class VI
　　　　－－－]s

G(*orgoneion*) *seal*. Stamped nearly upsidedown, chin pointing upward to the left. Same die as on **20**.

From a thin Class III or IV pinakion.

53 (Fig. 84) Athens, National Museum, Inv. Bronze 8085. P. Girard, *BCH* 2 (1878), 533, no. 15. (*IG* II, 937; II², 1916)

Right end. Recently stripped to bare metal. L. 2.3 cm., w. 2.1 cm., th. 0.2 cm.

Two or more uses:

a　　－－－]
　　　　－－－]　Ⓖ

b　　－－－]s　　Class VI
　　　　－－]εύs

G(*orgoneion*) *seal*. With long-haired profile. The degree of obliteration suggests that the last use was a stampless, Class VI use.

54 (Fig. 85) Athens, British School of Archaeology. George Finlay Collection. W. Vischer, *Beiträge*, 53, and pl. VI, 10 = *Kleine Schriften* II, 79, and pl. VI, 10, (Girard, no. 47; *IG* II, 875; II², 1836)

Originally a right end. Clean, bare metal. L. 4.1 cm., w. 2.1–1.9 cm., th. 0.18 cm. maximum to 0.1 cm. at break.

Two or more uses:

a　　－－－]ἐ
　　　　－－－]　Ⓖ

Inverted, to become a left end

b   A $\Delta\eta\mu$[– – –   Class VI
         $\Lambda\alpha\mu$[$\pi\tau\rho\epsilon\acute{u}s$

G(*orgoneion*) *seal.* Stamped right side up in the original lower right corner. Thoroughly erased (causing the surrounding metal to spread and split) by time of last use.

All that survives from an earlier text is the short diagonal which bisects the right hasta of the lambda in text *b*. This diagonal could be the upper bar of a final sigma or the right upper bar of an upsilon.

55 (Figs. 86–87) Athens, Peiraeus, Archaeological Museum, A. N. Meleto-poulos Collection. I. A. Meletopoulos, *Polemon* 3 (1947–48), 40, and pl. B′, no. 6 (photograph before cleaning).
  Right end. Recently stripped to bare bronze. L. 3.4 cm., w. 2.2 cm., th. 0.2 cm. at right to 0.15 cm. at left.
  Probably more than two uses:

a   – – – –]$A\Theta I$ Ⓖ
    – – – –]

b   – – –]$\rho\alpha\tau os$ Class VI
    – – –]Ω

G(*orgoneion*) *seal.* Only the faintest indications of a circular seal remain, but they are confirmed by text *a* which rises to the upper right corner in order to avoid encroaching on the seal. The omicron and sigma of the last use were inscribed directly through the then erased seal's upper half.

Some very fine scratches in line 1, too uncertain to be recorded, probably belong to letters of a still earlier use or uses. The letters of text *a* are from a patronymic, which was either curtailed or continued in line 2.

56 (Fig. 88) Paris, Cabinet des Médailles, Froehner Collection Inv. 618. "Athènes, 1907." L. Robert, *Coll. Froehner* I, 10, and pl. VI, no. 10n.
  Right end. Dark, clean metal. L. 3.4 cm., w. 2.0 cm. at right to 2.1 cm. at left, th. 0.2 cm. at right to 0.08 cm. at left.
  Three or more uses. The incompetent inscribing of the earliest legible text suggests that it is not the earliest text, which would have been inscribed by a professional in the state's employ.

a   – – –]
      – – –]   ⓖ

b   – – –]⅃*MO?*
      Ἀρα]φή(νιος)   ⓖ

c   – –κ]*ράτης*   **Class VI**
      Εὐω]νυ(μεύς)

G(*orgoneion*) *seal* (not mentioned in prior publication). Large, circular face with bushy hair and prominent, protruding tongue. Diam. ca. 1.05 cm. Because of the obscurity of the upper part of the seal, I have not been able to identify it with a die known from another pinakion, but see **33**.

Text b. Composed of some of the most poorly inscribed letters to be found in this corpus. The letterer made his rounded letters with short, straight lines, thereby producing a rectangular omicron (?) in line 1 and a diamond-shaped phi in line 2. Note also the ill-proportioned and crooked eta in line 2. The letters look as if they have been engraved or scratched into the metal, rather than having been formed with a straight punch.

Text c. Several centimeters may have broken from the original left end before the final inscription was added, if not earlier.

The position of the small carrying-hole at the lower right has a parallel on the imperfectly known **147**. I wonder, however, whether the hole here is original. It is much smaller than the standard pinakion carrying-hole and is rather reminiscent of small holes often found on ancient coins that were worn as ornaments or charms in ancient and more recent times.

57 (Figs. 89–90) Athens, National Museum, Inv. Bronze 8121. A. Dumont, *RA²* 17 (1868), 144. S. Bruck, *Philologus* 54 (1895), 70, n. 21, 78, n. 39. S. Dow, *BCH* 87 (1963), 664–666, with fig. 1 (enlarged photograph before cleaning). (Girard, no. 14; *IG* II, 933; II², 1912)
Right half. Broken in two. Clean brown bronze. L. 5.4 cm., w. 2.2 cm., th. 0.20 cm. at right to 0.08 cm. at left.
Probably four or more uses:

a   – – – –]ς
      – – – –]   ⓖ

b   – – – – – – – – –]$\underset{.}{O}K$ Ⓖ?

        – – – –]⫽ Σ

c   – – – –]ς   Ⓖ?   Class VI?

      —ᵖᵃᵗʳ·—A]ίθα(λίδης)

d   – – –]$M\underset{.}{\nu}ησίππο$ Class VI

      – – –]$\underset{.}{\;}$

G(*orgoneion*) *seal*. Head with pointed, V-shaped jowls, in field ca. 1.0 cm. diam. Traces of snakes knotted under the chin. Probably from the same die as the gorgoneia on **38**.

The traditional text (Dumont through the *Editio Minor*) conflated line 2 of our text *c* with line 1 of our text *d* to give a restoration with a wide gap in the first half of line 2, thus

nomen M]νησίππο

v v v A]ίθα

Bruck filled the gap with a hypothetical earlier demotic, on the dubious assumption that Mnesippos' son changed his deme and had his new demotic, *Aἴθα*, inscribed at the right of the earlier one. My texts *b–d* follow Dow, who was the first to see that we have to deal with a multiple palimpsest, that the lettering in *Mνησίππο* is different in character than the lettering in *A*]*ίθα*, and that these two elements therefore should be assigned to different uses, the approximately similar diameters of the omega at the right of line 1 (text *d*) and the theta at the left of line 2 (text *c*) notwithstanding.

Some additions and corrections should be made to Dow's texts: I add the remains of three earlier sigmas, which have been somewhat arbitrarily assigned in my texts *a*, *b*, and *c* (one of the sigmas survives only in a slanting hasta before the gorgoneion seal); in text *b* I read $\underset{.}{O}K$ for Dow's *Y*; and in text *d* the initial letter of the patronymic no longer need be restored, since the right-hand bar of a mu is now plainly visible.

58 (Figs. 91–92) Athens, National Museum, Inv. Bronze 8136. Unpublished.
Right end. Recently stripped to bare metal. L. 2.1 cm., w. 2.1 cm., th. 0.20 cm. to 0.10 cm.
Four or more uses:

a   – – – –] Ⓖ

      – – – –]

b   – – – – – –]$\overset{.}{\Phi}A$ Class VI
      – – – –]

c   – – – –]$\equiv$ Class VI
      – – – –]

d   – – – –]ς   Class VI
      $\overset{\text{dem.}}{- -}$ K]αλλι(—?)

G(*orgoneion*) *seal.* Mouth, tongue, and lower profile still visible.

Text a. We should probably restore at least one use during which the gorgoneion seal was left intact.

Text b. The phi and alpha were inscribed right through the upper third of the gorgoneion. The partial erasure of these letters has left in the upper right corner a concave depression that terminates abruptly in a line at the feet of the alpha and at about the eye level of the gorgoneion.

Text c. Three of the four short, partially erased strokes directly to the right of the sigma of use *d* were inscribed into the right half of the erased phi of use *b* and thus represent an intermediate use or uses between *b* and *d*.

59 (Figs. 93–96) Athens, National Museum, Inv. Bronze 8073. A. Dumont, *RA*[2] 17 (1868), 145 (last text only). (Girard, no. 23, but omitted from *IG* II and hence from *IG* II[2])

Originally a right end. Recently stripped to bare metal. L. 3.6 cm., w. 2.1 cm., th. 0.15–0.12 cm.

Five (or more) uses:

a   – – – – – –]$A\boxtimes AIO$ Ⓖ   Side A
      – – – – – –]

b   – – – –]ς   Ⓖ
      – – – –]

c   – – –]ς̣   Ⓖ
      – – –]

Back side, remains right end

d ‾‾^{nomen}‾‾]ᵥ Θωρα(—?)   Class VI
‾‾_{demotic}‾‾]

Back side, inverted, becomes left end

e   Αἰσχ[‾ ‾ ‾   Class VI
Αἰσχίν[ου

G(*orgoneion*) *seal*. From the same die as the gorgoneia on **63, 65, 66**, and possibly **22**. Large circular head, with smooth bands of hair. Diam. of field ca. 1.1 cm.

Text a. The patronymic terminates in –απαιο, as from Ἀγαπαῖος (*PA*, 90), or –αναιο, as from Παναῖος (*PA*, 11561–11563).

Text b. The sigma has been exposed to less erasure than the remains of text *a*.

Text c. This sigma is less erased still.

Text d. Surviving are the first four letters of an abbreviated patronymic rendered in stippled dots. By analogy with **68**, text *c*, also with a stippled patronymic, the nomen and demotic were probably inscribed with conventional, punched letters, the patronymic being an afterthought added by the owner himself. Several variants in Θωρα– are given by Pape-Benseler and Bechtel, but according to the prosopographical file at the Institute for Advanced Study, Θώραξ is the only one to date attested from Athens (335/4 B.C.: *IG* II², 1700, line 80).

Text e. Nomen and patronymic begin at the very edge of the inverted plate to avoid as much as possible conflicting with the remains of the earlier text extending in from the right. A section-letter may have been added at the right of the owner's name.

On side B are a number of fine lines, of which some may be erased remains of an intermediate text anterior to text *d*; others of these lines, however, are too randomly disposed to be anything but accidental scratches in the surface.

60 (Figs. 97–98)   Basel, Antikenmuseum, Inv. 1906.776. J. J. Bernoulli, *Katalog*, 189, no. 1084b. (*IG* II², 1901)
Right half. Recently stripped to bare bronze. L. 6.2 cm., w. 2.0 cm., th. 0.32 cm. at right to 0.25 cm. at left.

Two (or more?) uses:

a   – – – –]ς̣[.]η̣ς   Ⓖ
          – – – –]|Υ̣

b   – – –]τελης   Ⓖ
          – – –]υιεύς

G(*orgoneion*) *seal*. From a die related in style and proportions to the die or dies used for the gorgoneia of Class V: circular profile, short hair, finely modulated facial features, in a field, diam. 1.0–1.1 cm. Compared with the Class V gorgoneia, the present one has a shorter tongue and a narrower mouth, and his right cheek is malformed by two unconnected lines of relief apparently caused by a slip in the cutting of the die.

Several shallow pittings left of center (in and around the lambda of line 1 and the epsilon of line 2) conceivably could be erased remains of an earlier name that was inscribed with punched serifs at the terminations of letters in imitation of Class V lettering. If they are, the fragment would positively have belonged to Class IV since such lettering in imitation of Class V does not occur on Class III pinakia. But these pittings have more the look of natural pittings caused by corrosion and seem too randomly disposed to have belonged to letters.

The exceptional thickness of the piece cannot be paralleled by other Class III or IV pinakia.

Class IV

Section-letter in the upper left corner, triobol seal beneath, and gorgoneion seal at the right. Double-bodied owl secondary seal.

Class IV A

Triobol seals with AΘE, as in Classes I and II.

Gorgoneion seals from dies used in Class III or similar thereto, that is, not from a Class V gorgoneion die.

WITHOUT SECONDARY SEAL

61 (Figs. 99–100) Rouen, Musée Départemental des Antiquités. Ex coll. L. F. S. Fauvel. Found by Fauvel in the northern Peiraeus[12] "sur la poitrine

---

12. As Fauvel's statement that the tomb was located "soit à Phalère, soit à Pirée" makes amply clear. In the early nineteenth century Phaleron was commonly believed to be situated in the northeast corner of the Peiraeus peninsula.

du mort, dans un tombeau fermé." *Magasin Encyclopédique* 1807, III, 136–139 (letter from Fauvel dated November 11, 1806). Abbé Tougard, "Note sur quelques monuments grecs du Musée Départemental d'Antiquités de Rouen," *Revue de la Normandie* 1868, 237–241. J. H. Kroll, *BCH* 91 (1967), 379, 382, and 385–387, with fig. 3 (photograph before cleaning). (*CIG*, 209; Girard, no. 45; *IG* II, 879; II², 1843)

Whole. Inscribed area recently cleaned of patination. L. 11.9 cm., w. 2.2 cm. at right to 2.5 cm. maximum, th. ca. 0.1 cm.

Three or more uses. The nearly total erasure of the seal at the right and the plate's considerably distorted profile suggest erasure on more than two occasions, that is, more than three uses.

a   [[?]] [– – – – – –]
     ⓣ   [– – – – – –] ⓖ

b   Η   Φρύνος Εὐκλείδο
     ⓣ   Παιαν(ιεύς)   ⓖ

c   Β   Ἀντίχαρμος   Class VI
         Λ α μ π (τρεύς)

T(riobol) seal. With $\begin{smallmatrix}&[A]\\E&\Theta\end{smallmatrix}$. Double-struck, the second impression being 0.2 cm. to the left of the first one. Visible are the feet and tail of the owl, the lower letters of the ethnic, and lower segments of the olive wreath: three pairs of leaves and a terminal leaf on the right branch, four leaves, apparently representing three pairs, on the left branch. Diam. ca. 1.1 cm. Too many details have been distorted or are missing to permit the die to be positively identified or disassociated with triobol dies on other extant pinakia. The die, however, appears to be extremely close to that used on **18**.

G(orgoneion) seal. Only the long-haired profile of the head remains, but it is enough to show that the head was similar in size and appearance to the gorgoneia on **21**, **25**, and others.

Text a. An original use with a stamped section-letter, all traces of which have been destroyed by erasure, should be restored. To date, no Class IV pinakion is known to have been manufactured without a stamped section-letter.

Text b. Amplifies the incomplete readings printed in *BCH* 91 (1967). I owe the full patronymic and demotic to the recent cleaning by Mlle. Monique Mainjonet of the Cabinet des Médailles.

WITH SECONDARY SEAL

62 (Figs. 101–102)　London, British Museum, Inv. Bronze 329. Ex coll. Thomas Burgon. Excavated from a tomb in Peiraeus in 1809. E. Dodwell, *Tour* I, 437, with a commendable drawing. E. L. Hicks, *Manual*, 202, no. 119.2 = Hicks-Hill, *Manual*, 287, no. 151.2. H. B. Walters, *Catalogue*, 49, no. 329 (*CIG*, 208; Girard, no. 30; *IG* II, 886; II², 1850)

Complete. Broken in the middle and mended in antiquity. Recently stripped to bare metal. L. 11.9 cm., w. 2.0 cm., th. 0.2 cm. at ends to 0.1 cm. at break in center

Two or more uses:

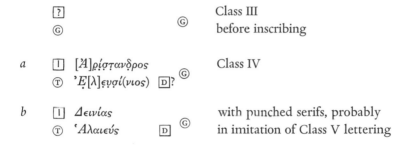

Iota section-letter (not a gamma as given in all previous publications). In ca. 0.75 cm. square field; twice broken from being stamped over an earlier letter in relief.

G(orgoneion) seals. From the best-known Class III–IV die; see **21**.

T(riobol) seal. With $\substack{A \\ E\ \Theta}$.[13] Owl with narrow head, proportionally long body, and short legs. The olive wreath is exceptionally well leafed, the right-hand branch with four pairs of fine leaves, above which (next to the owl's head) two single leaves, and a terminal leaf below. Only three pairs of leaves and the terminal leaf are visible on the left branch. Diam. ca. 1.15 cm. The die is highly distinctive and cannot be identified on other surviving pinakia.

D(ouble-bodied owl) seal. Hanging from the upper left corner are the lower terminations either of an alpha or of an olive spray. If the latter, possible suggestions of an epsilon would confirm that the seal is the sole extant example that exactly reproduces the type of a diobol coin with ethnic $\substack{[A] \\ E\ [\Theta]}$. But the

13. The indications of the epsilon are far from unambiguous, but an epsilon would have to be restored regardless since the seal bears no relation to the Class V type and would not therefore have borne an ethnic in AΘH.

epsilon is by no means certain and could be the illusory effect of corrosion, in which case the seal would be normal with an ethnic in two alphas (see Chapter II, n. 35, above). No clear parts of a letter can be distinguished in the field to the right of the head. Width of incuse square, 0.85 cm.

One cannot be sure whether the seal was added in an earlier use and was partially erased at the top with the erasure of an earlier name, or whether it was added with the last text and owes its incomplete survival to uneven striking. In favor of the second possibility, however, is the fact that erasure of the penultimate inscription was confined to the area of the letters themselves, as explained below.

Text a. The traces of letters at the left are practically invisible on the surface of the pinakion itself. My readings are taken from a plaster cast, which does not reflect light and therefore brings out the traces more clearly.

Text b. The last owner of the pinakion may be identified with the Deinias of Halai who was an epimeletes of the dockyards in 356/5 and who apparently died prior to the years 345/4–342/1 (*IG* II², 1622, lines 513–519, with my discussion above, pp. 66–67).

Like the celebrated Burgon amphora, this "Burgon" pinakion is unique among objects of its kind. Apart from the questions raised by its double-bodied owl seal and settled by the identity of its last owner, this is the only pinakion known to have been altered through the overstriking of one of its primary seals with a primary seal of a different kind. Originally stamped as a Class III pinakion with an identical gorgoneion seal at each end, it was converted by the addition of a triobol seal over the gorgoneion at the left. As the earliness of the style of the triobol seal (in relation to triobol seals of Class V) implies, the conversion probably took place before the pinakion was inscribed.

There are two final points of interest. As one sees particularly well at the right of line 1, the next to last inscription was erased not by hammering uniformly over the entire inscribed surface but by hammering or peening out each letter or stroke individually, thus giving the surface an exceptional unevenness. The four rivet holes in the middle were drilled after the last owner's name was inscribed and show that the pinakion broke and was repaired during its last use. Before the pinakion was cleaned, the outline of the mending strip that the rivets held in place was visible on the back as a rectangle, ca. 4.0 × 1.5 cm., differing in color from the surrounding patination.

63 (Figs. 103–105)   Paris, Cabinet des Médailles, Froehner Collection Inv. 615. "Athènes, 1895." L. Robert, *Coll. Froehner* I, 8, and pl. VII (photograph before cleaning), no. 10c (text *d* only).

Complete. Broken in two. Cleaned of heavy corrosion.[14] L. 12 cm., w. 2.25 cm., th. 0.1 cm.

Four or more uses:

a   Ⓐ [– – – – $\overset{\text{ca. 9-10}}{–\, –\, –\, –}$ – – – –Δ]ΩPO   (carrying-hole)

    Ⓣ [– – – – – – –] Ⓓ   Ⓖ

b   Ⓐ Δ[ι]ọ[νύ]σị[ο]ṣ?

    Ⓣ [$\overset{\text{ca. 2}}{–\,–}$]PẸⅠ⌐[.Φυ]λάσι(ος)   Ⓖ

c   Ⓐ Ẹὐθοịνίδης

    Ⓣ Φυλ**ą**σι(ος)   Ⓖ

d   B Εὐθυμένης

    Ⓣ Φυλάσι(ος)   Ⓖ

T(riobol) *seal*. Ethnic $\begin{smallmatrix}[\text{A}]\\ \text{E }\Theta\end{smallmatrix}$. Small-bodied, compact owl, similar in profile to the ones on Class V pinakia. All traces of the olive wreath are missing. The partial effacement of the seal would seem to be due more to the action of corrosion than to erasure. The stamped alpha section-letter directly above the seal has apparently not been subjected to much erasure and was simply inscribed into by the beta of text *d*.

G(orgoneion) *seal*. From the same die as the gorgoneia on **59**, **65**, **66**, and possibly the one on **22**.

D(ouble-bodied owl) *seal*. With A A. 0.85 cm. square. A demotic, which cannot be later than the antepenultimate use, was inscribed directly over the seal and was subsequently erased, thus causing the seal to be flattened. Apparently, then, the seal had no validity for at least the last three uses.

Texts a and b. The most legible parts of inscriptions earlier than text *c* occur at the right of the plate: in line 1, *ΩPO*, which should belong to a patronymic beginning or ending Δ]*ΩPO*; and, in line 2, *ΛΑΣΙ* from the demotic Φυ]λάσι-

14. I did not receive a photograph of the right half in its fully cleaned state. Fig. 103 shows the right half after partial cleaning.

(*os*) and inscribed, as mentioned above, over the double-bodied owl seal. These two parts of names belong to two separate texts since the second half of *Δωρόθεος*, the only compound Athenian male name beginning *Δωρο–*, is too short to fill the first 6–8 spaces in line 2 before *Φυ]λάσι(ος)*. Apart from their absence in Athenian prosopography, the few longer *Δωρο–* compounds listed by Bechtel do not fit the erased traces in the first half of line 2. The demotic belongs to a use later than the use for which the secondary seal was stamped. In my texts I have assumed that there were only four uses altogether and that the secondary seal and *Δ]ΩΡΟ* belonged to the earliest one. But, of course, if there were more than four uses, it becomes uncertain whether *Δ]ΩΡΟ* preceded or followed the use with the demotic.

The earliest traces in the left half of the plate are much less positive, and the remains of one well-erased text cannot be confidently distinguished from the remains of the other (or others). A few recognizable letters in line 1 at least imply a common name, which can be attributed to the antepenultimate owner, but in line 2 one can do no more than record the more prominent suggestions of letters.

Text c. Although its cognate Euthoinos is very well attested, the name Euthoinides is new to Greek prosopography. The correctness of my readings is supported by **123**, a Class VI pinakion last used by Euthoinides' son. The first two letters of the nomen and the first three of the demotic are mostly hidden by the identical letters of text *d*.

This is the sole known instance of a pinakion with three owners from the same deme. But, so long as some doubt exists as to the overall number of uses and the precise sequence of the demotic of text *b*, we cannot be altogether positive that the pinakion was owned by three Phylasioi in succession.

PRESENCE OR ABSENCE OF SECONDARY SEAL UNCERTAIN

64 (Figs. 106–107)   Athens, National Museum, Inv. Bronze 8087. P. Girard, *BCH* 2 (1878), 532, no. 9. U. Koehler, *IG* II, 902. Cf. S. Bruck *AthMitt* 19 (1894), 204, no. 8. (*IG* II², 1866)

Left end. Recently stripped to bare metal. L. 2.4 cm., w. 2.1 cm., th. 0.25 cm. at left to 0.18 cm. at right.

Three or more uses. The fragment has almost certainly been erased more than once.

a   ☐? [– – –
     ⓉT [– – –

b   ? |[– – –

    ⓣ   Ọ[– – –

c   E   *Γλ*[*αυκ—? vel –ύκων*   Class VI?

      "*Ω*[*αθεν*

T(riobol) seal.[15] With $\begin{smallmatrix}&[A]\\E&[\Theta]\end{smallmatrix}$. Indications of two pairs of leaves on the left olive branch. Diam. seems small, ca. 1.0 cm. The owl looks slightly shorter and stubbier in profile than the owls on Class V pinakia.

No traces of the original stamped section-letter or of the erasure that removed it are visible. The three shallow holes in the surface might survive from a use inscribed in imitation of Class V lettering, but since one of these holes is located within the area occupied by the section-letters, they are more likely natural pittings.

Class IV A or B

Ethnic of triobol seal uncertain. Gorgoneion seal as in Class III, that is, not from a Class V gorgoneion die.

WITH SECONDARY SEAL

65 (Figs. 108–110) Athens, National Museum, Inv. Bronze 13347 Λ. "Aus dem Peiraeus." Ex coll. University of Athens. L. Ross, *AllLitZeit* 1837, Intelligenz-blätter Nos. 84–85, 689–690 and 710, no. 7. Whence Ross, *Demen von Attika*, 72, no. 86. (Girard, no. 32; *IG* II, 904; II², 1868)

Whole. Erasure in the middle has caused the ends to curve slightly forward. Recently stripped of patination. L. 12.0 cm., w. 2.2 cm. except at left end where 2.4 cm.; th. 0.25–0.20 cm. at ends to minimum 0.15 cm. in middle.

Three uses, minimum:

a   ⊡'*O*[*νη*]*σί*[*κ*]*ρ*[*ι*]*τος*?

     ⓣ *O*[– – –]|[.]O|[– –   Ⓓ?   Ⓖ

b   ⊡ *Ἐπικράτης*

     ⓣ *Ἐρχιεύς Σατ(υρ—?)* Ⓓ?   Ⓖ

---

15. Correctly recognized as an "owl" seal by Koehler and Bruck. Girard had tentatively identified it as a "croissant(?)."

c   E: *Λυσιθείδης*
    ⓣ *Θριάσι(ος)*   ▯D   ⃝G

T(riobol) seal. In ca. 1.05 cm. diam. field. No positive traces of the ethnic are preserved, some tempting suggestions of an epsilon at the lower left not being sufficiently clear for a decisive reading. The owl itself is similar in profile and proportions to the triobol owls on Class V pinakia. The seal, nearly invisible before cleaning, was not detected by Ross, who was also unaware that the pinakion is a palimpsest.

G(orgoneion) seal. From the same die as the gorgoneia on **59, 63, 66,** and possibly **22.** All dimensions and details of cheeks, eyes, and hair are identical to theirs. Its nose looks more narrow, but this is the result of the present seal's comparatively high, three-dimensional relief. Not only was the die impressed more deeply on the present pinakion, but the nose of the gorgoneion on **59** has been flattened and spread by erasure.

D(ouble-bodied owl) seal. With A A. Stamped upside down. In field 0.8 cm. high × 0.85 cm. wide. Apparently from the same die as that used on **85** and **86.** It is impossible to tell with which use the seal was added. Since erasure of the penultimate text comes right up to the seal and stops at its left edge, the seal could have been added at any time before or after this name.

Text a. In the restoration of line 1, I have assumed that several faint diagonals within the final sigma of text *b* are remains of an earlier sigma and that the erased high horizontal within the final –*HΣ* of text *c* owes its exceptional length to the fact that it contains the horizontals of two taus, one from each of the two earlier uses.

Text b. Observe that both lines begin one letter space to the right of the initial letters of texts *a* and *c*. The patronymic is probably to be completed *Σατ(ύρου)* or *Σατ(υρίωνος)*, which are the only two possibilities attested in *PA*. A *Σατυρίσκος* is known from *IG* II², 12446, but his nationality is uncertain. Other possibilities from outside Attika are given by Bechtel. The owner would seem to be a relative (probably a brother) of the penultimate owner of **121,** a Class VI pinakion. A possible descendant is *PA*, 12569, Satyrion Erchieus, father of an ephebe of 106/5 B.C.

66 (Figs. 111–112)   Athens, Depot of the Second Archaeological Ephoria of Athens (Polynotos Street). Excavated from a necropolis at Tavros (outside the north Long Wall between Athens and Peiraeus) in February 1969. D. Schilardi, "*Ἀνασκαφὴ παρὰ τὰ Μακρὰ Τείχη*," *Deltion*, forthcoming.

Complete, except for two fragments missing along the upper edge. Mended from several broken pieces. In two large areas, toward the left of lines 1 and 2 and in the upper left corner, and in numerous smaller areas, the original surface metal is hidden by thick, encrusted patches of redeposited copper. In three small areas, namely under the kappa (where a white spot in the photograph), in the head of the double-bodied owl seal, and at the lower right corner, the surface metal has flaked away. Cleaned to bare, brown metal. L. 12.4 cm., w. 2.2 cm. at right to ca. 2.5 cm. in middle, th. 0.23 cm. at the lower left corner to a minimum 0.13 cm. in middle. Both the left and right ends have been slightly notched.

Three or more uses:

a   ⊟ $E[--\overset{ca.\ 6}{-----}-]\Sigma P[\overset{ca.\ 3}{---}]\Sigma$?   Ⓖ

       Ⓣ $\Pi[----\overset{ca.\ 8}{------}-]\|[..]\overset{..}{\equiv}\Sigma X$?

b   ⊟? $N[\iota\kappa]o[\overset{ca.\ 2}{--}]O\!/\!\overset{=}{=}\,[\overset{ca.\ 2}{--}]\|\Sigma$ Ⓖ   (carrying-hole)

       Ⓣ $\Gamma[----]$ ⅅ

c   ⊞ $K\alpha\lambda\lambda\iota\acute{\alpha}\delta\eta\varsigma\ M[\epsilon\iota]\delta\omega(-?)$ Ⓖ

       Ⓣ $\mathring{A}\gamma[\nu]\acute{o}\sigma\iota(os)$ ⅅ

T(riobol) seal. One cannot be sure whether or not the seal is from a Class V die. In size and profile, the owl is identical with the triobol owls of Class V, and there is a possible suggestion of the right vertical of an eta in the lower left field. Nevertheless, the surface there is very disturbed, and the indication of an eta could well be illusory. A triobol seal with a similar owl but with an ethnic in AΘE occurs on **63**, which shares a common gorgoneion seal die with the present pinakion.

G(orgoneion) seal. From the same die as the gorgoneia on **59, 63, 65**, and possibly **22**.

D(ouble-bodied owl) seal. With [A]A. Field 0.8 cm. high × 0.85 cm. wide. As explained below, the seal may not have been stamped until one of the later uses of the pinakion.

Section-letters. A layer of redeposited copper obscures all but the faintest suggestions of a theta stamped in incuse square and of a later letter inscribed over it. The inscribed letter would have been a delta, an epsilon, or a zeta.

Texts a and b. Although the sequence of letters at the beginning of lines 1 and 2 seems clear enough, it is impossible to be certain how most of the earlier letters and parts of letters at the middle and right are to be apportioned to texts. For instance, I am unsure whether the two sigmas—one heavily, the other weakly erased—at the right of line 1 respectively went with the antepenultimate and penultimate uses, as indicated above. Their apportionment to texts could be reversed; or, if there were more than three uses altogether, one or both sigmas might have come from still earlier uses. Similar uncertainties exist for the erased letters at the middle of line 1 and at the right of line 2.

The letters *ΣX* preceded by a vertical at the very end of line 2 can only have belonged to a patronymic. Because space for the name was giving out, the letters are run tightly together. The one well-attested root which can be restored from the letters is *AIΣX*, which begins numerous Athenian names and is used in the termination of *Παναίσχης*, PA, 11563–11564. On the other hand, if certain possible traces of erased letters between the double-bodied owl seal and *ΣX* actually belonged with the latter, the patronymic would have to be restored differently. These traces, though shown in Fig. 112, are too uncertain to be incorporated in the texts.

Another problem concerns the relationship of *ΣX* to the carrying-hole and the double-bodied owl seal. The carrying-hole seems clearly to be later than the letters since it encroaches on the vertical; cf. **15**, where a carrying-hole was added after at least one use. And if, as is probable, the letters completed a long second line containing a demotic and patronymic, the double-bodied owl seal, too, would not have been added until after the line was erased; for the seal extends into the area of line 2 but has not been subjected to erasure. However, there is an outside chance that *ΣX* is a broken continuation of line 1 (as on **68**, text *d*) and that the seal therefore might have been stamped in a vacant space to the left of the letters prior to their being erased.

The second line of text *b* began with epsilon or gamma.

Text c. The full patronymic was *Μείδωνος* or *Μειδωνίδου*. The horizontal line below the restored epsilon is the upper edge of the incuse square of the double-bodied owl seal and not part of the epsilon.

Context. Since it was recovered from a necropolis containing burials as late as the fourth century B.C., one assumes that the pinakion was originally buried there with its last owner. When excavated, however, the pinakion was found stratified in a layer of earth above the earth fill of a cremation pit of the sixth century B.C. (Pyre XIII). Hence the pinakion was probably removed from its owner's grave by tomb robbers or during some later leveling or grave digging in the immediate area.

67 (Figs. 113–115)   Athens, National Museum, Inv. Bronze 8126. "Trouvée au Pirée." P. Girard, *BCH* 2 (1878), 531, no. 2. Sketch showing last text published by S. Bruck, *AthMitt* 19 (1894), 206, no. 14. (*IG* II, 920; II², 1893)

Complete. Broken in four pieces, now mended. Metal heavily encrusted and blistered by bronze disease. Superficially cleaned; further cleaning was deemed inadvisable. L. 11.6 cm., w. 2.4 cm., th. ca. 0.20 to 0.15 cm. uneven.

Three or more uses:

a   ⊡ Γ[ᶜᵃ·²] | \ [– – –]
   Ⓣ [– – – – – – –]   Ⓓ? ᴳ

b   ? Ἀνδρο[– –ᶜᵃ·⁵– –]ς
   Ⓣ [– – – – – –]   Ⓓ? ᴳ

c   Ι. Καλλικύδης
   Ⓣ Αἰγιλιεύς   Ⓓ ᴳ

T(riobol) seal. Legend illegible. Almost totally effaced by corrosion.

G(orgoneion) seal. Although the metal in the area of the seal is blistered and flaking, enough of the seal remains to show that it is not from a Class V die.

D(ouble-bodied owl) seal. Still visible are the profile of the owl and the edges of the deeply impressed incuse square. As often with secondary seals, it is uncertain with which use the seal was added.

Texts a and b. In most areas it is impossible to distinguish positively actual remains of erased letters from cracks and other accidental disturbances in the rough surface. In the left half of line 1, however, there are clear indications of at least two inscriptions earlier than the final one.

68 (Figs. 116–120)   Athens, National Museum, Inv. Bronze 8063. From Kypseli. Edited independently by U. Koehler, *IG* II, 887, and K. D. Mylonas, "Δικαστικὰ πινάκια ἀνέκδοτα δύο," *BCII* 7 (1883), 30–33. Correct arrangement of the last two texts and recognition of an epsilon of an earlier, third text (text *b* below) by S. Bruck, *AthMitt* 19 (1894), 203, no. 3. (*IG* II 5, 887, corrects Koehler's first texts; II², 1851)

Complete. Broken in four pieces, now mended. Recently stripped to bare bronze. L. 12.7 cm., w. 2.05 cm. at right to 2.4 cm. maximum, th. ca. 0.15 to 0.10 cm.

Four or more uses:

a   Ⓖ *Τιμο*[. .³. .]*ος* [¹⁻²]| | |*O* Ⓖ   inscribed with added punched
    Ⓣ [– – –⁷⁻⁸– – –]*ς* Ⓓ   dots in imitation of Class V
                              lettering

b   Ⓖ [*Κηφι?*]*σοκλέης*   Ⓖ
    Ⓣ [– – – – – –]   Ⓓ

c   Ⓖ *Λυσίστρατος*   Ⓖ
       Κηφισοδώ(ρου)
    Ⓣ *Μελιτεύς*   Ⓓ

d   Γ *Παράμονος Φανοδήμ(ου)* Ⓖ
    Ⓣ *Αἰθαλίδης*   Ⓓ

T(riobol) seal. With ethnic $_{[?]}\overset{A}{}_{[\Theta]}$. The present profile of the owl and what appears to be the relief of a long olive leaf or stem in the left field strongly imply that the seal is not of the Class V type and that the pinakion probably belongs to Class IV A. However, the relief of the seal may have been distorted by some erasure and the owl's profile perhaps by a slight amount of re-touching. Diam. ca. 1.05 cm.

G(orgoneion) seal. Similar to the short-haired, Class V type with four promi-nent pairs of snakes, but clearly not from a Class V die. Here the snakes are thicker, and the two knotted under the chin are attached to the ends of the hair and continue down along the cheeks. Diam. ca. 1.05 cm.

D(ouble-bodied owl) seal. With A A. Width 0.8 cm. × height 0.7 cm. As indi-cated by the two right-hand profiles of the owl's head, one being about a millimeter to the left of the other, the seal was double-struck. The seal was probably added to the text inscribed in imitation of Class V lettering.

Stamped section-letter. A vertical and a horizontal in relief remain from the original gamma (or epsilon) section-letter. These relief lines were reinforced with three inscribed lines presumably at the time of the last use.

Texts a and b. Although the letters of these two earliest visible texts are easily disentangled, thanks to the punched dots attached to the letters of *a*, it is impossible to be sure which of the texts was the earlier. At the left of line 1, where text *a* is still partially legible, all of text *b* has disappeared; whereas toward the middle of this line, the letters of *b* (especially the epsilon) are generally heavier and look later than the remains of *a*. But, in either case, we must remember that the earlier of these two texts was not necessarily the earliest inscription on the pinakion altogether. The pinakion has obviously been subjected to much erasure (though not between texts *c* and *d*, because *c* is nearly intact), and a still earlier text (or texts) may have existed.

Text c. That the patronymic in stippled letters through the middle of the plate does in fact belong to this penultimate use is clear both from the unerased state of the stippled dots and from the way the dots were placed to avoid contact with the letters of Λυσίστρατος in line 1 and Μελιτεύς in line 2. Note especially the low positioning of the stippled phi (to avoid the upsilon in line 1) and the high placing of the iota (to avoid touching the epsilon in line 2). For another instance of a stippled patronymic, see **59**, text *d*.

The patronymic was an afterthought, added probably by the owner Lysistratos in order to distinguish himself from a fellow demesman with the same nomen. Hence we have good reason for assuming that there were two Lysistratoi of Melite active at the time of this use. One of them is mentioned, without patronymic, in a fragmentary catalogue from Eleusis, dated 350–300 (*IG* II², 1702, line 11), and the son of one of them was the Lysikrates, son of Lysistratos, of Melite who was honored in 304/3 (*IG* II², 488, lines 6–7) and who proposed a decree in about 302/1 (*IG* II², 506, line 1). As for the Lysistratos who owned the pinakion, he is probably the brother of Onetor, son of Kephiso-doros, of Melite, proposer of a decree in 376/5 (*IG* II², 1141, line 8); likely descendants are two bouleutai of Melite in the year 281/0 (*Hesperia* 38 [1969], 473, lines 13 and 14): Κηφισόδωρος Κ[ηφ]ισοδ[—] and Κηφισόδωρος Λυ[σ]ι[στ-ράτου] (?). The latter is almost certainly related and could conceivably be the son, at an advanced age, of our Lysistratos.

I assume that the final sigma in line 2, text *c* and *d*, was originally inscribed for text *c*, went virtually unerased (like the rest of text *c*), and was accommo-dated into the demotic of the final owner. The fainter sigma behind it must go with text *a* because of the punched dots at the terminations of its strokes, its small size, and its considerably erased state.

Text d. The tombstone of the last owner and his wife, that is, the tombstone that stood over the grave containing the pinakion, is extant (*IG* II², 5396). I illustrate it in Fig. 121, as it forms a kind of grave-group with the pinakion and has not been published with a photograph. It too is known to have come from Kypseli, and was dated by Kirchner to *med. s. IV a.*, which happens to agree quite well with my dating of late uses of Class IV pinakia. The stone is most notable for the punched holes used in place of crossbars in the alphas and etas of lines 2 and 3, somewhat reminiscent of the lettering conventions of Class V pinakia.

69 (Figs. 122–123) Basel, Antikenmuseum, Inv. 1941.126.4. Ex coll. Rouso-poulos-Pfuhl. F. Stähelin, *AA* 1943, 19, and pl. I, no. 4 (photograph before cleaning).

Right half. Recently stripped to bare metal. L. 5.0 cm., w. 2.2 cm., th. 0.2 cm. at right to 0.15 cm. at left.

Four or more uses:

a   – – – – – – –] ⫶< ⓖ
          – – – –]

b   – – – – – –]ος   ⓖ
          – –]|ΛΙΕΥΣ

c   – – –]ος 𝐃 ⓖ
          – –]

d   – –]σιας 𝐃? ⓖ?
          – –]Π

G(*orgoneion*) *seal*. With a large, bushy-haired profile.

D(*ouble-bodied owl*) *seal*. With [A]A. 0.8 cm. height. The seal has been subjected to erasure at the left, but to much less erasure than that which removed all traces of letters of texts *a* and *b* in the area directly above the seal. The seal was, therefore, almost certainly not added until after the erasure of text *b*.

Text a. Although the remaining letter strokes could perhaps have belonged to a terminal sigma, they are more suggestive of a kappa or chi from an abbreviated patronymic.

Text b. I assume that the nomen was of maximum eleven to twelve letter length, that an abbreviated patronymic began line 2, and that the demotic was probably Αἰγ]ιλιεύς or Ἐστ]ιαιεύς.

Text d. The only text recorded by Stähelin; he misread the pi in line 2 as tau. The nomen was presumably one of the longer names in –σιας, for example, Μελη]σίας (which is the longest), and the demotic Ἀλω]π(εκῆθεν), Κρω]π-(ίδης), Λαμ]π(τρεύς) or Προσ]π(άλτιος).

The crowding at the right of text *b* and the rather short restorations at the left of text *d* suggest that the pinakion was comparatively short to begin with, say ca. 10 cm. in length. We can be confident that an original 1 or 2 cm. with the essential triobol seal did not break off from the left end—at least not prior to the last use—for the triobol seal must have been retained until the double-bodied owl seal was added.

70 (Fig. 124) Athens, National Museum, Inv. Bronze 8099. From Kypseli. Edited independently by U. Koehler, *IG* II, 932, and K. D. Mylonas, *BCH* 7 (1883), 33. (*IG* II², 1911, with addendum)

Right fragment. Recently stripped to bare metal. L. 4.8 cm., w. 2.3 cm., th. (minimal) 0.05 cm.

Three or more uses:

a   – – – – – –]O
      – – –]   ⬚D   Ⓖ

b   – – – –]κράτης   Ⓖ
      – – –]   ⬚D   Ⓖ

c   – – – –]μος   Ⓖ
      – –]H   ⬚D   Ⓖ

G(orgoneion) *seal*. From the most frequently appearing Class III and IV die; see **21**.

D(ouble-bodied owl) *seal*. With A[A]. Small, 0.65–0.70 cm. square. Since sigmas of the last two uses were inscribed into this seal, it was stamped prior to these uses.

This is the sole surviving example of a positively identified Class IV pinakion of minimum thinness (cf. two thin Class III pinakia, **29** and **36**, and **52** from Class III or IV).

The omicron of text *a* (under the eta of *b* and a sigma of *c*) is probably the terminal of a patronymic.

71 (Figs. 125–126) Athens, National Museum, Inv. Bronze 8075. P. Pervano-glu, *AZ* 22 (1864), 284. Independently edited by A. Dumont, *RA*² 17 (1868), 143. Cf. S. Bruck, *AthMitt* 19 (1894), 207, no. 17. (Girard, no. 5; *IG* II, 935; II², 1914)

Right end. Recently stripped to bare metal. L. 3.1 cm., w. 1.8 cm. at right to 2.0 cm. at left, th. 0.20 cm. maximum to 0.15 cm.

Three or more uses:

a	– – –]s	⒟ Ⓖ	letters with punched serifs in
	– – –]		imitation of Class V lettering

b	– – –]‴	⒟ Ⓖ	
	– – –]O|		

c	– – –]os	⒟ Ⓖ	
	– – –]AP		

G(*orgoneion*) *seal.* Long-haired Class III–IV type, stamped upside down. Small, field ca. 0.9 cm. diam.

D(*ouble-bodied owl*) *seal.* With A A, stamped upside down. Field, 0.7–0.8 cm. square. The seal was probably added to the use inscribed in imitation of Class V lettering.

Text a. The earliest visible remains of an inscription. It may have been preceded by a use or uses inscribed in conventional lettering. The sigma is restored from the three punched dots indicated in Fig. 126.

Text c. This fragment and **50** came into the museum of the Archaeological Society together, in August 1864, and received the respective inventory numbers 49 and 50 (not 59 as printed by Dumont). Since line 2 of the present fragment can be restored Ἀχ]αρ(νεύς), on analogy with **50**, Bruck proposed that both fragments had been inscribed for a single owner and had been recovered from a single grave. In the apparatus to *IG* II², 1914, however, Kirchner pointed out that at least one other demotic can be restored in line 2, and to this we may add that the line may have terminated in an abbreviated patronymic. It is probable, moreover, that both fragments were surface finds and did not come from graves. Even if both were found together and happened to have been last used by Acharnians, there is still no reason for thinking that they had been used by the same owner, or even that their owners were related.

Class IV B

Triobol seal with AΘH, from a die similar to or identical with a die used in Class V. Gorgoneion seal as in Class III and IV A.

WITHOUT SECONDARY SEAL

72 (Fig. 127) formerly Berlin, Staatliche Museen, Inv. Bronze 3425. "Aus Aexone."[16] L. Ross, *AllLitZeit* 1837, Intelligenzblätter Nos. 84–85, 689–690, and 710, no. 7b. Whence Ross, *Demen von Attika*, 57, no. 37. C. Curtius, *RhM* 31 (1876), 284, no. 5, with a sketch. Photograph in Otto Kern, *Inscriptiones Graecae* (Bonn: Marcus and Weber, 1913), pl. 22 (whence Guarducci, *Epigrafia*, II, 449, fig. 101). (Girard, no. 31; *IG* II, 900, with an engraving; II², 1864)

Whole. Fine, green patina. L. 10.6 cm., w. 2.0 cm.; from the photograph the thickness looks average, ca. 0.2 cm.

Apparently one use. The photograph shows absolutely no indications of an earlier name, or, except in the upper left-hand corner, of erasure.

    Ⓣ   Ⓖ
                  before inscribing
    [?]

E: Ἀντικράτης : Εὐκτ(ημον—?)
Ⓣ *Αἰξωνεύς* Ⓖ

T(riobol) seal. With $_{H}^{[A]}{}_{[\Theta]}$. The profile of the owl (wide, flat head, small body) is identical in every respect to the profiles of Class V owls. Diam. ca. 1.1 cm.

G(orgoneion) seal. Similar to the long-haired gorgoneia of **21**, **25**, and others and of **24**, but, because of differences in hair and chin profiles, probably from a different die. The locks of hair terminate in snakes that must have been knotted under the chin. Diam. 1.0 cm.

Like **28**, this pinakion was originally provided with a stamped section-letter that was erased and replaced with an inscribed letter when the owner's name came to be added.[17] Evidence of the erasure is to be found in the spread

16. Not from the Peiraeus, as erroneously stated in *Demen von Attika*. In the original publication (699, n. 16, and 710) Ross twice gives Aixone as the place of finding. By "Aexone" ("Aexonischen Todenfelder," ibid., 702) Ross apparently means the entire vast necropolis reaching from Trachones "to Halai Aexonides" (ibid., 698–699) and not necessarily the site of the deme proper, which occupied only the southern half of this coastal stretch (see C. W. J. Eliot, *Coastal Demes of Attika* [Toronto: University of Toronto Press, 1962], 6–25).

17. Bruck (*Philologus* 54 [1893], 65) contended that the section-letter was added by a different hand than the hand responsible for the owner's name. To be sure, the middle bar of the epsilon section-letter is shorter than its counterparts in the name, and the section-letter was punched more deeply, but neither factor need evidence two hands. Two different forms of epsilons occur also on **122**, text *b*, which was almost certainly inscribed by only one letterer.

profile and depressed surface at the upper left corner of the pinakion. The lower edge of the depression is straight and can be distinguished between the lower bar of the epsilon and the top of the triobol seal.

The patronymic may be restored *Εὐκτήμονος* or *Εὐκτημονίδου*. The former is much more common in Attika generally, the latter the only full name in *Εὐκτ–* attested from Aixone (*IG* II², 5425, *tit. sep. s.* IV *a.*: *[Εὐ]κτημονίδης [Τε]λεσάνδρου [Αἰξ]ωνεύς*). Note the interpuncts between the section-letter and nomen and the nomen and demotic.

In the addenda to *PA* (II, p. 444), Kirchner restored *[Ἀντ]ικράτης* (Aixoneus) in line 14 of a fragmentary catalogue of tribesmen of Kekropis, dated 400–350 and eventually republished as *IG* II², 2375. In the latter he left the line unrestored, as did Robert in a more recent republication (*Coll. Froehner* I, 139–140, and pl. III, no. 93). Although Kirchner's restoration was, of course, conjectural, it was not without substance, since, in the list of demesmen of Aixone provided at the end of *PA*, the Antikrates known from this pinakion affords the only name that will restore *[. ? .]ικράτης*.

Class IV C

Both triobol and gorgoneion seal from dies indistinguishable from dies used in Class V.

WITH TWO SECONDARY SEALS

73 (Figs. 128–129)   Athens, National Museum, Inv. Bronze 8125. From a grave at Pykrodaphne, near Old Phaleron (A. S. Rousopoulos, "Scavi D'Atene," *BdI* 1864, 227). Full publication with a fine watercolor facsimile by A. Dumont, *RA*² 17 (1868), 142, and pl. V. 3. (Girard, no. 1; *IG* II, 909; II², 1878)

Complete. Broken into a number of fragments, now mended. Metal in a rather highly corroded state, both internally and on the pitted and rough green surface. L. 12.5 cm., w. 2.1 cm. at ends to 2.6 cm. in the middle, th. ca. 0.25 cm. at ends to 0.18 cm. in middle.

Two or more uses. Erasure by hammering has been most heavy in line 1, as is seen from the curve of the plate's upper edge.

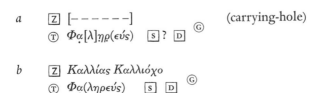

a   Z [– – – – – –]   (carrying-hole)
       T *Φα[λ]ηρ(εύς)*   S ?   D   G

b   Z *Καλλίας Καλλιόχο*
       T *Φα(ληρεύς)*   S   D   G

T(riobol) seal. With   A .

              H [Θ]

G(orgoneion) seal.

D(ouble-bodied owl) seal. With A A. Field ca. 0.75 cm. square. Stamped upside down and apparently subjected to partial erasure prior to the last use.

S(phinx?) seal.[18] In incuse square, ca. 0.8 × 0.8 cm. Visible is a feline creature with a small head and prominent breasts (or front haunches), seated right, tail curving up from behind. This seated, upright position is particularly characteristic of sphinxes in all periods of Greek art [19] and, together with the possible breasts, makes the identification probable. There are no positive indications of curved wings in the upper left field, but, if in low relief, they could have easily disappeared through corrosion, wear, and the like. The seal is unique, occurring on no other extant pinakion. To judge from the depth of its relief, the seal would seem to have been a late addition. It was certainly stamped later than the faint double-bodied owl seal and may not have been added until the last use.

Section-letter. Abnormally wide and rectangular, incuse field ca. 0.8 × 0.7 cm.

Text b. Owing to corrosion, the letters in the middle of line 1 are weak and look almost as if they had been subjected to erasure. The two legible letters in line 2 are weaker still and may in fact have been partially erased. The right-hand diagonal of the alpha is missing altogether. It will be observed further that certain possible traces of erased letters at the right combine with the phi and alpha to give a more complete demotic and that the phi was apparently formed with a smaller ring punch than the omicrons at the right of line 1. All of this suggests that the more complete demotic was originally inscribed for the penultimate owner and that it was erased preparatory to the last inscription, but was retained in its partially erased form when it was discovered that the last owner, too, was from Phaleron.

That the last owner was a Phalereus is confirmed by the rarity of his patronymic. The only other occurrence of Καλλίοχος in Greek prosopography is in the name of a relative, probably a nephew: Καλλίοχος Καλλιμάχου (Φαληρεύς), bouleutes in 303/2 (*Hesperia* 37 [1968], 14, line 202).

18. Identified by Dumont as a sphinx or a griffin, by Koehler, who also examined the pinakion in Athens, and hence by Kirchner, as a griffin. Griffins, however, were usually depicted in classical Greek iconography as walking or standing (F. Imhoof-Blumer and Otto Keller, *Tier- und Pflanzenbilder auf Munzen und Gemmen des Klassischen Altertums* [Leipzig, 1889], pl. XI, nos. 23–30), and when they are shown in a seated position (as on certain coins of Teos and Abdera [*ibid.*, nos. 24 and 27]), one front paw is invariably extended forward. The figure in our seal, if not a sphinx, is more likely to have been a seated lion or panther than a griffin.

19. Imhoof-Blumer and Keller, *Tier- und Pflanzenbilder*, pl. XIII, nos. 8–14, and XXVI, nos. 34–42.

Class IV B or C

PRESENCE OR ABSENCE OF SECONDARY SEAL UNCERTAIN

74 (Fig. 130) Athens, National Museum, Inv. Bronze 8078. A. Dumont, *RA²* 17 (1868), 141, and pl. V, 2. (Girard, no. 6; *IG* II, 881; II², 1845)

Left end. Recently stripped to bare bronze. L. 2.1 cm., w. 2.1 cm., th. 0.20 cm. at left to 0.15 cm. at right.

Two or more uses:

a Ⓑ [- - -
   Ⓣ 4̣[- - - -

b Ⓑ *E*[- - -   letters with punched serifs in imitation of Class V
   Ⓣ *A*[- - -   lettering

T(riobol) seal. With $\overset{[A]}{\underset{\text{H}\ \Theta}{}}$. The eta was read by Dumont from faint suggestions visible before cleaning and is supported by the size and profile of the owl, which is identical with owls on Class V pinakia.

Section-letter. Field ca. 0.75 cm. in height × ca. 0.7 cm. in width. Possibly from the same die as the beta section-letter on **107**.

Class IV A, B, or C

WITHOUT SECONDARY SEAL

75 (Fig. 131) formerly Athens, in a private collection.[20] "Fundort die Patissia-Strasse in Athen angegeben wird." S. Bruck, *AthMitt* 19 (1894), 210, no. 1 (with facsimile = our Fig. 131). (*IG* II 5, 877b; II², 1840).

Complete. Broken in two. Bruck's dimensions: L. 11.2 cm., w. 2.1 cm., th. ca. 0.15 cm.

Probably one or two uses:

Last Ⓐ *Νημονίδης*
use   Ⓣ *Εὐωνυ(μεύς)* Ⓖ

20. Bruck does not explicitly state the location of the collection, but the other pinakion that he published from the same collection (our **78**) was later obtained by the British Museum, from "Greece, 1895."

T(riobol) seal.

G(orgoneion) seal.

Bruck, although not infallible, did know what to look for and usually saw the obvious. It seems safe, therefore, to accept his facsimile as accurate. The facsimile permits no judgments about the styles of the stamped seals, but it does show that the shape of the plate had not been distorted by excessive erasure and that obvious traces of earlier inscriptions, that is, earlier letters or drilled holes (as would have certainly been visible had this been originally a Class V pinakion) were lacking.

To my knowledge, the name Nemonides occurs only on this pinakion.

PRESENCE OR ABSENCE OF SECONDARY SEAL UNCERTAIN

76 (Fig. 132)   Athens, National Museum, Inv. Bronze 8138. S. Bruck, *AthMitt* 19 (1894), 208, no. 3. (*IG* II 5, 915b; II², 1888)

Left end. Recently stripped to bare metal. L. 3.4 cm., w. 2.1 cm. at left to 2.5 cm. at right, th. 0.18 cm. at left to 0.06 cm. at right.

Probably more than two uses. The piece has been heavily erased and finally broke as a result.

a   ⊙ /[– – –

  Ⓣ [· – – –

b   ⊙ ∧|[– – –   erased

  Ⓣ *X*[– – –

T(riobol) seal. No letters of the ethnic visible. The owl has the standard flat-headed, small-bodied Class V profile, but compare the triobol seal on **63** with a similar owl but an ethnic in AΘE.

As Bruck recognized, the letters of the last use have been erased. The fragment, like **9,** is the discarded end of a pinakion that broke during erasure and was therefore certainly a surface find. The chi in line 2 has not been recorded previously.

77 (Figs. 133–134)   Basel, Antikenmuseum, Inv. 1941.126.5. Ex coll. Rouso-poulos-Pfuhl. F. Stähelin, *AA* 1943, 19, and pl. I, no. 5 (photograph before cleaning).

Left end. Recently stripped to bare metal. L. 3.4 cm., w. 2.4 cm., th.
0.18 cm. at left to 0.08 cm. at right.

Three or more uses. The piece has suffered much erasure.

a   Ⓩ $A\Lambda$[– – –
     Ⓣ [– – –

b   Ⓩ   /[– – –
     Ⓣ $E[i]\tau[\epsilon\alpha\hat{\iota}os$?

c   A $Ap\chi$[– – –   Class VI?
     Ⓣ? $M\epsilon[\lambda\iota\tau\epsilon\acute{u}s$?

T(riobol) seal. No letters of the ethnic remain. As on **76**, the profile of the owl is
of the Class V type. The seal has been subjected to some erasure, like the
stamped section-letter above it.

Class V

Same seal and section-letter format as in Class IV. Owners' names inscribed with added pierced holes, as diagramed in Table I, above.

All triobol seals from an uncertain number of virtually identical dies. As
on **78**: owl with flat, wide head, articulated from a small, stubby body.

Ethnic $\begin{smallmatrix} & A & \\ H & & \Theta \end{smallmatrix}$. Olive wreath with three pairs of leaves on each branch. Diam.

of field, 1.05–1.1 cm.

All gorgoneion seals from an uncertain number of virtually identical dies.
As on **78**: head with a relatively circular profile, finely modulated facial
features, and short, smooth bands of hair. A pair of confronting snakes' heads
above (where most prominent) and at each side of the head. A fourth pair
of snakes knotted under the chin, their loose ends writhing in the field to the
left and right. These last snakes appear to be attached to the creature's chin
(like the lower snakes on **29**), for there is no indication that they extend down
from the ends of the hair. Diam. of field, 1.1 cm.

WITHOUT SECONDARY SEAL

78 (Fig. 135) London, British Museum, Inv. Bronze 332. Acquired from
"Greece, 1895." First published from a private Athenian collection by S.

Bruck, *AthMitt* 19 (1894), 210, no. 2, with a facsimile drawing. H. B. Walters, *Catalogue*, 50, no. 332 (includes a superb engraving). (*IG* II 5, 908b; II², 1877)

Complete. Broken in two (possibly in this century, as neither Bruck nor Walters acknowledges or shows any breakage). Good, dark green patina. L. 10.8 cm., w. 2.1 cm., th. 0.25 cm.

One use:

> Z   Θουκυδίδης
> T   Λαμπτ(ρεὺς)˙Καθύ(περθεν)   G   (carrying-hole)

T(riobol) seal. With   H   A   Θ˙

G(orgoneion) seal.

Each of these seals is the best-preserved example of its type.

Section-letter. From the same die (field 0.66 cm. high × 0.75 cm. wide) as the zeta section-letters on **88** and **146**.

All of the full holes pierce completely through the plate except the lower right hole of the final sigma in line 1 and the rightmost hole of the final letter in line 2.

The owner is probably to be identified with Θουκυδίδης Θεοκύδου Λαμπ-τρεὺς Καθύπερθεν, bouleutes in 367/6 (*Hesperia* 11 [1942], 233, no. 43, line 54). The pinakion omits the patronymic, but this is compensated for in part by the knowledge that both documents refer to a Thucydides of Upper Lamp-trai, the smaller section of the deme (with five representatives in the boule as compared with nine from Lower Lamptrai).

79 (Fig. 136) Paris, Cabinet des Médailles, Froehner Collection Inv. 622. "Attique, 1905." L. Robert, *Coll. Froehner* I, 9, and pl. VI, no. 10j.

Whole. Slightly encrusted green patina. L. 10.8 cm., w. 2.0 cm., th. 0.22 cm.

One use:

> H   Μειξικράτης
> T   Προσπάλ(τιος)   G

T(riobol) seal. With   H   A   Θ˙

G(orgoneion) seal.

The incrustation would have to be cleaned from the section-letter before it could be positively associated with or dissociated from the only eta die identified in Class V, see **86**. The pierced holes of the letters are abnormally small. Except for the hole at the apex of the alpha in line 2, all holes that should pierce through the plate do.

According to the standard Greek prosopographies, the name Meixikrates, though composed of common elements, is otherwise unattested.

80 (Fig. 137)   Paris, Cabinet des Médailles. Anonymous Gift. Text and dimensions published by L. Robert, *Coll. Froehner* I, 11, no. 10s. Photograph in S. Dow, *BCH* 87 (1963), 673, fig. 4 (whence Guarducci, *Epigrafia*, I, 466, fig. 241).

Whole. Encrusted green patina. L. 11.1 cm., w. 1.9 cm., th. 0.26 cm.

One use:

    Ⓗ *Καλλίας*

    Ⓣ *Ἀλαι*(εὺς) : *Θογενίδ*(ου) Ⓖ   (large carrying-hole)

T(riobol) seal. Legend illegible.

G(orgoneion) seal.

Section-letter. With the same internal and external dimensions as the etas positively from the one eta die identified in Class V (see **86**) and therefore possibly from this die.

Θογενίδ(ου) for *Θεο–* or *Θου–γενίδ*(ου), neither of which is otherwise attested in Athenian prosopography, although the cognate *Θεογένης* (*PA*, 6702: *Θουγένης*) was common. Compare *Hesperia* 11 (1942), 233, no. 42 (367/6 B.C.), line 52: *Θογείτων* for *Θεο–* or *Θου–γείτων*.

This text, **84***a*, **89**, **91**, **93***a*, line 1, **94***b*, **96***a*, and **105***a* were inscribed with completely pierced holes added in principle to every other letter. The alternate letters received partially punched holes. Here, the principle is violated in line 2 where terminal letters of the demotic and patronymic received completely pierced holes in spite of their position in the alternating sequence. Also, by mistake, the lower left hole of the second alpha in line 1 and the lower right hole of the theta in line 2 were pierced completely through, although in the latter case the letterer probably had difficulty making up his mind whether or not he should begin the patronymic with fully pierced holes.

81 (Figs. 138–140)   Paris, Cabinet des Médailles, Froehner Collection Inv. 611. "Trouvée à Athènes." Ex coll. Rayet. O. Rayet, *AnnAssEtGr* 1878, 206–207, with a good drawing. Photograph (before the recent cleaning) in L. Robert, *Coll. Froehner* I, 8, and pl. VI, no. 10b. S. Dow, *BCH* 87 (1963), 661–662, and fig. 9b. (*IG* II, 887; II², 1839)

Complete. Broken in two. Now freed of most dirt and corrosion on the inscribed surface. The back side remains heavily diseased. The reddened, fused condition of the surface and the faintness of most letters, especially toward the middle of the plate, result from Rayet's ill-advised attempt to clean the surface with fire.[21] L. 11.9 cm., w. 2.2 cm., th. 0.25 cm. at ends to 0.10 cm. in the middle.

Five uses:

a	Ⓗ [– – – – – –] Ⓣ *Λαμπτρ(εύς)*	Ⓖ	Class V (carrying-hole)
b	Ⓗ [– – – – – –].Ọ Ⓣ [– – – – – –]*N*	Ⓖ	inscribed with added punched holes in imitation of Class V lettering
c	Ⓗ Λ[– – –⎯8–10⎯– –]ọ*s* Ⓣ [– – –⎯5–7⎯– –]*σι(ος)*	Ⓖ	conventional lettering
d	? *Φ*[– –⎯ca.5⎯–]*s* *Φ*ịλ*ω*(—?) *Σημạ(χίδης)*	Ⓖ	Class VI?
e	Α *Λύσων* *Στειρι(εύς)*	Ⓖ	Class VI?

T(riobol) seal.[22] Effaced by the initial sigma of line 2, text *d*. None of the letters of the ethnic have survived.

G(orgoneion) seal.

Nearly all editors have recognized this to be a palimpsest, although no one has suggested more than two uses. The unerased eta at the beginning of

---

21. "De plus, pour debarrasser la plaque de l'oxydation qui l'empâtait, on l'a fait rougir au feu et on l'a ensuite gratée avec un couteau." (Rayet.)

22. The body of the owl, distorted and damaged by the sigma inscribed over it, has taken on the appearance of a profile head facing right; hence Rayet's identification of the seal as containing a "tête presque effacée tournée à droite et qui semble feminine," which was accepted with misgivings by Bruck (*Philologus* 54 [1895], 74) and in both editions of *IG* II. Robert quotes Froehner's imaginative "Buste d'Hermès à dr., avec petase ailé et caducée."

line 2 (my text *d*) was cited by E. Caillemer (DarSag, "Dikastai," 189) as evidence that the last owner was assigned to two dikastic sections. Bruck (*Philologus* 52 [1893], 419) and Dow knew better, but nevertheless did not recognize the crucial sigma inscribed in front of it over the triobol seal and so were unable to connect it convincingly with a demotic.

Text a. Prior to my examination, all of the completely pierced holes were closed by corrosion and erasure and, if visible at all, appeared as shallow pittings in the surface. I was able to locate and clean enough holes in line 2 to recover the demotic, but have had less success with line 1, where several key holes doubtless remain undetected. In the present state of line 1, no one letter can be positively restored, and the length of the name itself remains uncertain; it may have continued beyond the last-detected hole at the right. In Fig. 139 I have indicated how the positive holes should probably be apportioned to letters. (Two of the holes indicated in position 6 were punched through since the photograph was taken.) The apportionment suggests a seven-letter name ending in –*ΩN* with *Θ*, *O*, *P*, or *Φ* in position 3, *T* or *Y* in position 4, and *A*, *Δ*, or *Λ* in position 5. But since I have been unable to find any attested Greek name that fits these requirements, I suspect that the apportionment or the length of the name was somehow different. It would be ideal if the pinakion could be X-rayed. An X-ray photograph should reveal more holes and might allow the nomen to be restored.

Text b. Although a fairly large number of shallow punched holes survive from this use, only three letters are recognizable: the intact nu at the right of line 2; and at the right of line 1 a rectangular letter, followed by three holes indicative of an omicron. The text, like text *b* of **83**, would also have utilized drilled holes from text *a* whenever possible.

Texts c, d, and e. Fig. 140 should be self-explanatory. In line 1 Dow correctly saw that the patronymic beginning with an erased phi should be dissociated from the name of the last owner since it clearly belongs with the identical erased phi (?) at the left of the line. Diagonals at the left and an *OΣ* under the patronymic at the right belong to a still earlier text. Also belonging to this intermediate text *c* in line 2 is the *ΣI*, which cannot go with the demotic of either of the last owners. The sigma of the *ΣI* had previously been read as an epsilon, and, in spite of its extreme faintness, had been assigned to the demotic of the last owner.

82 (Figs. 141–142) Athens, National Museum, Inv. Bronze 8068. P. Girard, *BCH* 2 (1878), 533, no. 12. Sketch provided by S. Bruck, *AthMitt* 19 (1894), 207, no. 18. (*IG* II, 936; II², 1915)

Right half. Recently stripped to bare metal. L. 5.9 cm., w. 2.0 cm. at right to 2.3 cm. at left, th. 0.17 cm. at right to 0.08 cm. at left.

Four or more uses:

a – – –]
   – – –]Ọ Ⓖ
   Class V
   (carrying-hole)

b – – – – – –]
   – – –]/ | | Ω | Ⓖ
   conventional
   lettering

c – – –]κτης
   – – –]ς Ⓖ
   conventional
   lettering

d – – –]πίδης
   – – –] Ⓖ
   conventional
   lettering

G(orgoneion) seal.

WITH SECONDARY SEAL ADDED AFTER THE FIRST USE

83 (Figs. 143–144) London, British Museum, Inv. Bronze 331. Probably from Sepolia (see n. 23, below). "Découvert depuis peu, vient d'être acquis par M. Phodiades-bey, ministre de la Porte en Grèce," A. Dumont, "Tablette judiciaire du tribunal des Héliastes," *Bulletin de l'école française d'Athènes* 2 (Aug. 1868), 27–30. Later acquired by Alessandro Castellani in Rome and announced by Georg Kaibel as a new pinakion in "Adunanze dell' Instituto, Decembre 20, 1872," *BdI* 1873, 4. Dumont replied in a letter published in *BAntFr* 1873, 177–179. Purchased by the British Museum in 1873. E. L. Hicks, *Manual*, 202, no. 119.1 = Hicks-Hill, *Manual*, 286, no. 151.1. H. B. Walters, *Catalogue*, 50, no. 331. (Girard, no. 33; *IG* II, 885, after a transcription sent from Rome by W. Helbig; II², 1849)

Whole. Recently stripped of all encrusting patination. L. 10.7 cm., w. 2.0 cm., th. 0.2 cm. even.

Two uses:

a Ⓖ Φιλοχάρης
   Ⓣ Ἁλαι(εύς) Ⓖ
   Class V
   (carrying-hole)

b Ⓖ Ἀριστοφῶν : Ἀρισ–
   Ⓣ τοδήμου : Κοθω(κίδης) Ⓓ Ⓖ
   inscribed in imitation of
   Class V lettering

T(riobol) seal. With H A Θ·

G(orgoneion) seal.

D(ouble-bodied owl) seal. With A A. Small, 0.7 cm. square; from the same die as the seal on **93**. The careful stamping of the seal sideways (top of the seal to the left) between lines 1 and 2 of the final inscription and between the carrying hole and the gorgoneion (actually cutting into the gorgoneion's field) implies that the seal was not added until after the second text had been inscribed. Had it been stamped earlier, with use *a*, the seal would have been placed in the ample space at the right of line 2.

Section-letter. From the same die as the gamma on **91**; field 0.7 cm. high × 0.75 cm.

Previous editors did not note either of the two seals at the right or the existence of the earlier inscription. About half of the pierced holes of text *a* were closed by dirt and corrosion, but were easily punched through with a pin before chemical cleaning. The second inscription is notable for its careful imitation of Class V lettering with large, shallow punches in place of the standard pierced holes.

The last owner, Aristophon, belonged to a family of Kothokidai, which is rather well known from the three grave monuments: *IG* II², 5479 (lost; commemorating our Aristophon, his sister Demokleia, and her husband);[23] 6474 (also lost; commemorating his brother Exekestides, who was trierarch in 353/2 [*IG* II², 1613, line 184]); and 6480 (commemorating another brother, Silanion, and dated by Kirchner to *init. s. IV a.*) See Kirchner's stemma *ad PA*, 1816. The Ἐξήκεστος Κοθωκίδης who was secretary of the poletai in 367/6 (*Hesperia* 10 [1941], 14, no. 1, lines 5–6) should be still another brother since he was probably the father of Ἀριστόδημ[ος Ἐξ]ηκέστου (Κοθωκίδης), bouleutes in 304/3 (*Hesperia* 35 [1966], 225, line 92).

Owing to its confused earlier history, the pinakion came to be listed as two separate pinakia by Josef Klein ("Epigraphisch-antiquarische Streifzüge: I, Heliastentäfelchen," *Jahrbücher des Vereins von Alterthumsfreunden im Rheinland* 58 [1876], 67–68, nos. 5 and 6) and was subsequently included by Bruck among the pairs of pinakia that were inscribed for a single owner (see Chapter II, n. 3, above).

23. The patronymic, Ἀριστοδήμου, is given only for his sister. This stele presumably stood over the grave that yielded the pinakion. If the stele was found in the region of Sepolia (on the Kephissos in the northwest part of modern Athens), where it was seen by Ross (*Demen von Attika*, 78, no. 106) and Koehler (*IG* II, 5478), this too would be the place of finding for the pinakion.

84 (Figs. 145–147)   Basel, Antikenmuseum, Inv. 1906.773. Ex coll. Vischer. W. Vischer, *Kleinigkeiten*, 14, no. 1, and pl. II, 63 = *Kleine Schriften* II, 286, no. 1, and pl. XV, 63 (drawing before cleaning). J. J. Bernoulli, *Katalog*, 189, no. 1084. (*IG* II, 923; II², 1897)

Complete. Broken in two. Recently stripped to bare bronze. L. 12.4 cm., w. 2.0 cm., th. 0.20 cm. at left to 0.08 cm. in center.

Three uses:

a   Ⓚ *Εὐφίλητ*[*ο*]*ς* [*Ἀ*]*ν*[*τ*]*ι*–
     Ⓣ *δ*[*ό*]*τ*(*ο*)? [*ἐ*]*κ Κολωνῶ*   Ⓖ   Class V

b   Ⓚ *Γλαύκων* : *Πυθέο*
     Ⓣ *Φαλη*(*ρεύς*)   Ⓓ? Ⓖ   conventional
                                            lettering

c   Ⓚ *Φιλόξενος* : *Φιλοφεί*(—?)
     Ⓣ *Ἀγρυλῆθεν*   Ⓓ   Ⓖ   conventional
                                            lettering

T(riobol) seal. With H ∴ Θ · (A above)

G(orgoneion) seal.

D(ouble-bodied owl) seal (not noted previously). With [A] A. Field, 0.82–0.84 cm. square. Stamped upside down, possibly not until use *c*, as it appears in places to have been added over the striations from the erasure of text *b*. It clearly does not belong with the first use. Had it been stamped literally into text *a*, the seal would have been noticeably affected by the erasure of this text. Besides, there was sufficient room for the seal at the lower right of text *a*.

Section-letter. The only kappa section-letter surviving from Class V, field 0.7 cm. high × 0.6 cm. wide.

Before cleaning the pinakion was covered with a thick, crusty patina through which it was difficult to make out even much of the last inscription; most all of the completely drilled holes from text *a* were filled with corrosion and dirt, and indications of the intermediate text were lacking altogether.

Text a. Inscribed like **80, 89, 91**, and others, with completely pierced holes added only to every other letter. In three instances—in the phi and sigma of line 1 and in the first kappa of line 2—a hole that should have been pierced completely through was only partially pierced. As Figs. 146–147 show, cleaning has revealed enough of the shallowly punched holes in the alternate letters of the nomen and demotic to make their restorations absolutely certain. On the other hand, I was unable to detect a single partially punched hole from the alternate letters of the patronymic so that it is necessary to restore from

the following: [.]$\underset{.}{N}$[.]$I/\underset{\Lambda}{\overset{A\quad T}{\Delta}}$[.]$Y$. I am unaware of any name other than Ἀντίδοτ(ος) that will fit these requirements satisfactorily.

Text b. The father or son of this second owner was Πυθέας Γλα[ύκω]νος Φαληρ[εύς], the second owner of **103**, another Class V pinakion. The [– – –]ς Πυθέου Φ. who appears in a *Ratio Centesimarum, IG* II², 1598, line 19, dated *post med. s.* IV, may be a brother of our owner. A descendant of the family may be the Pytheas of Phaleron who served as prytanis sometime between 199/8 and 189/8 (Dow, *Prytaneis*, 103, no. 48, line 81).

Text c. Line 2. It will be observed that misstrikings occurred in the stamping of the left hasta of the lambda and in the ring of the theta. I assume that similar misstrikings are responsible for the considerably finer lines paralleling the right vertical of the eta and the diagonal of the nu. Both lines (shown in Fig. 146) have the appearance of erased strokes, but neither will go with text *a* or *b*, and I regard it as quite improbable that they could represent yet a fourth inscription, all other indications of which are lacking.

The last owner's patronymic (or the present spelling of it) is otherwise unattested in the standard prosopographies. Vischer restored Φιλοφεί(δου) and noted that although the name was new it was constructed of common elements (cf. Bechtel, 444; *PA*, 9162: Λεωφείδης). Apparently assuming metathesis of aspiration, Koehler preferred to print the irregular formation Φιλοφεί(θου?). Kirchner subsequently incorporated Φιλοφείθου in *PA* (14702 and 14762) and in the apparatus to *IG* II², 1897, there citing *PA*, 4442, Διοφείθου (for Διοπείθου), which, according to Meisterhans-Schwyzer, 102, no. 915, is the sole exception of this particular kind in Athenian prosopography. Φιλοπείθης is known from Athens (*PA*, 14714). But since there is much to be said for Vischer's alternative solution, the completion of our patronymic is best left undecided.

Another Philoxenos of Argyle is mentioned on a second-century B.C. gravestone, *IG* II², 5284.

WITH SECONDARY SEAL ADDED IN FIRST USE

85 (Fig. 148)　Paris, Cabinet des Médailles, Froehner Collection Inv. 623. Ex coll. Rayet. O. Rayet, *AnnAssEtGr* 1878, 206 (with a drawing, which was later

reproduced in Caillemer, DarSag, "Dikastai," 190, fig. 2410, and in Sandys, *Constitution of Athens*, frontispiece). Photograph published by L. Robert, *Coll. Froehner* I, 5, and pl. VI, no. 10a. (*IG* II, 876; Ii², 1837)
   Complete. Broken in two. Green patina. L. 10.9 cm., w. 2.0 cm., th. 0.27 cm. One use:

[A] Διονύσιος : Δι–
(T) ονυ(σ—?) : ἐκ Κοί(λης)   [D]   (G)   (carrying-hole)

T(riobol) seal. With H $\overset{\text{A}}{\cdot}$ Θ·

G(orgoneion) seal.

D(ouble-bodied owl) seal. With A A. 0.8 cm. high × 0.85 cm. wide. From the same die as on **65** and **86**.

Section-letter. (Field 0.73 cm. high × 0.7 cm. wide) from the same die as the only other surviving alpha section-letter in Class V, on **94**.

   Except for the lower left-hand hole of the initial delta in line 1, *all* of the holes, including the holes at the middle of the epsilon and sigmas, pierce completely through the plate.

86 (Fig. 149)   New York, Brooklyn Museum, Inv. 34.678. Purchased from C. T. Seltman. Unpublished.
   Whole. Excellent, dark green patina. L. 11.0 cm., w. 2.0 cm., th. 2.5 cm. One use:

[H] Λυσανίας
(T) Εὐπυρί(δης)   [D]   (G)

T(riobol) seal. With H $\overset{\text{A}}{}$ [Θ]·

G(orgoneion) seal.

D(ouble-bodied owl) seal. With A A. From the same die as the seals on **65** and **85**.

Section-letter. (Field 0.66 cm. high × 0.68 cm. wide.) From the only eta die identified in Class V. The die appears also on **87**, **106**, and **110**, and there is no material reason why the etas on **79** and **80** might not have been stamped by it also.

Save for the lower hole on the final iota, all full terminal holes pierce completely through the plate.

The exquisite preservation of the plate and the preciseness with which the letters were formed (the holes look drilled rather than punched) make this surely the most attractive of all surviving Athenian pinakia. Its authenticity is upheld by the dies used for stamping its seals and section-letter, each of which has been recognized on other Class V pinakia. The metal and its patination have been studied and passed by technicians at both the Brooklyn Museum and the Institute of Fine Arts in New York.

A Λυσανίας Λυσιάδου Εὐπυρίδης served as bouleutes in 335/4 (*IG* II², 1700, lines 84–86), but it is highly doubtful whether he can be identified with the owner of the pinakion. Eupyridai was one of the smaller Attic demes, but my high chronology for stamped pinakia (Class V not later than mid-century) and the probability that the pinakion, which had only one use, was buried with its owner soon after the Class V issue require that the bouleutes be a younger relative (above, p. 67).

87 (Fig. 150)   Paris, Musée du Louvre, Inv. Bronze 4070. Full publication including an excellent drawing by E. Michon, *BAntFr* 1908, 356–358 (whence the notice in *AA* 1909, 417, no. 6). A. de Ridder, *Bronzes du Louvre* II, 217, no. 4070 (imperfect text, ignores Michon). (*IG* II², 1900, after de Ridder)

Whole. Slightly encrusted green patina. L. 10.7 cm., w. 2.0 cm., th. 0.25 cm. One use:

⊞ *Εἰρηνοκλέης*
Ⓣ *Ἀφιδνα(ῖος)*   ⊡   Ⓖ

T(riobol) seal. With H A [Θ]ˑ

G(orgoneion) seal.

D(ouble-bodied owl) seal. With A A, stamped upside down. Field ca. 0.8 cm. high × 0.85 cm. wide. Possibly from the same die as on the two preceding pinakia.

Section-letter. From the same die as on the preceding pinakion.

All terminal holes pierce completely through the metal.

88 (Fig. 151)   Athens, National Museum, Inv. Bronze 8064. From a grave in Kypseli. Independently edited by U. Koehler, *IG* II, addenda, 885b, and by K. D. Mylonas, "Ἀνέκδοτον δικαστικὸν πινάκιον," *ArchEph* 1883, 105–106, with a drawing. Corrections by Bruck, *AthMitt* 19 (1894), 207, no. 20. (*IG* II 5, 885b; II², 1876)

Whole. Encrusted dark green patina. L. 10.7 cm., w. 2.1 cm., th. ca. 0.25 cm. One use:

> Z͏ *'Επιχάρης*
> T͏ *Άλαιε(ύς)*   D͏ G͏

T(riobol) seal. With H Α Θ·

G(orgoneion) seal.

D(ouble-bodied owl) seal. With A A. 0.75 cm. high × 0.8 cm. wide. The die cannot be identified on any other pinakion.

Section-letter. From the same die as the zeta section-letters on **78** and **144**.

All terminal holes pierce completely through the plate.

The *'Επικράτης 'Επιχάρους Άλαιεύς* mentioned in a votive inscription dated 400–350 B.C. (*IG* II², 4884) could be the owner's son or father.

89 (Figs. 152–154)   Athens, National Museum, Inv. Bronze 8124. P. Girard, *BCH* 2 (1878), 534, no. 18. More complete readings provided by U. Koehler, *IG* II, 897. Drawn (Fig. 154) and described by S. Bruck, *AthMitt* 19 (1894), 204, no. 5; whence J. Kirchner, *IG* II², 1861.

Left end and two middle pieces missing. Composed of several badly diseased fragments, which nevertheless have been recently subjected to cleaning. L. 11.5 cm., w. 2.2 cm., th. 0.15–0.20 cm. The right end contains two notches.

One use:

> Δ͏ *Νικόδημος*
> T͏ *'Ελαόσιος*   D͏ G͏   (carrying-hole)

T(riobol) seal. Bruck wrote "Unterhalb des Sektionsbuchstabens (erhaben in verticftem Viereck) ist der Rest eines Stempels, wahrscheinlich Eule, deutlich erkennbar."

G(orgoneion) seal. Visible are segments of the raised circular relief.

D(ouble-bodied owl) seal. Clearly present are the upper and left edges of the incuse square, and the relief of the owl's head, upper left body, and perhaps the left-hand alpha.

It is not surprising that neither of the seals at the right had been noted previously.

In spite of the deteriorated condition of the piece, it is quite apparent from the pattern of punched holes that the pinakion was inscribed with completely pierced holes at the terminations of every other letter (see. **80**).

Line 2. Koehler printed //*ΛΛ*...*Σ* and restored [*Ἀ*]λα[ιεύ]ς, which was duly incorporated into *PA*, and which doubtless inspired Bruck to restore an upsilon in dotted lines in his drawing. Later, in the *Editio Minor*, Kirchner suggested from the drawing that the demotic be restored ʼΕλα[ι]ούσ(ιος). To be sure, this is the correct demotic, as is obvious from the first three letters. Only Kirchner's spelling needs revision. The remains observed by Bruck and myself show that the demotic was unabbreviated, that is, not curtailed, but was condensed by the consistent omission of the second vowel in both diphthongs. On the omission of intervocalic iota in the name of this very deme, see Meisterhans-Schwyzer, 33, no. 6. The holes belonging to the iota of *–ΙΟΣ*, no longer visible, were seen by Bruck and recorded by him as the two right-hand holes of his "upsilon."

90 (Fig. 155)   formerly, Berlin, Staatliche Museen, Inv. Bronze 7384. Published from an Athenian private collection by P. Girard, *BCH* (1878), 535, no. 28. Reedited as Berliner Museum 7384 by S. Bruck, *AthMitt* 19 (1894), 204, no. 6, with the drawing reproduced here. (*IG* II, 898; II², 1862)

Whole. No dimensions recorded, but they would have been regular. Bruck's facsimiles are always at a reduced scale and usually distort overall proportions; cf. our Figs. 152 and 154.

One use:

[Δ] *Χαρίας*
Ⓣ *ʼΟτρυν(εύς)* [D]   Ⓖ

T(riobol) seal.

G(orgoneion) seal.

D(ouble-bodied owl) seal. With A A.

This is one of three Berlin pinakia of which no photograph survives. It is, fortunately, the least problematic. Bruck's drawing serves to show that the pinakion was perfectly regular in all respects. Neither he nor Girard mentions a carrying-hole.

91 (Figs. 156–157)   Oxford, Ashmolean Museum, Inv. 1968.81. Purchased from Sotheby sale, December 11, 1967 (cf. **39**). H. W. Catling, "A Bronze Dikast's Pinakion in Oxford," *BCH* 93 (1969), 571–573, with 2 figs. (= our Figs. 156 and 157).

Broken in three pieces; the rightmost one (containing the gorgoneion seal) is missing. Partially cleaned of a crusty patination. L. 11.4 cm., w. 2.1–2.2 cm., th. 0.15 cm.

One use:

> Γ *Πεδίαρχος*   (carrying-hole)
> Τ *Ἀλαιεύς* D

T(riobol) seal. With [H] A [Θ]·

D(ouble-bodied owl) seal.

Section-letter. From the same die as the gamma section-letter on **83**.

The text was inscribed with regularly alternating fully and partially pierced letters (see **80**). The lettering is remarkably similar to the lettering on **94**, text *b*, in two respects: in the shapes of the epsilons and in the depth of the strokes generally. Note the angular rho (and omicron?).

For other occurrences of the name Pediarchos at Athens, see *Supplementum Epigraphicum Graecum* 3 (1929), no. 56 = *AthMitt* 67 (1942), 88–89, no. 142; and *IG* III 3, 29, line 5.

92 (Figs. 158–159)   Munich, Antikensammlung (Museum Antiker Klein-kunst), Inv. 399. Excavated by Edward Dodwell in the summer of 1805 from "amongst the bones" of a closed grave in the northern Peiraeus. Purchased by the Munich Museum after Dodwell's death (1832). J. D. Akerblad, *AttiAccRom* 1, 1 (1821), 39–41, and pl. I.1 (drawing, made before full cleaning, omits seals and holes from text *a*). Dodwell, *Tour* I, 433 (with an excellent engraving). Text *a* restored by Albert Rehm in a review of William Larfeld, *Griechische Epigraphik, Berliner Philologische Wochenschrift* 36 (1916), 300. (*CIG*, 207; Girard, no. 29; *IG* II, 893; II², 1857)

Complete. Cleaned to bare bronze. L. 10.7 cm., w. 2.0 cm., th. 0.23 cm. at ends to 0.18 cm. in middle.

Two uses:

> *a*   Δ *Φαίγιππος*   D G   Class V
>   Τ *Ὤαθεν*   (carrying-hole)

b $\boxed{\Delta}$ $\Delta\iota\acute{o}\delta\omega\rho o\varsigma$ $\boxed{\text{D}}$ Ⓖ conventional
     Ⓣ $\Phi\rho\epsilon\acute{\alpha}(\rho\rho\iota o\varsigma)$ lettering

T(riobol) seal. With $\begin{smallmatrix} & A \\ H & \Theta \end{smallmatrix}$·

G(orgoneion) seal.

D(ouble-bodied owl) seal. With A [A], height 0.75 cm., stamped unevenly (the right side did not take), at a tilt, and exceptionally far to the left. Since the top of the seal appears cut by the sigma of use *b*, but only touches a hole of use *a*, it appears that the seal was probably added during the first use.

Section-letter. The only fully preserved delta section-letter on a surviving Class V pinakion. Field, 0.7 cm. in height × 0.75 cm. wide.

This, the first pinakion to have been discovered, was also the first Class V palimpsest to have had its entire original inscription restored. Rehm's task of restoration was simplified by the survival of several of the original lines that connected the pierced holes. I have indicated these original connecting strokes with thicker lines in my reconstruction of the text in Fig. 159.

The last owner of the pinakion is probably to be identified with one or both of the following: Diodoros Phrearrios, father of the Peithiades who was prytanis *ante med. s. IV a. (IG* II², 1742, lines 49–50); Diodoros Phrearrios, father of the Euboulos who was prytanis *post med. s. IV a. (IG* II², 1752, line 19). Both references could, of course, refer to the same Diodoros. The Diodoros, son of Kallimachos, of Phrearrioi, an ephebe in or about 324/3 (*ArchEph* 1918, 75, line 8), was possibly a younger relative.

WITH SECONDARY SEAL, UNCERTAIN WHEN ADDED

93 (Figs. 160–161)   Leiden, National Museum of Antiquities, Inv. RO III 103. Excavated from a tomb in Attika during the early 1800s by L. F. S. Fauvel.[24] Purchased, probably from Fauvel in Smyrna, by B. E. A. Rottiers for the Leiden Museum in 1825. J. D. Akerblad, *AttiAccRom* I, 1 (1821), 61–62, and pl. I.2 (after a facsimile by C. R. Cockerell). L. J. F. Janssen, *Musei Lugduno-Batavi Inscriptiones Graecae et Latinae* (Leiden, 1842), 48–49, and pl. III.2, with an admirable drawing. First published photograph and restoration of text *a* by J. H. Jongkees, *BABesch* 20 (1945), 8–10. J. H. Kroll, *BCH* 91 (1967), 385 and 387–388, with figs. 4 and 5. (*IG* II, 884; II², 1848)

---

24. Janssen quoted Rottiers thus: "Sepulcrum, in quo lamina reperta est, continebat sarcophagum marmoreum, tegulis tectum, in quo defuncti ossa deposita jacebant."

Whole. Brown metal, except in three waxy green areas along the lower edge àt the left, center, and right. L. 11.6 cm., w. 2.1 cm., th. 0.2 cm. Two uses:

a   B *Δημ[ό]φιλ[ο]ς*   Ⓖ   Class V
      Ⓣ   *Εἰρεσί(δης)* D?   (carrying-hole)

b   B *Φρυνοκλέης*   Ⓖ   conventional
      Ⓣ *Θριάσι(ος)*   D   lettering

T(riobol) seal. With ᴴ • A • Θ.[25]

G(orgoneion) seal.

D(ouble-bodied owl) seal. With A A, stamped upside down, from the same small die as the seal on **83**.

Section-letter. Field 0.8 cm. high × 0.7 cm. wide. From a larger die than the beta section-letters on **74** and **107**.

Text a. The several deductions leading to the restoration are discussed in my article cited above. The most serious difficulty is provided by the hole I have connected to the lower extremity of the phi. A phi with such a long stem is irregular to be sure, yet a phi must be restored in the middle of line 1 even if there were no holes to which to fit it. The hole will not restore with any other combination of letters in line 2, and its connection with the phi is confirmed by the exceptional height of the upper terminal hole of the vertical. For a phi with a very long vertical in a conventionally lettered text, see **92**, text *b*.

Altogether, this is the most irregularly inscribed Class V text extant. Line 1 seems to have been treated according to the principle of alternating full and partially pierced letters, although individual letters themselves—more than in **94**, text *b*—were inconsistently treated as the punch occasionally pierced more shallowly or more deeply than it should have. The piercing of holes in the demotic, however, seems to be utterly haphazard. The demotic was probably indented to center it under the nomen. For another demotic indented two spaces, see **29**.

25. The letters have previously been read as KO or Λ̸O (Fränkel *apud IG* II) or Z̄Λ̸/IO (Bruck [*Philologus* 54 (1895), 74] from Janssen's engraving). In both instances leaves of the olive sprays above the H and Θ were mistaken as additional letters.

94 (Figs. 162–164)   Athens, National Museum, Stathatos Collection, No. 406. A. A. Papagiannopoulos-Palaios, *Polemon* 4 (1949), 76–80, and fig. 1. Claude Rolley, in *Collection Hélène Stathatos*, 3 vols. (Limoges: A. Bontemp; Strasbourg: n.p., 1953–1963), III, 105, and pl. XV, no. 105. Both publications with photograph before cleaning.

Whole. Recently stripped to bare metal. L. 11.3 cm., w. 2.3–2.4 cm., th. 0.2 cm. even.

Two uses:

a   Ⓐ $\Pi[\overset{ca.2}{--}]\Sigma[-\overset{ca.3}{--}-]O\Sigma$ Ⓓ? Ⓖ   letters with partially punched
     Ⓣ $E\rlap{/}{\rm E}\,[-\overset{ca.4}{--}-]$ "serifs" (carrying-hole)

b   Ⓐ *Εὐγείτων*   Ⓓ Ⓖ   Class V lettering
     Ⓣ *Ἀλαιεύς*

T(riobol) seal. With ${}_{\rm H}\!\overset{\rm A}{}\!{}_{\Theta}$·

G(orgoneion) seal.

D(ouble-bodied owl) seal. With A A, 0.8 × 0.8 cm. square.

Section-letter. From the same die as the other alpha section-letter in Class V, on **85**.

This is the only surviving pinakion known to have been inscribed with partially punched holes in its first use and with fully pierced holes in a later use. The implications of the puzzling reversal are discussed above, pp. 32–33. I note here merely that the style of the primary seals, the identity of the section-letter die, and the technique of the second inscription require that the pinakion be listed among the pinakia of Class V.

Text a. Previously undetected. Several of the dots and lines recorded in Fig. 163 may be actually pittings or scratches in the metal. The only positive letters in line 1 are the two sigmas and a penultimate omicron. At the beginning of the line is probably a pi. Taken together, these four letters could belong to at least three different Athenian names, none of which, however, exactly fits the remaining traces in the line. The remains toward the right of line 2 are too ambiguous to permit a restoration of the demotic.

Text b. Inscribed with completely pierced holes added in principle only to every other letter. The pattern is interrupted at the middle of line 2, and the two epsilons in line 1 were rather haphazardly treated. The half partially pierced, half fully pierced letters at the ends of both lines represent a conscientious attempt to terminate lines with fully pierced holes without doing violence to the alternating pattern (cf. the treatment of ends of names in line 2 on **80**).

95 (Figs. 165–167) Basel, Antikenmuseum, Inv. 1941.126.1. Ex coll. Rhousopoulos-Pfuhl. F. Stähelin, *AA* 1943, 16, and pl. I, no. 1.

Complete. Broken in two toward the left. Recently cleaned to the bare, pitted bronze. L. 11.1 cm., w. 2.1 cm., th. 0.30 cm. at ends to 0.22 cm. at the center.

Three uses:

a	E $K\lambda\epsilon\acute{o}\kappa\rho\iota\tau os$		Class V
	T $\Sigma o\upsilon\nu\iota(\epsilon\acute{\upsilon}s)$ D? ^{G}		(carrying-hole)
b	E $\overline{/\!/\!/}[-^{ca.3}-]\overline{/\!/\!/}[-^{ca.3}-]P[--]$ ^{G}		conventional
	T $\Pi\.[-----^{ca.7}----]\|$ D		lettering
c	E $K\alpha\lambda\lambda\acute{\iota}\sigma\tau\rho\alpha\tau os$		conventional
	T $\Gamma\alpha\rho\gamma\acute{\eta}\tau\tau\iota os$ D ^{G}		lettering

T(riobol) seal. With [A] / [H]   [Θ]˙

G(orgoneion) seal.

D(ouble-bodied owl) seal. With A A. Small rectangular field, 0.65 cm. high × 0.75 cm. wide.

Section-letter. Of exceptionally small size, field ca. 0.65 cm. square. Apparently from a smaller die than the epsilon on **104**.

The photograph of the pinakion in its uncleaned state is illustrated to show better the appearance of the seals and the last inscription. Stähelin noted that an earlier name was represented by a number of pierced holes, but made no effort to punch them clean or to restore the name. Evidence of the intermediate inscription was not visible until after chemical cleaning; its fragmentary survival is to be attributed as much to the pitted condition of the metal as to the heavily striating erasure.

96 (Figs. 168–171) Athens, Stoa of Attalos, Agora Excavations Inv. B 1352. Excavated in 1970 from Area I/5; context of fourth to sixth centuries A.D. Publication forthcoming in 1970 Agora report in *Hesperia*.

Whole, except for a small piece missing from the middle of the upper edge. Each end cut with a V-shaped notch at some time after the primary seals were added. Heavy erasure at the middle has warped the ends forward. Cleaned to bare metal. L. (distended by erasure) 13.9 cm., w. 2.15 cm. at right to 2.5 cm. at middle, th. 0.25 cm. maximum at ends to 0.10 cm. minimum in middle.

Six uses, minimum:

a	⊡ · [.] · [.]ι[.]s		Ⓖ	Class V
	Ⓣ 'Ẹ[λ]ε[υ]σί(νιος)	⊡?		(carrying-hole)
b	Γ [– – – – – –]		Ⓖ	conventional lettering
	Ⓣ [– – – – – –]	⊡		
c	K [– – – – – –]ης		Ⓖ	conventional lettering
	Ⓣ [– – – – – –]	⊡		
d	B [– – – – $\frac{7-9}{}$ – – – –]ρος		Ⓖ	Class VI?
	[– $\frac{3-4}{}$ –]Λ⫶[–$\frac{1-2}{}$–]Σ	⊡		
e	Κιχων[ίδ]ης		Ⓖ	Class VI
	Ⓗ Γαργήτ(τιος)	⊡		
f	Φιλόμνηστος		Ⓖ	Class VI
	Ⓚ 'Ικαριεύς	⊡		

T(riobol) seal. With H $\overset{[A]}{\Theta}$·

G(orgoneion) seal.

D(ouble-bodied owl) seal. With A A. In field ca. 0.85 cm. square.

Section-letters. The original stamped section-letter in the upper left corner has been heavily erased; nevertheless, traces remain to suggest that the letter was either an alpha or delta. This original letter was inscribed over by three subsequent letters: a gamma (or epsilon), a kappa, and a large beta. The beta was positioned rather low and cut through the head of the owl of the triobol seal; hence it is probable that the seal was no longer valid and that the pinak- ion was being used as a stampless Class VI pinakion by the time of its antepenultimate use, with which the beta belongs. Since all three inscribed letters have been subjected to some erasure, it is clear that they preceded the two stamped section-letters at the lower left of the pinakion.

After the inscribed beta was erased, an eta section-letter was stamped just to the right of the triobol seal. One assumes that this position was chosen so that the relief of the letter would not be distorted by the uneven surface at the upper left corner of the pinakion or by the relief of the triobol seal. For the last use, the eta was overstamped by a kappa, which cut slightly into the triobol seal. The incuse fields of both the eta and kappa section-letters are approximately 0.8 cm. square.

The irregular appearance of these stamped section-letters in uses following uses with inscribed section-letters has a parallel in **145** (see Chapter II, n. 26, above). The parallel with **145** tends to confirm that the last uses of the pinakion were indeed theoretically stampless Class VI uses.

Text a. The name of the original owner was inscribed with alternately fully and partially pierced letters. The pattern is broken at the end of line 2 to permit the line to end with a fully pierced letter. Erasure on the face of the pinakion has closed up some of the holes that originally pierced completely through the metal; these holes, however, show up clearly on the back where there was no erasure (Fig. 171). The demotic can be restored from the holes in line 2. Possibilities for the nomen in line 1 are Ἀκταῖος (PA, 483), Ἀμυνίας (PA, 737), Ἀστεῖος (PA, 2641–2642), and Λεύκιος (PA, 9053–9057).

Text e. The owner is the same Κιχωνίδης Διογείτονος Γαργήττιος who appears in a poletai inscription of 367/6 as representative of the association of the phratry of the Medontidai (*Hesperia* 10 [1941], 16, no. 1, lines 16–17). Because of the extreme rarity of the nomen, the identification may be regarded as certain. To my knowledge, there is only one other occurrence of the name Kichonides in Greek prosopography, see *ibid.*, 43, no. 11, lines 16–17.

Text f. The name Philomnestos is apparently new to Athenian prosopography.

97 (Figs. 172–174)   Athens, Stoa of Attalos, Agora Excavations Inv. B 12. Excavated in 1931 from Area H/5; context of fifth to second century B.C. *Hesperia* 2 (1933), 474, with photo = photo in *Art and Archaeology* 34 (1933), 27.

Left half. Cleaned to bare metal. L. 5.6 cm., w. 2.0 cm. at right to 2.2 cm. at left, th. 0.2 cm. at right to 0.1 cm. at left.

Four uses:

a   — —μ?]αχος   Ⓖ   Class V (carrying-hole)
    — — —]   Ⓓ?

b   – – – – – –]*N*   Ⓖ   conventional lettering
        – – –]   Ⅾ

c   – – – – –]*s*   Ⓖ   conventional lettering
        – – –]   Ⅾ

d   <u>nomen</u>]*Nικίο*   Ⓖ   conventional lettering
    <u>dem.</u>]   Ⅾ

G(orgoneion) *seal.*

D(ouble-bodied owl) *seal.* Stamped on back side; width ca. 0.8 cm. No alphas visible.

98 (Figs. 175–176) Paris, Cabinet des Médailles, Froehner Collection Inv. 621. "Athènes, 1912." L. Robert, *Coll. Froehner* I, 10, and pl. VI, no. 10p.

Right end. Partially cleaned of the encrusting patination. L. 2.8 cm., w. 2.0 cm., th. 0.2 cm.

One or more uses:

a   – – –]*s* Ⅾ Ⓖ
       – – –]   (carrying-hole)

G(orgoneion) *seal.*

D(ouble-bodied owl) *seal.* Large rectangular field, 0.8 cm. high × 0.9 cm. wide. No alphas visible.

Traces of one partially and three fully pierced holes of a final sigma survive in line 1.

Froehner mistakenly believed that this fragment and **173** belonged to the same pinakion. The two fragments were correctly dissociated by Robert.

99 (Figs. 177–178) formerly Berlin, Staatliche Museen, Inv. Bronze 6363.[26] S. Bruck, *AthMitt* 19 (1894), 209, no. 7, with the sketch reproduced in our Fig. 178. (*IG* II 5, 938e; II², 1920)

Right end. Heavily encrusted. L. ca. 3.0 cm., w. ca. 2.0 cm.; from the photograph th. looks normal, ca. 0.2 cm.

Probably more than one use.

26. According to Bruck. *IG* II² gives 6436.

Visible use:

$- - - -]X$ Class V or imitation of Class V lettering

$- - -]\Sigma$ ⒟ ⒢ (carrying-hole)

G(orgoneion) seal. Features clearly of the the Class V type.

D(ouble-bodied owl) seal. With A A.

    The fragment is so heavily corroded that for the surviving letters one must depend more on Bruck's sketch than on the photograph. Neither makes it clear, however, whether the holes at the terminations of letters would have pierced completely through the metal or were only partially punched as in "imitation" of the Class V technique. If the latter, the partially punched text would have been preceded by a regular Class V text with completely pierced letters—unless of course the fragment actually happened to belong to a Class IV C pinakion (cf. **73**). It is possible also that the letters, especially the one composed of three holes in line 2 (presumably a sigma), may have been subjected to erasure and thus were superseded by a later inscription.

100 (Figs. 179–180) Athens, National Museum, Inv. Bronze 8067. P. Girard, *BCH* 2 (1878), 533, no. 16. Drawing, identification of the stamped seal, and restoration of the demotic of text *a* by S. Bruck, *AthMitt* 19 (1894), 206, no. 16. (*IG* II, 924, with restoration of text *b*; II², 1898, with restoration of text *a*, line 1, from Bruck's drawing).

    Broken at both ends. Clean brown bronze. L. 3.8 cm., w. 2.2 cm., th. 0.18 cm.

    Two or more uses:

a $[-\overset{3-4}{-}-]\phi\iota\lambda o\varsigma$ ⧚ $[\overset{patro-}{---}$ Class V

          ⒟]?

    $[\overset{nym.}{---}]\Theta\rho\iota\acute{\alpha}\sigma\iota[os$

b $[\Pi o\sigma\epsilon]\acute{\iota}\delta\iota\pi\pi[os$ conventional lettering

    $[\overset{ca. 3}{---}]\alpha\sigma\iota(—?)$

D(ouble-bodied owl) seal. Stamped upside down. Hardly more than the left and bottom edges of the incuse square and the depressed surface within have survived. The relief of the owl has been almost totally obliterated during erasure of a text prior to the last use. Hence, if there were only two uses, the seal would belong to use *a*. But since the seal has been stamped partially over the first letter in the patronymic of text *a*, there is reason for supposing that it may have been added during a hypothetical use intermediate between texts *a* and *b*.

Text a. To Kirchner's restoration of line 1, I add two holes—most likely terminals of a vertical—from the first letter of the patronymic, and to Bruck's restoration of line 2, the iota at the right.

Although many names ending in –φιλος will restore in line 1, the only demesman of Thria with such a name in Kirchner's list at the back of *PA*, II is Ἀντίφιλος Βρυσωνίδο Θ., known from a votive inscription of 400–350 B.C. (*IG* II², 4352); Kirchner remarks *ad IG* II², 1898, that he may have been the first owner of the pinakion.

Text b. Permits the approximate number of letters missing at the left to be estimated for both uses: the minimum is two and a half letters left of ⩘ΣΙ in line 2 (the diagonal I read off the break); the maximum is the four spaces in line 1 required for Ποσείδιππος, according to Dornseiff-Hansen the longest personal name in –ιδιππος. Indeed, Ποσείδιππος is almost certainly the correct restoration, alternatives such as Φείδιππος all being too short. Koehler's restoration of the entire name [Ποσε]ίδιππ[ος Πρα]σι(εύς), which Kirchner accepted for *PA* 12132 and *IG* II², 1898, must be regarded as only a weak possibility, however. The name of another known Athenian that actually fits better is *PA* 12133: Ποσείδιππος Φυλάσιος (*IG* II², 2329, line 6, *c. 350 vel paullo post a.*) Even so, I think it best to leave the demotic unrestored, since it could also have been Θριάσιος.

101 (Figs. 181–182)   Athens, Stoa of Attalos, Agora Excavations Inv. B 847. Excavated in 1948 from Area B/19; fourth century B.C. fill. *Hesperia* 20 (1951), 201, and pl. 67c.

Broken at both ends. Green patina. L. 2.6 cm., w. 2.1 cm., th. 0.2 cm. at right to 0.1 cm. at left.

Three uses:

a	– – –]ọṣ [		Class V
	– – –]Υ̣ Ḍ]?[		
b	– – –] [		inscribed in imitation of Class V lettering
	– – –].ṣ Ḍ [		
c	– – –]λειδη[ς		conventional lettering
	– – –]ρρι Ḍ [		

D(ouble-bodied owl) seal. With A[A]. Field, o.8 cm. high.

Text c. The demotic was Κυθή]ρρι(ος), Μυ]ρρι(νούσιος), ἐκ Μυ]ρρι(νούττης) or Φρεά]ρρι(ος).

LEFT AND MIDDLE FRAGMENTS OR EQUIVALENTS: PRESENCE OR
ABSENCE OF SECONDARY SEAL UNCERTAIN

102 (Fig. 183)   formerly Berlin, Staatliche Museen, Inv. Bronze 7263.[27] P. Girard, *BCH* 2 (1878), 537, no. 34, from a private collection in Athens. U. Koehler, *IG* II, 921, after a transcription sent by Fränkel from Berlin.[28] Facsimile (reproduced below) published by S. Bruck, *AthMitt* 19 (1894), 206, no. 15. (*IG* II², 1894)

Apparently broken or encrusted at the right. No dimensions have been recorded; nor can they be taken from Bruck's drawing, which is undersize. One use:

[I]   *Παυσανίας Λευκ–*
ⓣ   *ονοεύς*

T(riobol) seal.

This is another Berlin pinakion that was not photographed. The three primary records are in agreement as to the lettering ("chaque lettre est percée de plusieurs trous du diamètre de 1 millimetre" [Girard]; the majuscule

27. Not 1263, as stated in *IG* II².
28. Girard mentions no provenience. Koehler, however, gives this curious notice: *Lamina Dodona Athenas translata, nunc in museo Berlinensi. Exscripsit Frankelius.* Now it is not unthinkable that an Athenian pinakion could have traveled with its owner to Dodona. An Athenian pinakion (**7**) did find its way to Olynthos. But since the alleged provenience of the present example is unverifiable we would do well to regard it with suspicion, as apparently did Bruck and Kirchner, neither of whom bothered to repeat Koehler's information. It is known that several small bronze inscriptions were stolen from Karapanos' excavations of 1873 in the sanctuary at Dodona, were sold on the Athenian market, and by 1878 had reached Berlin (Max Fränkel, "Inschrift aus Dodona," *AZ* 36 [1878], 71; and Constantin Carapanos, "Inscriptions et autres pièces provenant de Dodone," *ibid.*, 115). I suspect that our pinakion, which was purchased in Athens and brought to Berlin at about the same time, somehow became confused with this material, either in the correspondence between Fränkel and Koehler (in *AZ* 36 Fränkel refers to one of the Dodona inscriptions [now William Dittenberger, *Sylloge Inscriptionum Graecum*, 3d ed., 4 vols. (Leipzig, 1915–1921), I, 91, no. 73] as a "Bronzetäfelchen," the word commonly applied to pinakia) or by a dealer who may have sold the pinakion to an agent of the Berlin Museum together with the Dodona inscriptions. Some such error would easily account for Koehler's unlikely provenience for a pinakion that in all probability was found in Attika.

transcription in *IG* II confirms the slanted forms of the nu's) and as to the presence at the left of the owl seal and the absence of any seal at the right. We must assume, however, that either a centimeter or two of the right end had broken off or that corrosion and wear were such as to have obscured traces of a gorgoneion and perhaps a double-bodied owl seal. Even Bruck, who had a good eye for seals, missed the seals at the right of **89** and **104**. It is hardly probable that this pinakion would be the sole exception to the seal format so regularly attested by all surviving whole pinakia of Classes IV and V. The arrangement of the text with the demotic beginning in line 1 has no extant parallels but this slight anomaly cannot be regarded as significant.

The owner may be a descendant of the celebrated astronomer Meton, son of Pausanias, of Leukonoe (*PA*, 10093, active 433–415 B.C.).

103 (Figs. 184–186) Athens, Peiraeus, Archaeological Museum. A. N. Meletopoulos Collection. I. A. Meletopoulos, *Polemon* 3 (1947–48), 38, and pl. B', no. 4 (photograph before cleaning).

Left three-fourths of a pinakion. Recently stripped to bare bronze. L. 8.0 cm., w. 1.9 cm. at left to 2.0 cm. at right, th. 0.2 cm. at left to 0.15 cm. at right.

Two uses:

a Ⓘ *'Ἐπιχάρης v* .[– – –   Class V
Ⓣ *ϝος Εὐωνυ[μεύς*

b Ⓘ *Πυθέας : Γλα[ύκω–*   conventional lettering
Ⓣ *νος : Φαληρ[εύς*

T(riobol) seal. With H Ⓐ Θ·

Section-letter. Field, 0.7–0.75 cm. square. It is uncertain whether the present iota and the iota section-letter on **108** come from the same or different dies.

Text a. Not recognized by Meletopoulos. The drilled holes are more pronounced on the intact back side than on the inscribed face, which has been filed down and polished.

An Epichares of Euonymon was one of the ten Treasurers of the Sacred Monies in 398/7 (*IG* II², 1388, line 3; 1392, line 4) and has been identified by Werner Peek with the [*'Ἐπ*]*ιχάρης Εὐ*[*ωνυμεύς*] on the curse tablet he published in *Abhandlungen der Deutschen Akademie, Berlin, Klasse für Sprachen*, 1956, III, 59, no. 205. The nomen may be restored among the demesmen of Euonymon

in the bouleutic list of 336/5(?) (*Hesperia* 30 [1961], 31 and 36, line 4: [...]χάρης);
and perhaps also in the bouleutic list of 304/3 (*Hesperia* 35 [1966], 266, line 128:
Χαρῖνος Ἐπιχ[...]).

Text b. The father or son of this owner was the second owner of **81**, another
Class V pinakion.

104 (Figs. 187–188) Athens, National Museum, Inv. Bronze 8066. According
to the museum inventory, from Serpentzes, that is, from within the medieval
wall enclosing the upper south side of the Acropolis. P. Girard, *BCH* 2 (1878),
532, no. 8. U. Koehler, *IG* II, 899. Sketch by S. Bruck, *AthMitt* 19 (1894), 204,
no. 7; whence J. Kirchner, *IG* II², 1863.

   Left half (?), composed of two fragments, a smaller third one from within
the inverted V-shaped space below the vertical break now missing. Heavily
attacked with bronze disease throughout. Recent superficial cleaning; more
thorough cleaning would be hazardous. L. 6.5 cm., w. 2.1 cm., th. ca. 0.2 cm.
except at the upper right corner where flattened to 0.08 cm.

   Three (or more) uses:

a   E Νικ[– – –]   Class V
      T Πα[λλ(ηνεύς)?]

b   E [– –ᶜᵃ·⁴ –]ⳍΕΣ   G   conventional lettering
      T [– – – – –]

c   E Ἀθην(ίων)?   G   conventional lettering
      T Βησα[ι](εύς)

                    A
T(riobol) seal, [H]˙[Θ]˙

G(orgoneion) seal. Previously undetected.

Section-letter. May be from a slightly larger die than the epsilon section-letter
on **95**.

   The absence of pierced holes from the first use and of any certain letters of
the last use on the right half led Koehler and Bruck to conclude that the two
halves must belong to two different pinakia. One wishes this were so, for the
right half is the source of all the difficulties discussed below. The join, however, is perfectly tight at every point along and within the break and estab-
lishes beyond all question that the two fragments do belong to the same
continuous piece of metal.

From the presence of the gorgoneion seal, which was probably added prior to the letters of text *b*, and from the rounded, worn appearance of the right edge, it is clear that the pinakion was used in its present short length at least by the time of these letters. Whether the present length is original or not is impossible to determine. An original right end with another gorgoneion seal and possibly a double-bodied owl seal may have broken away; if so, the present gorgoneion seal would not have been added until after the breakage.

My readings and the remains of letters recorded in my tracing are substantially the same as reported by Bruck and his predecessors.

Text a. After repeated attempts I was unable to locate and punch through a single hole at the right. This, however, must not be taken to mean that the inscription did not continue or that other holes did not exist. The letterer may have failed to pierce the holes at the right of the plate completely through the metal, or such holes as might have been added may have been closed and hidden by erasure and the severe corrosion. We may cite **105** as a parallel instance of a Class V pinakion on which few holes have survived.

Several fine, partially erased strokes connecting the holes in the first two letters of line 1 are visible, but might belong to an intermediate text. The nomen probably read *Νικ–* in any case, though *Κικ–* or *Κιν–* are possible. Kirchner's *Σικ–* (restored from Bruck's sketch) cannot be supported. The demotic was probably *Παλληνεύς* rather than any of the other three demotics beginning in *Πα–* since the third letter in any of these would presumably have left a pierced upper terminal hole between the alpha and the right edge of the left fragment.

Text b. The letters ⟍*ΕΣ* (I am able to confirm the faint diagonal noted by Koehler) cannot belong with the first use. Apart from the absence of punched serifs, the letters have been inscribed in an area that had previously been flattened and widened by erasure. The partially erased character of the diagonal and of the left part of the epsilon indicate that the letters probably cannot be attributed to the last use either, and this is confirmed by the impossibility of restoring them with the letters of text *c* at the left of the plate. I know of no Greek name that will incorporate both *ΑΘΗ* and ⟍*ΕΣ*.

Text c. All scholars who have examined the piece at firsthand have read the second letter in line 1 as a theta, placed high in order to incorporate the punched hole of the first use. No indications of a rho's vertical can be made out, and, since all other strokes of the final letters in both lines at the left are plainly visible, the possibility that the name began in *Ἄρη–* may be considered slight. Such names are extremely rare; *PA* gives only one example, *Ἄρης Ἄρεως Κηφισιεύς*, and it is late, from the second century B.C.

On the other hand, among the relatively small number of known demesmen from Besa is an Ἀθηνίων, father of a Nikias whose mid-fourth-century gravestone is extant (*IG* II², 5906), and of a Mnesimachos who appears in a list of uncertain character (*not* of diaitetai) from the second half of the fourth century (*IG* II², 1927, lines 195–196). Since Kirchner believed that the right-hand fragment of the present piece did not belong, he did not hesitate to restore the name of this Athenion *off* the left fragment, thus: Ἀθη[νίων] Βησ[αιεύς]. For lack of any better solution I submit that the identification should still stand and that we have here an—to my knowledge—unparalleled instance of an abbreviated nomen. A priori, there is no reason why a nomen might not have been abbreviated like patronymics and demotics, especially in an ill-inscribed text (cf. the poor beta in line 2), and when the nomen came from a tiny deme like Besa where there was a good chance of there being only one member with a name in Ἀθην– at a given time.

This admittedly tentative solution at least has the firmest material and prosopographical support. Were it possible, however, to restore the first three letters in line 1 with ⋮\ΕΣ at the right, or if one could feel at all confident about restoring Ἄρη[ς], either of the latter two solutions would be preferable.

105 (Figs. 189–190) Athens, Stoa of Attalos, Pnyx Excavations Inv. M–1. Excavated in 1930–1931 from the filling of the Third Period of the Assembly Place. G. R. Davidson and D. B. Thompson, *Pnyx Small Objects* I, 12, and fig. 12, no. 1.

Left half of a pinakion. Cleaned to bare bronze. L. 6.0 cm., w. 2.1 cm. at left to 2.5 cm. at right, th. 0.2 cm. at left to 0.05 cm. at right.

Probably more than three uses, as indicated by its heavily striated and flattened condition.

a	Ⓑ	.[. . .].[– – –	Class V
	Ⓣ	.[.].[.].[– – –	
b	Ⓑ	[– – – –]ǀǀ[– – –	conventional lettering
	Ⓣ	Ἁλα[ι]ε[ύς	
c	⊦⊤⊣	Ἐπικράτ[ης	Class VI?
		Γαργή[ττιος	

T(riobol) seal. Partially erased by the time of the last use.

The holes of the first use seem to have been pierced completely through only for alternate letters, but even in those letters every hole cannot be located. Perhaps not all were regularly pierced through, and some may have been totally closed up by the severe erasure.

Text c. The last owner may well be the same Epikrates of Gargettos who served as trierarch in 377/6 (*IG* II², 1604, line 26), and his son the Πολυκράτης Ἐπικράτο[υ Γαργήτ]τιος mentioned in a "Catalogue of Silver Phialai," about 330 B.C. (*IG* II², 1571, lines 6–7).

106 (Figs. 191–192)   Paris, Musée du Louvre, Inv. Bronze 4071. "Acheté au Pirée en 1890." A. de Ridder, *Bronzes du Louvre* II, 217, no. 4071, whence *IG* II², 1910. Corrected by L. Robert, *Coll. Froehner* I, 7, n. 1.
  Left end. Encrusted green patina. L. 4.2 cm., w. 2.0 cm., th. 0.2 cm.
  Two uses:

a   Ⓗ Δίων *vel* Ọἰων[—? – – –   Class V
   Ⓣ νọς[– – ͞– ͞–͞   dem.

b   Ⓗ Πολ[– – –   conventional lettering
   Ⓣ Ἀνα[– – –

T(riobol) seal. With Η $\overset{\text{A}}{\Theta}$·

Section-letter. From the same die as the eta section-letters on **86**, **87**, and **110**.

Text b. The demotic may be any one of three beginning Ἀνα–.

107 (Figs. 193–195)   Basel, Antikenmuseum, Inv. 1941.126.3. Ex Coll. Rhousopoulos-Pfuhl. F. Stähelin, *AA* 1943, 19, and pl. I, no. 3 (photograph before cleaning).
  Left end. Recently stripped to bare metal. L. 3.3 cm., w. 2.1 cm., th. 0.2 cm. at left to 0.15 cm. at right.

Three or more uses:

a   Ⓔ Ἀρχ[– – –   Class V
   Ⓣ ΛΛ[– – –

b   Ⓑ]? Ἐπι[– – –   at least the first two letters inscribed with added
   Ⓣ Πρạ[σιεύς?   punched holes in imitation of the Class V technique

c   B Θρα[σ‐ ‐ ‐   conventional lettering
     T Φλυ[εύς

T(riobol) seal. With H A Θ˙

Section-letter. Height of field 0.75 cm. and hence from a smaller die than the beta section-letter on **93**; stamped over an earlier epsilon. One cannot be positive when the substitution was made.

Text a. Line 2. The absence of a hole directly above the surviving hole of the third letter shows that the third letter did not contain a perpendicular. Thus, if the line began with a demotic, it would have read Ἁλαιεύς, Ἁλωπεκῆθεν, or Λαμπτρεύς.

Text b. Combines all visible remains intermediate between texts *a* and *c*. These remains, however, might belong to two intermediate texts, one inscribed in imitation of the Class V technique and involving only the *ΕΠ* in line 1, the other inscribed without serifs.

108 (Figs. 196–197)   Athens, National Museum, Inv. Bronze 8083. P. Girard, *BCH* 2 (1878), 532, no. 10. Sketch published by Bruck, *AthMitt* 19 (1894), 205, no. 13. (*IG* II, 919; II², 1892)
     Left end. Recently stripped to bare metal. L. 2.6 cm., w. 2.0 cm., th. ca. 0.28 cm. at left to ca. 0.15 cm. at right.
     Three (or more?) uses:

a   I ..[‐ ‐ ‐   Class V
     T ..[‐ ‐ ‐

b   I Σ[‐ ‐ ‐   utilizes the drilled holes of use *a*, in imitation of
     T Λ[‐ ‐ ‐   Class V lettering

c   I ΑΕ[‐ ‐ ‐   conventional lettering
     T Π[‐ ‐ ‐

T(riobol) seal. With [H] A [Θ]˙

Section-letter. Field ca. 0.7 cm. square; see **103**.

Text a. The four holes belonging to the first letter in line 1 are puzzling. It is unlikely that the irregular lower hole was drilled for use *b* since the sigma of that use lacks a hole at the terminal of its upper stroke. Perhaps the first letter in text *a* was an omicron or theta with four rather than the canonical three drilled holes. Or perhaps the extra hole belongs to another intermediate use in imitation of Class V.

109 (Figs. 198–199)   Athens, National Museum, Inv. Bronze 8079. A. Dumont, *RA*² 17 (1868), 141, with pl. V.1 (a fine watercolor facsimile). (Girard, no. 7; *IG* II, 889; II², 1853)

Left end. Recently stripped to bare bronze. L. 2.3 cm., w. 2.1 cm., th. ca. 0.20 cm. at left to ca. 0.15 cm. at right.

Two or more uses:

a	Γ̲ *Σ*[– – –	Class V
	Ⓣ .[– – –	
b	Γ̲ [– – – –	conventional or imitation of Class V lettering
	Ⓣ *𝑚*[– – –	

T(riobol) seal. With H A Θ.

Section-letter. With exceptionally wide field (0.7 cm. high × 0.9 cm. wide). From a different die than the gamma section-letters on **83** and **91**.

The leftmost hole in line 2 is shallow and cannot be punched through. The hole might belong to the first use (as part of a phi) or might have been added in a second use with punched serifs in imitation of Class V lettering. If the latter, there would have been at least three uses altogether since the connecting lines to this hole have been erased.

110 (Figs. 200–201)   London, British Museum, Department of Coins and Medals. Earle Fox Bequest (1920), Inv. 521. Unpublished.

Left end. Green patina. L. 1.9 cm., w. 2.1 cm. at left to 2.2 cm. at right, th. ca. 0.2 cm.

Probably several uses. The deep, clustered gouges at the right imply intensive erasure.

a	H̲ .[– – –	Class V
	Ⓣ .[– – –	

T(riobol) seal. With H A Θ.

Section-letter. From the die known from **86, 87,** and **106.**

111 (Figs. 202–204)   Paris, Cabinet des Médailles, Froehner Collection Inv. 616. "Athènes, 1895." L. Robert, *Coll. Froehner* I, 10, and pl. VI, no. 10m (photograph before cleaning).

Half of a pinakion, broken at both ends. Surface recently cleaned of patination. A concentrated attack of bronze disease was probably responsible for the large gouge at the lower right. L. 5.6 cm., w. 2.0 cm., th. 0.2 cm. at right to 0.15 cm. at left.

Three or more uses:

a   ]Μόνιππο̣[ς   Class V
      Ἀ]χαρν(εύς)?[(carrying-hole)

Inverted
b   ]Λ[.]Λ[.]𝑚𝑚[conventional lettering
      Β]ησαι(εύς)[

Reinverted to original orientation
c   Δη?]μοχάρη[ς   in imitation of Class V lettering
      Κε]φαλῆθε[ν

Text a (new). Line 1. The other two personal names in [⁻¹⁻²]ονιππο[– – listed by Dornseiff-Hansen (pp. 155 and 278) are Λε– and Χι–όνιππος, both of which would require a pierced hole directly above the half hole on the break at the beginning of line 1. Μόνιππος does not. The name is new to Athenian prosopography, but has a good cognate in *PA*, 10414: Μονιππίδης.

Line 2. The two shallow lower holes of the eta of text c seem not to have been added until that use. The two full upper holes, from the first demotic, almost certainly belonged to an original eta, the two lower holes of which were not completely pierced and thus have disappeared. The alternative restoration, [᾿Ι]καριε(ύς), would require that four holes, the upper right hole of the epsilon, and all three lower holes of iota-epsilon, were not completely pierced.

Text b. (new). The first letter after the break, that is, the second letter in the name, may be a mu. The inversion of this inscription is a strange phenomenon. In spite of the upside down name, the stamped seals and original section-letter probably still remained intact and valid, as is implied by the reinverted orientation of the last text. Class V pinakia were, moreover, generally reused at least twice before losing their seals and becoming stampless Class VI pinakia.

Text c. The shapes of letters were distorted in order to incorporate all of the pierced holes from the first use. Additional holes were punched only when necessary, for example, at the right of the alpha in line 2 and on the circle of the theta.

The name, left uncompleted by Robert, was restored by Werner Peek (*AthMitt* 67 [1942], 165, no. 343), who identified the owner with Δημοχάρης Δημοκλέους Κεφαλῆθεν, known from a tombstone with mid-fourth-century letters (*IG* II², 6350). His father, Δημοκλῆς *K.*, was one of the Treasurers of the Sacred Monies in 398/7 (*IG* II², 1388, line 5; 1391, line 7; and 1392, line 5). The tombstone of a Νίκαιος Δημοχάρους *K.* (*IG* II², 6365) is known only from transcription and cannot be dated.

112 (Figs. 205–206) Athens, Stoa of Attalos, Agora Excavations Inv. B 987. Excavated in 1952 from Area J/11. Unpublished.

Middle fragment. Cleaned to the bare, very roughened metal. L. 3.9 cm., w. 2.0 cm., th. 0.18 cm.

Three or more uses:

a	– – –].[– – – –	Class V
	– – –].[– – – –	
b	– –*K*]αλλι[– – –	conventional lettering
	– – – –]*N*[– – –	
c	– – –]κος[– – –	apparently inscribed with punched serifs at the
	– – –]ος [– – –	terminations of letters in imitation of Class V lettering

The notch at the bottom edge and the hole almost directly above it are almost certainly survivals from a fully pierced, original Class V use. I am less confident about the shallow holes that appear to be attached to some of the letters of text *c*, namely the one at the topmost extremity of the kappa and those within the lower sigma. One or more of these partially punched holes might go back to an earlier use.

113 (Figs. 207–208) Athens, Stoa of Attalos, Agora Excavations Inv. B 1276. From a cremation burial near Daphni, excavated November 11, 1961, by

Rudi Bachmann of the Public Power Corporation (*Δ.E.H.*). The contents of the burial were turned over to the Third Archaeological Ephorate of Athens and were subsequently mended and inventoried by members of the Agora staff. Unpublished.

Nearly complete. Melted out of shape, buckled, and fragmented by fire. Painstakingly recomposed on a paraffin backing from many small pieces. L. 9.5 cm., w. 2.0–2.8 cm., th. ca. 0.25 cm.

One or more uses:

a   [[?]].....ca.10.....[– –?
                                     ©]
      [①].....ca.10...Σ[– –?

All traces of the section-letter, seals, and inscribed lines, whether connecting lines or, if the pinakion had been reused, of a later text, have been obliterated. Only the pierced holes survive, although they have, unfortunately, been too severely affected by fire to yield even a partial restoration. In too many instances damage to the plate has altered the original juxtaposition of holes, has undoubtedly caused some holes to disappear, and has opened cracks and pittings in the surface that are indistinguishable from holes of the text. Only one grouping of holes gives an unmistakable letter, a sigma toward the right of line 2. Possible traces of one or two holes to the right of it caution against reading it as a terminal sigma, however, and the uncertainty of the letters to its left precludes the restoration of a demotic around it. The full length of both lines indicates that the inscription probably contained a patronymic, but it is not even clear whether the presumed patronymic preceded or followed the demotic.

The large hole toward the left end was caused by fragmentation. If there was a carrying-hole, it would have been at the right.

Context. In spite of the illegible and crumbly condition of the pinakion, its fortunate discovery within a grave-group datable to the second quarter of the fourth century makes it one of the few truly crucial finds for narrowing the absolute chronology of Athenian bronze pinakia. The burial was accidentally discovered in a trench being dug by the Electric Company just to the east and north of the Daphni monastery (between the highway and the insane asylum).[29] The burial consisted of a mass of ashes and fire-blackened soil

29. A detailed record complete with excellent drawings remains on file in the Agora archives (Notebook *KTΔ* IV, 670–672). I am especially grateful to H. A. Thompson and the former Ephor of the Akropolis, Dr. N. Platon, for permission to include this unpublished material.

surrounded by an oval ring of stones (ca. 0.15 m. high and 1.0 to 1.45 m. across) and yielded small bits of bone and iron, fragments of two stone alabastra (Inv. ST 725–726), the pinakion, and a complete red-figure squat lekythos (Inv. P 27241, Fig. 209)[30]—all heavily burned and lying in no apparent arrangement. Dr. Klaus Vierneisel, who has been studying the chronological development of fourth-century lekythoi in the stratified graves of the Kerameikos, assures me that the shape of this lekythos should date about 360 B.C. or a little earlier and in any case cannot be later than 350.[31] This dates the interment of the pinakion before the middle of the century and is consistent with other chronological data discussed at the end of Chapter III, above.

Class VI

Pinakia without stamped seals.

SECTION-LETTER AT LEFT

114 (Fig. 210)   Athens, British School of Archaeology. G. Finlay Collection. W. Vischer, *Beiträge*, 53, and pl. VI.11. = *Kleine Schriften* II, 79 and pl. VI.11. (Girard, no. 46; *IG* II, 916; II², 1889)

Whole. Clean brown bronze; surface slightly flaked. L. 11.2 cm., w. 2.05 cm., th. 0.15 cm. at left to 0.19 cm. at right.

One use:

> Θ Νικόστρατος Νικοστ(ράτου)
> Ἀχαρνεύς

The positioning of the section-letter in front of the nomen suggests that this may have been one of the earlier Class VI pinakia, inscribed under the influence of the section-letter format of Class III–V pinakia. The pinakion, however, was not buried with its owner until after 331/0, the year in which the owner won a choregic victory. The small size of the section-letter

30. Height 8.5 cm.; diam. 4.7 cm. Broken but complete except for fragments of the mouth. Large red-figure palmette on front. Discolored by fire.

31. For purposes of comparison, Dr. Vierneisel has pointed out to me that the two lekythoi illustrated in *ArchEph* 1910, 132, fig. 17, having longer necks, are slightly later examples of the same squat, palmette lekythos type. They belong to an earlier burial in the plot of the "Herakleotai" in the Kerameikos and, according to Vierneisel, should date about 360–350 B.C., since the latest burial in the plot is dated by the Koralion relief to about 350–340.

(like the smallness of the theta section-letter on **125**) was dictated by the size of the letterer's ring punch.

The owner is Nikostratos III of the prominent Acharnian family diagramed in Kirchner's stemma *ad PA*, 12413 and discussed with fuller documentation by D. M. Lewis, "Attic Manumissions," *Hesperia* 28 (1959), 232–233. As Lewis has shown, our Nikostratos is to be identified with the successful boy's choregos of 331/0 (*IG* II², 2318, line 334) and was born prior to 371. One of his brothers, Pythodoros N. A., was born in 384/3 and lived at least until 325/4, when he served as diaitetes. It is uncertain, however, whether the Nikostratos who is mentioned in the lengthy catalogue edited by Lewis ("Attic Manumissions," 226, lines 332–333) and dated by him to the late 320s is our Nikostratos III or his nephew, Nikostratos II.

115 (Fig. 211)   Paris, Cabinet des Médailles, Froehner Collection Inv. 624. L. Robert, *Coll. Froehner* I, 8, and pl. VII, no. 10e (photograph before cleaning).

Complete. Broken in two. The green, slightly encrusted patina has now been partially cleaned from the inscribed surface. L. 11.0 cm., w. 2.0–2.3 cm., th. 0.2 cm. even.

One use:

$$\Delta: \quad \begin{array}{l} Eὐάγγελος : Δημύ(λου) \\ Ἀναφλύστι(ος) \end{array}$$

Cleaning has confirmed that the vertical stroke within the alpha of line 1 is an error in the inscribing of the present name. There are absolutely no other indications of an earlier text or of erasure.

116 (Fig. 212)   Paris, Cabinet des Médailles. Froehner Collection Inv. 614. Ex coll. Rayet. "Trouvée en 1873, Μαρουσίου Ἀττικῆς. Le deme Ἀθμονία près du village *Marusi*" (Froehner). O. Rayet, *AnnAssEtGr* 1878, 205 (with a drawing later reproduced in Caillemer, DarSag, "Dikastai," 189, fig. 2409). L. Robert, *Coll. Froehner* I, 8 and pl. VII, no. 10f. (*IG* II, 894; II², 1858)

Whole. In most areas the upper layer of diseased bronze has flaked away, leaving visible a smooth green surface. L. 10.2 cm., w. 2.1 cm., th. 0.10 cm.

One use:

$$\Delta \quad \begin{array}{l} Θάλλος \\ Ἀθμονεύς \end{array}$$

117 (Figs. 213–214)   Athens, National Museum, Inv. Bronze 8065. "Trouvée à Khaïdari, près de Daphni" (Girard), in 1867 (Dumont). A. Dumont, *RA*² 17

(1868), 144, and pl. V.4 (reproduced in our Fig. 214). P. Girard, *BCH* 2 (1878), 534, no. 17. (*IG* II, 903; II², 1867)

Formerly complete. Left end now missing. Composed of five fragments, too heavily diseased at the left to permit cleaning; lightly encrusted patination at the right. Original length given by Girard as 12.2 cm. (present length, 10.9 cm.), w. 2.2 cm., th. ca. 0.08–0.10 cm.

One use (?). The only visible suggestion of a possible earlier text is a faint vertical just before the rho in line 1.

E , $\begin{array}{l}\Delta\acute{\eta}\mu\alpha\rho\chi o\varsigma\\ \text{'}E\rho o\iota\acute{\alpha}\delta\eta\varsigma\end{array}$

"Lettre de série en creux; pas de sceau" (Dumont). In Dumont's and Girard's majuscule transcriptions the section-letter is located squarely between lines 1 and 2; in Dumont's facsimile it is slightly higher. Bruck's statement (*Philologus* 54 [1895], 65) that the section-letter was inscribed by a hand different from the one that inscribed the owner's name is suspect.

The son or father of the owner is – – –]ς *Δημάρχου* E., known from *IG* II², 6090, a lost gravestone also discovered at Chaidari and dated by Kirchner to *med. s. IV. a.*, although Kirchner allows that the letters, known solely from a majuscule transcription, are themselves to be dated only *s. IV.*

118 (Fig. 215) Paris, Cabinet des Médailles. Froehner Collection Inv. 612. Ex coll. Rayet. "Trouvée en 1874, à *Φάληρον*." O. Rayet, *AnnAssEtGr* 1878, 205 (with drawing). L. Robert, *Coll. Froehner* I, 9, and pl. VII, no. 10i (photograph before cleaning). (*IG* II, 907; II², 1874)

Whole. Both sides recently cleaned to bare metal. L. 10.4 cm., w. 2.3 cm., th. 0.05–0.10 cm.

Probably more than one use. Its thinness, uneven surfaces, and torn edges are indicative of erasure.

Last use:

Z $\begin{array}{l}\Delta\eta\mu\acute{o}\sigma\tau\rho\alpha\tau o\varsigma\\ \Lambda\upsilon\sigma\iota(-?)\ \upsilon\ E\mathring{\upsilon}\omega\nu\upsilon(\mu\epsilon\acute{\upsilon}\varsigma)\end{array}$

From the photographs taken after cleaning I am unable to detect any positive traces of erased letters on either side. However it was formed, the heavy diagonal indentation under the delta at the left is obviously not part of an earlier text. The minute hole at the left is a tear in the thin metal (cf. **123**).

The owner is probably the Demostratos of Euonymon who appears in the bouleutic list dated in all probability to 336/5 B.C. (*Hesperia* 30 [1961], 31 and 37, line 10). The list does not, unfortunately, give patronymics, but its date is about right for the owner of a Class VI pinakion. The patronymic cannot be completed. Three Euonymeis with different names in Λυσι– are known from fourth-century inscriptions (see IG II², 478, line 48; II², 1952, line 7; and *ArchEph* 1917, 41, line 10).

119 (Figs. 216–218)   Athens, Depot of the Third Archaeological Ephorate of Athens (at the Library of Hadrian). Excavated from a necropolis under Panepistimiou St. between Korai and Voukourestiou Sts., Athens. Inv. 79 (grave Δ₂). John Threpsiades, "Ἀνασκαφαὶ Λεωφόρου Πανεπιστημίου," *Deltion* 16 (1960), Χρονικά, 27 (text *b* only).

Whole, except at the lower left, Side A. Stripped to bare bronze. L. 11.5 cm., w. 2.4 cm., th. ca. 0.05 cm.

Two uses:

a   Ἀ̣ *vel* Δ̣   Διονυσόφιλος   Side A
           Σουνιεύ(s)

b   Ἀρχέδημος   Side B
      Δ   Περιθοί(δης)

Text a. According to the standard Greek prosopographies, the nomen of the first owner can be paralleled only by a contemporary Διονυσίφιλος [*sic*] Θουγείτονος Σουνιεύς, prytanis *post med. s.* IV *a.* (IG II², 1752, line 25). The difference in the stem vowel might mean that the owner and the prytanis were merely related, but it is more probable that they are to be identified as the same person. If so, the spelling in IG II², 1752, would be in error since at Athens the more common root is Διονυσο–, as always before phi in Διονυσο-φάνης (PA, 4304–4305). An exception is in the name Διονυσικλῆς (PA, 4081–4083), although not consistently (cf. PA, 4303: Διονυσοκλῆς).

Text b. Note the low position of the section-letter, which necessitated the indentation of the demotic.

Context. According to the excavation records at the Library of Hadrian Depot, the small black-glaze lekythos,[32] illustrated in Fig. 219, was found in the same

32. Excavations in Leophoros Panepistimiou, Inv. 57. Height 7.3 cm.; diam. 3.7 cm. Glaze chipped and handle missing. A small band in relief on the neck at the upper level of the handle.

grave as the pinakion. The lekythos is of a different variety than the squat palmette lekythos found with **113** (Fig. 209) and is less closely datable. Dr. Vierneisel of the Kerameikos excavations tells me that this thinner type was used in the second quarter of the fourth century—alongside palmette lekythoi —and continued with little change in shape into the third quarter. He believes that the present example is more likely to date from about 350 or earlier than in the third quarter of the century, although this is only a guess. But he assures me that it should not be later than about 338, after which vessels known as ungentaria replaced lekythoi in the Kerameikos graves.

120 (Figs. 220–222)   Munich, Antikensammlung (Museum Antiker Klein-kunst), Inv. 3493b. Purchased 1882. U. Koehler, *IG* II 5, 876b (after a transcription of Side B by G. Christ). (*IG* II², 1838)

Whole, having been much eaten by bronze disease. Stripped to bare metal and encased in plastic. L. 12.1 cm., w. 2.4 cm. maximum, th. ca. 0.05 cm.

Two (or more) uses. The plate has obviously been subjected to an exceptional amount of erasure.

a	Δήμαρχος	Side A
	Κ Φαληρεύς	
b	Α Καλλίας Θερδώρ(ου)	Side B
	Ἀγρυλῆ(θεν)	

Text a (new). Again the low position of the section-letter is notable. Observe that in a number of the erased letters hammering has flattened out the trough of the strokes without eliminating the sides of the strokes, which remain visible as more or less parallel incisions in the metal. Under magnification, the same phenomenon can be observed in some of the right-hand letters of line 1 of text *a* on **119**.

The son or the father of the first owner may be the *Διονύσιος Δημάρχου Φαληρεύς* whose gravestone, dated after the middle of the fourth century, was found in the Peiraeus, *IG* II², 7602. A possible descendant, *Δήμαρχος Φίλωνος Φ.*, is known from a *post med. s. III. a.* columella (*IG* II², 7598).

Text b. Kirchner identified the last owner as the father of *Θειοφάντη Καλλίου Ἀγρυλῆθεν*, who married into a family well known from a group of sepulchral monuments (*IG* II², 5678, with stemma = stemma *ad PA*, 1408). Since Kirchner's stemma of the family should probably be down-dated, in part perhaps as much as fifty years, the identification, though uncertain, is still possible.[33]

33. In Kirchner's stemma, Theiophante and her husband are dated around 370 and their grave monuments to mid-century. But this chronology seems to have been tenuously

121 (Figs. 223–224) Munich, Antikensammlung (Museum Antiker Klein-kunst), Inv. 3493a. Purchased in 1882. U. Koehler, *IG* II 5, 875b (text *b* after a transcription sent by G. Christ). (*IG* II², 1835)

Whole. Inscribed surface recently freed of heavy corrosion. L. 11.3 cm., w. 2.0 cm. at left to 2.2 cm. at right, th. 0.16 cm. at left, 0.13 cm. at the center, 0.06 cm. at right.

Two uses:

a A? , $\overset{\Sigma\acute{\alpha}\tau\upsilon\rho\text{os } \Sigma\alpha\tau\upsilon(\rho—?)}{\text{᾿}Ε\rho\chi\iota\epsilon\acute{\upsilon}s}$

b A Ἀνδροτέλης
     Ἀχαρ(νεύς) Ἀνδροκλέ(ους)

As one sees from the unhammered left end, the pinakion was originally of medium thickness and perfectly rectangular, like **114–116**. Erasure has given it a shape and a thinness comparable to other Class VI palimpsests (e.g., **118–120**). A horizontal tear has opened between lines 1 and 2 at the right.

Section-letter. The alpha at the left is quite certainly the only section-letter ever to have been added to the pinakion. Although substantial traces of every letter of the first owner's name have survived the heavy erasure, no indications of an earlier section-letter exist at the left (which has not been ham-mered) or at the right. The problem, then, is whether the present alpha was inscribed for use *a* and was left intact for use *b* or whether it was not added until use *b*, in which case use *a* would have lacked a section-letter entirely. The question cannot be resolved by letter forms; the alpha may or may not have been inscribed by the same hand that produced the inconsistent letters of the second owner's name. But in my texts I have tentatively assumed that it was not, since most Class VI texts received section-letters and since the retention of a section-letter here would explain most cogently why the left end of the pinakion was untouched by erasure. It is true that Class VI pinakia regularly changed section-letters with every change in owners' names, but these pinakia were ordinarily erased and reinscribed by the state. As can be seen from the unprofessional lettering of the name of the second owner, the

---

anchored to the 373/2 date of a trierarch thought to be the father of another woman who married into the family (*Χρυσίον ῾Υπεράνθου ᾿Αχαρνεύς*) and in any case was devised before a firm date could be given to the prytany list, *IG* II², 1750, on which appears the name of ᾿Απολλόδωρος ᾿Ολυμπιόχου ᾿Αναφλύστιος. This list is now dated securely to 334/3, and if Kirchner was correct in identifying Apollodoros as the brother-in-law of Theiophante, a date in the second half of the fourth century could apply to her also.

present pinakion may have changed hands privately, so that some kind of irregularity in respect to its section-letter might be expected.

It should be remembered, on the other hand, that none of the above arguments are decisive. The left end could be intact simply because the pinakion was held by that end during erasure and because there might have been no section-letter there to be erased. And, to judge from the absence of a section-letter in the last, Class VI use of **47**, some uses of pinakia during the Class VI period apparently did lack section-letters.

Text a. On the patronymic, see **65**, the penultimate owner of which was a relative, probably a brother, of the present owner.

Text b. The owner's father was very likely the last owner of **12**. The father and two of the owner's brothers are commemorated on a lost fourth-century grave stele, IG II², 5782; cf. stemma *ad PA*, 859, to which should be added the owner's nephew, Ἀνδροκλείδης Ἀνδροσθένους Ἀχαρνεύς, who is mentioned around 330 B.C. in the manumission inscription IG II², 1576, lines 46–48, and who is probably *PA*, 849, a witness in Demosthenes 48.11, about 341, and trierarch, around 323 (IG II², 1632, lines 174 and 181–182).

122 (Figs. 225–226) Paris, Cabinet des Médailles. Froehner Collection Inv. 625. "Vente J. P. Lambros, 1912." L. Robert, *Coll. Froehner* I, 9, and pl. VII, no. 10g (photograph before cleaning).

Whole. Both sides recently cleaned of encrusted patination. L. 10.7 cm. w. 2.1 cm., th. ca. 0.05 cm.

Two uses:

a   ?   Σωγένης Φυλάσι(ος)
       Παιδείο

b   E   Δημόδοκος
       Περγασῆ(θεν)

This is the only surviving Class VI pinakion with a carrying-hole. The hole is square, its sides having been punched through with a short chisel blade. The pinakion is also notable for the irregular arrangement of the earlier inscription, with nomen and demotic in line 1 and the patronymic below.

Text a. Not previously noted. There are no suggestions of a section-letter to go with the remarkably distinct letters of the name. The first use may have lacked a section-letter altogether, or remains of a letter such as an iota or gamma could be hidden under the later epsilon section-letter.

Παιδείας (or Παιδειος) is new to Greek prosopography. But compare Παιδέας Σολεύς, a metic of Cilician origin, who served on a board of hieropoioi in third-century B.C. Athens (*IG* II², 2859, line 4). A possible late descendant of our owner is Ἀπολλοφάνης Σωγένους Φ., known from a tombstone of the first or second century A.D. (*IG* II², 7743).

Text b. In spite of a short middle bar, the epsilon section-letter was inscribed by the same hand as the letters of the last name; this is clear from the profile and texture of the letters and from the fact that the left end had been distended and thinned by hammering before the epsilon was added.

123 (Figs. 227–228)   Basel, Antikenmuseum, Inv. 1941.126.2. Ex coll. Rhousopoulos-Pfuhl. F. Stähelin, *AA* 1943, 16, and pl. I, no. 2 (photograph before cleaning).

Whole. Recently stripped to bare metal. Surface superficially pitted throughout. L. 10.8 cm., w. 2.3 cm., th. 0.05–0.08 cm.

Two uses:

a   ? [– – – –] $\overline{III}$ [– – – – –]ς
$\overset{\text{ca.4}}{}$ $\overset{\text{ca.5}}{}$
Π̣ε̣ρ̣ι̣θ̣ο̣[ίδης] ?

b   B: Καλλιγένης
Εὐθοινί(δου) ⋮ Φυλάσι(ος)

The irregularly shaped hole at the right appears to be a tear in the thin, hammered metal and not a carrying-hole.

Stähelin believed that the pinakion was reused, although for the wrong reasons: "die vier Punkte hinter dem Sektionsbuchstaben rühren von früheren Buchstaben her, ebenso vielleicht das E vor Φυλασι in Z. 2." However, the four dashes to the right of the beta and the three before the demotic are interpuncts, exceptionally close to the letters they separate because they were added after the text proper had been inscribed; they are linear in form because they were punched with a chisel rather than with a round, pointed punch. And the vertical before the interpunct in line 2 is certainly an iota in the last owner's patronymic. I do not know quite what to make of the lunate impression just above the second interpunct, but it may be a misstriking of some kind.

Text a. The thorough erasure combined with the pitted condition of the metal allows us to regard very few of the possible traces indicated in my Fig. 228 with complete certainty. I have had to depend on the photograph and a cast, and I am aware that it is not always possible to distinguish between lines left by letters and rows of natural pittings on the surface of the metal.

Text b. Euthoinides, the last owner's father, was the penultimate owner of **63**, a Class IV pinakion. His name, or any other in Εὐθοινι–, is otherwise unattested in the standard Greek prosopographies.

The daughter of a Kalligenes of Phyle is known from *IG* II², 6931, a tombstone with the following text:

ante med.	Καλλίππη Ἱερωνύμο Ξυπεταιόνος
s. IV a.	Πύθιλλα Καλλιγένος Φυλασίο

Kallippe was, presumably, either the mother or daughter of Pythilla, and thus either Kalligenes' wife or his granddaughter. Whichever is the case, if Kirchner's dating of the inscription (from a squeeze) is correct, the Kalligenes it mentions could be our owner probably only if both women died young, or at least before Kalligenes himself. According to my chronology for Class VI pinakia, the present pinakion would not have been buried with its last owner until sometime in the second half of the fourth century.

124 (Figs. 229–230) formerly Berlin, Staatliche Museen, Inv. Bronze 6313. "Im jahr 1873 von Lambros in Athen angekauft." C. Curtius, *RhM* 31 (1876), 283, no. 1 (with sketch). (Girard, no. 41; *IG* II, 878; II², 1841)

Complete. Heavily corroded. L. 10.5 cm., w. 2.2–2.4 cm., th. appears from the photograph to be less than average, ca. 0.05–0.10 cm.

Two (or more?) uses:

a ? $\overline{\text{/////}}$ /≡ [– $\underline{4\text{-}5}$ –]ος
[$\overset{ca.2}{--}$]|[$\overset{ca.2}{--}$]εύς

b A Πολυκλῆς
Φλυε(ύς)

The lack of any trace of a stamped seal at the right, where the encrustation is relatively light, leaves little doubt that this was a Class VI pinakion originally.

This pinakion, **29**, and **125** (the latter two belonging to the same Polymnestos Phlyeus) were purchased together and presumably were excavated
from the same necropolis. The fact that all three were heavily, if not identically, corroded may indicate that all had been exposed to identical conditions
during burial. From the last owners' demotics it would be natural to suppose
that the pinakia were found in the vicinity of ancient Phlya (modern Chalan-
dri). But the question is complicated by the likelihood that the last owner of
the present pinakion is to be identified with the Polykles of Phlya who, with
his wife, daughter, and son-in-law, is commemorated on a grave stele (*IG* II²,
7702) dated after the middle of the fourth century and discovered in the
Peiraeus. (See the photograph of the stele in Fig. 231). If the identification is
correct, and if *IG* II², 7702 was originally set up in the Peiraeus and was not
brought there in medieval or modern times, it becomes probable that the
pinakia of Polykles and Polymnestos also came from the Peiraeus. It would
be probable, too, that the graves of these two Phlyeis were close together and
that the men may even have been related.

125 (Fig. 232) formerly Berlin, Staatliche Museen, Inv. Bronze 6314. "Im
Jahr 1873 von Lambros in Athen angekauft." C. Curtius, *RhM* 31 (1876), 283,
no. 2 (with sketch). Photograph in Kern, *Inscriptiones Graecae*, pl. 22. (Girard,
no. 40; *IG* II, 917; II², 1890)

Whole. Heavily encrusted with bronze disease. L. 10.5 cm., w. 2.0–2.2 cm.,
th. appears from the photograph to be less than average, ca. 0.05–0.10 cm.
Two or more uses. The pinakion has been erased by hammering.

a	?	𝝙𝝙[– – – – – –]	Class VI?
		[– – – – – – –]	
b		Πολύμνηστος	Class VI
		Θ Φλυεύς υ Ἀρι(—?)	

I cannot be positive that this was a Class VI pinakion originally. Well-
erased traces of a stamped letter and seals could be hidden under the thick
patination, but at least at the left this looks unlikely. There can be no doubt,
however, that its important final use was stampless. The section-letter is
abnormally low. On its small size, see **114**.

A second pinakion owned by Polymnestos and doubtless found in the same
grave as the present pinakion is **29**. The patronymic was inscribed only on the
present example. Apparently guided by its extreme brevity, Curtius saw fit
to restore Ἀρι(μνήστου?), which was retained in *IG* II and *PA*, 1620 and 12051,

although in the *Editio Minor* Kirchner printed simply Ἀρι. The restoration may be correct. On a still incompletely published third-century B.C. prytany list from the Athenian Agora (see *Hesperia* 3 [1934], 61, no. 50) there is mentioned [. . .]μνηστ[ος] Ἀριμ[- - -] (Φλυεύς), which A. E. Raubitscheck has restored [Ἀρί]μνηστος Ἀριμ[νήστου] (Φ.) (*Hesperia, Index to Volumes I–X* [Athens: American School of Classical Studies, 1946], 19). The restoration is plausible and would give us a younger relative of the owner. But in view of the many other possibilities for the owner's patronymic—in addition to numerous names in Ἀριστ-, PA gives Ἀρίγνωτος, Ἀρίδηλος, and Ἀρίζηλος— it is certainly better to leave the patronymic unrestored.

SECTION-LETTER AT RIGHT

126 (Fig. 233) Paris, Cabinet des Médailles. Anonymous gift. L. Robert, *Coll. Froehner* I, 10, no. 10q (text and measurements only). Photograph published by S. Dow, *BCH* 87 (1963), 672–673, fig. 4.

Whole. Exceedingly corroded; light green bronze disease turning to a fine, white powder. L. 10.0 cm., w. 2.2 cm., th. 0.05 cm.

One use? Where preserved, the original edges are perfectly straight as if untouched by erasure.

Στράτων
Πήληξ   Z

There was room for a section-letter of average size at the left, but the letterer seems to have preferred to fill the space at the right with a larger, more conspicuous one. The fragile, diseased condition precludes cleaning.

127 (Fig. 234) Paris, Cabinet des Médailles. Froehner Collection Inv. 613. Published from a private collection in Athens by P. Girard, *BCH* 2 (1878), 538, no. 43. L. Robert, *Coll. Froehner* I, 9, and pl. VII, no. 10h. (*IG* II, 905; II², 1869)

Whole. Heavily diseased and covered with dirt on both sides; too fragile for cleaning. L. 9.7 cm., w. 2.2 cm., th. 0.05–0.10 cm.

Probably more than one use. Uneven shape and thickness attest erasure by hammering.

Last use:

Λυσικράτης : Λυσα(νίου)
Ἀτη(νεύς)   E

In this case no room for a section-letter remains at the left. The letter had to be placed at the right.

A son of Lysanias of Atene is listed in a catalogue of uncertain character (not of diaitetai) that dates from the second half of the fourth century B.C. (*IG* II², 1927, lines 181–182). His nomen is missing from the text of the inscription, but Kirchner (first in *PA*, 9451) saw fit to identify him with the owner of the present pinakion and thus restored the nomen Lysikrates in line 181 of *IG* II², 1927. The identification and restoration, which may well be correct, rest on the assumption that Lysanias had only one son. If he had more than one, it is possible that the catalogue mentioned a brother of our owner rather than the owner himself. Kirchner suggests (*ad PA*, 9451) that a contemporary Lysikrates Ateneus, son of Lysimachos, was perhaps a cousin.

128 (Figs. 235–238)   Athens, National Museum, Inv. Bronze 8091. Unpublished.
Fragment from near the original right end; broken at both ends. Recently stripped of patination. L. 2.3 cm., w. 2.3 cm., th. 0.1 cm.
Three uses:

a   [– – – – – – – –]Δ   whole; section-letter at right
      [– – – – – – – –]⋮   Δ

Inverted to become a left end

b   ] Φαιν[– – –   whole; section-letter at right?
      ] Ἀλω[πεκῆθεν

c   K   N[– – –   broken at left
         Πℵ[– – –

It is curious that the delta section-letter of use *a* and the left-hand letters of use *b* have not been noticeably erased, if at all.

Text a. For the two deltas, both upside down when the fragment is oriented to the later uses, see the tracing, Fig. 236.

Text c. The left end having broken off, the pinakion in this use was a centimeter or so shorter.

RIGHT END MISSING, POSSIBLY WITH SECTION-LETTER AT THE RIGHT

129 (Fig. 239)   Athens, National Museum, Inv. Bronze 13035. From a privately conducted excavation of a large necropolis "on the Ilissos at the place where the middle Long Wall crosses the river, west of the spur of the Mouseion Hill." Reported with **157** in "Funde," *AthMitt* 25 (1900), 453–454 (transcription without section-letter; no dimensions). *PA*, 11062, but omitted from *IG* II².

Left three-fourths of a pinakion. Recently stripped to bare bronze. L. 9.4 cm., w. 2.3 cm., th. 0.12 cm.

One use (?):

$$Νικοτέλης \ [$$
$$Ἀχαρνεύς \ [$$

The possibility of an earlier, remarkably well-erased text is raised by the faint suggestions of the three lower bars of a sigma at the middle of the plate's width between the final sigmas and the break at the right.

For our purposes the left end of the plate may be regarded as intact. The three diagonal grooves at the middle of the end are clearly accidental and can have nothing to do with a section-letter. Nor do they have the appearance of striations caused by erasure. The large pitting below them seems to have resulted from an imperfection in the metal, like the smaller pitting between lines 1 and 2 below NI. If nothing else, it is certain that the present text lacked a section-letter at the left.

Evidence of a section-letter is lacking also along the break at the right of the name. (What misleadingly appears in the photograph as a tail end of a large inscribed alpha is actually a small diagonal mound of metal that is raised *above* the inscribed surface.) Thus, if the present text was provided with a section-letter at all, it would have been to the right of the preserved length, on the missing right end. Room was available for a section-letter at the left, but the imperfections in the surface there may have encouraged the addition of a section-letter at the other end.

130 (Fig. 240)   Athens, Stoa of Attalos, Agora Excavations Inv. B 822. Excavated in 1947 from under the floor of the third period of House C³⁴ in Area B/19. R. S. Young, "An Industrial District of Ancient Athens," *Hesperia* 20 (1951), 216, and pl. 71b. Photographs published in *Archaeology* 6 (1953), 143, and *The Athenian Citizen*, Agora Picture Book No. 4 (Princeton: American School of Classical Studies at Athens, 1960), fig. 22.

34. The third period of the house is dated to "about the middle of the fourth century, or slightly later." Young writes: "From below the third floor level . . . the latest object was the lower part of a characteristic black-glazed skyphos of the mid-fourth century, of the sort found at Olynthos and attributed to the last years before its destruction in 348."

Nearly whole; only ca. 1 cm. missing at right. Bent and very fragile. Green, encrusted patina. L. 10.2 cm., w. 2.1 cm., th. 0.05 cm.

More than one use. Erasure by hammering is evidenced by the uneven edges.

Last use:

$Δημοφάνης:Φιλι[—?$
$Κηφισιεύς$ [

I have been unable to ascertain which lines on the surface properly belong to an earlier text and which might be cracks in the metal or patination. The more conspicuous possible remains of an earlier name are all in line 1, for example, a diagonal after the initial delta of the last text, another after the first eta, and a vertical between the nu and eta at the end of the nomen.

Last use. There was room for a section-letter at the right. A descendant of the last owner may be the Demophanes of Kephisia who was prytanis between 211/10 and 202/1 B.C. (*IG* II², 913, line 17; for the date, see Dow, *Prytaneis*, 85, no. 37).

BROKEN AT LEFT OR RIGHT?

131 (Fig. 241)   Athens, Stoa of Attalos, Agora Excavations Inv. B 974. Excavated in 1952 from Area J/11; fourth-century B.C. context. Unpublished.

Half of an original pinakion(?). Partially disintegrated in cleaning to six joining fragments. L. 5.7 cm., w. 2.2 cm., th. ca. 0.18 cm.

More than one use (?).

Last use:

$Κρατιάδης$
$Κ?$
$Θοραι[ε]ύς$

The name Kratiades is new to Athenian prosopography.

In its final use this plate was apparently no longer than its present length. The comparative smallness of the letters allowed the full nomen and demotic to be accommodated, and the positioning of the two lines of text at the top and bottom of the plate may have been intended to allow room for a section-letter between the lines. Owing to the rough surface at the left, however, the presence and identity of a kappa section-letter between lines 1 and 2 are not entirely certain. If the kappa is illusory, it is doubtful whether the pinakion had a section-letter at all.

132 (Figs. 242–243) Athens, Stoa of Attalos, Pnyx Excavations Inv. M–6. Excavated in 1930–1931 from the filling of the Third Period of the Assembly Place. G. R. Davidson and D. B. Thompson, *Pnyx Small Objects* I, 14, and fig. 12, no. 6.

Left half. Cleaned to bare metal. L. 5.0 cm., w. 2.0 cm., th. ca. 0.15 cm. at left to 0.08 cm. at right.

Two (or three?) uses:

a   *E*
         $Λυσι \overset{\leq}{\vDash} [---$
         $Δαμάσο[υ$

b $Ξενο \vDash [---$
       $Παιονί[δης$

The faint vertical within the second alpha of line 2, text *a*, and certain minor components in the section-letter of text *a* suggest that there may have been a third, earliest use in addition to the two uses recorded by the original editors. But the vertical may, of course, be a scratch of some kind, and any attempt to assign the components of the section-letter to two successive letters, for example, a beta and a later gamma, is really no more satisfactory than accepting a single epsilon. A high horizontal within the second letter of line 1 is probably a misstriking of the upper bar of the epsilon in text *b*.

Text a. Except for minor differences at the end of line 1, it is as read by the original editors. Another occurrence of the name Damasos in classical Athens is in a casualty list of around 411 B.C. (*IG* I², 950, line 64).

Text b. The section-letter at the left having been erased, the letter for this final use may have been located at the right end.

133 (Figs. 244–247) Athens, Stoa of Attalos, Agora Excavations Inv. B 62. Excavated in 1932 from Area F/16; context of the last quarter of the fourth century B.C. Unpublished.

Left half. Cleaned to bare metal. L. 5.9 cm., w. 2.1 cm., th. tapers from 0.08 cm. at left to 0.05 cm. at right.

Three or possibly more uses:

a   ? Ṇ[.]/[– – –
         Φαληρ[εύς

b   Θ Ἀντιχ[άρης?
         Ἀχαρν[εύς

c   Z Ἱππο[– – –
         Φαλη[ρεύς

The readings are those first disentangled by Mabel Lang.

Text a. Only the first two letters of the demotic are certain. To judge from them, the text was inscribed in smaller letters than usual, and line 2 was placed exceptionally low.

Text b. An alternative restoration, Ἀντίχ[αρμος], is possible, but an Antichares of Acharnai is known, as diaitetes in 325/4 (*IG* II², 1926, line 101), and it is not improbable that he is to be identified with the penultimate owner of this pinakion.

Text c. According to *PA* and the prosopographical file at the Institute for Advanced Study in Princeton, the only known Phalereus with a name in Ἱππο- is a Ἱππο(—?), father of a bouleutes between about 340–323 B.C. (*IG* II², 2423, line 18; identified as a bouleutic list and dated by D. M. Lewis, *BSA* 50 [1955], 26–27).

134 (Figs. 248–250) Athens, Peiraeus, Archaeological Museum. A. N. Meletopoulos Collection. I. A. Meletopoulos, *Polemon* 3 (1947–1948), Σύμμεικτα, κβ', no. 15, figs. 9 and 10 (photographs before cleaning). S. Dow, *BCH* 87 (1963), 667–668.

Left half. Recently stripped to bare metal. L. 5.3 cm., w. 1.9–2.1 cm., th. ca. 0.05 cm.

Three uses, minimum:

a   [..]OḳK[– – –   Side A
       [ἐ]κ Ḳο[ίλης *vel* –λωνοῦ ?

b   Σατυρ[– – –   Side A
           Κριωεύ[ς

c   Ϙ   *AIM*[̲ [– – –   Side B
           Ἀθμ[ονεύς

The large notch in the left end has a parallel in **96**.

Text a. Not visible before cleaning.

Text b. Line 1. Meletopoulos read [Θ]ρασυ[– – –]. On the nomen, see discussion of **65**, text *b*.

Text c. Line 1 presents two difficulties: the interpretation of the "phi" at the left; and the restoration of the root of the owner's nomen. As my text indicates, I have been unable to arrive at a satisfactory solution for either.

Much like myself, Meletopoulos printed Φ(?)αιμ[– – –]. Dow saw that the "phi" should be dissociated from the letters that follow, proposed that it was either a malformed theta section-letter or belonged to an earlier use, and concluded that the owner's name must have begun with the root Αἱμο– or Αἱμυ–. (The only other regular Αιμ– root listed in Pape-Benseler is Αἱμι–, which occurs exclusively in transliterations of the Latin *Aemil*–.) The recent cleaning, however, has disclosed an unmistakable vertical along the break at the right, which requires us to restore the nomen from *AIM*[̲ [– – –, but it has not revealed any possible traces of an earlier text on Side B to which the "phi" can be attributed.

Little can be said about the nomen. The letters *AIM*[̲ (or, for that matter, *ΦAIM* or *ΘAIM*) simply do not belong to any of the Greek roots in the standard prosopographies or lexicons. Line 1 may, therefore, involve an error in spelling, although I am unable to suggest what the error may be.

As for the "phi" at the left, it apparently was not inscribed by the same hand as produced the owner's name. Compare the theta in the second line of the name. It was produced by a series of straight punch impressions unlike the "phi" that is composed of thinner strokes and was formed with a ring punch. This should be enough, not only to exclude the "phi" from being read with the name, but also to eliminate the possibility of interpreting it as a theta section-letter for the last use. But although the thinness of the "phi's" strokes could be explained as the result of partial erasure, I cannot feel confident about attributing the letter to a hypothetical earlier use when no other evidence for such a use on Side B exists.

135 (Figs. 251–253) Athens, National Museum, Inv. Bronze 8130. Unpublished.

Left end. Recently stripped to bare metal. L. 4.2 cm., w. 2.2 cm., th. 0.2 cm. at left to 0.1 cm. at right.

Two uses:

a Γ 'Επα[– – –   Side A
      'Ερικ[εεύς

b K Εὐθ[– – –   Side B
      ἐκ Κ[– – –

Text a. Cf. *PA*, 4765: 'Επαμείνων 'Επαινέτου 'Ερικεεύς, prytanis, 341/0 B.C. (*IG* II², 1749, line 47). Either he or his father was probably the first owner of the pinakion.

136 (Fig. 254) Athens, National Museum, Inv. Bronze 8077. A. Dumont, *RA²* 17 (1868), 144. (Girard, no. 20; *IG* II, 890; II², 1854)

Left end. Recently stripped to bare metal. L. 2.0 cm., w. 2.4 cm., th. ca. 0.13 cm.

Probably more than one use.

Last use:

Δ Ἀ[– – –
    Ἀ[– – –

137 (Fig. 255) Athens, Stoa of Attalos, Agora Excavations Inv. B 1047. Excavated in 1953 from Area I/12; context of late fourth–early third century B.C. Unpublished.

Upper left end. Stripped to bare metal. L. 3.4 cm., w. 2.2 cm., th. ca. 0.05 cm.

Number of uses uncertain.

Last use:

Z Στ[– – –
    [– – –

The sigma is without a lower bar.

138 (Figs. 256–257) Athens, National Museum, Inv. Bronze 8097. U. Koehler, *IG* II, 931 (text *b* only). (*IG* II², 1909)

Left end, originally. Recently stripped to bare metal. L. 3.8 cm., th. 0.18 cm. at left to 0.10 cm. at right.

Two (or more) uses:

a   A $\underset{\cdot}{E}$ ⅏ [– – –
    ⅏ [– – – –

Inverted, to become a right end

b   – – – –]ρατος
    patro.
        – – – –]Αἰγιλιε(ύς)

RIGHT ENDS

139 (Figs. 258–259)   Athens, National Museum, Inv. Bronze 8128 and 8132. Unpublished.

Right half. Mended from two fragments. Recently stripped of patination. L. 6.2 cm., w. 2.4 cm., th. 0.2 cm. at right to 0.1 cm. at left.

Two or more uses:

a   – – –]ΟΝΙ$\cancel{E}$[.]ΗΣ
    patro.
    – – –]Σφή[τ]τιος

b   – – –]χος Λυσ–
    – – –]Άθμο(νεύς)

The fine diagonal at the left of line 2 is likely a survival from a use earlier than use *a*.

Text a. It would seem that the nomen was long (about four to six letters appear to be missing at the left) and that it ended in (–ο, –ρ, or –ω)νιαδης or –νιατης. I have been unable, however, to locate a name that both fits these requirements and that is attested from Athens.

140 (Fig. 260)   Athens, Stoa of Attalos, Agora Excavations Inv. B 898. Excavated in 1949 from Area D/16; fourth-century B.C. context. Unpublished.

Right half. Cleaned to brown metal. L. 5.7 cm., w. 2.2 cm., th. ca. 0.08 cm. at right to 0.05 cm. at left.

More than one use (?).

Last use:

– – – –]ληϛ   inscribed with punched serifs
– – –]σιοϛ

Along the right edge of the fragment is a slightly encrusted area of lighter brown, which at the lower corner extends left in a shape reminiscent of a long-haired, Class III–IV gorgoneion stamped on its side with the chin pointing left. Since the photograph was taken, I have cleaned this area further and am satisfied that the configuration is a superficial and accidental result of corrosion, and, not being accompanied by any traces of relief or outline in the metal itself, does not represent an erased seal.

Since there is no stamped seal at the right, this fragment must be from the only known Class VI pinakion inscribed with punched serifs. The serifs were perhaps inspired by the pierced lettering of Class V.

141 (Fig. 261)   Athens, Stoa of Attalos, Agora Excavations Inv. B 1083. Excavated in 1953 from Area N/16; Hellenistic context. Unpublished.

Right half. Bent. Cleaned to bare metal. L. 6.0 cm., w. 2.2 cm., th. ca. 0.05 cm.

More than one use (?).
Last use:

– – –]όδημοϛ
– – –]

142 (Fig. 262)   Paris, Cabinet des Médailles, Froehner Collection Inv. 619. L. Robert, *Coll. Froehner* I, 10, and pl. VI, no. 100.

Right end. Green patina. L. 4.2 cm., w. 2.2 cm., th. 0.08 cm.
More than one use (?).
Last use:

– – –]μποϛ
– – –]Υ̣

The most popular –μποϛ name in classical Athens was Theopompos (thirty-eight entries in *PA*). Much less common were Kleopompos and Olympos.

143 (Fig. 263)   Athens, National Museum, Inv. Bronze 8100. From Attika. Unpublished.

Right end. Recently stripped to bare bronze. L. 4.7 cm., w. 2.0 cm., th. 0.25 cm: at right to 0.10 cm. at left.
Three uses:

a   – – –]ων
        – – –]

b   – – –]χης
        – – –]

c   – – –]ης   *Καλλιμ(—?)*
        dem.
        – – –]

Unclassified (A)

Three highly anomalous left ends with a section-letter stamped in the upper left but lacking evidence of a stamped seal beneath.

AFFILIATED WITH CLASSES IV AND V

144 (Figs. 264–265)   Athens, National Museum, Inv. Bronze 8090. P. Girard, *BCH* 2 (1878), 534, no. 21. (*IG* II, 910; II², 1880)
    Left end. Recently stripped to bare metal. L. 2.6 cm., w. 2.0 cm., th. 0.22 cm. at left to 0.18 cm. at right.
    Three uses, minimum:

a, line 1   Z   Σ[– – –
                 .

b, line 1   Z   E[– – –
                 .

a or b, line 2   E.[– – –   inscribed with punched serifs in
                                      imitation of Class V lettering

c   Z   Σ[– – –
                     ΣG[– – –

Section-letter. The internal measurements demonstrate beyond any reasonable doubt that it was struck with the same die as the section-letters on **78** and **88**, both Class V pinakia.

Texts a and b. In line 2 the only visible traces of letters earlier than text *c* belong to a text inscribed with punched serifs. In what little remains of line 1, there are traces of two earlier texts, but since no indications of serifs have survived, it is impossible to ascertain which of the traces goes with the serifed letters of line 2.

Text c. If line 2 began with a demotic, it could be any of the three beginning *Σο–* or *Σφ–*.

As is clear from the photograph, the metal in the lower left corner is smooth and undisturbed and must never have received a seal impression.[35] The intact condition of the section-letter shows, moreover, that the extreme left end has not been subjected to erasure.

The fragment is affiliated with Class IV and V pinakia on three counts: by its early text in imitation of Class V lettering; by the retention of the original section-letter through several uses; and by the identity of the section-letter die on two Class V pinakia. The first two features occur as a rule only on pinakia with triobol seals and not in Classes III and VI. Thus it seems quite certain that the fragment comes from a pinakion that was issued and reused as a dikastic pinakion and that it bears no relation to **145** and **146**. Furthermore, as the identity of its section-letter die requires, the present fragment was manufactured close in time to the Class V pinakia. The small size of the section-letter alone eliminates any chance that we have here a Class I or II fragment with a section-letter that happened to have been struck higher than usual. According to all principles of classification and behavior of seals discussed in the earlier part of this study, a triobol seal should have been stamped below the section-letter at the left.

In view of the importance of the triobol seal for certifying dikastic pinakia, I would imagine that a triobol seal was stamped at the missing right end, in place of a gorgoneion seal, which would have been omitted. We know from several Class II pinakia last used soon after the Class V issue that gorgoneion seals were not essential to dikastic pinakia. Triobol seals were, however, and one was probably stamped somewhere on the pinakion from which this fragment survives.

AFFILIATED WITH CLASSES III OR VI

145 (Figs. 266–267)   Athens, National Museum, Inv. Bronze 8135. Unpublished.

35. Before the pinakion was cleaned, Bruck could write: "Bei dem jetzigen Zustande des Fragmentes ist die Existenz eines Stempels underhalb des Sectionsbuchstabens keineswegs ausgeschlossen, wenngleich Spuren davon nicht sichtbar sind." (*AthMitt* 19 [1894], 205, no. 10.)

Left end. Stripped to bare bronze. L. 3.5 cm., w. 2.0 cm., th. 0.15 cm. at left tapering to 0.10 cm. at right.

Two (or more) uses:

a   A M[– – – –

       [.]|[– – –

b   ⊡ Διε[– – –

       ᾽Ελευ[σίνιος

Two section-letters are visible at the upper left: a conspicuous theta stamped in an incuse square [36]; and a barely discernible alpha inscribed within it. The strokes of the alpha have been weakened and lightly broken, indicating that the alpha was partially erased and then over-stamped by the theta. Thus the fragment provides the second known instance of an inscribed section-letter superseded by a stamped one (cf. **96**).

The fact that no traces of a seal impression can be found in the lower left corner implies that the last two uses, the only uses for which we have evidence, were stampless Class VI ones. It must be admitted that the surface of the metal is a bit rough so that the possible existence of a gorgoneion seal in a hypothetical use earlier than use *a* cannot be excluded absolutely. But this is of little consequence for understanding the fragment in its final state. However many uses, the last two were without a seal, yet the second of them received a stamped section-letter rather than the inscribed one normally expected in a Class VI use. On this phenomenon, see my remarks in Chapter II, n. 26, above.

146 (Figs. 268–269) Athens, Stoa of Attalos, Pnyx Excavations Inv. M–3. Excavated from a disturbed context below the great polygonal wall on the Pnyx, 1930–1931. G. R. Davidson and D. B. Thompson, *Pnyx Small Objects* I, 13, and fig. 12, no. 3.

Left half. Cleaned to bare bronze. L. 6.2 cm., w. 2.3 cm. at left to 2.15 cm. at right, th. 0.1 cm. except at the extreme left end where the original 0.2 cm. th. is preserved.

---

36. Its dimensions (0.6 cm. outside diam. of the theta) compare closely to those of the stamped thetas on **21** (Class III) and **76** (Class IV), but the imperfect preservation of the incuse fields of all these thetas precludes identification of their dies with one another.

Three uses, minimum:

a   B   [-- -- -- -- --
    A?   Ἀχ[.]ρ[-- -- --

b   B?   ΑΓA̧̮Ņ͘ᵈ ᴎ[-- -- --
    A   Κ ο λ λ υ[τεύς

c   A   Ἁγνόθεος   right end broken away;
    A   Ὀῆθεν A   reused at half length

The stamped letters are similar in size to those in Classes III–V: incuse field of the alpha 0.75–0.8 cm. square; of the deltas (both from the same die) 0.85 cm. square. The field of the beta cannot be measured.

Text a. The beta section-letter and earlier demotic (restored Ἀχ[α]ρ[νεύς] or Ἀχ[ε]ρ[δούσιος]) had not been noted previously. Some of the remains in line 1, which I have recorded under text *b*, doubtless belong to this earliest detected use.

Text b. Davidson and Thompson printed

ΑΓΝ.Η
A   Κολλυ(τεύς)

My text of line 1 merely includes other remains that cannot be excluded from consideration; some, but it is uncertain which, belong to text *a*. So far as I can determine, however, no combination of the visible traces in the line leads to a convincing restoration of the nomen. Although the nomen began with the same initial two or three letters as the nomen of text *c*, it is clearly to be associated with the penultimate demotic Κολλυ[τεύς, since the alpha in line 1 and the lambdas of the demotic all have the same curiously flattened and spread character. Because the omicron in the demotic has a flattened shape also, the spreading of the letters may have been caused by erasure.

Text c. The sequence in which the elements of the last use were added is quite apparent: First, the pinakion broke at the right, compelling the letterer to begin the nomen exceptionally far to the left and actually to inscribe the initial alpha of the nomen into the original beta section-letter. Second, after the name was inscribed, a delta section-letter was stamped in the customary upper left corner, thoughtlessly, perhaps, since it partially obliterated the left half of the first letter of the nomen, but unsuccessfully in any case since the shape of the delta was distorted by the underlying relief of the earlier beta section-letter. Third, for greater clarity the same delta die was stamped at the lower right corner in the space remaining after the demotic. The drilled carrying-hole at the right was probably added sometime after breakage also.

The stamped alpha. It may be regarded as certain that the beta section-letter in the upper left corner was stamped for the first use and that the two delta section-letters belong with the last use. This makes it tempting to assign the stamped alpha in the lower left-hand corner to the intermediate text *b*, as it was in the *editio princeps*. The alpha was not erased before the last use, but one could assume that the presence of two delta section-letters may have excluded any possibility of mistaking the alpha for the correct section-letter during use *c*.

The difficulty with this solution, however, is that the beta section-letter of use *a* was apparently not subjected to erasure (that is, it had not been flattened) prior to being overstamped by the left-hand delta of use *c*, as is clear from the remarkable amount of the beta's relief that was picked up in the relief of the delta. (In order to appreciate the extent to which the delta has been deformed by the high relief of the beta within it, one must see a cast or the pinakion itself; the photograph is misleading.) Thus, if the stamped alpha was added prior to the last use (as it would have been on any interpretation), both it *and* the stamped beta above it would have been visible in use *b*, just as it was visible along with the delta section-letters during use *c*. The thickness at the lower left seems to be original, and there are no indications of a stamped seal within the relief of the stamped alpha. These considerations, together with the position of the alpha, lead me to question whether the alpha here was really intended as a section-letter. It is possible, I believe, that the stamp may have been added at the time of manufacture as a variant for a gorgoneion seal, since alpha was the city's initial and, like the gorgoneion seals, denoted the citizen body at large. If this is the case, the restored pinakion would probably have been provided with two such alpha stamps, one at the original right end as well as the present one at the left.

Such would be a strange pinakion indeed, but there is something strange about the fragment however the stamped alpha is interpreted. I do not know whether the second interpretation is the correct one, but it has the advantages of explaining why a primary seal was apparently omitted from the lower left corner, why the stamped alpha was placed below the beta section-letter of use *a* and not over it, why the beta section-letter was not erased prior to use *b*, and why the stamped alpha was not erased prior to the last use. If the alpha is accepted as a section-letter, these anomalies would remain unsolved.

One thing seems clear, however: the pinakion lacked a triobol seal in its last use and probably in its earlier uses also. Hence the pinakion is not a dikastic pinakion and should be associated with the nondikastic pinakia of Classes III and VI.

Unclassified (B)

Lost pinakia known only from incomplete transcriptions.

RECORDED WITH A STAMPED SEAL AT THE RIGHT; FROM CLASSES I–V

147 (Figs. 270–271) formerly Athens, Collection of L. F. S. Fauvel. J. D. Akerblad, *AttiAccRom* 1, 1 (1821), 61–64, and pl. I.3 (after a drawing by William Gell). J. H. Kroll, *BCH* 91 (1967), 388–391, with figs. 1 (= Akerblad's pl. I) and 2 (= page from a notebook of Col. W. M. Leake). (*IG* II², 1895)

Two nonjoining, badly corroded fragments. No dimensions recorded. Three uses, minimum:

a ? [------]   Ⓢ
       [------]

                 ca. 8
b ? |[---------]ης   Class VI?
       |[-] ⥾ [---]
                 vel
       |[----]

c   κ Σώσ[τρ]ατος   Class VI?
        Π α [λ] λ(ηνεύς)
                 vel
        Πρα[σιε]ύ(ς)

S(eal). Triobol or gorgoneion.

Until the sketch reproduced here in Fig. 270 was recently discovered among the Leake papers at Cambridge University, the sole record of this piece was the one published by Akerblad. As I have argued in the article cited above, Akerblad's engraving is suspect in a number of particulars, including the owl seal he shows at the right of the pinakion. The Leake sketch shows that the seal was partially obscured by a later sigma. The pinakion apparently had at least three uses, one with the seal, one with the sigma inscribed over the seal, and one with the name of Sostratos. To judge from the effacement ⌐f the seal at the right, the last two uses were probably stampless, Class VI ones, and their section-letters therefore would ordinarily have been inscribed, as the Leake record shows for the last use. Since the recent discovery of **96**, which was provided with stamped section-letters in its latest uses, however, it is now quite uncertain which of the two facsimiles is the more faithful in respect to the technique of the section-letter. Akerblad's stamped kappa cannot be dismissed out of hand. One detail neglected in the Leake sketch but provided by Akerblad is a carrying-hole at the lower right of the pinakion, below and just to the left of the stamped seal.

Text c. Following Leake, there are two possibilities for Sostratos' demotic. Akerblad and Kirchner printed a doubtful 'Η[φ]α[ιστι]ά(δης).

148 (Fig. 272)   formerly Berlin, Staatliche Museen, Inv. Bronze 6222. Missing since 1897, according to the museum inventory. S. Bruck, *AthMitt* 19 (1894), 210, no. 8, whence our Fig. 272. (*IG* II 5, 938f; II², 1921)
   Right half of a pinakion. No dimensions recorded.
   Apparently three uses, minimum:

a   — — — — — —] Ⓢ
         — — — — — —]

b   — — — —]ρος Ⓢ
         — — — —]

c   — —]λος Ⓢ
         — —]

S(eal). Triobol or gorgoneion, Bruck's "Undeutlicher Stempel." Fortunately, his indications of erasure in both lines help clarify the history of the fragment.

RECORDED WITH AN INSCRIBED SECTION-LETTER IN THE UPPER LEFT
CORNER, IMPLYING THE ORIGINAL PRESENCE OF A SEAL BELOW;
ALL OR MOST CLASS III–V PINAKIA IN A FINAL CLASS VI REUSE

149 and **150** (Fig. 273)   formerly Würzburg. Two pinakia from a single grave
(Ross) and belonging to the same owner. Ex coll. Bayerischen Legations-
secretar Herr Faber, in Athens, where recorded by L. Ross, *Demen von Attika*,
54, no. 25, with the transcriptions reproduced in Fig. 273. L. Ulrichs, *Ver-*
zeichnis der Antikensammlung der Universität Würzburg II (Würzburg, 1868),
3 (texts and measurements only). Cf. S. Bruck, *Philologus* 54 (1895), 73. Lost as
a result of the Allied bombing of the museum during the last war. (Girard,
nos. 36–37; *IG* II, 914–915; II², 1887)

149 Complete. Broken in two (Ulrichs). L. 12.0 cm., w. 2.0 cm.
   Two or more uses:

a	? $[- - - - - -$ Ⓖ $]$	
	Ⓖ? $[- - - - - -$ Ⓖ $]$	Class III?

b	Θ Καλλίας Κηφισοδώ(ρου)	Class VI
	Ἀγνόσι(ος)	

G(*orgoneion*) *seals* (?). The one at the right is my restoration. The one at the
left was recorded and described by Ross as a "half-moon" seal, but was
probably a partially erased gorgoneion, as Bruck deduced. In venturing this
correction, Bruck apparently had in mind Koumanoudes's drawing and description of the partially erased right-hand gorgoneion on **37** as a "half-moon,"
although in all fairness I should point out that the first editor of **64** hesitatingly
identified its erased *triobol* seal as a "half-moon" seal also.

   Fortunately for our purposes, the identity of the seal is of less importance
than the fact that the seal was eventually subjected to partial erasure (as
were the "half-moon" seals on both **37** and **64**) and thus belonged to a pinakion that was finally used as a stampless Class VI pinakion.

150 Complete. L. 11.0 cm., w. 2.2 cm.
   One or more uses.
   Last use:

Θ Καλλίας Κηφισ(οδώρου)	Class VI
Ἀγνού(σιος)	

According to Ross, no seals were visible.[37] The high position of the section-letter, however, warns that a seal may have originally been stamped in the lower left corner.

The father (or possibly the son) of the last owner of the pinakia is Κηφισ-όδωρος Καλλίου Ἁγνούσιος honored by the demos in 346/5 B.C. (*IG* II², 215, lines 9–10).

151 (Fig. 274)   A. Dumont, "Tablette judiciaire récemment découvert en Attique," *RA*² 19 (1869), 225, with the transcription reproduced in Fig. 274. (Girard, no. 44; *IG* II, 892; II², 1885)

Whole. "Conservation excellente. Belle patine verte." L. 12.0 cm., w. 2.3 cm.

Probably two or more uses.

Last use:

> Δ Ἀντιφῶν   Class VI
>   Ἁλαιεύς

Dumont writes: "L'inscription occupe les deux tiers de la tablette à gauche; le dernier tiers ne porte pas de lettres . . . La lettre de série est en creux. Les deux traits à droite et à gauche indiquent qu'on a voulu tracer un encadrement rectangulaire resté inachevé. Ce petit document n'a jamais reçu de timbre d'aucune sorte. C'est ce qui en fait l'intérêt . . . La tablette . . . n'a pas non plus été percée de trous."

As the size and technique of the last section-letter indicate, the last use clearly belongs to the stampless Class VI period. The lines to the left and right of this final letter should belong to an earlier section-letter with perhaps the initial letter of an earlier owner's name. The fact that at least two successive section-letters were positioned in the upper left corner implies that there was almost certainly an erased seal in the lower left corner that was invisible to Dumont.

152 and **153** (Figs. 275–276)   from graves ἐν Τράχονες (Mylonas).[38] Formerly in the possession of Komninos, whose estate was within the ancient deme of

37. The transcription of this pair of pinakia by A. R. Rangabe (*Antiquités Helléniques*, 2 vols. [Athens, 1842–1855], II, 825, no. 1302), which gives a half-moon seal at the right of **150** while omitting one at the left of **149**, involves a typographical error. There is no reason to think that Rangabe had any independent knowledge of these or of the other two pinakia published in his *Antiquités* (nos. 1300 and 1301, our **35** and **72**). From the concordance on his page 1059, his selection of pinakia, and his comments on them, it is clear that he was copying directly from Ross, *Demen von Attika*.

38. This may not be altogether accurate. According to Eliot (*Coastal Demes of Attika*, fig. 1), the town of Trachones lay within the deme of Euonymon, slightly to the north of Halimous.

Halimous.[39] K. D. Mylonas, "Σύμμικτα Ἀρχαιολογικά," *BCH* 3 (1879), 178–179, nos. 4 a and b (transcriptions and brief comments). U. Koehler, *IG* II, 892 and 906 (texts reproduced in Figs. 275–276) after transcriptions by Arthur Milchhoefer *apud Comnenum*. (*IG* II², 1856 and 1872)

152 Broken at right?
Probably more than one use.
Last use:

Δ Ἀριστοτέλης   Class VI?
ʾΑλιμόσιος

153 "Lamina a parte dextra fracta esse videtur" (Koehler).
Apparently more than one use, as implied by the erased or damaged area at the right of line 2.
Last use:

Ε Τελέσων Τελεσ(—?)   Class VI?
ʾΑλιμόσι(ος)

Τιμοκράτης Τελέ⟨σ⟩ωνος ʾΑλιμούσιος, bouleutes in 335/4 (*IG* II², 1700, line 78), should be either a brother or a son of the pinakion's last owner.

The Mylonas and Milchhoefer-Koehler transcriptions agree that the section-letter of **152** was positioned in front of line 1. Mylonas, however, did not note the epsilon section-letter of **153**, so we may well doubt the value of his statement that neither of the pinakia bore stamped seals in their lower left corners.

Mylonas gives one set of dimensions for both pinakia, 12.2 cm. × 2.1 cm., implying that both were complete. Koehler shows both as broken, although he does not comment on this aspect of **152** and qualifies his statement about **153** with a "videtur." Perhaps both pinakia were whole, but Milchhoefer's transcription somehow suggested to Koehler that they were not.

154 "Found in a grave in the northern Peiraeus, May 10, 1856, in the excavations of the English Col. C. Campbell" (cf. **155**). K. S. Pittakys, *ArchEph* 1865, 1470, no. 3038. (whence *IG* II², 1883)
Complete (?). Width given as 2.0 cm. Pittakys transcribed in majuscules:

‖ΛΥΣΙΑΣΔΗΜ
‖ΦΑΛΗ

Probably more than one use.

39. Mr. J. Geroulanos informs me that the estate was near Chasani and is now covered by the Athenian Airport.

Last use:

Ͱ? *Λυσίας Δημ*(—?)   Class VI?
Φαλη(ρεύs)

It is uncertain whether the two verticals at the beginning of line 1 belong to an eta section-letter. They, like the verticals in front of line 2, may be remains of letters from an earlier use.

Since Pittakys identified this and **155** as segments of inscribed headbands (*ταινίαι*), both of them were presumably quite thin. This pinakion apparently did not find its way into the hands of Captain Jones of Bangor with **155**.

LAST USE CLEARLY BELONGING TO CLASS VI

155 formerly Bangor, Wales. Collection of Captain Jones. "Found in a grave in the northern Peiraeus, May 10, 1856, in the excavations of the English Col. C. Campbell" (cf. **154**). K. S. Pittakys, *ArchEph* 1856, 1470, no. 3039 (whence *IG* II², 1879).

Obtained by "Captain Jones" of Bangor and displayed with his collection at the Fourteenth Annual Meeting of the Cambrian Archaeological Association, August 27–September 1, 1860, at Bangor where it was erroneously said to have been discovered on the island of Anglesey, *Archaeologia Cambrensis* 3d Ser., 6 (1860), 370,[40] whence its publication as a Greek inscription found in Britain, *Corpus Inscriptionum Latinarum* VII, p. 220, and *IG* XIV, 2546.

Complete and apparently thin (see **154**). No dimensions recorded. Pittakys transcribed in majuscules:

$$\text{I} \quad \begin{array}{l} ΓΟΛΥΣΤΡΑΤΟΣ \\ ΑΛΑΙΕΥΣ \end{array}$$

Number of uses uncertain.

Last use:

$$\text{Z} \quad \begin{array}{l} Πολύστρατος \\ Ἀλαιεύs \end{array} \quad \text{Class VI}$$

40. "A bronze strap, with trilobated ends, inscribed in Greek capitals
    ΠΟΛΥΣΤΡΑΤΟΣ
    ΑΛΑΙΕΥΣ
A piece of a similar but smaller strap, with square ends, inscribed *INO*. These two inscribed plates of bronze are said to have been discovered very lately in Anglesey." I have listed this second piece below as **178**. The reference in *Archaeologia Cambrensis* I owe to Professor M. L. Clarke.

Pittakys confirms that the zeta section-letter was positioned "in front of line 2, just above the line." I assume that it was inscribed and not stamped and that the visible text, therefore, belongs to Class VI. The pinakion nevertheless may still have been a palimpsest and originally stamped, like **42** and **61**. The statement in *Archaeologia Cambrensis* that the ends were "trilobated" indicates that the pinakion was notched like **57** and **89**.

The owner may be the Πολύστρατος Χαρμαντίδου Ἁλαιεύς, priest of Apollo Zoster, who was honored by his deme in an inscription that has been dated on the basis of letter forms toward the end of the fourth century (*Deltion* 11 [1927–1928], 40, no. 4, lines 1, 7, and 15).

As for the loss of this pinakion and **178**, I quote from a letter (February 13, 1968) of Professor M. L. Clarke of the University College of North Wales, Bangor, who generously looked into this matter for me:

"Captain Jones was a sea captain of Bangor who collected curios on his travels. His collection was housed in a small museum in the town until about 60 years ago when it was transferred to the town library. A former librarian decided it was of no value, and wanted the space for other purposes, and the objects were dumped in the foundations of the building and forgotten about until a few years ago when they were discovered and sent to the National Museum of Wales at Cardiff. The City Librarian has shown me a list of the objects found and sent away which appears to be full and careful, and the allotment plates are not among them."

Professor Clarke has since assured me that the pinakia are not to be found in the remnants of the collection still kept in the Bangor library, and the museum at Cardiff has written that there is no record of the objects there either.

156 (Fig. 277) (?) formerly Eleusis. A. N. Skias, "'Ἐπιγραφαὶ Ἐλευσῖνος,'" *ArchEph* 1899, 171, no. 1, with the facsimile reproduced in Fig. 277. (*IG* II², Addenda, 1871a).

Left half. L. 6.5 cm., w. 2.2 cm.
Number of uses uncertain.
Last use:

E $\quad$ Παυσ[– – – $\qquad$ Class VI
$\quad$ Ἀνδοκ[ίδου

The fragment may still be at Eleusis, but I was unable to find it in the display cases in the museum. The storerooms there are too disorganized for a systematic search.

NO SECTION-LETTER RECORDED

157 The second of "zwei Plättchen (aus Bronze) mit den Inschriften" from the excavations of a necropolis along the Ilissos that produced **129**. *AthMitt* 15 (1900), 454. *PA*, Addenda, 1457a, but omitted from *IG* II². The anonymous author of the report in *AthMitt* transcribed

$$ΑΓΟΛΛΟΔΩΡΟΣ$$
$$ΧΟΛΛΕΙ(δης)ΦΥ$$

Last use:

$$Ἀπολλόδωρος$$
$$Χολλεί(δης)\ Φυ(—?)$$

For all we can tell, the pinakion may have been broken at one end (like **129**, although this fact was not noted in the original publication of **129**) or may have contained an obscure section-letter (and seals). It is probable that line 2 was not indented two spaces as the transcription shows, since the demotic in the original transcription of **129** is also indented two spaces—incorrectly as we find from the pinakion itself.

The two letters that I have tentatively considered an exceptionally abbreviated patronymic at the right of line 2 may in fact be survivals of an earlier inscription. A possible descendant is an Apollodoros of Cholleidai, prytanis around 50 B.C. (*IG* II², 1754 = Dow, *Prytaneis*, 172, no. 103, line 13).

158 formerly Helsinki (?). J. Sundwall, *Nachträge*, 167: "(Φ)ιλόστρατος Κολων(ῆθεν). Heliastentäfelchen in meinem Besitz (4 Jahr.). Derselbe *P.A.* 14734."

Last use:

$$[Φ]ιλόστρατος$$
$$Κολων(ῆθεν)$$

Because there are too many letters for a one-line text, we are justified in assuming that the name was inscribed in two lines. The restored phi at the left of line 1 may or may not indicate that the original left end had broken away; corrosion could also have been responsible for the missing or undetected letter. Enough of the pinakion was preserved, however, to suggest that it was substantially complete and that it was probably recovered from a grave.

The loss of this pinakion is to be especially lamented, for, as Sundwall points out, there is a strong probability that it belonged to the well-known orator Philostratos, son of Dionysios, of Kolone. The identification would be particularly attractive if the pinakion happened to be of the Class VI variety. The orator Philostratos is known to have died about 330, and if he was buried with a bronze allotment plate, it would have to have been a Class VI one.

The present location of the pinakion is a mystery. On my behalf, Dr. C. A. Nordman, Director of the National Museum, Helsinki, contacted Sundwall's daughter, who explained that the scholarly materials of her late father had been sent to the Åbo Akademi, Åbo, Finland. Professor Rolf Westman of the Akademi has since written me the following (April 29, 1969): "Professor Sundwall did bequeath his library to the Åbo Akademi, but of any collection of antiquities we have no knowledge, with the exception of some small objects of rather modern origin (e.g., medals). I have checked this both with our Chief Librarian and with Sundwall's family . . . In spite of our efforts we have not been able to find the bronze plate you refer to. I may mention that I looked through Sundwall's personal copy of *IG* II² (1835–1923) in the hope of finding some marginal notes, but there were none."

Unclassified (C)

Fragments broken at both ends

WITH A TEXT INSCRIBED IN IMITATION OF CLASS V LETTERING AND
THEREFORE FROM A CLASS IV OR V PINAKION

159 (Figs. 278–279)   Athens, National Museum, Inv. Bronze 8088. P. Girard, *BCH* 2 (1878), 535, no. 25. (*IG* II, 930; II², 1908)

Middle fragment. Recently stripped of patination. L. 3.0 cm., w. 2.0 cm., th. 0.06 cm.

Two or more uses:

a	– – –] . . . [– – –	inscribed with punched serifs at terminations
	Συπα]λήτ [τιος?	of letters in imitation of Class V lettering
b	– – –]ς ῾Εστ[ι – – –	
	– – –]ς [	

The letters of text *a* were not visible before cleaning.

Since texts inscribed in imitation of Class V lettering are frequently not the earliest texts on the pinakia on which they are found, the earliest legible letters on this fragment may have been preceded by an earlier text. Perhaps some of the fine lines in a diamondlike configuration at the lower right belong to such an earlier use.

OTHER "MIDDLE" FRAGMENTS

160 (Fig. 280)   Athens, Stoa of Attalos, Agora Excavations Inv. B 111. Excavated in 1933 from Area K/7; context of the second half of the fourth century B.C. Unpublished.

Fragment from near the left end. Cleaned to bare metal. L. 3.4 cm., w. 2.2 cm., th. 0.15 cm. at left to 0.10 cm. at right.

More than one use, as shown by the tapering thickness.

Last use:

]Φρυνι[– – –
] Εἰρε[σίδης

The nomen read Φρυνίχος, Φρύνισκος, or Φρυνίων.

161 (Fig. 281)   Athens, Stoa of Attalos, Pnyx Excavations Inv. M–4. Excavated from the filling of the Third Period of the Assembly Place, 1930–1931. G. R. Davidson and D. B. Thompson, *Pnyx Small Objects* I, 13, and fig. 12, no. 4.

Probably from near left end. Cleaned to bare metal. Bent. L. 4.4 cm., w. 2.0 cm., th. ca. 0.05–0.08 cm.

Probably more than one use.

Last use:

]Στρατ[– – –
]Βουτ(άδης)[

162   formerly Athens, Stoa of Attalos, Agora Excavations Inv. B 1212. Found in 1957 northwest of the Pnyx in dumped earth from elsewhere in Athens. Lost before photographing. Unpublished.

Broken at both ends. L. 2.8 cm., w. 2.3 cm.

Number of uses uncertain.

Last use:

Λ]ΥΣΙΣ[– – –
Ἀ]πολλ[– – –

The nomen read Λ]ῦσις or Λ]υσίσ[τρατος.

163 (Figs. 282–283)   Athens, National Museum, Inv. Bronze 8093. U. Koehler, IG II, 926. (*IG* II², 1903)

From near left end. Recently stripped to bare bronze. L. 3.3 cm., w. 2.0 cm., th. 0.12 cm.

Two or more uses.

Last use:

Θε?]ογένη[ς
᾿Ερ]χιε[ύς

Traces of a single vertical in each line remain from an earlier use.

Last use. Line 1. The restoration is Kirchner's (*PA*, 6707 and *ad IG* II², 1903). A Theogenes of Erchia, basileus around mid-fourth century B.C. (Demosthenes 59.84), is the sole member of the deme with a name in –ογένης in Kirchner's list of Erchieis at the back of *PA* II. Bechtel gives, moreover, only two other possibilities for restoring a two-letter gap at the beginning of the line, Διογένης and ῾Ηρογένης, and the second of these is not attested at Athens. Of course, if the first letters of the nomen and demotic were not perfectly aligned, the gap at the beginning of line 1 might have consisted of three letter spaces, in which case the possibilities for restoration would be multiplied considerably.

164 (Figs. 284–285)   Athens, Stoa of Attalos, Pnyx Excavations Inv. M–5. Excavated from the filling of the Third Period of the Assembly Place, 1930–1931. G. R. Davidson and D. B. Thompson, *Pnyx Small Objects* I, 13, and fig. 12, no. 5.

From near left end. Cleaned to bare metal. L. 3.5 cm., w. 2.2 cm., th. 0.08 cm.

Two or more uses:

a   [ᶜᵃ·²]ησι/ἓ[– – –
      [Ἀ]θμο[νεύς

b   [ᶜᵃ·²]ἓδων Τἓ[– – –
      [Κο]λλυ(τεύς)[

Text a. The remains in line 1 probably belong to one of the several Athenian names in –ησιας (e.g., ῾Ηγήσιας, Κτήσιας) but a name such as ῾Ηγησίλεως, Μνησίλοχος, or Τλησιμένης, all listed in *PA*, would also fit.

Text b. The likely restorations are [Με]ίδων, [Φε]ίδων (so Dow, *BCH* 87 [1963], 667), or [Κ]ήδων. Dow points out that a relative of the last owner may be the [.]είδων [Κ]αλλιστράτου K. who is commemorated on a fourth-century B.C. tombstone (*IG* II², 6505).

165 (Fig. 286) Athens, National Museum, Inv. Bronze 8089. P. Girard, *BCH* 2 (1878), 535, no. 24. (*IG* II, 927; II², 1904)

From near left end. Stripped to the bare metal, which is cracked and fragile. L. 3.3 cm., w. 2.2 cm., th. ca. 0.08 cm.

Probably more than one use.

Last use:

$$[\overset{2-3}{-}]οδωρ[ος \; vel \; -ίδης$$
$$[\overset{2-3}{-}]μογέ(νους):[\overset{dem.}{-}-$$

The interpunct shows that the demotic follows in line 2. The patronymic probably read Δημο-, Ἑρμο-, Θεσμο-, or Τιμο-γέ(νους).

166 (Fig. 287) Athens, National Museum, Inv. Bronze 8094. Unpublished.

Probably from near left end. Recently stripped of patination. L. 3.5 cm., w. 2.1 cm., minimal th. ca. 0.05 cm.

One (or more?) uses.

Last use:

$$]\; μαίν[ετος$$
$$]\; ΑΝΤΑ[---$$

The nomen was Δημαίνετος (*PA*, 3265-3277) or Τιμαίνετος (*PA*, 13598). Line 2 probably began Παιαν(ιεύς) Τα- or with a patronymic in Παντα-.

167 (Fig. 288) Athens, National Museum, Inv. Bronze 8140. S. Bruck, *AthMitt* 19 (1894), 209, no. 4. (*IG* II 5, 928b; II², 1906)

Probably from near left end. L. 3.3 cm., w. 1.9 cm., th. 0.08 cm.

More than one use, as evidenced by diagonal erasure striations.

Last use:

$$---]\; ΣΘΕ[---$$
$$Με]λιτ(εύς)[$$

Line 1 probably should restore [$\overset{2-3}{-}$]ισθε[νης] although $--$]ης Θε[$--$ is possible.

The remains of an erased omicron (?) appear between the I and T in line 2.

168 (Fig. 289)   Athens, National Museum, Inv. Bronze 8095. U. Koehler, *IG* II, 925. (*IG* II², 1902)

From the left end or middle. Stripped of patination. L. 2.4 cm., w. 2.0 cm., th. ca. 0.05 cm.

More than one use.

Last use:

]ΙΠΠΙ[
] *Α* [

169 (Fig. 290)   Athens, Stoa of Attalos, Agora Excavations Inv. B 1003. Excavated in 1952 from Area R/10; second-century B.C. fill. Mentioned with regard to findspot in *Hesperia* 23 (1954), 59, n. 42.

Middle fragment. Cleaned to bare metal. L. 4.3 cm., w. 2.1 cm., th. 0.18 cm.

Two or more uses.

Last use:

$---$]ⵄ|λος Ευ[$--$
$---$ ε]ύς   [

An earlier use is evident from the upright within the epsilon in line 1.

170 (Fig. 291)   Athens, National Museum, Inv. Bronze 8092. U. Koehler, *IG* II, 928. (*IG* II², 1905)

Middle fragment. Recently stripped of patination. L. 3.0 cm., w. 2.3 cm., th. ca. 0.10 cm.

Probably more than one use.

Last use:

[$-\overset{ca. 5}{--}-$]ς[
[Κηφ] ισιεύ[ς

The hitherto undetected vertical along the left break permits the restoration of the demotic.

171 (Fig. 292)   Athens, National Museum, Inv. Bronze 8081. "Trouvée près de Vari." A. Dumont, *RA²* 17 (1868), 145. Sketch published by S. Bruck, *AthMitt* 19 (1894), 207, no. 19. (Girard, no. 22; *IG* II, 938; II², 1917)

Middle fragment. Recently stripped of patination. L. 3.6 cm., w. 2.25 cm., th. 0.12–0.15 cm.

More than one use.

Last use:

$$- - -]^{\overline{m}}\, \omega\nu : \varLambda\upsilon[- - -$$
$$- - -\varAlpha\lambda?]\alpha\iota[(\epsilon\acute{\upsilon}s?)$$

Because of the findspot, Dumont restored the demotic $\Theta o\rho]\alpha\iota[\epsilon\acute{\upsilon}s$. But according to this reasoning a much more convincing restoration is that given above, as Halai Aixonides nearly reached Vari (which is actually in Anagyrous). Thorai lay some ten kilometers to the southeast (cf. Eliot, *Coastal Demes of Attika*, 33–34, 44–46, and 65–68).

Traces of an earlier text or texts are visible in several diagonals in line 1 and an erased vertical in the alpha in line 2.

172 (Figs. 293–296)   Athens, National Museum, Inv. Bronze 8129. Unpublished.

From near right end and ultimately reused as a right end. Recently stripped to bare metal. L. 5.0 cm., w. 2.2 cm., th. 0.15–0.08 cm.

Four uses, minimum:

a	$- - -]\iota\alpha s$ [		Side A
	$- - -]\lambda\eta(-?)$ [		
b	$- - -]os$ [		Side A
	$- - -]\nu\alpha\hat{\iota}(os)$ [		
c	$- - -]\iota\kappa\lambda\hat{\eta}s\ \Sigma[^{\underline{patro}-}$		Side A
	$^{\underline{nym.}}\varPhi\lambda]\nu\epsilon\acute{\upsilon}s$ [		
d	$- - - - -]\iota\lambda os$ ⊢	Class VI	
	$- - -]\upsilon\ {}^{\backprime}E\kappa\alpha\lambda\hat{\eta}(\theta\epsilon\nu)$	Side B	

The original was almost certainly stamped with seals on the much-reinscribed Side A, and, on analogy with **59**, another much-reused opisthographic palimpsest, was probably of the Class III or IV type.

Text a. Line 2 presumably concludes the abbreviated demotic Παλλη(νεύς), Συπαλή(ττιος), or one of the five demotics terminating in –λῆ(θεν).

Text b. Line 2 probably contained the demotic Ἀφιδναῖ(ος) or Οἰναῖ(ος)

Text d. The break at the right of the fragment did not occur until just before the inscribing of this use. The section-letter at the right is typical of a number of Class VI pinakia.

173 (Fig. 297)   Paris, Cabinet des Médailles, Froehner Collection Inv. 620. "Athènes 1912." L. Robert, *Coll. Froehner* I, 10, and pl. VI, no. 10p (cf. **98**) S. Dow, *BCH* 87 (1963), 671–672, with fig. 9.

Fragment from near the right end. Inscribed surface has recently been cleaned. L. 2.8 cm. w. 2.0 cm., th. 0.10 cm.

More than one use.

Last use:

    – – – –]νης   [
    <u>patro.</u>
    – – – Π]λωθε(ύς)[

A sigma from an earlier use can be made out within the present sigma of line 1. Cleaning has confirmed Dow's reading and restoration of line 2.

174 (Fig. 298)   Athens, National Museum, Inv. Bronze 8096. U. Koehler, *IG* II, 929. (*IG* II², 1907)

From near right end. Recently stripped clean. L. 3.4 cm., w. 2.1 cm., th. ca. 0.10 cm.

More than one use, as the unevenness of the top and bottom edges shows.

Last use:

    – – –]ς : Ἀρχεℵ[– – –
    – – –]ς   [– – –

The half circle of the rho was made with about a half-dozen short, controlled blows of a straight punch.

175 (Fig. 299)   Athens, Stoa of Attalos, Agora Excavations Inv. B 76. Excavated in 1933 from Area I/13. Unpublished.

From near right end. Cleaned to bare metal. L. 3.4 cm., w. 2.1 cm., th. 0.1 cm.

More than one use. Diagonally striated by erasure.

Last use:

$$- - -]\eta\varsigma \quad [$$
$$- - -] \quad\quad [$$

176 (Fig. 300)   Athens, National Museum, Inv. Bronze 8139. Unpublished.
From near right end. Stripped of patination. L. 2.4 cm., w. 2.0 cm., th.
0.15 cm. at right to 0.05 cm. at left.

More than one use. Thickness tapered by erasure.

Last use:

$$- - -]o\varsigma \quad [$$
$$- - -] \quad\quad [$$

Unclassified (D)

Identity as fragments of allotment plates uncertain or doubtful.[41]

177 (Fig. 301)   Athens, National Museum, Inv. Bronze 8142. S. Bruck, *AthMitt*
19 (1894), 209, no. 5, with sketch. (*IG* II 5, 938c; II², 1918)

Right end. Recently stripped to bare metal. L. 3.9 cm., w. 1.9–2.0 cm., th.
ca. 0.20 cm.

One (or more?) uses.

Last use:

$$- - - \omega]\nu : A\chi\alpha\rho(\nu\epsilon\dot{\upsilon}\varsigma)$$
$$\text{patro.?} \quad]$$

41. One item mistakenly recorded as an Athenian pinakion by Boeckh (*CIG*, 210) and
subsequently by Girard (*BCH* 2 [1878], 537, no. 38) and in both editions of *IG* II (II, 939, and
II², 1922) is a bronze weight with an owl symbol in relief and the letters Θ $\begin{smallmatrix}\text{T}\\ \Delta\text{Y}\text{A}\end{smallmatrix}$, now in the
British Museum (Walters, *Catalogue*, no. 2998). The weight, known to Boeckh from an
engraving in P. M. Paciaudi, *Monumenta Peloponnesia*, 2 vols. (Rome, 1761), I, 254, has yet
to be convincingly attributed. The curious style of the owl and the perplexing inscription
both rule out an Athenian origin. Koehler rightly omitted Girard's no. 27 (now Athens,
National Museum, Inv. Bronze 8082) from the list of pinakia in *IG* II. Although similar in
size to many of our fragments (length 2.7 × width 2.5 cm.), it is inscribed with a single row
of crude, large letters (height: 1.0–1.2 cm.) on each side and is a fragment of a bronze
inscription of some other kind.

The consistently early look of the letters (slanting nu, asymmetrical alphas, chi with a horizontal crossbar, and rho composed of three straight strokes) led Hommel (*Heliaia*, 43) to regard this as the earliest pinakion extant. But, of course, if the fragment were to be dated by letter forms alone, it would ordinarily have to be pushed back well into the fifth century. Other factors that suggest that it may not be a fragment of an allotment plate are the inscribing of nomen and demotic in a single, upper line; the relatively narrow width; and the crenulation of the upper and lower edges, which is without parallel among the positively identified pinakia.

None of these factors is necessarily decisive, however. For other slanted nus, see, for example, **102** and **130**; for tilted chis, see **16c**, **25b**, **37c**, and **121b**; and for the angular rho, see **91**. For a parallel in the arrangement of the name, see **122a**, which is a Class VI text, as the present one would be if it were indeed from a pinakion. Finally, the width is not excessively narrow, and the crenulation, I suppose, could somehow be the result of erasure.

178 formerly Bangor, Wales. Collection of Captain Jones. *Archaeologia Cambrensis* 3d Ser., 6 (1860), 370 (see n. 40, above).
Broken at one or both ends.
Last use:

]*INO*[

Since this piece was probably purchased by Captain Jones along with **155** (one of the two pinakia excavated by Col. C. Campbell), it is likely to have been a fragment of a pinakion. From the three letters, we see that it is not a part of Campbell's other pinakion, **154**.

179 (Fig. 302) Athens, National Museum, Inv. Bronze 8076. A. Dumont, *RA*² 17 (1868), 145. (Girard, no. 26; *IG* II, 940; II², 1923)
Middle fragment. Recently stripped of patination. L. 2.6 cm., w. 1.6 cm., minimal th. ca. 0.05 cm.
Last use:

‒ ‒ ‒]*IEPO*⫶[‒ ‒ ‒

The width of the fragment is exceptionally narrow, by some 0.3 to 0.4 cm. There is barely enough room for a second line of text. Moreover, the preserved letters suggest the restoration, Ἱερόν, a word that is often found on inscribed plaques associated with dedications (cf. *IG* I², 460). It would seem, therefore, that previous editors have erred in ascribing this fragment to an allotment plate.

180 (Fig. 303)   Athens, Stoa of Attalos, Agora Excavations Inv. B 1028. Excavated in 1953 from Area I/13. Unpublished.

Only one edge preserved. Uncleaned. L. 1.5 cm., w. 1.8 cm., th. 0.05–0.10 cm.

Letters, if read as from a bottom edge:

$$---]\underset{.}{Y}\Phi|[---$$

The phi was formed with several blows of a straight punch and, hence, is square. Cf. the similarly formed, diamond-shaped phi on **56**, text *b*.

181 (Fig. 304)   Athens, Stoa of Attalos, Agora Excavations Inv. B 863. Excavated in 1947 from Area A–B/19–20. Unpublished.

Broken into five pieces. Encrusted brown bronze. L. 5.7 cm., w. 2.6 cm., th. ca. 0.12 cm. If the piece is not from an allotment plate, its length may be original.

Possible letters:

$$| \;_{vel}\; \Gamma? \quad \begin{array}{l} \varDelta IO[.] \\ [.]|\Gamma\square \end{array}$$

Owing to the blistered and cracked condition of the surface and the fact that the letters seem lightly scratched into the metal, few of the above letters or parts of letters can be regarded as certain. The suggestions of a possible section-letter are especially doubtful. On the other hand, there can be no mistaking the square letter (?) in line 2, although I do not know how it is to be reconciled with what seems to be a circular omicron in line 1.

In addition to the irregularly scratched and angular lettering, the piece's width is exceptional by 0.3–0.5 cm., and there are no indications of a demotic. The combination of all these factors makes it highly unlikely that the piece belonged to an allotment plate.

Unclassified (E)

Attribution to Athens uncertain.

182 (Figs. 305–306)   formerly Athens. Lost since reported in the collection of L. F. S. Fauvel during the early 1800s. J. D. Akerblad, *AttiAccRom* 1, 1 (1821),

61–64, and pl. I.4. Emendation proposed by Karl Keil in a review of Akerblad *AllLitZeit* 1846, Intelligenzblatt No. 35, 283–284. Attributed to Dodona in Epiros by J. H. Kroll, *BCH* 91 (1967), 388–396, and figs. 1 (= Akerblad's pl. I) and 2 (= page from a notebook of Col. W. M. Leake). (*IG* II², 1899)

Whole. No dimensions recorded.

As recorded by Akerblad (after William Gell) and Leake (after an unidentified transcription):

> Κλεόκριτος   carrying-hole at lower left
> Δωδωνεύς   ⓢ

As possibly to be emended:

> ? Κλεόκριτος
>   ⟨Ἀθμο⟩νεύς ?   ⓢ

S(eal). As drawn by Akerblad, after a transcription by Gell: owl standing right, facing, in incuse circle; located more than a centimeter from the right end of the plate. Since Akerblad shows an almost identical owl seal in his patently overrestored facsimile of **147**, however, the accuracy of the present representation is highly suspect. The Leake transcript gives an incuse circle containing a design that was clearly intended to be noncommittal, but that could be interpreted as the head and body of a facing owl or as a gorgoneion (with bulging forehead and cheeks).

Absence of section-letter? Although the pinakion may have lacked a section-letter, there is an equal probability that a section-letter may have been hidden by heavy corrosion at the left end.

Since obscuring corrosion can be suspected at the left, Keil proposed that the initial letters of line 2 were misread and should be emended ⟨Κολ⟩ωνεύς. Kirchner accepted the emendation. In my discussion of the pinakion I pointed out that the singular Κολωνεύς is not well enough attested to provide a confident solution, but I had neglected the possibility of Ἀθμονεύς, which is perfectly regular and might do excellently. I had also overlooked one other point in favor of the possible correctness of Akerblad's owl seal: the carrying-hole at the left of the pinakion. Among surviving Athenian pinakia, the only example with a carrying-hole at that end is **16**, which belongs to Class II, the very class suggested by Akerblad's drawing, whether his owl seal be interpreted as an inaccurate rendering of a triobol seal or of a circular double-bodied owl seal (such as occurs also on **16**).

These reconsiderations, plus the possibility that the Akerblad and Leake texts might derive from the same intermediary source, and the general likelihood that the pinakion was discovered in one of Fauvel's many excavations of Attic cemeteries and a priori should be Athenian, leave little to recommend my prior attribution to Epiros other than some arguments of a purely circumstantial nature. I have found it difficult, nevertheless, to erase all lingering doubts and think it best to list the pinakion as possibly non-Athenian.

183 (Figs. 307–308) Nauplion, Archaeological Museum. University of Pennsylvania Excavations at Porto Cheli, ancient Halieis, Inv. HM. 29. Excavated in 1963 from late fourth-century B.C. destruction debris in the eastern unit of the Industrial Terrace. Notice by M. H. Jameson, "Excavations at Porto Cheli and Vicinity," *Hesperia* 38 (1969), 324.

Right fragment. Stripped to bare bronze. L. 4.4 cm., w. 2.0–2.1 cm., th. 0.15 cm. at right to 0.05 cm. at left.

Probably more than two uses. The heavily striated surface and tapering thickness attest to a considerable amount of erasure.

a   − − − − −]I   ⓢ?
        − − − −]Ọ

b   − − −]ΛΕΥ
       − − −]Ⓐ

S(eal)? There are suggestions only, but it would be difficult to explain the configurations of lines and depressions at the middle of the right end unless they belonged to the border of an erased, circular seal. The remains are reminiscent of effaced gorgoneia on many well-erased Athenian pinakia of the Class III type (cf. **34–43**), but the device of the seal(?) is illegible and cannot prove or disprove an Athenian origin for the fragment. The pinakion from Sinope (Fig. 309) bears a Sinopean seal at the right.

Stamped alpha. Height of incuse square, 0.75 cm. The die cannot be identified with any of those used on the extant Athenian pinakia. Untouched by erasure, the stamped alpha is the freshest looking detail on the fragment and would seem not to have been added until the last use. The stamping of the alpha apparently weakened the metal and ultimately caused the pinakion to break where it did.

The letter is most reasonably interpreted as the section-letter of the last use, added at the right for want of space or of a smooth striking surface at the left.[42] By Athenian standards, the position of the letter is highly irregular and

42. When the pinakion first came to my attention, I thought that it might be Argive and that the alpha might be a state seal reproducing at a smaller scale the Argive coin-

has a parallel only in the delta stamped at the right (also for the last use) of **146**, the most anomalous of all Athenian pinakia. It is doubtful, however, whether the position of the letter on the present fragment would be any more regular if the fragment happened to be non-Athenian.

Text b. The inscribed letters recorded in my text *b* look relatively weak, as if possibly subjected to some slight erasure, and thus they may belong to a use prior to the use with the stamped alpha. Although the letters are suggestive of the termination of an Athenian demotic, their position in the first line of what was presumably a two-line text implies rather that they should belong to a patronymic, abbreviated or continued in line 2. The letters of text *b* cannot, therefore, be brought to bear on the question of the pinakion's origin either.

Uncertain Attribution. Small, of comparatively minor importance, and located deep in the southeast Argolid, well outside the usual sphere of Athenian interest during the fourth century, Halieis is a most surprising place for the discovery of an allotment plate of any kind. Had the fragment been found in Attika, one would not hesitate to identify it as the right end of an Athenian pinakion with an irregularly stamped section-letter. Its dimensions and multiple reuse are in keeping with good Athenian practice, and its effaced seal (?) and abnormally positioned section-letter are paralleled on erased Class III pinakia and on the anomalous **146**, respectively. There is, on the other hand, nothing about it to prove an Athenian origin, and its place of discovery raises the distinct possibility that the fragment, although closely modeled on Athenian prototypes, was local, made and used either in the town of Halieis, where it was discovered, or in some nearby place like Argos. The government of fourth-century Argos is known to have been democratic and can be expected to have imitated innovations in Athenian democratic procedure.

Beyond this it is impossible to go. As we know from **7**, the fragment of an Athenian pinakion lost at Olynthos, some Athenian pinakia did travel with their owners beyond the borders of Attika. But at least Olynthos was a place that many Athenians would have had good reason to visit. The fourth-century pinakion from Sinope, which imitates Athenian pinakia in a number of particulars, and the pinakia that are being found in increasing numbers from other Hellenistic centers (including possibly Arkadia, see Appendix B,

---

type of an alpha in incuse square (B. V. Head, *Historia Numorum*[2] [Oxford: Clarendon Press, 1911], 437, 439–440). But if the alpha were a state seal, its position and the fact that it was added after the first use would require it to be a secondary seal of some kind. Although this interpretation is not impossible, it is hardly preferable to interpreting the alpha as a section-letter.

below) make a local attribution tempting. But until a positively attributed non-Athenian pinakion should be discovered from a city in the Argolid—or until an Athenian pinakion should be found stamped with the same die as was used for the stamped alpha on the present fragment—the question of the fragment's origin had best remain open.

ADDENDA

Since the manuscript for this book went to the printer's, Athenian prosopographical studies have been greatly enriched by the appearance of J. K. Davies, *Athenian Propertied Families 600–300 B.C.* (Oxford: Clarendon Press, 1971), which exhaustively treats a number of the families of Athenians who appear on the pinakia. The relevant discussions are to be found at Davies' no. 849 (pinakia 12c and 121b), no. 3248 (pinakia 149/150), no. 4719 (pinakion 83b), no. 4889 (pinakion 105c), pp. 183–184 (pinakion 88), pp. 196–197 with addendum (pinakion 23b), no. 10093 (pinakion 102), no. 11473 with addendum (pinakion 68c), no. 12132 (pinakion 100b), no. 12413 (pinakion 114), no. 13905 (pinakion 120b), and no. 14734 (pinakion 158).

In addition, pinakion 86 has now been published by Kevin Herbert, *Greek and Latin Inscriptions in The Brooklyn Museum* (Brooklyn: Brooklyn Museum, 1972), 73–75 and pl. xxiv, no. 42. Pinakion 96 has appeared in T. L. Shear, Jr., "The Athenian Agora: The Excavations of 1970," *Hesperia* 40 (1971), 279. And the second allotment plate from Pamphylia (below, p. 269) has been published by Claude Brixhe, "Un nouveau Document épichorique de Side," *Kadmos* 8 (1969), 143–151. The last has the same curious form as the other Pamphylian pinakion, but is inscribed in the local tongue and alphabet of Side. At the left is an alpha section-letter; at the right a pomegranate, the state symbol of Side, in relief. It is a palimpsest and is dated not later than the end of the third century B.C.

Appendixes   Registers

Appendix A   Status of Dikastai

All fourth-century B.C. statements on the subject agree that a substantial proportion of the Athenian dikasts were poorer citizens who derived an important share of their livelihood from their three-obol pay and other state subsidies (Isokrates 7.54, 8.130; Demosthenes 21.182, 24.123; cf. *AthPol* 27.4). About this, even making allowance for the antidemocratic coloring of some of the testimony, there can be little doubt. Three obols on random court days could support only the meanest subsistence,[1] but for men who had little or nothing, it was not to be spurned. And, as A. L. Boegehold has rightly observed,[2] Isokrates (7.83) is probably telling the truth when he says that the number of needy citizens was greater than that of the prosperous. Boegehold's unpublished comments seem to me to be entirely reasonable:[3] "In the fourth century city-dwelling folk assumed a preponderance in numbers over the earlier more numerous farmers,[4] and the extremes of wealth and poverty that one finds in the city came to represent more faithfully the general character of Athenian citizenry than did the earlier distinction between city and farm people. The needy city people would unquestionably form a large percentage of the dikasts applying each day for a seat in the courts, if only because they were actually more numerous."

Whether the poorest element of the population regularly dominated all court sessions is another question altogether, and one that as yet cannot be answered with much confidence.[5] Middle- and upper-class citizens surely participated, possibly in large numbers also. They had a vested interest in many judicial decisions and shared with all Athenians the city's famed

1. See Jones, *Athenian Democracy*, 37 with n. 86, 50, 80–81 with n. 20.
2. A. L. Boegehold, "Aristotle and the Dikasteria" (Ph. D. diss., Harvard University, 1957), 100, n. 101.
3. *Ibid.* I am grateful to the author for permission to include this quotation.
4. See Chapter IV, n. 21, above.
5. Hommel's solution (*Heliaia*, 47–48) has the virtue of happy compromise. He suggests that the poorer dikasts predominated on days of routine litigation, but that when cases of exceptional public interest were placed on the docket the men applying to be allotted would have contained a much higher proportion of prosperous citizens. This view accords with Aristotle, *Politics* 1320a.17–29, where it is observed that richer citizens were occasionally willing to take time off to attend the courts, but could not afford to attend on a very regular basis.

philodikia. The only evidence for the participation of the richer citizens, however, are the several passages in the orators, gleaned by Bruck and Jones,[6] which make an appeal to upper-class sentiments, and the slight prosopographical testimony of the bronze pinakia. Bruck knew of at least one surviving pinakion that belonged to a citizen of fairly high social standing (**83***b*, see Table 3 *a*).[7]

Although the amount of prosopographical material has grown prodigiously since Bruck's day, the evidence now at our disposal adds little to the above considerations. As a result of our division of the pinakia into dikastic and nondikastic groups, about half of the names attested on the surviving pinakia must be removed from the roster of known Athenian dikastai. This loss in numbers, however, does not seem to be accompanied by any serious loss in the evidence the pinakia might afford for the social makeup of the Athenian dikasteria, for, as is apparent from Tables 2 and 3, the social status and public activity which can be documented for owners of the surviving nondikastic pinakia is quantitatively and qualitatively very much the same as that which can be documented for the owners of the surviving dikastic pinakia. In both groups the number of owners identified from prominent families is uniformly low (Table 2a) whereas the number of owners who are otherwise altogether unknown or whose families are unknown is uniformly high (Table 2d). The latter number in fact comprises over half of the legible names on the surviving pinakia (Table 2e). The overall similarity in status of the dikastic and nondikastic owners is underlined further by the families represented by more than one pinakion (Table 4). In one instance, two dikastai are known from the same family (**103***b* and **84***b*). But in three or possibly four others, a father or brother known from a dikastic pinakion has a son or brother known from a nondikastic pinakion (**16***c* and **37***c*, **63***c* and **123***b*, **65***b* and **121***a*, and possibly **12***c* and **121***b*).

On the whole, our owners, dikasts and nondikasts alike, are not a distinguished lot. Though there are a few exceptions who serve to prove the rule, the average owner of a surviving pinakion came from the lower strata of the Athenian citizenry. Because the poorer classes constitute a majority in virtually every society, this is to be expected. But it is perhaps even less surprising when we reflect that the fully preserved pinakia, from which most of the legible owners' names are drawn, have survived from graves. If a pinakion was buried with an Athenian as a symbol of his proud participation in democratic government (see above, p. 9), such owners as took pinakia with

---

6. Bruck, *Philologus* 52 (1893), 310–311; Jones, *Athenian Democracy*, 36–37 with nn. 81–85, 60, 124.

7. Bruck, *Philologus* 52 (1893), 311–312.

them to their graves can be suspected of being particularly ardent democrats, and surely democratic ardor burned strongest among the Athenian poor. Thus, because a selective process may have operated in the burial and survival of pinakia, the prosopographical evidence must be used with care. If anything, it is likely to be weighed toward the lower elements of the demos. It should be remembered on the other hand that any such selective process would have operated indiscriminately upon the survival of both dikastic and nondikastic pinakia.

The available prosopography shows that well over half of the known jurors were men of minimal status or resources, but that the courts by no means consisted of such men exclusively. Since the sociology of the owners of surviving nondikastic pinakia is similar to that of the dikastic owners, and since the nondikastic pinakia should be to the entire Athenian male population what the dikastic pinakia are to the body of jurors, the composition of that body would seem to have reflected closely the social and economic composition of the citizen population at large.

Table 2.   Prosopographical conspectus

	Dikastic pinakia	Nondikastic pinakia
a. Owners of surviving pinakia known to have belonged to upper-class families (Table 3 a–b)	4–5	3–6
b. Owners or families of owners known from public documents (Table 3 a–d)	15–18	13–19
c. Total owners or families of owners known from sources other than pinakia (Table 3 a–e)	18–21	17–23
d. Approximate total owners or families of owners unknown from sources other than pinakia*	29–32	37–43
e. Approximate total owners known from pinakia*	50	60

* Exact totals are precluded by the fact that some pinakia or uses cannot be firmly classified as dikastic or nondikastic and also because it is difficult to be consistent in determining how many of the fragmentary names should be counted.

Table 3.   Athenians known from pinakia and other sources
(identifications in brackets especially tentative)

Dikastic pinakia	Nondikastic pinakia
a. Owners from wealthy families known to have borne liturgies	
83 (V) *b* Aristophon Aristodemou Kothokides: family well known; one brother trierarch 353/2; another brother secretary of the *poletai* 367/6	**114** (VI) Nikostratos Nikostratou Acharneus: choregos 331/0; from a prominent family of trierarchs
? **12** (II) *c* [And]rokles [Acha]rneus	**121***b* (VI) Androteles Androkleous Acharneus: nephew manumitted a slave around 330 and was probably trierarch about 323; owner's father probably the last owner of **12**, a Class II pinakion, but it is unclear whether this last use was dikastic or a theoretically stampless nondikastic use
	? **105***c* (VI?) Epikrates Gargettios: probably trierarch 377/6; son manumitted a slave around 330; it is not perfectly certain that use *c* of **105** was a nondikastic use, however
	[**158** (VI?) Philostratos Kolonethen: possibly the prominent orator who was trierarch about 342]
	[**120***b* (VI) Kallias Theodorou Agrylethen: daughter may have married into a prominent family of Anaphlystos, but dates uncertain]
b. Owners from families known to be of the hoplite census or higher	
111 (V) *c* [De]mochares Kephalethen: father probably treasurer of	**133***b* (VI) Antich[ares] Acharneus: probably diaitetes 325/4

Table 3 *cont.*

Dikastic pinakia	Nondikastic pinakia
the sacred monies 398/7	
103a (V) Epichares Euonymeus: he or an older relative possibly treasurer of the sacred monies 398/7	
2 (I) Demetrios Pteleasios: possible descendant diaitetes 325/4	

c. Bouleutai or relatives of known bouleutai

Dikastic	Nondikastic
78 (V) Thoukydides Lamptreus Kathyperthen: bouleutes 367/6	23b (VI) Eukolion Pyrrakou Anagyrasios: bouleutes 367/6; mentioned in a list pertaining to liturgies, in the 380s
92 (V) b Diodoros Phrearrios: father of a bouleutes *ante* or *post med. s.* IV *a*	
86 (V) Lysanias Eupyrides: a younger relative of a bouleutes of 335/4	119a (VI) Dionysophilos Sounieus: probably bouleutes *post med. s.* IV *a.*
73b (IV) Kallias Kalliochou Phalereus: probably a nephew bouleutes 303/2	118 (VI) Demostratos Lysi(- -?) Euonymeus: probably bouleutes 336/5
68c (IV) Lysistratos Kephisodorou Meliteus: brother probably proposer of a decree 376/5; a younger relative, possibly the owner's son, bouleutes 281/0	135a (VI) Epa(- -?) Erikeeus: he or his father bouleutes 311/0
	[41c (VI) Philochar[es] Acharneus: possibly bouleutes 303/2]
16 (II) c Eupolemos Timodo[.]ou Erchieus: descendant bouleutes 256/5	37c (VI) Timodo[.]os Eupolemou Erchieus
[Cf. also 72 (IV)]	[Cf. also 153 (VI?)]

d. Owners or relatives of owners known from public documents in other connections

Dikastic	Nondikastic
4b (I) Protarchos Peiraieus: probably owner of a house in the Peiraeus, about 342/1	96e (VI) Kichonides Gargettios: represented the phratry of the Medontidai 367/6
62b (IV) Deinias Halieus: probably epimeletes of the dock-	149/150 (VI) Kallias Kephisodorou Hagnousios: father

Table 3 *cont.*

Dikastic pinakia			Nondikastic pinakia
	yards 356/5		honored by the demos 346/5
104 (V)c	Athe(nion?) Besaieus: if his nomen is correctly restored, he is to be identified as father of a man in a *post med. s. IV* list of uncertain character	**28** (III)	Pedieus Theoxe(nou) Eleusinios: father or son probably *symproedros* of the Samian cleruchs 346/5
103 (V) *b*	Pytheas Glaukonos Phalereus (father?)	**155** (VI)	Polystratos Halaieus: possibly priest of Apollo Zoster in the late fourth century
84 (V) *b*	Glaukon Pytheou Phalereus (son?): another son(?) mentioned in a *Ratio Centesimarum, post med. s. IV a.*	**127** (VI)	Lysikrates Lysaniou Ateneus: he or a brother mentioned in a catalogue of uncertain character *post med. s. IV a.*
[Cf. also **100** (V) *c*]		[**38c** (VI)	Aristion Timo(– –?) Pergaseus: possibly *lampadephoros* at Rhamnous *post med. s. IV a.*]

e. Owners known from private monuments

88 (V)	Epichares Halaieus: known from a votive inscription *ante med. s. IV a.*	**117** (VI)	Demarchos Eroiades: known from gravestone of his son or father
68d (IV)	Paramonos Phanodemou Aithalides: known from his gravestone	**120a** (VI)	Demarchos Phalereus: known from gravestone of his son or father
		124b (VI)	Polykles Phlyeus: probably known from his gravestone
63c (IV)	Euthoinides Phylasios	**123b** (VI)	Kalligenes Euthoinidou Phylasios: possibly known from gravestone of his (?)daughter

Table 4. Families represented by more than one pinakion

Dikastic pinakia	Nondikastic pinakia
16 (II) *c*, father	**37***c* (VI), son [see Table 3c]
63*c* (IV), father	**123***b* (VI), son [see Table 3e]
65*b* (IV), Epikrates Sat(yr—?) Erchieus, brother(?)	**121***a* (VI), Satyros Saty(—?) Erchieus, brother(?)
(?) **12** (II) *c**, father	**121***b* (VI), son [see Table 3a]
103 (V) *b*, father(?) **84** (V) *b*, son(?) [see Table 3d]	

* It is uncertain whether the last owner of **12** was in fact a dikastes.

Appendix B   Non-Athenian Pinakia

Although a bronze allotment plate from Sinope and others from Myrina have been known since the 1880s, only in recent years has it become clear just how widely the Athenian institution of allotment by kleroteria and pinakia had spread throughout the Greek world. Kleroteria at Smyrna (around 243 B.C.) and at Kyrene (7/6 B.C.) are attested in inscriptions.[1] Since 1928, when Henri Seyrig identified and published the first pinakion from Thasos, the French excavations on the island have raised the total of Thasian pinakia to five. And as recently as the 1960s pinakia have become known from Rhodes and Pamphylia. The implications are that pinakia or evidence of kleroteria can now be expected from a large number of other Greek cities. No doubt many of the non-Athenian pinakia are dikastic, but one can no longer be sure that all of them were. As at Athens, pinakia must also have been used in allotments not connected with the courts.

My investigation of the Athenian pinakia has given rise to several new observations about the pinakia from Sinope and Thasos, which are republished below. For non-Athenian pinakia from elsewhere, the following remarks may suffice:

Rhodes. The pinakion was excavated from a necropolis east of the city of Rhodes in 1968. Text, measurements, and a photograph are published in Gr. Konstantinopoulos, "Ἀρχαιότητες καὶ μνημεῖα Δωδεκανήσου," *Deltion* 24 (1969), *Χρονικά* 480, with pl. 478a.

The plate is shaped rather like a miniature cricket bat, with a rounded right end and a small protruding tongue at the left for insertion into a klero-terion with very narrow slots. The owner's name, patronymic, and demotic are inscribed (by stippling) in three lines. A Rhodian rose is engraved (not stamped) at the right end. The pinakion seems not to have had a section-letter, unless one or part of one is represented by a large vertical at the right of the two lower lines of the name. Letter forms, including lunate epsilons and sigmas, indicate a date relatively late in the Hellenistic period. I under-

---

1. Dow, *HSCP* 50 (1939), 13–14; cf. *BCH* 87 (1963), 682 (notice of the stone kleroterion from Athenian Delos).

stand that a similar Rhodian pinakion has been found in more recent excavations and is scheduled for publication in the *Deltion* for 1970.

Pamphylia. Paris, Cabinet des Médailles, Inv. 1965/686. The publication, by Claude Brixhe, "Une tablette de juge d'origine probablement pamphylienne," *BCH* 90 (1966), 653–663, with figs. 1–4 (whence Guarducci, *Epigrafia*, II, 458, fig. 106), is exhaustive. The plate bears an alpha section-letter, an owner's name, including tribal ethnic, in four lines, and has a curious T-shaped attachment on its back side, which presupposes a kleroterion with T-shaped slots. The letter forms date "de la fin du IIIe ou de la première moitié du IIe siècle av. J.-C."

In a review of Brixhe, Jeanne and Louis Robert have shown an understandable uneasiness about the object's authenticity ("Bulletin Épigraphique," *REG* 80 [1967], 548, no. 603). But I am informed that a second pinakion, very similar to the first, has come into the hands of the Cabinet des Médailles and will soon be published by Brixhe. It is to be hoped that the new pinakion will help to settle any doubts on this score.

Aeolis. Twenty-nine inscribed bronze nameplates from late Hellenistic graves at Myrina were published by Edmond Pottier and Salomon Reinach, *La Nécropole de Myrina* (Paris, 1887), 206–209, with fig. 21, and 581–582. The authors noted that the plates belonged to men exclusively and therefore were probably analogous to the bronze pinakia of Athens; this supposition is firmly supported by the circumstance that many are palimpsests. The Myrina plates lack section-letters (as do some of the Thasian pinakia), date from the first century B.C. or A.D., and display such a wide range of shapes that it is doubtful whether they could have been used with kleroteria (*pace* the premature statement in the summary of my "Bronze Allotment Plates from Aeolis," a paper read at the Seventieth General Meeting of the Archaeological Institute of America, *AJA* 73 [1969], 239). I assume that they were employed in the more primitive kind of allotment whereby names were simply drawn out of a container. Nameplates of identical type and date have been recovered from graves at the nearby Aeolic cities of Kyme and Pitane. A full publication will appear presently.

Incerta. Although I am no longer confident of my earlier attribution of **182** to Epiros, chances are perhaps greater than 50 percent that the fragment of a reused pinakion from Halieis, **183**, is non-Athenian. Two fragments of unknown origin that are certainly not Athenian are discussed below; of these, one may be from Arkadia.

Sinope (Fig. 309)

Paris, Musée du Louvre, Inv. 4072. Acquired in 1889. Reported to have come from Sinope.[2] E. Michon, *BAntF* 1908, 356 (description and text). A. de Ridder, *Bronzes du Louvre* II, 217, and pl. 123 (minuscule photograph), no. 4072. Reedited with corrections, commentary, and a legible photograph by Louis Robert, *Études anatoliennes* (Paris: E. de Boccard, 1937), 296–297, no. 13, and pl. VIII. 4 (whence Guarducci, *Epigrafia*, II, 458, fig. 105). Cf. S. Dow, *BCH* 87 (1963), 676.

Whole. Rough green patina remaining at left; cleaned to bare bronze at right. L. 9.3 cm., w. 1.8 cm., th. ca. 0.18 cm. even.

One use:

Δ $\Sigma\tau\eta\sigma i\lambda\epsilon\omega\varsigma$ ⓢ   Inscribed with finely punched serifs
  $\Delta\acute{a}\mu\epsilon o\varsigma$

S(eal). Sea eagle bearing off dolphin to left. An indistinct circular symbol, probably a gorgoneion, below.[3] Diam. 1.4 cm.

As first pointed out by Robert, the eagle-dolphin device reproduces the state badge of Sinope. The type occurs on the extensive Sinopean drachm coinage of the fourth and late fifth centuries B.C.[4] as well as on fourth-century Sinopean amphora stamps.[5] The seal was apparently stamped on the pinakion

2. Although four rather obvious—and superficially patinated—forgeries of Athenian pinakia appeared on the Paris market between 1878 and 1920 (J. H. Kroll, "The 'Paris' Forger of Dikasts' Pinakia," *BCH* 91 [1967], 397–400), there are no good reasons for associating the Sinopean piece with them or for doubting its authenticity. Mme. S. Delbourgo of the laboratoire de recherche des Musées de France has written me (December 14, 1966) that upon spectrographic analysis the bronze alloy was found to have a "composition classique" (about 15 percent tin) and that from a microscopic examination of both the surface and a section "the thickness and quality of the corrosion attest to a slow and progressive process of mineralization from the outside surface into the sound metal." Contrast the report of the Metropolitan Museum on the shallow, artificial patination of its forgery from Paris, quoted in Dow, *BCH* 87 (1963), 686.

3. The two small bumps along the left circumference of the seal, identical to similar warts in the area of the inscription, were raised by corrosion and have nothing to do with the design of the seal.

4. W. H. Waddington, E. Babelon, and Th. Reinach, *Recueil général des monnaies grecques d'Asie Mineure*, 4 fascicules (Paris: Leroux, 1904–1910), I.1, pls. XXIV, nos. 13–37, and XXV, nos. 1–21. Cf. E. S. G. Robinson, "A Find of Coins from Sinope," *NC*[4] 20 (1920), 1–16, and pl. I, and "Sinope," *NC*[5] 10 (1930), 1–15, and pls. I and II; E. T. Newell, *The Küchük Köhne Hoard* [*Numismatic Notes and Monographs*, No. 46] (New York: American Numismatic Society, 1931).

5. See Virginia Grace, "Stamped Wine Jar Fragments," in *Small Objects from the Pnyx: II* [*Hesperia* Suppl. X] (Princeton: American School of Classical Studies at Athens, 1956), 164–165, with bibliography, 175–176. Most abundantly illustrated by B. N. Grakov, *Ancient Greek Pottery Stamps with Names of Astynomoi* [in Russian] (Moscow, 1929), pl. 3. Miss Grace informs me that this group of stamps, the earliest from Sinope, are now believed to date about 360–320 B.C.

simply as a mark of official certification. Since the round symbol under the dolphin has no parallel on Sinopean coins, no reference to a particular denomination of coinage was intended. The reverse dies of the above-mentioned drachms bear an inscribed ethnic instead of the gorgoneion (?) and have diameters, moreover, that are 2–3 millimeters larger than the diameter of the seal on the pinakion.

Although the gorgoneion (?) symbol is reminiscent of the gorgoneion seals on Athenian pinakia, it should probably be understood as a magistrate's symbol, such as appear on Greek coins and amphora stamps as signatures of eponyms or officials with a particular responsibility for the stamped objects. Should another pinakion from Sinope ever come to light with a different symbol below the dolphin, we would be bound to assume that each symbol stood for an eponym or at any rate the particular year for which a pinakion was issued.

Text. A faint vertical at the beginning of line 2 was included by Michon and de Ridder in their unlikely reading 'Ιδάμεος. The vertical, however, has more the appearance of a fine scratch than a letter, lacks the letters' serifs, and was correctly dissociated from the patronymic by Robert. Dow suggested that the pinakion was perhaps a palimpsest, the vertical being a partially erased remainder of an earlier text. But I was unable to detect any evidence of erasure or, in the areas cleaned of corrosion at the middle and the right, of other possible earlier letters, and I am inclined to agree with Robert that the vertical should be regarded as a "trait accidentel," possibly a scratch made in modern times during cleaning. A still fainter vertical scratch is to be found extending down from the lower left corner of the delta section-letter.

Date. That we have here a respectably close imitation of stamped Athenian pinakia goes without saying. The arrangement of seal and section-letter on the Sinopean pinakion reproduces the Class I and II format of Athens, and the serifed letters may have been inspired by Athenian Class V lettering or lettering in imitation of Class V lettering. The differences are in the comparatively small size of the Sinopean piece and in the fact that, unlike the section-letters on most stamped Athenian pinakia, its section-letter is inscribed. All of this suggests that the Sinopeans borrowed various features from several Athenian prototypes and freely combined them to suit their particular needs and tastes. The pinakion was probably manufactured after inscribed section-letters were introduced on Athenian pinakia but while Athenian pinakia still bore stamped seals, that is, roughly around the middle of the fourth century. The lettering looked like that of the fifth or fourth century to Robert, and fourth century, probably first half rather than second, to Dow.

What little is known about Sinope for most of the fourth century is mainly deduced from its coinage. The autonomous drachms with changing magistrates' names began in the later fifth century and continued until about 320[6] with only a brief interruption by an issue signed by the satrap Datames, who controlled the city sometime between around 370 and 362. The pinakion attests that the free city was in close touch with the latest democratic innovations in Athens and in all probability was democratic itself. Sinope's special relationship with Athens went back to the previous century when Perikles freed the city of a tyrant and settled 600 Athenians on the tyrant's property.[7] At the same time, an Athenian colony was established at another site on the southern coast of the Black Sea, at Amisos, then renamed Peiraieus.[8] Its fourth-century coins, inscribed *ΠΕΙΡΑ* and bearing an owl,[9] demonstrate the continuity of the Athenian tradition there for several generations in the same way as the present pinakion would seem to demonstrate the continuing influence of the Athenian settlers at Sinope.

Thasos

The fundamental treatment is by Dow in *BCH* 87 (1963), 676–684, to which little can be added, even though two of the pinakia listed here (2) and (5) were not available when the article was written.

All but one of the pinakia from Thasos are palimpsests. The pinakia are alike in respect to the technique of their lettering (by stippling) and in having a tapering prong at their upper left ends. These prongs were for insertion into kleroteria that had rows of small, drilled holes, instead of the horizontal slots that received pinakia on Athenian kleroteria (*ibid.*, 682–684).

As Dow observed, the Thasian pinakia admit of division into two groups (*ibid.*, 680): the widths of 1 and 2 are just under 2 cm., and are 1–2 mm. in thickness; 3 and 4 are much wider (by more than 1 cm.) and thinner. Although

6. See the chronological discussions of Robinson and Newell, n. 4, above. Concerning the history of Sinope generally, see D. M. Robinson, *Ancient Sinope* (Baltimore: Johns Hopkins Press, 1906); and David Magie, *Roman Rule in Asia Minor* (Princeton: Princeton University Press, 1950), 183, 1074–1077, nn. 18–23.

7. Plutarch, *Perikles* 20. The date of the Athenian expedition to the Black Sea is discussed exhaustively by B. D. Meritt, H. T. Wade-Gery, and M. F. McGregor, *The Athenian Tribute Lists*, 4 vols. (Princeton: American School of Classical Studies at Athens, 1939–1953), III, 114–117.

8. Strabo 12.3.14, quoting Theopompus. Appian, *Mithradates* 8 and 83, adds that the "ancestral" constitution of Amisos-Peiraieus was democratic, and Plutarch, *Lucullus* 19.6, states that Amisos remained a favorite refuge for dissident Athenians as late as the time of Mithradates.

9. Waddington, Babelon, and Reinach, *Recueil*, I.1, pls. VI, nos. 16–32, and VII, nos. 1–4.

the *original* dimensions of **3** and **4** have doubtless been distorted from erasure by hammering, such hammering alone could hardly have caused the full divergence in width between these last pinakia and the smaller **1** and **2**. There are two further points of differentiation: **1** and **2** seem to have been intentionally cut in two, and they are inscribed with some letters in addition to the names of their owners. The extra letter, a gamma, of **1**, use *b*, is a good, large section-letter of the kind that we know from Athens and Sinope, and to the left of the name in use *a* we read the letters *ΘYP*, presumably belonging to θύρ(α) or one of its cognates and referring to an entrance of the Thasian courts (*ibid.*, 680–681). The two isolated letters, *ΘE*, at the right of **2** should also refer to some kind of division among the owners of the pinakia and are perhaps to be understood θ(ύρα) έ. On the other hand, **3** and **4** show no evidence of being cut; nor do they bear letters or any information apart from the names of their owners.

To judge from the progressive simplification from stamped to stampless bronze pinakia at Athens, the smaller and more elaborate Thasian pinakia **1** and **2** should have preceded the cruder **3** and **4**. And this, too, is as one would expect from the presence of a section-letter on **1**; the section-letter was a direct borrowing from Athenian practice, but one that was eventually discontinued (section-letters do not occur on the much later allotment plates from Aeolis). **3** has been dated by its letter forms and orthography to the later fourth or early third century B.C., a time that suits the stratigraphic evidence for the finding of **4**. Though **1** and **2** are earlier, it is surely not by much, for the shapes of their letters do not differ appreciably from those of **3** and **4** (*ibid.*, 679). And **1** and **2**, moreover, should date after around 350 when seals and stamped section-letters were abandoned on Athenian pinakia.

Thasos 1 (Figs. 310–311)   Paris, Cabinet des Médailles. Anonymous gift, ca. 1937. Discovered by a peasant among the remains of bones in a grave in the necropolis of Patargia, south of the ancient city of Thasos. Henri Seyrig. "Tessère d'un juge thasien," *BCH* 52 (1928), 392–394, with fig. 1 (enlarged drawing); whence *IG* XII, Suppl., 515. S. Dow *BCH* 87 (1963), 676–678,[10] no. 1 (cf. 680–681), with figs. 6 (enlarged photo) and 7 (Seyrig's fig. 1, our Fig. 311).

Left half. Light green patina. The right edge looks cut, not broken; along the top edge is the beginning of another cut. L. (including the 0.8 cm. prong) 4.5 cm., w. 1.9 cm., th. 0.18 cm. except for prong, the th. of which is 0.20 cm.

---

10. A misprint should be noted: on p. 678, n. 1, read "Eight other names . . . are known," for "No other name . . . is known."

Two uses minimum. Texts as read by Seyrig and arranged by Dow:

a   ΘΥΡ   Σωσίων   Inscribed with fine punch marks
          Βίωνο[ς

b   Γ   Πολυφα[ντος *vel* -ντης   Inscribed with heavier punch marks

I doubt that there would have been room for a patronymic at the right of text *b*. The text probably contained a nomen only, located in line 2 perhaps in order to avoid the cut at the top of the plate.

Because of the different sized punch marks with which they were inscribed, Dow recognized that the letters ΘΥΡ and the gamma section-letter should be dissociated. Yet this dissociation raises an obvious difficulty in the interpretation of ΘΥΡ as "door." Thus Dow writes (p. 681) "it is hard to understand why no section-letter, such as gamma, appears before ΘΥΡ in Use 1. The only explanation I can suggest is that the gamma, despite its larger dots, belongs with ΘΥΡ and that both alike apply to Use 1 and Use 2: both owners belonged in this case to the same section." This solution is not without its attractions, but it clearly would not be valid if the punch marks in ΘΥΡ and the earlier name happen to look fine because they have been subjected to some erasure, as I rather suspect that they have been. I am unable to propose a solution that will allow ΘΥΡ to become fully intelligible without a section-letter; nor is it clear to me how the question is affected by the isolated letters ΘΕ at the right of 2, however they are to be interpreted. One can only hope that these difficulties will be resolved by future discoveries.

Thasos 2 (Fig. 312)   Thasos Excavations, Inv. 2619. Olivier Picard, in "Chronique des fouilles en Grèce en 1967," *BCH* 92 (1968), 1087–1090, with fig. 8. Excavated in 1967 from "sondage Apostolidis"; Hellenistic fill.

Complete, cut or broken in two. Stripped to bare metal. L. (including the 0.9 cm. prong at the left) 8.4 cm., w. 1.7 cm., th. 0.15 cm. even. Two notches and a carrying-hole at the right.

Apparently, one use:

Δεινοκράτης   ΘΕ
Σατύρου

Picard has confirmed for me that there are no indications of erasure by hammering, nor of an earlier text to which the letters ΘΕ at the right could be attributed. These letters are larger than the letters of the name and, as

Picard suggests, probably pertain to some kind of division or section to which the owner belonged, like the Γ/ΘΥΡ on **Thasos 1**. In a review of Picard, Jeanne and Louis Robert suggest that the letters may represent θ(ύρα) ἑ ("Bulletin Épigraphique," *REG* 82 [1969], 495, no. 442).

Thasos 3 (Fig. 313)   Thasos Excavations, Inv. 1310. Excavated in 1954 "in the region east of the Hall of Pillars in the Agora." Notice with photograph by Jean Pouilloux, in "Chronique des fouilles en Grèce en 1954," *BCH* 79 (1955), 366, and fig. 39. Full publication by Christiane Dunant and Jean Pouilloux, *Recherches sur l'histoire et les cultes de Thasos*, II [Études thasiennes, V] (Paris: E. de Boccard, 1958), 235, no. 412, and pl. 56.3. S. Dow, *BCH* 87 (1963), 678–679, no. 2.

Whole.[11] Damaged at both ends of the bottom edge. The surface has been cleaned. L. (including the 1.2 cm. prong at the left) 10.6 cm., w. 3.3 cm., th. of the plate uneven, maximum 0.05 cm. (not 0.2 cm. as previously recorded, unless this figure applies to the th. of the prong only). O. Picard examined the hole just below the middle of the plate and writes me that it appears to be the accidental result of corrosion.

More than one use (?). The unevenness of the upper edge suggests that the pinakion has been erased by hammering.

Last use:

> Ἀρισταγόρας
> Ἡρακλείδευς

Dunant and Pouilloux remark that the forms of the letters look like those of the fourth or third century and that the genitive of the patronymic in -ευς would suit a date from the second half of the fourth to the beginning of the third century B.C.

Thasos 4 (Fig. 314)   Thasos Excavations, Inv. 1702. Excavated "in 1961 in a sondage at the east of the Basilica in the Agora, in a level corresponding to habitations of the fourth or of the third century B.C." Paul Bernard and François Salviat, "Inscriptions de Thasos," *BCH* 86 (1962), 605–606, no. 21, with fig. 25 (photo before the more recent cleaning). S. Dow, *BCH* 87 (1963), 679, no. 3.

Nearly whole. A few millimeters are apparently missing from the original right end. Recently stripped to bare bronze. L. (including the 1.5 cm. prong

---

11. Dunant and Pouilloux state that the pinakion is broken at the right, but apparently because they assumed that the pinakion should have had a prong at each end.

at the left) 10.5 cm., w. 3.5 cm. maximum at the right, th. of the plate 0.08–
0.05 cm. (not 0.2 cm. as previously recorded, unless this figure applies to the
th. of the prong).

Three or more uses. Erasure by hammering evidenced in the tapering
width and thickness.

a   [------
     [---]...[---

b   [.]ᶄΑΣΟ𝑚[.]....[
     [.]ᶓ[.]ᵮΑΤΟ|ᶓ

c   Ἀρχέλεως
     Κιβᾶδος

In previous publications only the last text had been noted. I owe the cleaning and the clarification of the remains of earlier letters to O. Picard. He
observes (by letter of 1968) that the punches at the right of line 2 are too
numerous to have belonged to a single earlier text, so that the pinakion must
have had at least three uses.

Text b. Picard writes that line 1 may involve the letters, $\alpha\sigma\theta\varsigma$ and that line 2
probably terminates in -$\alpha\tau\sigma\varsigma$. However, -$\alpha\tau\sigma\kappa$ or -$\alpha\tau\sigma\upsilon$ seem to be possible
also.

Thasos 5 (Fig. 315)   Thasos Excavations, Inv.? Apparently the pinakion mentioned by Jean Pouilloux, *Recherches sur l'histoire et les cultes de Thasos*, I [Études
thasiennes, III] (Paris: E. de Boccard, 1954), 393, no. 2: "parmi les petites
bronzes trouvés sur l'agora en 1950 on a découvert une lamelle analogue à
celle que H. Seyrig avait publiée, mais tellement endommagée qu'on n'a
pu déchiffrer les charactères marqués, de la même façon, au pointillé."
According to O. Picard, the fragment could not be located in 1968.

Fragment of uncertain position. Dimensions estimated from the photograph, ca. 2.3 × 3.7 cm.; th. looks exceptional, perhaps as much as 0.3 cm.

Two or more uses. Texts illegible.

The stippled punches of the earlier text (or texts) have not been appreciably erased and cannot be confidently distinguished from the punches of
the last text. I have not, therefore, been able to identify a single letter from
any text. Nor have I been able to ascertain the fragment's proper orientation;
from the photograph it is unclear which edges are original and which have

been broken or cut. Still, the identity of the fragment as part of an allotment plate seems assured by the fact that it is a palimpsest.

Uncertain[12] (Fig. 316)

Athens, National Museum, Inv. Bronze 8069. Purchased on the Athenian antiquities market. Unpublished.

Right end. Recently stripped to bare bronze. L. (including the prong [?] at the right) 3.5 cm., w. 2.1 cm., th. 0.15 cm.

One use visible:

$$
\begin{array}{l} \text{---]} \\ \text{---]} \end{array} \; \mathrm{K}
$$

This would seem to be a fragment of a pinakion with a prong (which was perhaps originally longer and has broken) and an inscribed kappa section-letter at the right. The prong (?) is reminiscent of those on the pinakia from Rhodes and Thasos (whose prongs are shaped or positioned differently, however) and cannot be paralleled on any known pinakion from Athens. Hence if the fragment is indeed part of an allotment plate, it should be neither from Athens, Rhodes, or Thasos.

Arkadia (?) (Figs. 317–318)

Basel, Antikenmuseum, Inv. 1906.777. Ex coll. Vischer. W. Vischer, *Kleinigkeiten*, 15, no. 4, and pl. II, 66 = *Kleine Schriften* II, 687, no. 4, and pl. XV, 66 (drawing before cleaning = our Fig. 318).

Left end. Recently stripped to bare bronze. L. 3.5 cm., w. 2.8 cm., th. 0.18–0.24 cm.

Reused (?); the thickness is uneven.

Visible text:

ⓢ Φιλ[---
Εὐ[---
Ἡρ[---

12. Robert, *Coll. Froehner*, 11, and pl. IV, no. 10u is not part of an allotment plate, as Dow assumed it was (*BCH* 87 [1963], 684). The object, with late lettering and a metal loop at one end, is one of three that are listed as "amulettes de bronze" in Froehner's hand-written inventory at the Cabinet des Médailles. One of these amulets is noted as having come from Syria, and a reference is given to Gustave Schlumberger, *Mélanges d'archéologie byzantine* (Paris, 1895), 125–128.

S(eal). Monogram containing the letters *AR* or *APK*, in incuse circle. Diam. 0.8 cm.

   Vischer published this fragment of unknown provenience with his Athenian pinakia, but cautioned that it may not be the same kind of object, or even Athenian. On the former question there is still room for doubt, although the position of the stamped monogram suggests some kind of section-letter. Or, is the monogram actually a state seal? It is identical to the $\overline{APK}$ monogram used as a state badge by the Arkadian League in the fourth century B.C. The monogram occurs both on the reverses of the fourth-century coins of the league (see *British Museum Catalogue of Greek Coins: Peloponnesus* [London, 1887], pl. XXXII, 10–12) and in the headings of two inscribed stelai that were set up at Delphi in the fourth century in honor of Arkadian *proxenoi* (see Guarducci, *Epigrafia*, I, 402-404, with fig. 218). The third line of the text, moreover, can be restored with the ethnic ʿΗρ[αιεύς] or ʿΗρ(αιεύς). Arkadian Heraia was one of the members of this league. At any rate, the text in three lines poses no difficulty, as the pinakion from Rhodes is inscribed in three lines, and the one from Pamphylia is inscribed in four. The width, though exceptional by Athenian standards, would be permissible for use with a kleroterion with wide slots.

Registers

I. Pinakia by Collections

Numbers in the right-hand column refer to numbers in the Catalogue. Non-Athenian pinakia and objects wrongly identified as pinakia are listed in parentheses.

Athens

British School of Archaeology, Finlay Collection	54
	114
Depot of the Second Archaeological Ephoreia of Athens	66
Depot of the Third Archaeological Ephoreia of Athens	119
Paul Kanellopoulos Collection	6
	48

National Museum,
Inv. Bronze

8060	20	8081	171	8123 + 8127	37
8061	16	(8082 See Cata-		8124	89
8062	28	logue, n. 41)		8125	73
8063	68	8083	108	8126	67
8064	88	8085	53	8128 + 8132	139
8065	117	8086	44	8129	172
8066	104	8087	64	8130	135
8067	100	8088	159	8131	9
8068	82	8089	165	8133	46
(8069 Appendix B,		8090	144	8134	26
uncertain attri-		8091	128	8135	145
bution)		8092	170	8136	58
8070	52	8093	163	8137	42
8071	11	8094	166	8138	76
8073	59	8095	168	8139	176
8074	50	8096	174	8140	167
8075	71	8097	138	8141	25
8076	179	8098	43	8142	177
8077	136	8099	70	13035	129
8078	74	8100	143	13347A	65
8079	109	8121	57	13347B	35
8080	10	8122	1	15173	14
				16308	30

National Museum, Karapanos Collection,	Inv. 1198	31
National Museum, Stathatos Collection,	Inv. 406	94

279

Formerly Berlin (East)
Staatliche Museen, Antikenabteilung,

Inv. 3425	72	6315	29
6222	148	6363	99
6313	124	6504	8
6314	125	7263	102
		7384	90

Hannover
Kestner-Museum, Inv. 1928.265   13

Formerly (?) Helsinki
Collection of Johannes Sundwall   158

Leiden
National Museum of Antiquities, Inv. RO III.103   93

London
British Museum, Department of Greek and Roman Antiquities,

Inv. Bronze 329	62
330	36
331	83
332	78
1905.6–7.4	41

British Museum, Department of Coins and Medals, Fox Bequest,

Inv. 521   110

Munich
Antikensammlung,

Inv. 339	92
3493a	121
3493b	120

Nauplion
Archaeological Museum, University of Pennsylvania Excavations at Porto Cheli,   Inv. HM 29   183

Newcastle upon Tyne
The Greek Museum   39

New York
Brooklyn Museum, Inv. 34.678   86
Metropolitan Museum of Art, Inv. 07.286.95   4

Oxford
Ashmolean Museum, Inv. 1968.81   91

Paris
Cabinet des Médailles, Froehner Collection,

Inv. 609	34	617	12
610	2	618	56
611	81	619	142
612	118	620	173
613	127	621	98
614	116	622	79
615	63	624	85
616	111	625	122

	Anonymous Gift	23
	Anonymous Gift	80
	Anonymous Gift	126
	(Anonymous Gift	Appendix B, Pamphylia)
	(Anonymous Gift	Appendix B, Thasos 1)
Musée du Louvre,	Inv. 4070	87
	4071	106
	(4072	Appendix B, Sinope)

Rouen
Musée Départemental des Antiquités   61

(Thasos

Excavations of the École Française d'Athènes,	Inv. 1310	Appendix B, Thasos 3
	1702	Thasos 4
	2619	Thasos 2
	?	Thasos 5)

Thessalonika
Archaeological Museum,   Inv. 1207   7

Toronto
Royal Ontario Museum,   Inv. 939.42   38

Urbana
University of Illinois Classical and European Culture Museum,
     Inv. 907   18

Utrecht
Archaeological Institute,   Inv. 136   17

Formerly Würzburg
Antikensammlung der Universität   149
     150

II. Pinakia by Prior Publication

IG II²,

1835	121	1848	93	1861	89
1836	54	1849	83	1862	90
1837	85	1850	62	1863	104
1838	120	1851	68	1864	72
1839	81	1852	28	1865	36
1840	75	1853	109	1866	64
1841	124	1854	136	1867	117
1842	37	1855	151	1868	65
1843	61	1856	152	1869	127
1844	35	1857	92	1870	17
1845	74	1858	116	1871	1
1846	43	1859	10	1872	153
1847	34	1860	8	1873	25

IG II², *cont.*

1874	118	1892	108	1910	106
1875	27	1893	67	1911	70
1876	88	1894	102	1912	57
1877	78	1895	147	1913	50
1878	73	1896	40	1914	71
1879	155	1897	84	1915	82
1880	144	1898	100	1916	53
1881	44	1899	182	1917	171
1882	16	1900	87	1918	177
1883	154	1901	60	1919	52
1884	20	1902	168	1920	99
1885	11	1903	163	1921	148
1886	2	1904	165	(1922	see Cata-
1887	149 + 150	1905	170		logue, n. 41)
1888	76	1906	167	1923	178
1889	114	1907	174	Addenda	
1890	125	1908	159	1864a	41
1891	29	1909	138	1871a	156

Not in *IG* II²

AA 1943, 16–19, no. 1	95
no. 2	123
no. 3	107
no. 4	69
no. 5	77
no. 6	51
AJA 36 (1932), 292–294	18
Archaeological Reports 16 (1969–1970), 58, no. 10	39
ArchEph 1939–41, Χρονικά 17, no. 5	14
AthMitt 25 (1900), 453–454	129
	157
BCH 2 (1878), 535, no. 23	59
(no. 27	See Catalogue, n. 41)
87 (1963), 674–675	38
93 (1969), 571–573	91
Deltion 16 (1960), Χρονικά 27	119
forthcoming	66
Hesperia 2 (1933), 474	97
20 (1951), 201	101
216	130
38 (1969), 324	183
forthcoming	96
Suppl. VII, 12–14,	

no. 1	105	no. 4	161
no. 2	33	no. 5	164
no. 3	146	no. 6	132

UNPUBLISHED

9, 13, 15, 19, 26, 30, 32, 42, 45, 46, 47, 48, 49, 58, 86, 110, 112, 113, 128, 131, 133, 135, 137, 139, 140, 141, 143, 145, 160, 162, 166, 169, 172, 175, 176, 180, 181

III. OWNERS' NAMES

A̤[– – –] [– – –], 9a
A̤[– – –] A̤[– – –], 136
A⫶[.]||[– – –] [ᶜᵃ˙ ³]||[– – –], 41b
A⫶[– – –] Π[– – –], 108c
A⫶[– – –] Φ[– – –], 44b
A̤Λ[– – –] [– – –], 77a
Ἀβρ[– – –] K[– – –], 45b
A̤ΓA̤ỻ⌐[| [– – –] or A̤ΓN̤ỻ⌐[|[– – –] Κολλυ[τεύς], 146b
Ἀγνόθεος, ’Οῆθεν 146c

Ἀθην(ίων)? Βησα[ι](εύς), 104c
ΑΙΜ[⫤][- - -] Ἀθμ[ονεύς], 134c
Αἰσχ[- - -] Αἰσχίν[ου] [- - -], 59e
Αἰσχ[- - -] Ἐπιμ[- - -] [- - -], 25b
Αἰσχίν[ης] ([- - -]), father of Αἰσχ[- - -]. 59e
Ἀνδοκ[ίδης] ([- - -]), father of Παυσ[- - -], 156
Ἀνδρο[-ca. 5-]ς [- - -], 67b
Ἀνδροκλέ(ης) (Ἀχαρνεύς), father of Ἀνδροτέλης, 121b
[Ἀνδ?]ροκλῆς [Ἀχα]ρνε(ύς), 12c
Ἀνδροτέλης Ἀνδροκλέ(ους) Ἀχαρ(νεύς), 121b
Ἀνθεμίων Με(ι)δυ(λίδου) Προσπάλτι(ος), 6b
[Ἀ]ν[τ]ίδ[ο]τ(ος)? (ἐκ Κολωνοῦ), father of Εὐφίλητ[ο]ς, 84a
Ἀντικράτης Εὐκτ(ημον- -) Αἰξωνεύς, 72
Ἀντιφῶν Ἁλαιεύς, 151
Ἀντιχ[άρης] Ἀχαρν[εύς], 133b
Ἀντίχαρμος Λαμπ(τρεύς), 61c
Ἀρι(- -) (Φλυεύς), father of Πολύμνηστος, 125b (cf. 29)
Ἀρισταγόρας Ἡρακλείδευς, of Thasos, Appendix B, Thasos 3
[Ἀ]ρίστανδρος Ἐ[λ]ευσί(νιος), 62a
Ἀριστίων Τιμο(- -) Περγα(σῆθεν), 38c
Ἀριστόδημος (Κοθωκίδης), father of Ἀριστοφῶν, 83b
Ἀριστ[ο]κράτης Στε(ι)ρ(ιεύς), 4a
Ἀριστοτέλης Ἁλιμο(ύ)σιος, 152
Ἀριστοφῶν Ἀριστοδήμου Κοθω(κίδης), 83b
Ἀριστοφῶν Φλυεύ[ς], 7d
Ἀρχ[- - -] ΛΛ[- - -], 107a
Ἀρχ[- - -] Με[λιτεύς], 77c
Ἀρχε[⫤][- - -] ([- - -]), father of [- - -]ς, 174
Ἀρχέδημος Περιθοί(δης), 119b
Ἀρχέλεως Κιβᾶδος, of Thasos, Appendix B, Thasos 4c
Ἀρχίλοχος Φαληρεύς, 36b
[Ἀ]πολλ[- - -] ([- - -]), father of [Λ]ΥΣΙΣ[- - -], 162
Ἀπολλόδωρος ?Φυ(- - -) Χολλεί(δης), 157

Βίων, of Thasos, father of Σωσίων, Appendix B, Thasos 1a
Βλεψίδης Τειθράσιος, 30b

Γλ[αυκ- or -ύκων] Ὠ[αθεν], 64c
Γλα[ύκω]ν (Φαληρεύς), father of Πυθέας, 103b
Γλαύκων Πυθέο(υ) Φαλη(ρεύς), 84b

Δάμασος ([- - -]), father of Λυσι⫤[- - -], 132a
Δάμης, of Sinope, father of Στησίλεως, Appendix B, Sinope
Δεινίας Ἁλαιεύς, 62b
Δεινοκράτης Σατύρου, of Thasos, Appendix B, Thasos 2
Δημ[- - -] Λαμ[πτρεύς], 54b
Δημ(- -) (Φαληρεύς), father of Λυσίας, 154

[Δ]ημαίν[ετος] or [Τ]ιμαίν[ετος] [-]⫶ΑΝΤΑ[- - -], 166
Δήμαρχος Ἐροιάδης, 117
Δήμαρχος Φαληρεύς, 120a
Δημήτριος Πτελε(άσιος), 2
Δημόδοκος Περγασῆ(θεν), 122b
Δημόστρατος Λυσι(- -) Εὐωνυ(μεύς), 118
Δημοφάνης Φιλι[- - -] Κηφισιεύς, 130
Δημ[ό]φιλ[ο]ς Εἱρεσί(δης), 93a
[Δη]μοχάρη[ς] [Κε]φαλῆθε[ν], 111c
Δημύ(λος) (Ἀναφλύστιος), father of Εὐάγγελος, 115
Δι[- - -] Φ/⫶ [- - -], 26c
Διε[- - -] Ἐλευ[σίνιος], 145b
ΔΙΟ[.] [.]|ΠΟ ?, 181
Διόδωρος Φρεά(ρριος), 92b
Διονυ(σ- -) (ἐκ Κοίλης), father of Διονύσιος, 85
Διονύσιος ([- - -ε]ύς), father of [- - -]s, 15c
Δ[ι]ο[νύ]σι[ο]s? [ᶜᵃ·²]ΡΕ|Γ[. Φυ]λάσι(ος), 63b
Διονύσιος Διονυ(σ- -) ἐκ Κοί(λης), 85
Διονύσιος Κλε(ι)μά(- -) Τρικορύ(σιος), 35b
Διονυσόφιλος Σουνιεύ(s), 119a
Διρολις Κρωπίδ(ης), 39b
Δίων or Οἴων[- -] [- - -]νος [- - -], 106a
[---ᶜᵃ·⁹⁻¹⁰--Δ]ΩΡΟ [- - -], 63a

Εᵂᵂ[- - -] ⫶⫶⫶ [- - -], 138a
Ε⫶⫶[- - -] Φ|⫶[- - -], 24b
Ε[--ᶜᵃ·⁶-]ΣΡ[ᶜᵃ·³]Σ? Π[---ᶜᵃ·⁸---]|[..]⫶ ⫶ ΣΧ?, 66a
Εἰρηνοκλέης Ἀφιδνα(ῖος), 87
Ἐπα[- - -] Ἐρικ[εεύς], 135a
Ἐπι[- - -] Εὐω[νυμεύς], 42b
Ἐπι[- - -] Πρα[σιεύς?], 107b
Ἐπικράτ[ης] Γαργή[ττιος], 105c
Ἐπικράτης Σατ(υρ- -) Ἐρχιεύς, 65b
Ἐπικράτης Σκα⟨μ⟩βω(νίδης), 4c
Ἐπίκτ[ητος] Ἐρχι[εύς], 27b
Ἐπιμ[- - -] ([- - -]), father of Αἰσχ[- - -], 25b
Ἐπιχάρης Ἀλαιε(ύς), 88
Ἐπιχάρης [- - -]νος Εὐωνυ[μεύς], 103a
Ἐρυξίμ[αχος] ([- - -]), father of Εὐθύμα[χος], 32c
Ἑστ[ι- - -] ([- - -]s), father of [- - -]s, 159b
Εὐ[- - -] [- - -], 22a
Εὐ[- - -] ([- - -ε]ύς), father of [- - -]⫶λος, 169
Εὐ[- - -] (Ἡρ[αιεύς?]), of Arkadia(?), father of Φιλ[- - -], Appendix B, Arkadia(?)
Εὐ[- - -] Τ⫶[- - -], 43b
ΕΥ[.]Ε[..]|[- -] Κολωνῆ(θεν), 30a
Εὐάγγελος Δημύ(λου) Ἀναφλύστι(ος), 115

Εὐγείτων Ἁλαιεύς, 94b
Εὐθ[– – –] ἐκ Κ[– – –], 135b
Εὐθοινίδης Φυλάσι(ος), 63c
Εὐθοινί(δης) (Φυλάσιος), father of Καλλιγένης, 123b
Εὐθύμα[χος] Ἐρυξιμ[άχου] [– – –], 32c
Εὐθυμένης Φυλάσι(ος), 63d
Εὐκλείδης (Παιανιεύς), father of Φρύνος, 61b
Εὐκολίων Πυρρά(κου) Ἀναγυρά(σιος), 23b
Εὐκτ(ημ– –) (Αἰξωνεύς), father of Ἀντικράτης, 72
Εὐπό(λεμος) (Ἐρχιεύς), father of Τιμόδο[.]ος, 37b
Εὐπόλεμος Τιμοδό(.ου) Ἐρχιεύς, 16c
Εὐφίλητ[ο]s [Ἀ]ν[τ]ιδ[ό]τ(ου)? [ἐ]κ Κολωνο(ῦ), 84a

Ἡρακλείδης, of Thasos, father of Ἀρισταγόρας, Appendix B, Thasos 3

Θάλλος Ἀθμονεύς, 116
[Θε?]ογένη[s] [Ἐρ]χιε(ύς), 163
Θεόδωρ(ος) (Ἀγρυλῆθεν), father of Καλλίας, 120b
Θεόξε(νος) (Ἐλευσίνιος), father of Πεδιεύς, 28
Θογενίδ(ης) (Ἁλαιεύς), father of Καλλίας, 80
Θουκλ(ῆς or -είδης) ([– – –]), father of [– – –]ων, 51b
Θουκυδίδης Λαμπτ(ρεὺς) Καθύ(περθεν), 78
Θρα[σ– – –] Φλυ[εύς], 107c
Θωρα(– –) ([– – –]), father of [– – –], 59d

Ἱππο[– – –] Φαλη[ρεύς], 133c

Κ[⫯[– – –] Κ[⫯[– – –], 19b
Καλλι(– –) ([– – –]), father of [– – –]s, 58d
[Κ]αλλι[– –] ([– –]Ν[– –]), father of [– – –], 112b
Καλλιάδης Μ[ει]δω(– –) Ἀγ[ν]ο(ύ)σι(ος), 66c
Καλλίας Θεοδώρ(ου) Ἀγρυλῆ(θεν), 120b
Καλλίας Θογενίδ(ου) Ἁλαι(εύς), 80
Καλλίας Καλλιόχο(υ) Φα(ληρεύς), 73b
Καλλίας Κηφισοδώ(ρου) Ἁγνούσι(ος), 149–150
Καλλιγένης Εὐθοινί(δου) Φυλάσι(ος), 123b
Καλλικύδης Αἰγιλιεύς, 67c
Καλλίοχος (Φαληρεύς), father of Καλλίας, 73b
Καλλίστρατος Γαργήττιος, 95c
Κηφισόδω(ρος) (Ἁγνούσιος), father of Καλλίας, 149–150
Κηφισόδω(ρος) (Μελιτεύς), father of Λυσίστρατος, 68c
[Κηφι?]σοκλέης [– – –], 68b
Κιβᾶς, of Thasos, father of Ἀρχέλεως, Appendix B, Thasos 4c
Κιχων[ίδ]ης Γαργήτ(τιος), 96e
Κλέανδρος (ἐκ Κεραμέων), father of Κλεόφαντος, 14b
Κλε(ί)μα(– –) (Τρικορύσιος), father of Διονύσιος, 35b
Κλεόκριτος ⟨Ἀθμο⟩νεύς?, 182

Κλεόκριτος Σουνι(εύς), 95a
Κλεόφαντος Κλεάνδρου ἐκ Κεραμέων, 14b
Κο[⫶[– – –] ῎Οαθ[εν], 42a
Κρ[– – –] [– – –], 10c
Κρατιάδης Θοραι[ε]ύς, 131
ΚΥ[⫶⩘[.]Σ Ἀναγ[(υράσιος)], 7a

Λυ[– – –] ('Αλαιεύς?), father of [– – –]‾‾‾‾‾ων, 171
Λυσ[– – –] (Ἀθμονεύς), father of [– – –]χος, 139b
Λυσ[– – –] ΦΕΝ[– – –] [– – –], 42c
Λυσα(νίας) (Ἀτηνεύς), father of Λυσικράτης, 127
Λυσανίας Εὐπυρί(δης), 86
Λυσι(– –) (Εὐωνυμεύς), father of Δημόστρατος, 118
Λυσι⩘[⫶[– – –] Δαμάσο[υ] [– – –], 132a
Λυσίας Δημ(– –) Φαλη(ρεύς), 154
Λυσιθεΐδης Θριάσι(ος), 65c
Λυσικράτης Λυσα(νίου) Ἀτη(νεύς), 127
[Λ]ΥΣΙΣ[– – –] [Ἀ]πολλ[– – –] [– – –], 162
ΛΥΣ[Ι]Σ‾‾‾ΡΑΤ⩘[Σ Δευ(κονοεύς), 14a
Λυσίστρατος Κηφισοδώ(ρου) Μελιτεύς, 68c
Λύσων Στειρι(εύς), 81e

Μ[– – –] [.]‖[– – –], 145a
Μ[– – –] Κ[– – –], 24a
Με(ι)δυ(λίδης) (Προσπάλτιος), father of Ἀνθεμίων, 6b
Μ[ει]δω(– –) (Ἀγνούσιος), father of Καλλιάδης, 66c
Μείδω(ν?) (Κηφισιεύς), father of Μειδωνΐδης, 20
Μειδωνΐδης Μείδω(νος?) Κηφισιεύς, 20
Μειξικράτης Προσπάλ(τιος), 79
Μενεκράτης Λαμπτ(ρεύς), 17b
Μένιππο[ς Σ]φήττι(ος), 6a
Μνησικλ[ῆς or -είδης] [– – –], 8
Μνήσιππος ([– – –]), father of [– – –], 57d
Μνησίστρατος Σφήττι(ος), 13b
Μολ[– – –] ᾿Ερχ[ιεύς], 46c
Μόνιππο[ς] [Ἀ]χαρν(εύς)?, 111a

Ν[– – –] Π[⫶[– – –], 128c
Ν[.]/[– – –] Φαληρ[εύς], 133a
Ν[⫶[– – –] ἐκ [– – –] or ῾Εκ[αλῆθεν], 10b
Νεοκλείδης [‾‾ca. 4‾‾]‖[⫶, 16b
Νημονΐδης Εὐωνυ(μεύς), 75
Νικ[– – –] Πα[λλ(ηνεύς)?], 104a
Νικίας ([– – –]), father of [– – –], 97d
Ν[ικ]ο[‾‾ca.2‾‾]Ο[⫶ [‾‾ca.2‾‾]‖Σ Γ[– – –], 66b
Νικόδημος ᾿Ελα(ι)ο(ύ)σιος, 89
Νικόστ(ρατος) (Ἀχαρνεύς), father of Νικόστρατος, 114

Νικόστρατος Νικοστ(ράτου) Ἀχαρνεύς, 114
Νικοτέλης Ἀχαρνεύς, 129
Νικοφῶν Ὑβά(δης), 1

Ξενο|≋[– – –] Παιονί[δης], 132b

Ο[– – –] Ι[– – –], 45a
Ο[– –<u>ca. 7</u>– –]s [– – –], 16a
 Οἴων[– –], see Δίων
Ὀλυμπ[– – –] Ἀναγ[υράσιος], 22b
Ὀ[νη]σί[κ]ρ[ι]τος? Ο[–<u>4–5</u>–]Ι[.]ΟΙ[– – –], 65a
Π[<u>ca.2</u>]Σ[<u>ca. 3</u>]ΟΣ Ε|≋[–<u>ca. 4</u>–], 94a
Παιδείας or Παιδειος (Φυλάσιος), father of Σωγένης, 122a
Πάμφι[λος] Παυσί[– – –] [– – –], 33b
Παράμονος Φανοδήμ(ου) Αἰθαλίδης, 68d
Παυσ[– – –] Ἀνδοκ[ίδου] [– – –], 156
Παυσανίας Λευκονοεύς, 102
Παυσι[– – –] ([– – –]), father of Πάμφι[λος], 33b
Πεδίαρχος Ἁλαιεύς, 91
Πεδιεὺς Θεοξέ(νου) Ἐλευσίνιος, 28
Πίτταλος Προσπάλτιος, 34c
Πολ[– – –] Ἀνα[– – –], 106b
Πολυκλῆς Φλυε(ύς), 124b
Πολύμνηστος Ἀρι(– –) Φλυεύς, 29 and 125b
Πολύστρατος Ἁλαιεύς, 155
Πολυφα[ντος or -ντης], of Thasos, Appendix B, Thasos 1b
[Ποσε]ίδιππ[ος] [<u>ca. 3</u>]ασι(– –), 100b
Πρώταρχος Πειραι(εύς), 4b
Πυθέας (Φαληρεύς), father of Γλαύκων, 84b
Πυθέας Γλα[ύκω]νος Φαληρ[εύς], 103b
Πύρρα(κος) (Ἀναγυράσιος), father of Εὐκολίων, 23b

Σ̣[– – –] [– – –], 11b
Σ[– – –] [– – –], 109a
Σ[– – –] Λ[– – –], 108b
Σ̣[– – –] Σ|≋[– – –], 9b
Σ[– – –] Σ◁≋[– – –], 144c
Σ[– – –] (Φλυεύς), father of [– – –]ικλῆς, 172c
Σατ(υρ– –) (Ἐρχιεύς), father of Ἐπικράτης, 65b
Σατυ(ρ– –) (Ἐρχιεύς), father of Σάτυρος, 121a
Σατυρ[– – –] Κριωεύ[s], 134b
Σάτυρος, of Thasos, father of Δεινοκράτης, Appendix B, Thasos 2
Σάτυρος Σατυ(ρ– –) Ἐρχιεύς, 121a
Σήλων Πρασι(εύς), 3
Σ̣τ̣[– – –] [– – –], 137
Στησίλεως Δάμεος, of Sinope, Appendix B, Sinope

Στρὰτ[- - -] Βουτ(άδης), 161
Στράτων Πήληξ, 126
Σωγένης Παιδείο(υ) Φυλάσι(ος), 122a
Σώσαν(δρος) (Πειραιεύς), father of Σωταιρίδης, 31
Σωσίων Βίωνο[ς], of Thasos, Appendix B, Thasos 1a
Σώσ[τρ]ατος Πα[λ]λ(ηνεύς) or Πρα[σιε]ύ(ς), 147c
Σωταιρίδης Σωσάν(δρου) Πειραιεύ(ς), 31

Τ[ῖ̧[- - -] (Κολλυτεύς), father of [ᶜᵃ·²]∰δων, 164b
Τεισίας "Ωαθεν, 21b
Τελεσ(- -) (Ἁλιμούσιος), father of Τελέσων, 153
Τελέσων Τελεσ(- -) Ἁλιμο(ύ)σι(ος), 153
Τιμαν(- -) (Φλυεύς), father of Τιμοκράτης, 7c
[Τ]ιμαίν[ετος], see [Δ]ημαίν[ετος]
Τιμο(- -) (Περγασῆθεν), father of Ἀριστίων, 38c
Τ̣ιμο[.³.]ος [¹⁻²]||||Ο [--⁷⁻⁸--]ς, 68a
Τιμόδο(.ος) ('Ερχιεύς), father of Εὐπόλεμος, 16c
Τιμόδο[.]ος Εὐπο(λέμου) 'Ερχιεύς, 37b
Τιμοκράτης Τιμαν(- -) Φλυεύ[ς]. 7b and c
Τ[ι]μόστρατος ['Ι]καριεύς, 38b
Τιμοφῶν Παιανι(εύς), 18d

Φ[- - -] Ε[- - -], 44a
Φ[-ᶜᵃ·⁵-]ς Φιλω(- -) Σημα(χίδης), 81d
Φα[- - -] Φα[ληρεύς?], 11c
Φαίδιμος Φανο(- -) Παια(νιεύς), 18c
Φαιν[- - -] Ἀλω[πεκῆθεν], 128b
Φαίνιππος "Ωαθεν, 92a
Φανο(- -) (Παιανιεύς), father of Φαίδιμος, 18c
Φανόδημ(ος) (Αἰθαλίδης), father of Παράμονος, 68d
Φείδυλ[λος] 'Ιωνίδη[ς], 40c
Φιλ[- - -] Εὐ[- - -] 'Ηρ[αιεύς],? of Arkadia(?), Appendix B, Arkadia(?)
Φιλι̣[- - -] (Κηφισιεύς), father of Δημοφάνης, 130
Φ[ι]λοκύδης 〈Ἀ〉λω(πεκῆθεν), 47b
Φιλόμνηστος 'Ικαριεύς, 96f
Φιλόξενος Φιλοφεί(- -) Ἀγρυλῆθεν, 84c
[Φ]ιλόστρατος Κολων(ῆθεν), 158
Φιλοφεί(- -) (Ἀγρυλῆθεν), father of Φιλόξενος, 84c
Φιλοχάρης Ἁλαι(εύς), 83a
Φιλοχάρ[ης] Ἀχα[ρνεύς], 41c
Φιλω(- -) (Σημαχίδης), father of Φ[-ᶜᵃ·⁵-]ς, 81d
Φρυνι̣[- - -] Εἰρε[σίδης], 160
Φρυνοκλέης Θριάσι(ος), 93b
Φρύνος Εὐκλείδο(υ) Παιαν(ιεύς), 61b
Φυ(- - -), possibly (Χολλείδης), father of Ἀπολλόδωρος, 157
Χα[- - -] Σο[υνιεύς?], 9c
Χαρίας 'Οτρυν(εύς), 90

Broken Names Containing Demotics

[$\overset{ca.2}{--}$]ησι/ᷤ [– – –] [Ἀ]θμο(νεύς), 164a
[– – –]χος Λυσ[– – –] Ἀθμο(νεύς), 139b

[– – –]ρατος Αἰγιλιε(ύς), 138b

[– – –]ς [Α]ἰθα(λίδης), 57c

[– – – –]ΙΙ[– – –] Ἀλα[ι]ε[ύς], 105b
[– – –]⫶⫶⫶ων Λυ[– – –] [Ἀλ]αι(εύς)?, 171

[– – –] Ἀλωπε(κῆθεν), 37a

[.]/[–$\overset{ca.\,6}{----}$–]ς Ἀρ[α]φ[ήν]ιος, 18b
[– – –]\MO? [Ἀρα]φή(νιος), 56b

[– – –]μος [– – –]ο Ἀχαρ(νεύς), 50b
[– – –ω]ν Ἀχαρ(νεύς), 177

[– – –] Ἀχ[α]ρ[νεύς] or Ἀχ[ε]ρ[δούσιος], 146a

[.]Λ[.]Λ[.]⫽⫽[– –] [Β]ησαι(εύς), 111b

/[– – –] Ε[ἰ]τ[εαῖος], 77b

[– – –]ιλος [– – –]υ Ἑκαλῆ(θεν), 172d

Ἀ[κ]τ[α]ῖ[ο]ς, Ἀ[μ]υ[ν]ί[α]ς, Ἀ[σ]τ[ε]ῖ[ο]ς, or Λ[ε]ύ[κ]ι[ο]ς Ἐ[λ]ε[υ]σί(νιος),
    96a

[$\overset{2-3}{--}$]⸗ινος [Εὐ]ωνυ(μεύς), 49b
[– – –κ]ράτης [Εὐω]νυ(μεύς), 56c

[$\overset{3-4}{--}$]φιλος [– – –] Θριάσι[ος], 100a
Ο[.]ΛΟΚ[..]ᷤΣ ἐ[κ Κε]ραμ[μ]έ(ων)?, 34b

[–$\overset{ca.\,5}{----}$–]ς [Κηφ]ισιεύ[ς], 170

[$\overset{ca.2}{--}$]ᷤδων Τᷤ[– – –] [Κο]λλυ(τεύς), 164b
ᷤᷤᷤ Ε[– – –] Κολλυ[τεύς], 40b

[..]ΟᷤΚ[– – –] [ἐ]κ Κο[ίλης or -λωνοῦ?, 134a

[– – –] Λαμπτρ(εύς), 81a
[– – –]ς Λαμ(πτρεύς), 12a

[– – –]ᷤΣΘΕ[– – –] [Με]λιτ(εύς), 167

[$\overset{ca.\,4}{--}$]⫶⫶⫶[–$\overset{ca.\,5}{----}$–]ς Περιθο[ίδης]?, 123a

[– – –]νης [Π]λωθε(ύς), 173

[– – –] [Συπα]λήτ[τιος]?, 159a

[– – –]ΟΝΙ/ᷤ[.]ΗΣ Σφή[τ]τιος, 139a

[– – –] Φα[λ]ηρ(εύς), 73a

[– – –]ικλῆς Σ[– – –] [Φλ]υεύς, 172c

Plates

Fig. 1   **1** (Athens, National Museum)

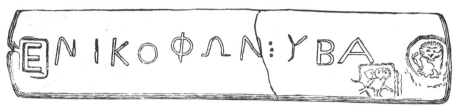

Fig. 2   **1** Reproduced from Koumanoudes

Fig. 3   **2** (Paris, Cabinet des Médailles)

Fig. 4   **3** (Peiraeus, Archaeological Museum), before cleaning

Fig. 5   **3** after cleaning

Fig. 6   **4** (New York, Metropolitan Museum of Art, Rogers Fund, 1907)

Fig. 7   **4**, text *a*

Fig. 8   **4**, text *b*

Fig. 9   **5** (Basel, Antikenmuseum)

Fig. 10   **5**, texts *a* and *b*

Fig. 11   **6** (Athens, Paul Kanellopoulos Collection)

Fig. 12   **6**, text *a*

Fig. 13　**7** (Thessalonika, Archaeological Museum)

Fig. 14　**7**, text *a*

Fig. 15　**7**, text *b*

Fig. 16　**7**, text *c*, line 1

Fig. 17　**8** (formerly Berlin, Staatliche Museen)

Fig. 18　**9** (Athens, National Museum)

Fig. 19   **9**, texts *a–c*

Fig. 20   **10** (Athens, National Museum)

Fig. 21   **10**, text *b*

Fig. 22   **11** (Athens, National Museum)

Fig. 23   **12** (Paris, Cabinet des Médailles)

Fig. 24   **12**, texts *a* and *b*

Fig. 25   **13** (Hannover, Kestner-Museum)

Fig. 26   **13**, text *a*

Fig. 27   **14** (Athens, National Museum)

Fig. 28   **14**, text *a*

Fig. 29   **15** (Athens, Agora Excavations)

Fig. 30   **15**, texts *a* and *b*

Fig. 31   **16** (Athens, National Museum)

Fig. 32   **16**, texts *a* and *b*

Fig. 33   **17** (Utrecht, Archaeological Institute)

Fig. 34   **17**, text *a* and profile

Fig. 35   **18** (Urbana, University of Illinois Classical and European Culture Museum)

Fig. 36   **18**, texts *a–c*

Fig. 37   **19** (Athens, Numismatic Museum)

Fig. 38   **20** (Athens, National Museum)

Fig. 39   **21** (Peiraeus, Archaeological Museum)

Fig. 40   **22** (Peiraeus, Archaeological Museum)

Fig. 41   **22**, text *a*

Fig. 42   **23** (Paris, Cabinet des Médailles)

Fig. 43   **23**, text *a*

Fig. 44   **24** (Peiraeus, Archaeological Museum)

Fig. 45   **25** (Athens, National Museum)

Fig. 46   **26** (Athens, National Museum)

Fig. 47   **27** (Basel, Antikenmuseum)

Fig. 48   **28** (Athens, National Museum)

303 *Plates*

Fig. 49 **29** (formerly Berlin, Staatliche Museen)

Fig. 50 **30** (Athens, National Museum)

Fig. 51 **30**, text *a*

Fig. 52 **31** (Athens, National Museum)

Fig. 53 **32** (Athens, Agora Excavations)

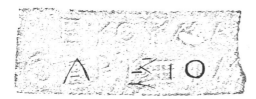

Fig. 54 **32**, texts *a* and *b*

Fig. 55   **33** (Athens, Pnyx Excavations)

Fig. 56   **34** (Paris, Cabinet des Médailles), Side A

Fig. 57   **34**, Side B

Fig. 58   **35** (Athens, National Museum)

Fig. 59   **35**, text *a*

Fig. 60   **36** (London, British Museum)

Fig. 61   **37** (Athens, National Museum)

Fig. 62   **38** (Toronto, Royal Ontario Museum)

Fig. 63   **38**, texts *a* and *b*

Fig. 64   **39** (Newcastle upon Tyne, Greek Museum), before cleaning

Fig. 65   **39**, after cleaning

Fig. 66   **40** (Basel, Antikenmuseum)

Fig. 67　**40**, text *b*

Fig. 68　**41** (London, British Museum)

Fig. 69　**41**, texts *a* and *b*

Fig. 70　**42** (Athens, National Museum)

Fig. 71　**42**, text *a*

Fig. 72　**42**, text *b*

Fig. 73   **43** (Athens, National Museum)

Fig. 74   **43**, text *a*

Fig. 75   **44** (Athens, National Museum)

Fig. 76   **45** (Athens, Agora Excavations)

Fig. 77   **46** (Athens, National Museum)

Fig. 78   **47** (Athens, Agora Excavations)

Fig. 79 **48** (Athens, Agora Excavations)

Fig. 80 **49** (Athens, Paul Kanellopoulos Collection); photo of an imperfectly impressed plaster cast

Fig. 81 **50** (Athens, National Museum)

Fig. 82 **51** (Basel, Antikenmuseum)

Fig. 83 **52** (Athens, National Museum)

Fig. 84 **53** (Athens, National Museum)

Fig. 85   54 (Athens, British School of Archaeology)

Fig. 86   55 (Peiraeus, Archaeological Museum)

Fig. 87   55, text *a*

Fig. 88   56 (Paris, Cabinet des Médailles)

Fig. 89   57 (Athens, National Museum)

Fig. 90   57, texts *a–c*

Fig. 91   **58** (Athens, National Museum)

Fig. 92   **58**, texts *b* and *c*

Fig. 93   **59** (Athens, National Museum), Side A

Fig. 94   **59**, Side B

Fig. 95   **59**, texts *a–c*

Fig. 96   **59**, text *d*

Fig. 97 **60** (Basel, Antikenmuseum)

Fig. 98 **60**, text *a*

Fig. 99 **61** (Rouen, Musée Départemental des Antiquités)

Fig. 100 **61**, text *b*

Fig. 101 **62** (London, British Museum)

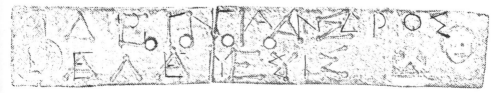

Fig. 102 **62**, text *a*

Fig. 103   **63** (Paris, Cabinet des Médailles); right fragment photographed before complete cleaning

Fig. 104   **63**, texts *a* and *b*

Fig. 105   **63**, text *c*

Fig. 106   **64** (Athens, National Museum)

Fig. 107   **64**, text *b* and other details

Fig. 108   **65** (Athens, National Museum)

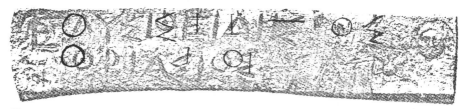

Fig. 109   **65**, text *a*

Fig. 110   **65**, text *b*

Fig. 111   **66** (Athens, Depot of the Second Archaeological Ephoria)

Fig. 112   **66**, texts *a* and *b*

Fig. 113   **67** (Athens, National Museum), before cleaning

Fig. 114   **67**, after cleaning

Fig. 115   **67**, texts *a* and *b*

Fig. 116   **68** (Athens, National Museum), before cleaning

Fig. 117   **68**, after cleaning

Fig. 118   **68**, text *a*

Fig. 119   **68**, text *b*

Fig. 120   **68**, text *c*

Fig. 121 *IG* II², 5396 (Athens, Epigraphical Museum)

Fig. 122 **69** (Basel, Antikenmuseum)

Fig. 123 **69**, texts *a–c*

Fig. 124 **70** (Athens, National Museum)

Fig. 125   **71** (Athens, National Museum)

Fig. 126   **71**, texts *a* and *b*

Fig. 127   **72** (formerly Berlin, Staatliche Museen)

Fig. 128   **73** (Athens, National Museum), before cleaning

Fig. 129   **73**, after cleaning

Fig. 130   **74** (Athens, National Museum)

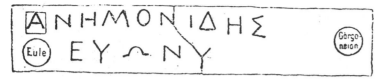

Fig. 131   **75** Reproduced from Bruck

Fig. 132   **76** (Athens, National Museum)

Fig. 133   **77** (Basel, Antikenmuseum)

Fig. 134   **77**, texts *a* and *b*

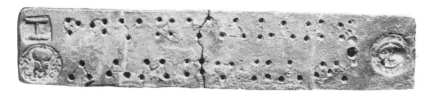

Fig. 135   **78** (London, British Museum)

Fig. 136   **79** (Paris, Cabinet des Médailles)

Fig. 137   **80** (Paris, Cabinet des Médailles)

Fig. 138   **81** (Paris, Cabinet des Médailles)

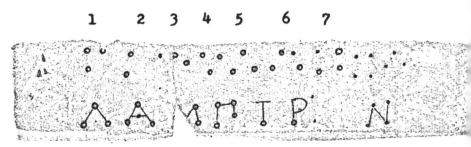

Fig. 139   **81**, texts *a* (remains and restoration of line 2) and *b* (remains)

Fig. 140   **81**, texts *c–e*

Fig. 141   **82** (Athens, National Museum)

Fig. 142   **82**, texts *a–c*

Fig. 143   **83** (London, British Museum)

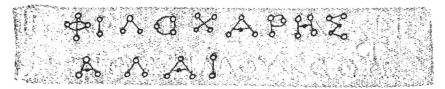

Fig. 144   **83**, text *a* restored

Fig. 145   **84** (Basel, Antikenmuseum)

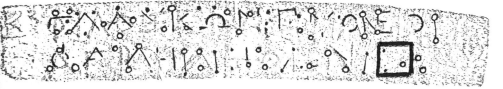

Fig. 146   **84**, remains of texts *a* and *b*

Fig. 147   **84**, text *a*, positive letters restored

Fig. 148   **85** (Paris, Cabinet des Médailles)

Fig. 149   **86** (New York, Brooklyn Museum)

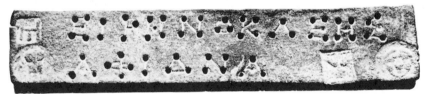

Fig. 150   **87** (Paris, Musée du Louvre)

Fig. 151   **88** (Athens, National Museum)

Fig. 152   **89** (Athens, National Museum)

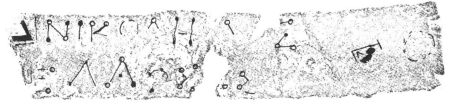

Fig. 153   **89**, visible details

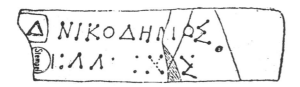

Fig. 154   **89** Reproduced from Bruck

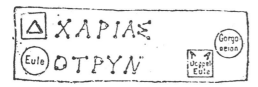

Fig. 155   **90** Reproduced from Bruck

Fig. 156   **91** (Oxford, Ashmolean Museum)

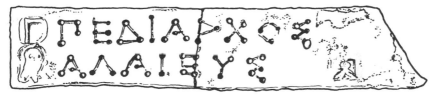

Fig. 157   **91** Reproduced from Catling

Fig. 158   **92** (Munich, Antikensammlung)

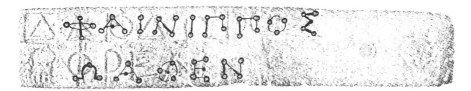

Fig. 159   **92**, text *a* restored

Fig. 160   **93** (Leiden, National Museum of Antiquities)

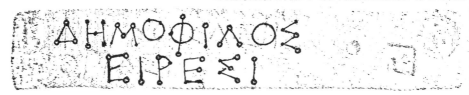

Fig. 161   **93**, text *a* restored

Fig. 162   **94** (Athens, National Museum)

Fig. 163   **94**, remains of text *a*

Fig. 164   **94**, back side, showing fully pierced holes of text *b*

Fig. 165   **95** (Basel, Antikenmuseum), before cleaning

Fig. 166   **95**, after cleaning

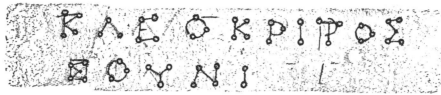

Fig. 167   **95**, text *a* restored and remains of text *b*

Fig. 168   **96** (Athens, Agora Excavations)

Fig. 169   **96**, texts *b–e*

Fig. 170   **96**, remains of text *a* with positive letters restored

Fig. 171   **96**, back side

Fig. 172   **97** (Athens, Agora Excavations)

Fig. 173   **97**, back side

Fig. 174   **97**, text *a* restored and remains of texts *b* and *c*

Fig. 175   **98** (Paris, Cabinet des Médailles)

Fig. 176   **98**, remains of text *a*

Fig. 177   **99** (formerly Berlin, Staatliche Museen)

Fig. 178   **99** Reproduced from Bruck

Fig. 179   **100** (Athens, National Museum)

Fig. 180   **100**, text *a* restored

Fig. 181   **101** (Athens, Agora Excavations)

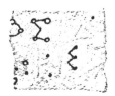

Fig. 182   **101**, text *a* restored and remains of text *b*

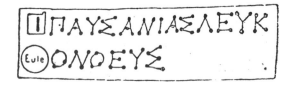

Fig. 183   **102** Reproduced from Bruck

Fig. 184   **103** (Peiraeus, Archaeological Museum)

Fig. 185   **103**, text *a* restored

Fig. 186   **103**, back side, showing fully pierced holes from text *a*

Fig. 187   **104** (Athens, National Museum)

Fig. 188   **104**, remains of texts

Fig. 189   **105** (Athens, Pnyx Excavations)

Fig. 190   **105**, remains of text *a*

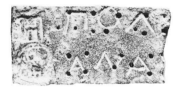

Fig. 191   **106** (Paris, Musée du Louvre)

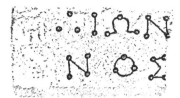

Fig. 192   **106**, text *a*, positive letters restored

Fig. 193   **107** (Basel, Antikenmuseum)

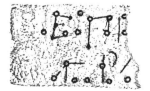

Fig. 194   **107**, remains of texts *a* and *b*

Fig. 195   **107**, text *a*, positive letters restored

Fig. 196   **108** (Athens, National Museum)

Fig. 197   **108**, remains of texts *a* and *b*

Fig. 198   **109** (Athens, National Museum)

Fig. 199   **109**, remains of text *a*

Fig. 200   **110** (London, British Museum)

Fig. 201   **110**, remains of text *a*

Fig. 202   **111** (Paris, Cabinet des Médailles)

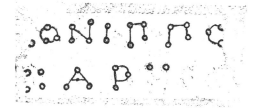

Fig. 203   **111**, text *a*, positive letters restored

Fig. 204   **111**, text *b*

Fig. 205   **112** (Athens, Agora Excavations)

Fig. 206   **112**, texts

Fig. 207   **113** (Athens, Stoa of Attalos Museum)

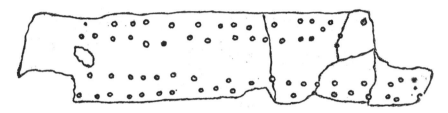

Fig. 208   **113**, sketched as if flattened out; visible holes and their approximate disposition

Fig. 209   Squat lekythos (Athens, Stoa of Attalos Museum), buried with **113**

Fig. 210   **114** (Athens, British School of Archaeology)

Fig. 211   **115** (Paris, Cabinet des Médailles)

Fig. 212   **116** (Paris, Cabinet des Médailles)

Fig. 213   **117** (Athens, National Museum)

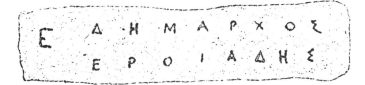

Fig. 214   **117** Reproduced from Dumont

Fig. 215   **118** (Paris, Cabinet des Médailles)

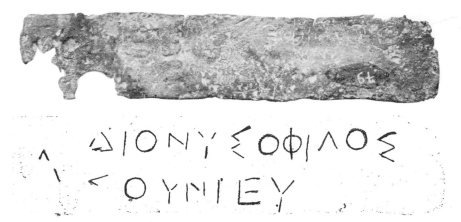

Figs. 216–217 **119** (Athens, Depot of the Third Archaeological Ephoria), Side A

Fig. 218 **119**, Side B

Fig. 219 Black-glaze lekythos (Athens, Depot of the Third Archaeological Ephoria), buried with **119**

Figs. 220–221   **120** (Munich, Antikensammlung), Side A

Fig. 222   **120**, Side B

Fig. 223   **121** (Munich, Antikensammlung)

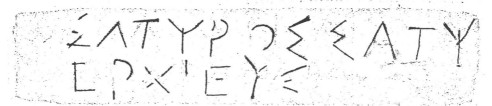

Fig. 224   **121**, text *a*

Fig. 225   **122** (Paris, Cabinet des Médailles)

Fig. 226   **122**, text *a*

Fig. 227   **123** (Basel, Antikenmuseum)

Fig. 228   **123**, text *a*

Fig. 229   **124** (formerly Berlin, Staatliche Museen)

Fig. 230   **124**, text *a*

Fig. 231 *IG* II², 7702 (Athens, Epigraphical Museum)

Fig. 232 **125** (formerly Berlin, Staatliche Museen)

Fig. 233 **126** (Paris, Cabinet des Médailles)

Fig. 234 **127** (Paris, Cabinet des Médailles)

Fig. 235   **128** (Athens, National Museum)

Fig. 236   **128**, text *a*

Fig. 237   **128**, text *b*

Fig. 238   **128**, text *c*

Fig. 239   **129** (Athens, National Museum)

Fig. 240   **130** (Athens, Agora Excavations)

Fig. 241   **131** (Athens, Agora Excavations)

Fig. 242   **132** (Athens, Pnyx Excavations)

Fig. 243   **132**, text *a* and other possible remains

Fig. 244   **133** (Athens, Agora Excavations)

Fig. 245   **133**, text *a*

Fig. 246   **133**, text *b*

Fig. 247   **133**, text *c*

Fig. 248   **134** (Peiraeus, Archaeological Museum), Side A

Fig. 249   **134**, Side B

Fig. 250   **134** text *a*

Fig. 251   **135** (Athens, National Museum), Side A

Fig. 252   **135** Side B

Fig. 253   **135** text *a*

Fig. 254   **136** (Athens, National Museum)

Fig. 255   **137** (Athens, Agora Excavations)

Fig. 256   **138** (Athens, National Museum)

Fig. 257   **138**, text *a*

Fig. 258   **139** (Athens, National Museum)

Fig. 259   **139**, text *a*

Fig. 260   **140** (Athens, Agora Excavations)

Fig. 261   **141** (Athens, Agora Excavations)

Fig. 262   **142** (Paris, Cabinet des Médailles)

Fig. 263   **143** (Athens, National Museum)

Fig. 264   **144** (Athens, National Museum)

Fig. 265   **144**, texts *a* and *b*

Fig. 266   **145** (Athens, National Museum)

Fig. 267   **145**, text *a*

Fig. 268   **146** (Athens, Pnyx Excavations)

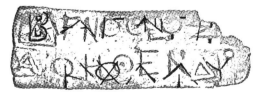

Fig. 269   **146**, texts *a* and *b*

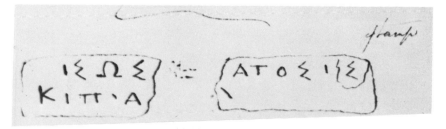

Fig. 270   **147** Reproduced from a notebook of Col. W. M. Leake

Fig. 271   **147** Reproduced from Akerblad

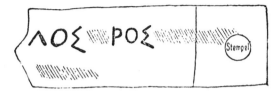

Fig. 272   **148** Reproduced from Bruck

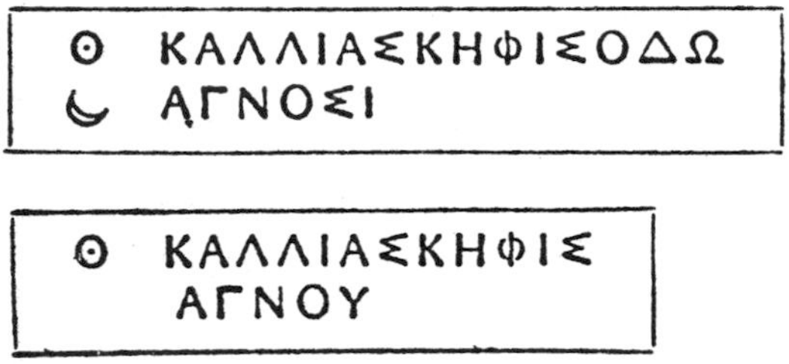

| Θ | ΚΑΛΛΙΑΣΚΗΦΙΣΟΔΩ |
| ☽ | ΑΓΝΟΣΙ |

| Θ | ΚΑΛΛΙΑΣΚΗΦΙΣ |
| | ΑΓΝΟΥ |

Fig. 273   **149** and **150** Reproduced from Ross

 ΑΝΤΙΦΩΝ
Α ΛΑΙΕΥΣ

Fig. 274   **151** Reproduced from Dumont

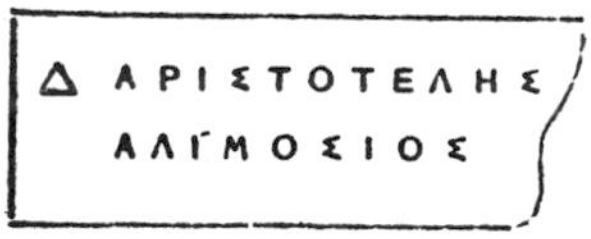

| Δ | ΑΡΙΣΤΟΤΕΛΗΣ |
| | ΑΛΓΜΟΣΙΟΣ |

Fig. 275   **152** Reproduced from *IG* II

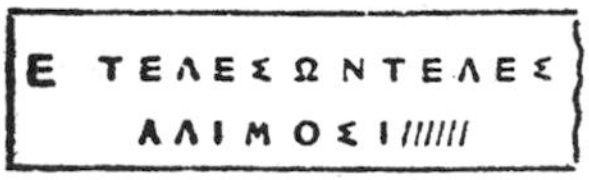

| Ε | ΤΕΛΕΣΩΝΤΕΛΕΣ |
| | ΑΛΙΜΟΣΙ ////// |

Fig. 276   **153** Reproduced from *IG* II

Fig. 277 **156** Reproduced from Skias

Fig. 278 **159** (Athens, National Museum)

Fig. 279 **159**, text *a*

Fig. 280 **160** (Athens, Agora Excavations)

Fig. 281 **161** (Athens, Pnyx Excavations)

Fig. 282 **163** (Athens, National Museum)

Fig. 283　**163**, erased remains

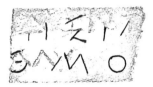

Fig. 284　**164** (Athens, Pnyx Excavations)

Fig. 285　**164**, text *a*

Fig. 286　**165** (Athens, National Museum)

Fig. 287　**166** (Athens, National Museum)

Fig. 288　**167** (Athens, National Museum)

Fig. 289   **168** (Athens, National Museum)

Fig. 290   **169** (Athens, Agora Excavations)

Fig. 291   **170** (Athens, National Museum)

Fig. 292   **171** (Athens, National Museum)

Fig. 293   **172** (Athens, National Muscum), Side A

Fig. 294   **172**, Side B

Fig. 295   **172**, text *a*

Fig. 296   **172**, text *b*

Fig. 297   **173** (Paris, Cabinet des Médailles)

Fig. 298   **174** (Athens, National Museum)

Fig. 299   **175** (Athens, Agora Excavations)

Fig. 300   **176** (Athens, National Museum)

Fig. 301   **177** (Athens, National Museum)

Fig. 302   **179** (Athens, National Museum)

Fig. 303   **180** (Athens, Agora Excavations)

Fig. 304   **181** (Athens, Agora Excavations)

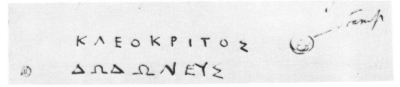

Fig. 305   **182** Reproduced from a notebook of Col. W. M. Leake

Fig. 306   **182** Reproduced from Akerblad

Fig. 307 **183** (Nauplion, Archaeological Museum)

Fig. 308 **183**, text *a*

Fig. 309 **Sinope** (Paris, Musée du Louvre)

Fig. 310 **Thasos 1** (Paris, Cabinet des Médailles); actual size

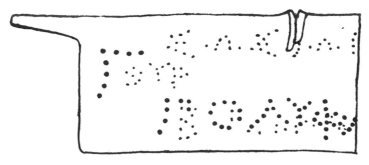

Fig. 311 **Thasos 1** Reproduced from Seyrig

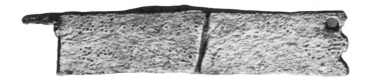

Fig. 312   **Thasos 2** (Thasos Excavations)

Fig. 313   **Thasos 3** (Thasos Excavations)

Fig. 314   **Thasos 4** (Thasos Excavations)

Fig. 315   **Thasos 5** (Thasos Excavations)

Fig. 316   **Uncertain attribution** (Athens, National Museum)

Fig. 317   **Arkadia(?)** (Basel, Antikenmuseum)

Fig. 318   **Arkadia(?)** Reproduced from Vischer

Index